From Blind Obedience
to a Responsible Faith

From Blind Obedience to a Responsible Faith

The Memoir of a Cradle Catholic

Donald F. Fausel

iUniverse, Inc.
New York   Bloomington

From Blind Obedience to a Responsible Faith
The Memoir of a Cradle Catholic

iUniverse books may be ordered through booksellers or by contacting:

iUniverse
1663 Liberty Drive
Bloomington, IN 47403
www.iuniverse.com
1-800-Authors (1-800-288-4677)

Because of the dynamic nature of the Internet, any Web addresses or links contained in this book may have changed since publication and may no longer be valid. The views expressed in this work are solely those of the author and do not necessarily reflect the views of the publisher, and the publisher hereby disclaims any responsibility for them.

ISBN: 978-1-4502-4457-2 (sc)
ISBN: 978-1-4502-4459-6 (dj)
ISBN: 978-1-4502-4458-9 (ebk)

Printed in the United States of America

iUniverse rev. date: 08/27/2010

To my mother, father, and brother, who have completed their earthly journey and have entered into eternity.
And
to my dear wife, Jane, the love of my life.

You have a duty and an obligation to write, not because you have "the truth" and must share it with others, but because we need to discover truths and we need all the help we can get, yours included. You write because you have an obligation to do so.
—James E. Porter, *Audience and Rhetoric*

If you think you're too small to make a difference, try getting in bed with a mosquito.
—Anonymous

When I was a child, I spoke and thought and reasoned as a child. But when I grew up, I put away childish things.
—I Corinthians 13:11, New Living Translation, 2007

Contents

Preface. ix

Acknowledgments. xi

Introduction 1

In the Beginning. 4

Love Thy Neighborhood 20

Family Ties 45

School Dazes. 92

The Seminary Years 124

The New Priest 152

Back Home Again. 183

The Turbulent 1960s. 215

Turning Points 247

Life in Post-Vatican II 284

Go West, Young Man 315

The Seventies and Eighties. 344

The Nineties and the New Millennium. 364

Notes 405

Preface

When I first told my friends and relatives that I was going to write my memoir, I usually added a little sheepishly, "I know that's a little presumptuous of me." They of course automatically but supportively replied something to the effect of, "I think that's a great idea. You've had a very interesting life, and I think a lot of people would find your story interesting and inspiring." Of course that was just what I hoped they would say.

As I thought about it, I realized that I had two life stories to tell. Unlike some other memoirs I've read, the content of my stories do not include overcoming physical abuse or traumatizing emotional events. They focus on the circumstances that influenced who I became as a person and how I grew spiritually. My journey often led me down paths I had to retrace or re-create. Struggling through major changes can produce its own brand of pain.

My first life story took place during my years growing up in pre-Vatican II. That time of my life was guided by blind obedience to the "prescribed beliefs" that I learned from my family of origin, Irish Catholic culture, Catholic education, and my protected life experiences. I don't blame anyone for that. I take responsibility for having been content in believing what I was taught was indeed *the* truth. It was years later that I began to challenge what I had been taught and engage in an intellectual and spiritual struggle to integrate a more experiential and scientific worldview with my religious faith—what I refer to in the title as "a responsible faith."

The story of my second life began when I was introduced to critical thinking as a master's student in the social work program at Fordham University. What a welcome change it was for me to be living in an atmosphere that was based on democratic values, in contrast to the authoritarian, hierarchical organization that Rome had become. I found these democratic values much more compatible with my spiritual journey. It became important for me to be able to internalize a belief system that acknowledged that there was not just one faith tradition that had a monopoly on truth; that acknowledged and encouraged exploration; that embraced diversity; that was open to spiritual experiences as well as intellectual discovery; and that could tolerate dissent and was open to substantive change.

While I was doing research on the theology that underlies the concepts of beliefs and faith, Harvey Cox's book, *The Future of Faith*, helped me put into words what I had been thinking but hadn't been able to articulate. I learned, rather late in life, that being able to distinguish between beliefs and faith is the key to our understanding the history of the church from the earliest days of Christianity to the present time. After reading Cox's book, I realized that most people who think they've lost their faith have not lost it, but have lost their belief in many of the doctrines they have been taught and blindly accepted. Following our conscience and not accepting all the prescribed beliefs does not mean that we can no longer practice our faith and follow what Jesus taught: to love one another, have compassion for the poor and sick, and pursue justice for the disenfranchised.

I hope my memoir will help you understand the culture I grew up in, with its strengths and weaknesses and its joys and sorrows, and how it contributed to making me who I am. Hopefully, it will assist you in your journey to a responsible faith.

Acknowledgments

I 've been fortunate to have a circle of relatives, friends, and colleagues who took the time to review and critique each chapter of this book as it was completed. They have all been very helpful and patient with me over the last two years. At one point, my cousin Walter McCarroll observed, "I think I know you better than I know myself." Our good friend Philomena Avona, whom Jane and I met with her husband, Vince, on a transatlantic cruise on the QE2, told me she was going to miss receiving each chapter on a regular basis. Bob Byars kept me on track with his prompt and thoughtful critiques. Cousin Bob Brew, as a professor who had corrected hundreds of term papers, sent me detailed reports on each chapter. Jean Brew provided me with genealogies of the McCarroll family. John Rusnak gave me his perspective as a fellow seeker, professor, psychologist, and friend. My cousin Mary Anne passed chapters on to the Tammany family. My nieces Laura Li, Angela Rodela, and Lisa Prout were helpful with their technical knowledge whenever my computer was not cooperating.

I owe a special debt of thanks to Larry Prout, who worked his magic in formatting all the chapters from individual files, placing the pictures in their proper places in the manuscript, and helping out when I thought I lost a chapter or two in cyberspace.

Most of all, I appreciate the patience of my wife, Jane, as I sequestered myself in my office, day after day. She never complained about the time I was spending on the memoir or my messy office. She was also the first reader of every chapter.

Introduction

M y memoir is a combination of stories of my life and my reflections on them. Each chapter includes a section on reflections, in which I look back at the content of the stories in that particular chapter and describe how those events affected my spiritual journey. The stories were easy to write. I had access to my journals, treasured albums of photos, report cards, letters, home movies, and my long-term memory, which is fortunately still intact. My only problem was choosing what to include, since I obviously had to be selective. Although the stories will perhaps hold more interest for my relatives and friends, my hope is that they will resonate with those of us who are part of the "Depression Generation" and that they may contribute a bit of history for other generations.

The reflections often required considerable research. In some instances they are based on the theological, philosophical, sociological, or political underpinnings that were part of my reasoning; in others they simply describe the impact the events in the stories had on me. I don't intend the reflections to be systematic theological treatises in the strict sense of the term. They provided me with an opportunity to expand my views of religion and spirituality beyond my early religious background and education. I believe that, as part of the "People of God," we have a responsibility to do what we can, within our sphere of influence, for the renewal of the church. That includes being able to express dissent when it is appropriate. My reflections are not always in disagreement with the magisterium of the church. Nor do my conclusions rely solely on the teaching of the magisterium. In my opinion a responsible faith relies on the primacy of conscience for its conclusions.

In addition to the primacy of conscience, my reflections cover: the differences between faith and beliefs; abortion and artificial birth control; the doctrine of infallibility; the danger of relying solely on the magisterium; the charism of celibacy and mandatory celibacy; the place of women in the church and the ordination of women; the effect of the new cosmology on our image of God; the importance of other faith traditions in our search for truth; the need for the church to abandon its hierarchical structure and to become more democratic. I believe that the reflections may help others who have struggled with particular prescribed beliefs and are looking for another way of resolving their uncertainties.

I've organized my pilgrimage into several sections. The first three chapters cover my recollections of my earliest years and their impact on my development, beginning with my birth that according to my father heralded the start of the Great Depression of 1929. I then introduce you to the neighborhood in which I spent the first eighteen years of my life, my family of origin, the Fausels, and the McCarrolls.

Chapters four and five describe and appraise my formal education from grammar school through high school. This period covered three decades, from the 1930s through the 1940s. I next examine how each decade, with its unique history and experiences influenced my development. Chapters six, seven, and eight discuss my life as a seminarian and Catholic priest, pre- and post-Vatican II, and the struggle leading up to my departure from the active priesthood. The remaining chapters are devoted to my life after leaving the ordained ministry. I describe my life as an academic;

an agent of social change; and a serious spiritual seeker, who critically examined the beliefs that were prescribed by the church and moved toward a more responsible faith, which I believe, is compatible with the tradition of my Catholic faith.

Chapter 1
In the Beginning

Knickerbocker News
Albany, New York
November 27, 1929

Birth Announcements:

On November 22, 1929, a son, Donald Frederick Fausel, was born at the Brady Maternity Hospital to Jane McCarroll Fausel and James Otto Fausel of 8 Judson Street. Mr. Fausel works for the Howard B. Stark Insurance Co.

Not exactly breaking news by today's standards, but in the 1920s birth announcements seemed to be of great public interest in many communities. If for no other reason, they satisfied the curiosity of the busybodies, who had nothing better to do than count the months from your parents' marriage to your birth. After all, they didn't have television and all our other modern distractions to occupy their minds. Since my parents had been married on February 8, my birth date was a few weeks over nine months. Thankfully, that put an end to any speculation or rumors about my legitimacy. The announcement also gave a little free publicity for my father's new position at the Howard B. Stark insurance company.

I obviously don't remember the circumstances surrounding my arrival except what I've been told. When I was growing up, my father frequently told me the story of how he anxiously paced the floor in the hospital waiting room to learn how my mother was doing after my birth and whether he had a son or daughter. I can almost hear him reciting the details as I write. As many times as I listened to him reminisce, I never tired of hearing him recalling that eventful morning.

"I brought your mother to the Brady Maternity Hospital just after dinner on Thursday. I had to call my brother Ken to take us; we didn't have a car in those days. He dropped us off, and it was just the two of us—and you. It was scary! I checked your mother in and then waited until the next morning before I got any news of how either of you was. I spent that night in this gloomy waiting room with another expectant father, whose wife worked with your mother at the telephone company. Your mother and his wife had been telephone operators together. You know, 'Number please'? They called them 'old plugs,' since they sat at a switchboard and plugged the calls into a board. Anyway, about four o'clock on Friday morning, Dr. Kircher came into the waiting room. I couldn't tell by the expression on his face whether the news was going to be good or bad. I never felt more anxious in my life."

"Well, Ott, you have a son. It wasn't an easy delivery, but both your son and Jane are doing okay. Jane is resting right now, but you can see her in a little while. We had to use instruments for the delivery, so when you see your son, don't be upset because he has bandages on his head."

"You're sure he's okay?"

"We're as sure as we can be. He might have some scars, but they should heal in a few weeks."

"He wasn't exactly reassuring, but he wasn't negative, either. I asked if I could see the baby." (I didn't even have a name! I was "the baby.")

"Dr. Kircher said, 'Certainly, but like I said, don't be shocked when you see him. He's going to be okay.'

"I felt a little more reassured. When I got to the nursery, the nurse brought you to the window, but, despite Dr. Kircher's warning, I was taken aback. The bandages covered most of your head, and there were traces of blood seeping through. I could hardly see your face, but I could hear you crying. I hoped that was a good sign. The nurse smiled at me as she held you in her arms and then mouthed though the glass that you were doing just fine. That was a bit of a relief."

Later that day they brought me downstairs to meet my mother. My father prepared her for the shock by reassuring her that Dr. Kircher had told him I would be fine and that they didn't have to worry about any permanent damage. At that point, my mother was just glad to meet me and hold me in her arms after carrying me for nine months. My father told me that he wished he had a picture of that first meeting. My mother cried tears of joy and relief, and Dad was just as proud as can be of their accomplishment. It was just dawning on them that they were parents. It also dawned on him that they didn't have a name for this bundle of joy. There were no ultrasound machines, as there are today, so they had had no idea what my gender would be. My father asked, "What are we going to call him?" He described my mother's response as automatic: "Donald! Donald Frederick! I chose Frederick, after your father." My father agreed but asked, "Where does the 'Donald' come from?" My mother reminded him that one of her favorite radio soap opera characters was named Donald. (I'm not sure, but I think the soap was called *The Romances of Helen Trent.*)

My father shook his head and said, "Okay with me, as long as we don't call him Otto." His first name was James, but everyone called him by his middle name, Otto. He hated the name but said it was good for business, since no one ever forgot his name. Also because Otto spelled backward was Otto.

Years after, my father presented me with the original itemized bill for the two weeks my mother and I spent in the hospital.

I understand it was not unusual in those days for a woman to spend a week or more recovering in the hospital after childbirth. What surprised me was that the total cost for my mother's room was $68.00—just $4.00 a day. I suspected I knew the answer but asked, "Do you want me to reimburse you?"

He responded, "Oh, you think you're funny! Of course I don't want your money. I just thought you might want to keep it to show your kids how reasonable the cost of having a baby was back in the dinosaur age. You were worth every nickel. Just imagine how much you would cost today."

Not So Happy Days

Years later I came to appreciate how difficult it must have been for my parents to bring me home and start their life as parents. To make matters worse, I wasn't one of those good babies who slept through the night. My father frequently reminded me that I had been a crybaby with a touch of colic.

Just imagine—in 1929 my parents were both twenty-one years old. At least my father thought they were both the same age. He didn't find out that his dear wife was a couple of years older until he filed for her Social Security benefits some forty years later. I remember him confiding in me, "Guess what? I went to the Social Security office to start the paperwork for your mother's Medicare, and I found out she was born in 1904. All these years I thought we were the same age. That little devil! When we started dating, she told me she was nineteen. It wouldn't have made any difference to me, but I guess she thought I might not want to marry an older woman." He chuckled and went on, "I wonder if I should tell her?" I knew he wasn't asking for my advice; the question was more rhetorical and didn't require my wisdom. So I let him answer it himself.

"Nah, she'd be too embarrassed if I even mentioned it." That was the end of that conversation, except for my having to swear I would never let her know that I knew "the secret." To his credit, he never told her he had discovered that she was an older woman. He never even put her age in her obituary. Now that's true love.

So, there they were, the honeymoon was barely over, and along I came. They hardly had time to get to know one another as a married couple and now more adjustments. My mother was forced to quit her job at the telephone company when it was evident that she was pregnant. That lowered their income. My father had never finished high school and, after some dead end jobs, had started to work for an insurance company at the lowest rung on the ladder, earning $25 a week. Twenty-eight dollars of his monthly wages were for rent. Now they had to purchase all the paraphernalia that little babies need. Not to mention another mouth to feed. Plus, my father was taking night courses to learn the insurance business. I remember him telling me it was a luxury for him to take the trolley car to work. He would usually walk the three miles to save the dime fare. Don't get me wrong. We were never on the verge of knocking on the door of the poorhouse. If we were poor, I didn't know it. But I know now that it was not easy for my parents to start a new family in 1929.

Just to put my birth in perspective, Herbert Hoover was elected president of the United States in 1928. He ran on the platform that "We in America today are nearer to the final triumph over poverty than ever before in the history of this land ... We shall soon with the help of God be in sight of the day when poverty will be banished from this land."[1] One of his slogans was, "A chicken in every pot and a car in every garage." His opponent was Alfred Smith, the first Roman Catholic to run for the presidency. The two major issues in the campaign were religion and prohibition. Smith campaigned against prohibition, while Hoover was in favor of continuing the Eighteenth Amendment. The Republicans attacked Smith, claiming that if he were elected he would make Catholicism the national religion.[2] Growing up, I remember the adults talking about how it was a blessing that Al Smith didn't win the election, since otherwise all the Protestants would be blaming the depression on the Catholics and the pope.

Hoover took the oath of office on March 15, 1929. On October 29, 1929, known as Black Tuesday, the stock market crashed, and the Great Depression was underway. That was the end of "a chicken in every pot and a car in every garage." People were lucky if they had a pot to put a chicken in. The optimism that Hoover had inspired came crashing down with the stock market. Remember, I was born on November 22, less than a month after the crash. Nevertheless, my father always blamed me for the Great Depression. Even though he said it in jest, I can still hear him saying to his friends, "That Don, if it wasn't for him, we wouldn't have had the Great Depression."

How bad was it? During the worst years of the Depression, 1933–34, the overall jobless rate was 25 percent, with another 25 percent of breadwinners with their wages and hours cut. That translates into almost one out of every two United States households directly experiencing unemployment or underemployment. This was catastrophic for workers and their families.[3]

Songs of the Great Depression

I have a tape recording that I love to replay of my father singing one of the most popular ballads of the day, "Brother Can You Spare a Dime?" by E. Y. Harburg and Jay Gorney. It's a sad song about a man called Al, who had obviously bought into the hopes of the American Dream, only to have those hopes dashed by the tremendous personal losses of the Great Depression. Al symbolized thousands of wage earners who were down on their luck, as they used to say. I'm sure most people who lived during the depression could identify with the despair and sadness that Al expressed when he was forced to beg on the streets. The song was so popular it was even recorded by two of the most popular vocalists of the twenties, Rudy Vallee and Bing Crosby. Every time my dad sang it, he would recount his recollections of the Great Depression. He seemed to make it his own song. It was a song that somehow helped him and others through those years.

I think one of the reasons the song was so special for my father was that one of his very good friends for over fifty years was Al Port. Marge and Al Port eventually became good friends of mine. Marge and my mother had worked at the telephone company before my mother got pregnant with me. In those days women were not permitted to work once it was apparent that they were "in a family way." As a matter of fact, it was considered unseemly for a pregnant woman to be seen in public, except for going to church on Sunday. Anyway, Marge was another of the "old plugs" from my mother's days with the telephone company. She and my mother were also sorority sisters. Not to be outdone by the college girls, they started their own Greek sorority. They called it "Tau Nu Signa," or, in English, "Twenty Necking Sisters." I suspect it was the only chapter in the country. I can picture them in their flapper outfits, going out to the "speakeasies" to meet fellows on the weekends after a hard week at the New York Telephone Company.

Al and my father became friends through dating the founders of the "Twenty Necking Sisters." The connection with Al Port and the Al of the song is that one day, before he was married, Al Port just took off for six months and became a hobo. The hobo population thrived during the Great Depression. Although there isn't much agreement on the etymology of the word, its roots are thought to be associated with the phrase "**ho**meless **bo**dy." Hoboes traveled from city to city mostly by railroad boxcars, which they hopped on when the authorities were not watching. According to Al Port, it was a dangerous life. The economy was so bad that they would work for money, food, or shelter. I remember Al describing what appeared to be a hobo subculture. He told me that the hoboes had their own language that was foreign to non-hoboes. They had their own code of ethics; for example, "Help runaway children and try to convince them to go home." They also had signs that they would place outside homes where they had asked for food or work. A sign of two shovels indicated work was available. A drawing of a cat meant that a kind lady lived there and would offer food. Eventually, Al got tired of being what he called a "bum" and went back to Albany to marry Marge. His story had a happy ending. After working as plumber for small companies, he started his own company, Al Port Sprinklers, and did very well financially.

My mother told me that she and Dad had a special depression song that they used to sing when they were first married. It was "their song." It was a song that was popular in the twenties, and I suspect that their song was adopted by many other young couples trying to look at a brighter side. The song was "Side by Side," written by Harry Wood, who wrote other uplifting songs during the Depression.

Besides being "their song," it was one that we used to sing growing up, when we took a Sunday ride in my Uncle Ken's car or had gatherings with our extended families and friends. It was always—and still is—one of my favorite old songs. As we say, "They don't make songs like that anymore." I was very touched and pleased when my mother shared how meaningful their song was to her and Dad. I could imagine the two of them singing "Side by Side" and suddenly realizing that it would no longer just be the two of them—that there would be someone else to share their lives.

Reflection

In reflecting on my birth, I was reminded of one of Albert Einstein's frequently quoted dicta, "There are only two ways to live your life. One as though nothing is a miracle. The other as though everything is miracle." It might be a cliché to refer to the birth process as the "miracle of birth," but as I pondered my own birth, it became more and more apparent that it was a miracle. I became more convinced that miracles can range from a supernatural happening or vision to a wondrous experience that fills us with awe. In that sense, every birth is certainly awesome.

I realized that just writing about my birth was an opportunity for me to appreciate it as I never had before. Even though I had spent years studying different approaches to meditation, engaging in

Native American spiritual teaching and practices, reading spiritual works from a variety of sources, practicing tai chi and other Eastern mind-body experiences, this encounter with my own birth was different for me. After spending hours meditating on the complexity of my own birth, I came to a special realization of the intricacy of every little detail that goes into the creation of each person and felt an awe that was overpowering. Wow! How did that one little spermatozoon reach the one special ovum and produce the DNA that eventually became me? It seemed improbable that it happened by accident. I was filled with gratitude—gratitude to my parents that, despite all the financial pressures they were under, they hadn't aborted me, and gratitude to God for giving them the strength to bring me into the world. The feelings were so strong and different that I asked myself whether I was having a mystical experience. If not mystical, it was certainly a spiritual experience. It was suggestive of what Abraham Maslow refers to as a "peak experience."[4]

To Be or Not to Be, That Is the Question

Another issue that recalling my birth experience brought to mind and that caused me to engage in more meditation, research, and soul-searching was abortion. I started to wonder whether my parents might have considered abortion when they discovered that my mother was pregnant. I wondered how they felt about assuming the responsibility for this miracle. I even had a dream that I saw as symbolic of my trying to reach them as an unborn child. I was outside our house on Judson Street, banging on the door, silently screaming for them to let me in. I wasn't able to see myself, except for my little arms banging against the door, but I knew it was me. The door finally opened slowly, and I was able to feel that it was okay for me to come in and join my parents. Even though we did not exchange any words, I had a strong feeling of being welcomed. This was comforting.

I realized that there were many questions that I wished I had discussed with my parents. Abortion was only one of them. Even if I had asked the question, adult to adult, I'm not sure if they would have given me an answer. They might have just discounted my question. They might have been shocked that I even asked the question. Given the times, and their Catholic background, I suspect that they never seriously considered abortion. The only reason for my entertaining the question was that I just wanted them to know that I certainly would have understood if it had been an option they had considered.

This reflection prompted me to revisit my own position on abortion. I don't mean to be overdramatic, but Shakespeare's Hamlet came to mind. Hamlet's soliloquy is probably the most famous line in English literature. "To be or not to be, that is the question" is a question of life and death. On a metaphysical level, his question was not, "Shall I kill myself or can I live like this?" "To be or not to be" debates existence itself. It is a conflict between reason and feelings/passions.[5] The question with which Hamlet was wrestling was one for which he couldn't find an answer that had the same clarity and purity as the question itself.

My struggle with the ethics of abortion has been a Hamlet-like struggle, and I've agonized about the issue over and over again. My effort is not unlike that of many others who believe they are making a judgment from an informed conscience. At the risk of sounding like John Kerry in a political debate, I personally have been against abortion. Up to this point, however, I've struggled with the church imposing its position on other people of good will whose consciences differ from Rome's on a woman's right to choose to have an abortion. I have been concerned that to take a position of imposing our beliefs in our pluralistic society, where the majority of people do not share the same beliefs, could make it appear that we were trying to change our democracy into a theocracy, where the religious beliefs of a minority are imposed on the majority. Wouldn't that be the same kind of fear that many Americans have about the agendas of radical Muslims in attempting to create theocracies in pluralistic/democratic societies? Given the seriousness of that concern, I decided I needed to pursue my dilemma in greater depth.

My background as an academic for over forty years suggested that if I were to have an informed conscience on abortion, I needed to do more empirical research on the morality of abortion. I also had to reread what I thought I understood. So, I put my writing on hold for several months to immerse myself in research, which included collecting and digesting data from both sides of the abortion debate. It was my earnest and heartfelt attempt to be open to what my reason and research revealed. I had no intention of being either an apologist for, or an opponent of, the church's teachings. I realized that, in discussing any particular issue of faith or belief, it is always a temptation to look just for research that supports one's position. I've tried to avoid that hazard and will discuss the findings that had the most influence on my final conclusions.

My conclusions are not intended to speak for anyone but myself. I believe that each one of us needs to take responsibility for developing our individual consciences, based on reliable sources, including both faith and reason. Only then can we make a decision.

Before I started my research, I invoked the Holy Spirit to give me an open mind that would lead me in the right direction, put on my research cap, and sequestered myself with books, reports, articles, and resources from the Internet. I will focus my reflections on what I believe are the most important, but certainly not the only considerations from my research.

Abortion and an Informed Conscience

Assuming I've practiced due diligence in arriving at an informed conscience and granted the primacy of conscience, which I will discuss in detail in chapter 9, I began my search to resolve my conscience on the moral, ethical, and political issues involved in an induced abortion.

This search started with a review of the teaching of the magisterium, the church's deposit of beliefs. I also needed to examine the positions of those who are for abortion and describe themselves as pro-choice, and those against legal abortion, who call themselves pro-life. I've always thought that the titles of the two groups would be more forthright if they referred to themselves as pro-abortion and anti-abortion. Both pro-choice and pro-life are loaded terms that reduce what is complex to a bumper sticker slogan. No one wants to say they are anti-choice or anti-life. For the purposes of these reflections, however, I'll use the common terms, pro-life and pro-choice.

One of the major issues that divide the two groups is the question, "At what point does the fertilized egg become a human person?" In reviewing the positions of each advocacy group, I had not only to appraise their positions but also to update my knowledge of the biology of birth. If what follows sounds a little pedantic and elementary, I apologize, but it was part of the process of reeducating myself.

Most of the pro-lifers believe that human life begins at the time of conception, when one lucky spermatozoon out of 500 becomes one with the ovum and forms a genetically unique entity called a zygote.[6] The zygote contains all the genetic information (DNA) necessary to become a child. Half of the genetic information comes from the mother's egg and half from the father's sperm. The zygote spends the next few days traveling down the fallopian tube and divides to form a ball of cells. Further cell division creates an inner group of cells with an outer shell. The cells at this stage are called a "blastocyst." The inner group of cells will become the embryo, while the outer group of cells will become the membranes that nourish and protect it. The blastocyst reaches the uterus at roughly the fifth day, and implants into the uterine wall on about day six. At this point in the mother's menstrual cycle, the endometrium (lining of the uterus) has grown and is ready to support a fetus. The blastocyst adheres tightly to the endometrium, where it receives nourishment through the mother's bloodstream.[7] The question remains, is this combination of the sperm and ovum at conception, now with its own unique DNA, a person?

When I went back to the magisterium to refresh my memory about the traditional teaching of the church, I found that what I once thought was true needed to be verified. It was apparent that the teaching of the church had not always been anti-abortion. In modern political jargon, the teaching of the church might be characterized as a flip-flop. I suspect that most Catholics are not aware of any major change in the church's doctrine over time. I'm not suggesting that a change in dogma over time demonstrates the fallibility of the present teaching of the church on abortion. Of course, none of the modern elements such as the benefits of ultrasound, modern embryological observations, and DNA were available to the early fathers of the church. I thought it would be helpful for me to consider this information as I formed my conscience. Incidentally, I don't think framing the church's changing its doctrine as a flip-flop is helpful. I would like to see the church consider other doctrines that need to be changed. But that's for a later chapter.

There is no question that there are writings of many of the early Christian philosophers and church fathers opposing abortion (all in the first three centuries), including: Clement of Alexandria, Tertullian, and St. Basil the Great, to mention a few, who equated abortion with infanticide. In addition, the *Didache*, also known as *The Teaching of the Twelve Apostles,* which dates from the first half of the second century, admonishes the faithful very clearly that, "Thou shall not murder a child by abortion."[8]

Other theologians and fathers of the church had different opinions. At the risk of oversimplifying their positions: both St. Augustine and St. Jerome based their beliefs on "ensoulment," i.e., when the human soul was infused in the body. For SS. Augustine and Jerome, the fetus held no greater moral significance than an irrational animal. They both believed that the destruction of the fetus would not be considered a homicide until the fetus was fully formed. Their opinions of what point in the gestation process the fetus was a person varied, but they did not believe the fetus was a person at conception.[9]

St. Thomas Aquinas was considered *the* official church theologian for over 600 years. When I was in the seminary, his magnum opus, the *Summa Theologica,* was our primary resource for dogma and moral theology study. St. Thomas had a similar view as Augustine and Jerome, with a different understanding of the process of gestation. Briefly, he followed the steps of Aristotle, who believed that it is the faculty of reason that distinguishes humans from all other animals and that only a human person has the ability to reason because they have a human soul. Reason for Aquinas was the defining essence of what it means to be a human person. His conclusion rests on ensoulment. He also did not believe that the fetus was a human person from the time of conception. His belief was that since the newly formed zygote did not have a soul until it was eight weeks old, it was not yet a person.[10] Therefore it was not murder or infanticide to abort a zygote. To put his reasoning in the terms of an Aristotelian syllogism:

> Major: To commit murder, infanticide, the zygote must be a human person.
> Minor: Since zygotes do not have a human soul, they are not human persons.
> Conclusion: Therefore, aborting a zygote is neither murder nor infanticide.

Without any scriptural guidance, St. Thomas Aquinas again relied on Aristotle's view of three different kinds of animation.

The church actually codified Aquinas's teaching on abortion into law at the Council of Trent, when it convened between December 13, 1545, and December 4, 1563. It became the teaching of the church for the next 306 years that the fetus did not become a person until late in the course of gestation.[11] It was in 1869 that, in his encyclical *Apostolicae Sedes,* Pope Pius IX declared that those who caused abortion at any stage were subject to excommunication. I am not suggesting that under all circumstances the magisterium is wrong when it changes its position, but rather that before we blindly say, "Well the magisterium says so, therefore I must believe it, " we need to carefully examine what the magisterium has taught over a period of time.

Even though the magisterium had indeed changed its position, I focused on other sources for forming my conscience. After viewing the sketches of a late-term or, as it is also called, partial-birth abortion—i.e., after the first two trimesters, or six months—I was convinced that to abort a fetus at that stage of gestation was certainly infanticide. Up to that point, I had only a vague knowledge of exactly what the procedures entailed. According to the Web site LifeDoc, the procedure for performing a partial-birth abortion is: first, guided by ultrasound, the abortionist grabs the baby's legs with forceps and delivers the baby's body through the birth canal, except for the head; then scissors are jammed into the baby's skull and opened to enlarge the hole in the head; the baby's brains are then sucked out, and the head is removed from the womb.[12]

I had no question that this was murder. Although they didn't refer to it as murder, the Supreme Court in its 1973 *Roe v. Wade* decision put limits on abortion. They established a cutoff at the third trimester, unless the woman's health was at risk. In subsequent rulings the Court rejected the trimester cutoff altogether in favor of a cutoff at the point of fetal viability (*Planned Parenthood v. Casey*). At this time, given the composition of the Supreme Court and cases in the lower courts, it's uncertain whether *Roe v. Wade* will be overturned, even though opinion polls consistently show that most Americans accept the court's decision.[13]

Conclusions

Once I eliminated late-term abortion as an option, I needed to look again at the gestation process to see if it were even possible to determine when a human person was present in the mother's womb. The more I read, the more I was convinced that at this point, no one can apodictically prove when a human person comes into existence. The opinions range all the way from conception to the existence of a viable fetus—i.e., one that could live outside the mother's womb. Given the reality that no one can prove either position, it was now my responsibility to apply my conscience to abortion. My conclusion is based not just on religious dogma or legal decisions but on a reasonable interpretation of all facts as I understand them at this time.

The experience of the last four decades has proven that it has been fruitless for one side to try to convince the other side when a person is present in the womb. It's just not going to happen. In the face of lack of certainty of when a fetus becomes a person, I believe that the presumption should be in favor of the potential living person, with its own DNA embodied in the fetus.

I decided that I will fight for that life but will not fight against choice. I believe that this position against abortion is a reasoned one. I also believe that it is correct to give those who don't agree with me the right to make their own choices based on their consciences.

I'm sure my position opens me up to the criticism, from those who believe that, since I don't condemn those who are making choices that I don't agree with, that I am supporting abortion. One more time: I do not support abortion. I am against abortion. I would like others to agree with my opinion. I do not, however, intend to join the picket lines marching outside abortion clinics or the court building because others believe that everyone should believe as they do.

When I finished my reflections on what I believed to be issues of existence and nonexistence, I felt more aware that the end of my own journey was in sight. I experienced a deep sense of gratitude for the time I've had and an appreciation for any time I had left. I promised myself that I would continue to devote whatever time I have left to adoption programs. Throughout my professional life I've been involved in adoption programs both national and international. I plan to maintain my efforts to make sure that the needs of those who chose adoption versus abortion are cared for and that they have the opportunity to have their children placed in good, loving families.

Chapter 2
Love Thy Neighborhood

My parents brought me home from the Brady Maternity Hospital to 8 Judson Street. They had recently rented a second-floor "flat" owned by my Uncle John and Aunt Liz, who lived on the first floor. The flat included three bedrooms; a living room with a bay window and an alcove; one bathroom, with a tub, no shower; a dining room off the bedrooms; a kitchen with a pantry, and an old-fashioned washer with a ringer; and an enclosed back porch, where my mother hung her laundry out on a line that reached to a pole at the end of the backyard. My bedroom was in the front of the house, my parents' in the middle, and my brother Jim's, at the back, was waiting for him to occupy it in 1934. This was going to be my home, my world, for the first eighteen years of my life, until I left for the seminary in 1948.

I'd like to tell you a little bit about my neighborhood. Our block was bordered by Clinton Avenue on the west and First Street on the east. The area our family lived in was named Arbor Hill. The name is deceiving. You might think that Arbor Hill was one of the city's more elite sections, with tree-lined streets, front lawns, and perennial flowers, all enclosed with a white picket fence, and a garage for the family car. Far from it! The houses on our block were mostly two-story wooden frame row houses, all painted in drab colors—mostly gray or brown—and bordering on a cement sidewalk. My father always referred to Arbor Hill as Cabbage Town. I can only guess why he called it Cabbage Town. I suspect it was because we lived not too far from the West Albany Shops. The Shops, as they called them, were where the New York Central Railroad fixed their broken-down railroad cars. When the wind was blowing the wrong way, there was an odor that drifted from the Shops, which my father thought smelled like cabbage cooking.

In the early forties there was an epidemic in our neighborhood: one homeowner after another had his house covered with fake brick tiles. My Uncle John, not to be outdone by his neighbors, soon followed suit, and 8 Judson was covered in a facade of brown "brick." It didn't take an astute eye to determine that this was not the real thing and that it was just a cover-up. We weren't kidding anyone with our phony bricks.

Unlike the houses on the next three blocks of Judson Street, which had front porches, the houses on our block only had front stoops. In the summertime our parents were part of a block of stoop sitters. The stoop sitters were a microcosm of the northeastern United States. Practically every country from Eastern Europe was represented on our block.

Our house was in the middle of the block. To the right was an older couple, Ray and Martha Richardson. They didn't have any children, so they weren't very involved in the neighborhood. Next to them was the Franconi family. They were second-generation Italian. Frankie Franconi was about my age and was part of our Judson street gang of kids. I remember that he was the first one of us boys to graduate from knickers to long pants. I envied him so much that I added the sin of feeling envy of Frankie's long pants to my weekly list of sins that I told the priest in confession. "Bless me, Father, for I have sinned. I envied my friend having long pants." For those who have never had to endure the low status of being the last kid in their neighborhood who wore knickers, let me enlighten you. Everyday knickers were usually made of corduroy. They came down just below your knees and were worn with high socks that tucked under an elastic band. The band was either too tight or too loose. If the band was too loose, your socks would fall down to your ankles. Corduroy knickers had a very distinctive sound. Swish, swish as your legs rubbed together. I can almost hear the swishing of my corduroy knickers as I walked down the street.

Wearing long pants was a sign of coming of age. Despite my protests, I wore knickers until I was in the seventh grade. I can clearly remember my feeling of pride when I donned my first pair of long pants. The pants were part of a green, itchy, tweed suit that came with two pairs of pants. My father probably charged them at Spector's Men's and Boy's Quality Clothing store, on Central Avenue. They were an Easter present, along with my first fedora hat and Buster Brown shoes with crepe soles. I must say, I looked pretty spiffy all dressed up for the Easter parade. I finally was one of the big kids on the block.

The Gillette family lived next to the Franconi's. Their youngest daughter, Lois, was a year or two older than I. I know she had an older sister, but I can't remember her name. Lois was one of the guys until she began to develop at puberty. She could beat us all at stickball, kick the can, and most of the other games we played in the street. One day, when several of us were hanging out on her front stoop, she announced, "I guess I can't wear T-shirts anymore. I don't like the way some old men stare at me." No one acknowledged her announcement; we just sort of went on with whatever we were talking about. Up to that point, I hadn't paid much attention to how she was developing into an adolescent. She was just Lois, who hung out with us. I learned later that girls develop earlier than boys. I guess Lois was a textbook case of a girl turning into a women right in front of my pre-teen eyes. But from then on I took more notice.

Now I had to add another sin to my weekly confession. "Bless me, Father, I stared at my friend Lois's breasts." Soon Lois didn't hang out with us guys. I remember when she was in the first year of high school, she dated a senior. Ray Chapman was a star basketball player for Albany High School. A few years later, they married, and I hope lived happily ever after. I lost track of her, but for several years she remained the object of my adolescent fantasies. More sins to confess. "Bless me, Father. I had impure thoughts."

The Kemmers lived at 10 Judson Street. They were second-generation Germans. There was an alley between the houses just wide enough to get a two-wheel bicycle through. My bedroom window only had a view of the Richardson's blank wall. The window in our dining room looked right into Dolores Kemmer's bedroom. To my adolescent dismay, she was always very discreet about keeping her shades down at night. Dolores was my age, but we never really hung out together. I'm not sure why. She was attractive, with long, blonde hair, which she usually wore in a ponytail. She was always friendly and seemed to be popular with her school chums. Perhaps we never really connected, because we went to different grammar schools and both had our own circle of friends. I guess I'll never know for sure.

Down the block on our side of the street were the Harders, Grant and Dee. Their children were just babies, so they weren't part of my peer group. Grant and Dee became good friends of my parents even after we moved out of the neighborhood. They remained good friends up to the time my mother died in 1989. Even after her death, they kept in close contact with my father and invited him to their family celebrations of birthdays, Christmas, and other holidays. If I happened to be back in Albany for one of their celebrations, I used to accompany my father. I always felt welcome. I can picture Grant behind their homemade bar in the basement, dispensing drinks, while Dee and her now-grown daughters prepared the usual fare of salads, stuffed eggs, ham, and a variety of fresh vegetable dishes. Looking back with nostalgia, it's heartwarming to recall that the ties that bound us together were established forty years ago in Cabbage Town.

Next to the Harders were the Ouderkirks. I'm not even sure what Mr. and Mrs. Ouderkirk's first names were, but I remember they had a daughter, Margaret, who was close to my age. The Ouderkirks pretty much kept to themselves. They were not stoop sitters like the rest of our block. I don't ever remember them actually being part of the neighborhood. I do remember Margaret playing hopscotch with Dolores Kemmer, but she rarely played with the rest of the kids. She even seemed reluctant to establish eye contact if you passed her on the street. A "Hi Margaret" might receive a nod, but that was about it. She would come home from school, neatly dressed in her Our Lady of Angels school uniform and high socks, clutching her books to her chest and, rather than joining us kids playing in the street, retreat immediately into her house. We never made fun of her or teased her, but she was certainly the object of our behind her back tittle-tattle. Another sin to confess, "Bless me, Father. I talked uncharitably behind my neighbor's back."

Years later my mother told me she had heard that Mrs. Ouderkirk had pushed Mr. Ouderkirk through their front window and that he had to be rushed to the hospital. That's thirdhand information that I haven't been able to verify. I did wonder what ever happened to Margaret. I Googled her not too long ago on the chance that she hadn't married or that she kept her maiden name. I fantasized that she might have become a famous scientist or an academic. I was able to find the *Ouderkirk Family Genealogy* and several Margaret Ouderkirks, but none of them were close to my age. One of the Margaret Ouderkirks moved from Albany, New York, to Canada, but it was not the Judson Street Margaret. What I did find out is that the Albany branch of the Ouderkirk family traced it roots back to before the Revolutionary War to Johannes Ouderkirk, born in 1670. Not much help, but I tried. I hope that Margaret emerged from the isolation of her youth and lived a long and happy life.

On the corner of Judson and First Street was Brownstein's Grocery Store. In those days there weren't any big supermarkets like Safeway or the A&P. Each neighborhood had its own small mom-and-pop grocery. Max and Rose Brownstein lived over their grocery store in our neighborhood. They carried most of the items the supermarkets carry today, except on a much smaller scale.

The Browsteins were a very friendly Jewish couple who had moved to Albany from New York City to start their own business years before we moved into the neighborhood. I don't think they had any children. If they did, they were already grown. If you were a good customer, they would have an individual receipt book with your name on it, and you could charge your purchases until your next payday. They had a cash register but no adding machine. When all your items were lined up to check out, Max or Rose would take a pencil from behind his or her ear, write the price of each item on a paper bag, and add up your total faster than a computer. They'd put your groceries in the bag with their figures on it, and that was your receipt.

I have several strong memories of embarrassing experiences at their store. The first was during the summer before I made my first confession and Holy Communion. My parents and I were getting ready to go out somewhere. My mother had just combed my hair when she noticed something protruding from the pocket of my little linen summer shorts.

"Donald, what's that in your pocket?"

My not-so-automatic reply was, "Ah, ah, ah, nothing."

"Donald, you look me straight in the eyes. I'm going to ask you one more time, and I want the truth. What's that in your pocket?"

"Nothing," I persisted.

"Donald, you lie like a rug. What's in your pocket?"

Thinking she had some magical power to read my mind, I sheepishly sort of looked her in the eyes and mumbled, "A pack of gum."

"A pack of gum! Where did you get the money to get a pack of gum, young man?"

I was tempted to lie again, but I intuitively figured out it would get me in more trouble. I knew the gig was up, so I came clean. "I took it from Max's grocery store."

"Well, mister, you just take it right back to Max's store, and tell Mr. Brownstein you're sorry for stealing from him and ask him what he wants you to do to make it up to him."

My tears of remorse had no effect on my mother. So, off I went on the three-minute walk to the store, which seemed like an hour. What was I going to say to Max? Like any good crook, by the time I got to his store, I had an angle that I prayed would work. Even though it seemed unlikely that God would answer my prayer for a successful lie.

Max greeted me with his usual friendly, "What can I do for you, Donnie?"

I compounded the situation by saying, "Mr. Brownstein, my father needs a cardboard box and asked me to see if you had any to spare."

"Sure, just a minute. I'll get one from the back room."

As planned, that gave me the chance to replace the unopened pack of gum in the spot from which I had pilfered it. When Max came back with the box, I thanked him and made my way back home. I discarded the box on the way and prepared a deceitful story for my mother. As soon as I got back home, I was ready with yet another lie to answer my mother's anticipated question, "Well, what did Mr. Brownstein have to say?"

"Oh, he just said he was glad I was honest enough to bring it back and made me promise I'd never steal anything again."

Looking back, I can't believe how devious I was for a six-and-a-half-year-old kid. I had the skills to be a first-class criminal. Not surprisingly, my mother found out the real story from Max the next time she went to the store. I was properly punished, and that was end of my career of crime. Of course as I prepared for my first confession, I thought I'd really have an earful for the priest. Stealing, lying, lying again, and then again. I thought I was probably going to be the biggest sinner in my first-communion class. "Bless me, Father, for I have sinned. I'm a thief and a liar, and I disobeyed my mother."

Now that I think about it, I might have learned my evil ways from my mother. She would send me to Max's store to get ten cents' worth of boiled ham or a loaf of bread, or whatever she needed. Sometimes two or three times a day. That was no problem, but the one thing that I felt guilty about was when she would send me on a liver run. In those days, butchers gave away calf's liver to their customers for free. My mother instructed me to tell Max that I'd like some liver for my cat. The only thing was, I didn't have a cat! But off I'd go on my deceitful mission to get our free liver, feeling that this wasn't exactly kosher. Even so, devious Don would brazenly approach Max with a smile on his face and say, "Hi Max, can we have some liver for my cat?" If Max suspected me of obtaining liver under false pretenses, he never let on. He would cheerfully wrap up a portion of liver and send me on my way. I don't think I included that in my growing list of sins to confess to the priest. But to this day, I'm not able to eat liver. It gags me. No matter how it's prepared, I can't even swallow it. Not liver and bacon, not liver and onions—it is still liver. I don't even like to see it on a menu in a restaurant. To make matters worse, my mother used to serve it for dinner and tell me and my brother it was steak. One bite, and I was able to discern that this was a counterfeit steak. Gaggg! I mustn't be too hard on my dear mother. After all, it was the Great Depression, and every dime counted.

Later on, in my first year of high school, we had to read Victor Hugo's novel *Les Miserables*. I remember a recurring dream that I had after completing the book. In my dream I was hounded for stealing liver to feed my family. I was just like that other thief, Jean Valjean, who was hounded for stealing a loaf of bread to feed his family. His relentless pursuer, inspector Javert, eventually sacrificed himself for Jean Valjean, because Javert discovered all the good deeds Jean Valjean had done throughout the years. Unlike Jean Valjean's story, my dream always ended before I discovered whether my inspector Javert sacrificed himself to save me. I'm not sure of the meaning of the dream; I'll leave that for the Freudian or Jungian analysts to interpret. What I do know is that, once I began to have the wet dreams that adolescent boys experience, I never had another dream about the "sins" of my youth.

On the Shady Side of the Street

On the other side of the street on our small block was Frank Mosher and Sons' Garage. It was right on the corner of Judson Street and Clinton Avenue. The Moshers didn't live there, but it was a hangout for the men on weekends to kibitz or play poker. Otherwise they would meet at one another's homes for some serious poker. Next to the garage was a vacant lot where Frank used to rent out spaces for folks from the neighborhood to park their cars. When my father got his first car, a 1928 Chevrolet, in 1938, he paid Frank Mosher $3.00 a month to park in his lot. This also entitled him to have his name painted on the wall of the garage to designate that it was his parking place. The last time I went back to Albany, I could still see Fausel on the wall—a little worn with age but nevertheless readable. By the way, my father was proud of that 1928 Chevy. Every chance he got, he was over there in Mosher's lot washing or polishing it, so it would be ready to take his mother and us for a Sunday ride to the lake. His mother would sit in the backseat and if he went over twenty-eight miles an hour yell, "Otto, you're going too fast."

Louie C., his younger brother, Jerry, and his mother lived across the street. Mrs. C. was a single mother, so while she was at work, we had open access to her house. Louie was a couple of years older and wiser than me. Since my parents never enlightened me about s-e-x and sex education wasn't taught in Catholic grammar schools, Louie became the source of my sexual education during my early years. I remember one rainy day, my friend Muggsy McGraw and I attended our first sex class from Louie. We must have been about eight or nine, He ushered us down to his cellar and gave us a lecture about a woman's anatomy. I don't know where he got his information, but he certainly didn't make the female body sound very appealing. My eight-year-old mind couldn't understand how girls could take care of business when they were missing a part. After the anatomy lesson, he told us to show him our "things" (penises) and he would show us his thing.

We obediently followed his instructions, even though I thought that this didn't seem right. There was no touching, but after proudly showing us "his," he made a remark that I've never forgot. "Don't worry; yours will get as big as mine someday." Now I had a new sin to tell the priest in confession. "Bless me, Father, for I have sinned. I let someone look at my thing." I guess the priest knew what I meant by "my thing," because he didn't ask me any questions, and to my surprise, gave me my regular penance—three Hail Marys and three Our Fathers. Muggsy and I remained friends all through high school but never discussed the incident again. Nor did Louie give us any more lessons in sex education. The fact that I remember it all these years later is probably an indicator of my intuitive sense that there was something about the demonstration that wasn't quite right.

Clayton and Betty Benson and her mother, Mrs. Van Damure, lived directly across the street from us. The Bensons had a grown daughter who lived with them, had gentlemen callers, and took the Belt Line trolley to work every day. They were on the periphery of the neighborhood activities. They were friendly, but at the same time aloof. The only interaction I remember was when my cousins twice removed, Kate and Elizabeth (I'm not sure what twice removed means, but they were Uncle John and Aunt Liz's grown daughters, who at that time still lived at home), dressed me up like a little girl when I was about four or five and brought me across the street to the Bensons and introduced me as their cousin Donna from Springfield. Apparently the Bensons never suspected it was me. I don't remember the gambit, but Kate told me about it so many times, even into adulthood, that I assume it happened.

There was one more house on the block that I can remember. It was next to the Benson's. The family had an Irish name—it was either Kelly or Casey—and several small kids who were always screaming and yelling. I do remember that Mrs. Kelly/Casey always seemed mad at them, especially when she chased them down the street screaming and yelling.

The Backbone of the American Economy

Like most of the families in those days, the fathers were the main source of income. Most of the men on our block worked at the West Albany Shops, where the New York Central sent their railroad cars that needed repairs. I remember whispers about how our next-door neighbor, Mr. Kemmer, lost his arm when it was crushed as he tried to uncouple two railroad cars. I was always curious about the stump he had on his left arm, but I never saw it uncovered. I made a promise to myself that I would never work at the Shops.

I still can picture the men making their way home from the Shops after a hard day's work, covered with grease and grime, carrying their empty lunch boxes and thermos bottles and smelling like they needed a good bath. They were hardworking, blue-collar men; they were indeed the backbone of the American economy.

My father was the only man on our block who was a white-collar worker. He was twenty years old when he started working as a clerk in an insurance agency. He left every day dressed in a suit and tie, a fedora hat, with twenty-five cents for his lunch in his pocket. He usually walked forty-five minutes to the office to save the ten-cent trolley fare. Remember, this was during Great Depression.

While the fathers were bringing home the bacon, as they used to say, mothers took care of the house and children, prepared meals, darned socks, and did the family laundry. They had their coffee klatches during the day to exchange recipes and gossip and compare notes on what was going on with their favorite radio soap opera heroes. I wouldn't be surprised if many of them lived vicariously through characters on *As the World Turns* or the *Romances of Helen Trent*. Several times a week, a few of them would get together to play cards, usually canasta or bridge, or Scrabble. Doesn't sound too stimulating, but it was very much the norm in our neighborhood. I've never seen the TV program *Desperate Housewives,* but I suspect that the lives of the women in our neighborhood were nowhere near as complicated as those of the women in that series. I never asked my mother, but now I wonder how she would have felt if she had had the same opportunities that women have today. If I had had that conversation, I think it might have gone something like this:

"Mom, this might seem like a strange question, but when you look around and see all the opportunities that women have in the workforce today, how do you feel about having to give up your position at the telephone company as soon as they realized you were pregnant with me? Would you have liked to have pursued a career?"

She would probably look at me a little puzzled and say, "Donald, that's a silly question. It's two silly questions. First of all, my job at the telephone company wasn't so great. Repeating 'Number, please' over and over, all day long, was boring. Second, when I was growing up, the only thing I wanted was a husband and family. That's all us girls ever talked about. Your father and I were lucky to find one another and have two wonderful sons."

"But what if you ..."

"What's the point of 'what if?' I was lucky to do what I wanted to do, to be a wife and mother. No more with the 'what ifs'."

"I get your point, Ma, but ..."

"Donald!"

"Okay! What's for dinner?"

So much for trying to do an oral history! Perhaps that's why I never tried to do one. But I'll never know for sure.

Everything Is within Walking Distance

Today's realtors put a lot of emphasis on "location, location, location." Well, we were well located. Most of the men could walk to work. If we wanted to go downtown, where the major department stores were, there was a trolley stop at the end of our block. There were several local pubs within two blocks of us. Leo Moore's Grill was one of the favorites. In addition to having our corner grocery store so handy, there was a family-run bakery on

Clinton Avenue across from Mosher's garage. Milk was delivered every other day by the milkman, and Freuhoffer's Bakery delivered bakery products in a horse-drawn wagon. There was even an umbrella man who came by periodically with a pushcart that had all the equipment he needed to fix umbrellas, sharpen knives, and fix tools and about anything else that needed his handiwork. He'd walk up and down each block yelling, "Umbrellas fixed, knives sharpened!" over and over. I remember he even fixed my roller skates. They were the type of skates that attached to your regular shoes, and you'd size them yourself to fit your shoes. Once you had them on, you adjusted them with a skate key. They were a far cry from the fancy skates that kids have today.

Before we got an electric refrigerator, we had an ice box. It looked a little bit like a refrigerator, but it was on the back porch where the ice man, carrying large blocks of ice in iron tongs, would deposit a block of ice every few days. If you wanted ice before his regular delivery, you'd put a sign in your window that simple said, ICE. For years after we got our first GE refrigerator, we all kept referring to it as an ice box. Old habits are hard to break.

Then there was the life insurance man, who came right to your house to pick up a payment once a month. He kept track of your seventy-five-cent payment in a big book he carried from door to door. Sometimes when my mother didn't want to bother coming down stairs, she'd tell me, "Donald, here's seventy-five cents. Go down and pay Mr. Conlon, and make sure he marks it in his book." I'd dutifully pay Mr. Conlon and would double-check to see if he marked us paid. I thought this was a major responsibility. I hadn't the slightest idea of why we were giving him that much money and not getting anything in exchange. Later on I found out that that money was well spent. It was for life insurance policies for my brother Jim and me. I was happy that my parents thought our lives were worth that much money.

Another delivery was from the coal man, twice a year. You might order a half a ton of coal or even a ton. If money was tight, you might even order by the bag. These were big canvas bags that the coal man would bring to your cellar window and pour down a chute to your coal bin. My job, when I learned my numbers in school, was to sit in the window and count the number of coal bags he sent down the chute. If my mother ordered ten or twenty bags, I sat there patiently counting the bags and then reported to my mother. She'd usually ask, "Are you sure?" "Yes ma'am!" I'd reply in a tone that expressed a little bit of irritation. I really wanted to say, "How dare you question my honesty! I'm a responsible eight-year-old."

Churches and Schools

There were four Catholic churches, two with grammar schools, within walking distance of our house: St. Patrick's, which was the Irish church; Our Lady of Angels, the German church; St. Casmir's, the Polish church; and St. George's, the Lithuanian church. We went to the Irish church. Glory be to God, as my sainted mother might say, what would the Kellys (my father's mother's maiden name) and the McCarrolls (my mother's maiden name) be doing in the German or, even worse, the Polish church. Having a German name would at least have qualified us to go to the German church— but the Polish church! In this day and age it might seem like I'm mistaken about the number of Catholic churches, with so many ethnic backgrounds in one neighborhood. It's so different today with many churches and schools closing or being turned into either senior centers or social service providers.

Sports and Recreation

Many of our sports and recreation needs were met at the Catholic Youth Organization's (CYO) center. All I had to do was go to the end of our block, turn right on First Street, walk a half a block, and there I was, 340 First Street, my second home. It used to be called the Patrician Club because it was built by St.

Patrick's Church for the recreation needs of its parishioners. The CYO took it over in the forties, and it became the diocesan CYO organization's headquarters, as well as providing sports and other activities for the neighborhood's youth. The CYO had the underlying mission of building young people's character. I don't think any of us kids went there to have our character built but rather to enjoy the competition of games and sports.

On the bottom level, they had eight bowling alleys. When I was older, I earned fifteen cents per game for setting up pins. There were no automatic pin setters in those days—just us kids who were lucky enough to earn a few cents to go to the movies or buy candy.

On the second floor, there were the diocesan offices and a regulation basketball court with bleachers for spectators. On the third floor, there were rooms for ping pong, pool, and weight lifting. They say that a good pool shooter is a sign of a misspent youth. If that's so, it was there that I spent hours and hours learning how to misspend my youth, courtesy of the Catholic Youth Organization. With all that practice, I was able to pick up another few bucks for spending money.

The CYO did not develop baseball or football as an organized sport for several years after I graduated from grammar school. This was before the days of the Little League and Pop Warner football. There was a "sandlot" field at the end of Judson Street and Livingston Avenue. Then it really was a sandlot. No grass, no bases, no backstop, no umpires, no coaches, no adults, just a bunch of kids with their own bats and balls, often covered with tape, who would choose up sides and make believe they were playing at Hawkins Stadium, the home of the Albany Senators.

Most of the other games we played were in the street under the watchful eyes of our parents and neighbors, who occupied reserved seats on their stoops. Stickball; dock on the rock; Mother, may I?; hide and seek—games that might not be familiar to everyone today, but for us, they were fun to play, and for the adults, just as much fun to watch.

Movies

There were two movie theaters in our immediate area. The Paramount Theater was a block and a half away. When I was first able to go to the movies alone or with friends, the price for admission was ten cents. On Saturdays you could see a double feature plus a serial. The serials were thrillers that would continue their story line from week to week. They would always leave you wanting to come back the following week to see whether the hero escaped from an impossible situation. Usually it was a situation like his being tied up on a railroad track, with a train about to chop him in pieces. How could you resist not coming the next Saturday?

As I got older, the price increased to thirteen cents. My motivation also changed, as I became interested in girls. A couple of us guys would go with the hope that we could pick up a girl who would neck with us in the back of the theater. It predictably never worked, but just having the intent to "sin" was another item for confession.

On certain evenings they gave away dishes. If you went often enough, you could eventually have a whole set of dishes. This of course was for adults.

The other movie theater was the Colonial on Central Avenue. The one thing I remember about the Colonial was that it was where I had my first cigarette. You could smoke in the balconies, so Muggsy McGraw and I spent fifteen cents to buy a pack of Wings cigarettes. They weren't on the market very long, which was okay by me. After several butts, I ended up sick as a dog and threw up in the balcony of the Colonial. That ended my smoking for the next twenty years.

Health Care

Raymond Kircher, MD, lived around the corner on Clinton Avenue, no more than a four-minute walk to his house/office. He was available virtually day or night. No waiting in a crowded emergency room. Dr. Kircher and his family lived in a three-story brownstone-type house that was unlike the houses on our block. His office and waiting room, with a bathroom, were on the main floor; the living room, dining room, study, kitchen, and another bathroom were on the second floor, along with a room for the live-in maid. On the top floor were four bedrooms and two more bathrooms. The reason I'm so familiar with his living quarters is that his son, Raymond Jr. was a couple of years older than I, and we played together when we were younger. When we were teenagers, he was a junior and I was a freshman, and we went to the same high school and would walk to school together. I would stop by his house, and the maid would let me in and bring me up to the dining room. Ray would be sitting at a large dining table with a white tablecloth, a white napkin on his lap, reading the morning paper, sipping his freshly squeezed orange juice and eating his buttered toast with jam.

The first time I saw him sitting in what to me was the lap of luxury, I thought, *Wow, this is uptown, and it is only around the corner from me.* I don't think we ever got the morning or evening newspaper until I was in college. I know I never sat at the living room table with a little bell to summon the maid if I needed a refill of coffee or more toast. For Ray it just seemed natural. He and his family never put on airs; this was just the way things were. I had been his friend since I was eight years old, and sometimes I would stay overnight. I was always surprised with the fresh flowers all over the living quarters. Ray's mother was a very refined, well-educated, handsome woman, and his two older sisters went to the finest schools and, not surprisingly, married well, as they used to say.

Ray and I were like brothers growing up. A very blatant example of this was when my father was drafted into the army during World War II. Dr. Kircher invited me to the Annual Father and Sons dinners, even after Ray Jr. had graduated. In my sophomore year, when I was boxing in the annual tournament, I reached the finals of my division. Dr. Kircher volunteered to act as my "second" and was at ringside to give me encouragement. Boy, did I feel special. I won the championship, by way. Just to set the record straight, I wasn't as good a boxer as being a champion might suggest, the very next year I was eliminated in my first fight. The guy I was fighting was left-handed, and it took me three rounds to figure out where his punches were coming from.

There is one incident that helped me pinpoint how long Ray Jr. and I were friends. It was May 6, 1937. I would be eight in November. Ray was ten. We were playing on the swings in his backyard in the late afternoon, while his sister Jean read. As Ray and I were playing the ill-fated German zeppelin, the *Hindenburg* suddenly appeared on its way to a disastrous mooring at the Lakehurst Naval Air Station in New Jersey. I needed to Google the date and circumstances of the disaster, but what I do remember clearly was Jean Kircher shouting to us, "There goes the *Hindenburg*!" I had to take her word for it, but I was very impressed by the sheer majesty of the fishlike ship. It seemed huge. The swastikas on its tail would become more familiar in the next three or four years. Over the years I have heard recordings of radio announcer Herbert Morrison frantically trying to give an eyewitness report to his listeners, but his emotion spoke more clearly than the words that seemed reluctant to leave his lips. Crying, "Oh my God, it burst into flames!" and trying to hold back his tears, he seemed devastated by what he was observing and trying to report.

It was comforting to have Dr. K. so accessible. My parents told me about an accident that I had when I was about three, that required Dr. K's skills. I was downstairs watching my Aunt Liz iron when she left the iron standing upright to answer the doorbell, only to return to my screams as she ran back to find the iron stuck to my left arm. As the story goes, I was immediately picked up by Uncle John and rushed to Dr. Kircher's office with the iron still stuck to my arm. I have the scar to show for my not listening to Aunt Liz's caveat not to touch the iron.

Another incident that stands out is my brother Jim coming down the winding back stairs to join us in the yard. He must have been three or four years old. Precocious child that he was, he paid no attention to the rule that he was not to come down the treacherous back stairs by himself. As my mother and I sat in our backyard swing, swinging away, what to our wondering eyes should appear but a little redheaded four-year-old crashing through the glass pane of one of the windows. I panicked and ran for Uncle John, while my mother retrieved my brother's head from the broken glass. There was blood all over the place, and Jim sobbed all the way to Dr. K's.

This medical report would not be complete without my telling you about my tonsillectomy. I was about five years old. As I sat in Dr. Kircher's waiting room with my parents, I could not help but think that the adults in the waiting room didn't look near as sick as I felt. I had had a sore throat for the last couple of days, and our family remedies of gargling with salt and drinking orange juice that my mother spiked with cod liver oil hadn't worked. I was sure it was the liver in the cod liver oil that made me barf. After what seemed like hours, we were finally called into the office. There was my friend's father, sitting behind his desk in a white coat, wearing his familiar bow tie, a cigarette burning in an ashtray. After examining my throat with a wooden tongue depressor, looking in my ears, and listening to my heart, even though they weren't my problem, he was ready to pronounce the verdict. He made light of my diagnosis that I needed to have my tonsils removed, focusing on all the ice cream I'd have after the operation. My father paid the two-dollar fee—there was no health care then—and the next day, before I knew what tonsils were, or if I'd be okay without them, I was off to St. Peter's hospital.

I've never forgotten the fear that I felt as they wheeled me into the operating room. *Why was my mother crying if this was supposed to be a piece of cake? Would I ever see my parents again?* The doors closed, and there I was in this room with all these bright lights shining down on me. Why were all these masked people hovering over me? Then, with no warning, one of the masked men put this smelly cloth over my nose and mouth. I found out later that he was administering ethyl ether. Ether was the only anesthetic they had in the thirties to put people to sleep for an operation. If you never had the ether experience, let me try to explain it. The whole room was whirling and twirling around me, or was it my head that was whirling and twirling around the room? Add the weird, buzzing sounds that attacked my ears and, worst of all, the sickening odor.

Once I was back in my hospital room and had stopped throwing up, then the ice cream came to appease me for the ordeal I had been through. It took me a while for Dr. Kircher to regain my trust.

So now you know a little bit about my neighborhood and the people who contributed to my early years. I enjoyed recalling the memories of neighbors and our activities and the opportunities I had as a kid growing up in Cabbage Town. I really did love my neighborhood.

Reflections

After reminiscing about the old neighborhood and realizing how fortunate I was to grow up in such a close-knit and caring environment, I had a strong longing to go back and visit my old haunts. It had been probably half a dozen years since I had made that pilgrimage, and I suspected that it had changed even more. I wondered if our name was still on the wall of Mosher's garage, where my father used to park his car, and whether I would even recognize any of the once-familiar houses that made up our block of Judson Street.

I had planned to make an East Coast tour in July 2008, so I alerted my relatives and some old friends. One of those friends was Pete Young, who had lived several blocks west of us, at 72 Judson Street. That was one of the blocks where they had front porches, as opposed to our block of stoops and stoop sitters. My father used to call those folks "lace curtain Irish." Pete is now Father Peter G. Young, a priest of the Diocese of Albany, who is approaching the fiftieth anniversary of his ordination. Not only did we both grow up on Judson Street together; we also went to the same high school, and I was two years ahead of him in the seminary. Coincidentally, his parents are buried in the same cemetery, right in back of my parents. Over the years, we have stayed in touch, and when I do go back East, we get together and pick up right where we left off. In between we correspond by e-mail to keep up to date on our lives. When I told him I was going to visit Albany, he e-mailed me and confirmed my memory about where he lived on Judson Street and gave me his observations about the old neighborhood of my youth as it is now, in the twenty-first century.

"Donald, some of the memories you described bring back good times. Yes, we lived at 72 Judson and we did have a large front porch. We weren't stoop sitters like the Fausels. When you come back to visit, don't go near Judson Street. The neighborhood is a hotbed for drugs, many shootings and not a safe place to visit. The CYO center on First Street, where we spent so much time shooting hoops, and pool, is shut down."

O Tempora, O Mores!
(Oh, the changed times, Oh, the changed morals!)
Cicero, 106–43 BC

What's that old saying, "You can never go home again?" I wasn't sure, so I looked it up on a Web site called "clichés.com," and sure enough, there it was. Their explanation was that "Once you make a big change in your life, like leaving your childhood house, things will not be the same." Well, they got that right!

I didn't heed Pete's advice. Not that I doubted his assessment, but my curiosity got the best of me. So, as soon as I arrived at the Albany airport, I rented a car and started making my way to Judson Street. I got on Central Avenue and carefully made my way south until I got to my grammar school, St. Patrick's Institute (SPI). As I looked up at the three-story building, I was surprised to see how much it had shrunk. As a grade-school scholar, I thought it was huge. What stood out was the wrought iron fire escape that hugged the building from the third floor to the sidewalk. I had a flashback to 1940 with Sister Mary Carmelita shepherding us fifth graders as we made our way in silence down the fire escape during our periodic fire drills. If you dared whisper a comment to one of your classmates, you would be kept after school to write one hundred times, "I will not talk during a fire drill." Apparently that was supposed to be a cure for those who couldn't keep their mouths shut.

I was brought back from my reverie to 2008 when I saw a gaggle of senior citizens making their way from the school to a van, to go on an outing, I guessed. The seniors had replaced the hoots and hollers and high-energy of us kids when we were released at lunchtime, with the snail's pace of the elderly, carefully making their way down the stairs as if every step might be their last.

Yes, the school had been turned into a senior center, and the church that still stood proudly with its single tower raised to the sky was no longer accepting worshippers. With a twinge of sadness, I said a quick prayer, took a fast picture, and turned left onto Lake Avenue to trace the route I used to follow on my way to and from school from 1934 to 1943.

After going several blocks on Lake, I turned onto Clinton Street and realized that my walk to school hadn't been as long as I remembered it to be. So far it was only four blocks, and I was heading down the home stretch. As I got closer to Judson, I passed Dr. Kircher's house. Except for a different color of paint, it looked pretty much the same. I made a left-hand turn onto Judson, assuming that there would not be any stoop sitters out, since it was the middle of the day. Not so! If I didn't know any better, I might have thought I was in the middle of Spanish Harlem in the Bronx. I didn't stop to take pictures as I had planned. I made a furtive glance to the left to check out our old house and another to the right to see whether our name was still on Mosher's garage wall. Yes, our name is still on the wall and our house is still there. But the stoop sitters were mainly males who looked like gangbangers. I didn't get too good a look, but from the sound of the music coming from their boom box and their uniform dress code of baggy, sagging pants, they certainly had the appearance of gangbangers. In a matter of seconds, I was at the end of the block and saw what used to be Max Brownstein's corner grocery store all boarded up. I made a quick right turn onto First Street only to find the CYO Center in a state of disrepair.

It was another sad moment for me to realize that things had deteriorated so much in the last sixty years. But the physical deterioration, the obvious poverty, and the fact that so many stoop sitters were hanging out in the middle of the day, paled in comparison to what I was to find out from my cousin Rita.

Cousin Rita's house was my home base while I was back East. Rita Byrne was one of my Uncle Vincent and Aunt Rita McCarroll's five children. (I'll have more about the McCarrolls in the next chapter.) She was a wonderful hostess, and we spent hours talking about the family. When the topic turned to my old neighborhood, she mentioned a shooting that had occurred there a month or so ago. She couldn't remember the ten-year-old girl's name, but she promised to send the clippings. I recently received two stories from Rita of shootings in the neighborhood, both within a period of five weeks.

I was shaken to read the headline for the first shooting: "This is what I get for my birthday: a dead sister." These were the words of the sixteen-year-old brother of Katrina Thomas as quoted in the *Albany Times Union* on May 30, 2008. He expressed his feelings as the family mourned his ten-year-old sister's sudden and shocking death. According to the article, Katrina was "standing on her stoop when she was struck by a .45-calibre bullet, which is a large hand gun round that lodged in her, a high-ranking law official said today." The mayor of Albany, Jerry Jennings, made this comment at City Hall the next morning: "It takes a lot out of you, it really does. I've been through some tough times, but this is one of the toughest if not the toughest." The fact that the random killing of a child was the latest of twenty-one murders that year made the mayor's statement even more significant.

The second shooting in the Judson/First Street neighborhood appeared in the *Albany Times Union* on August 4, 2008. The story starts off by reporting that, "The small yellow house at 11 Judson Street was cordoned off by police tape Sunday." That address—11 Judson Street—was right across the street from where we lived. It used to be the Bensons' home. Unbelievable! Unfortunately, it's too believable, given the changes over six decades. The story ends with a statement that the victim, Nathan Walcott, was killed "less than a block away from where the fatal bullet was shot at First and Judson streets that killed 10 year old Katrina Thomas in May."

When I compare the neighborhood that I grew up in, where I was wrapped in the security of a loving family; where neighbors looked out for one another; where we never even had to lock our doors; where I could sit on our stoop without being afraid that some gangbanger terrorist might randomly chose to shoot me; where the only pusher was the Good Humor Man in his little white truck with ice cream treats; it's difficult for me to begin to fathom how terrifying it must have been for Katrina Thomas or any of the other children on the block to live with that constant fear.

Blaming the Victim

I know that it's not just my old neighborhood that has gone downhill in the past six decades. But seeing just how much the neighborhood had deteriorated—from the safe, stable, and secure block that I remember to the war zone it is today—forced me to check my hasty reactions and precipitous judgment of the values and way of life of the new generation of stoop sitters on Judson Street.

Over the years I've worked with homeless people, welfare recipients, alcohol and drug abusers, chronically mentally ill and violent people, but the difference was not just that those folks weren't destroying "my neighborhood" and were not a threat to my way of life. The difference was that I found that some of my old stereotypes were still alive. I realized that I was indeed blaming the victims. I know it's hard for many people of good will to think of anyone who grew up in abject poverty as a victim, but that is what the majority of those folks are—victims. I could never convince my father that it wasn't always a failure on the part of an individual that causes his/her poverty, so I'm not going to try to convince you. I just wanted to give you an example of how my knee-jerk reaction about the new generation of stoop sitters, was just that a knee-jerk reaction, not a reasoned response . I hope that you can take a few minutes of reflection to check your reactions when you see or hear about someone who was brought up in a culture of poverty.

Chapter 3
Family Ties

They say we can choose our friends but not our relatives. Well, I'm quite happy with the relatives that were chosen for me, both my immediate family and my extended family. We're not all perfect, by any stretch of the imagination, but we've always been there for one another in good times and bad times and in between. I have the fond memories and the home movies to prove it. Baptisms, birthdays, first holy communions, confirmations, graduations, weddings, reunions, sickness and hospital visits, wakes, funerals, and visits for no particular reasons, except to be with folks whom I've known and who have known me all my life.

It's quite clear from even a cursory review of the sociology of the family that it plays a major role in contributing to how we think, feel, and act. In this chapter I will give you a more detailed picture of my family. I am indebted to both my family of origin and the extended family of Fausels and McCarrolls for providing me with a childhood and adolescence that helped me develop to be the person I am today and the person I hope to be. Their unconditional acceptance and support, even when they didn't agree or were disappointed with the diverse paths I chose, was a clear expression of their love.

First, I would like you to know more about my birth family, then my extended family. Not just for you to have a better understanding of where I've come from, but because these folks are people you would enjoy spending time with. Unfortunately, I don't have space to go into great detail about all my relatives. So, if my numerous relatives are reading this and you find that I don't do you or your parents justice, I'm sure you will understand.

My Fausel Roots

My father was the middle child of five siblings—Chuck, Ken, Otto, Ed, and Frances—born to Frederick Fausel and Mary Frances Kelly. I don't have very much information about my grandfather in his early days. I know that his parents were Bertha and Christian Fausel. In the 1880 United States Census, Christian is listed as having been born in 1829 in Wurttemberg, Germany, and lived in Troy, New York. As a small child, I did meet my Great-Grandmother Bertha once at her home in Troy. She was a small woman who was bent over and seemed all shriveled up. Christian must have died by then; at least I don't recall his being around. But I do know from my Aunt Frances that he was a well-known lithographer and at least one of his pictures was displayed in the Albany Museum of History and Art. My grandfather was also a lithographer. Their artistic skill never reached my generation.

I did get more information about my grandfather from a talk I had with my father back in the 1970s. I was in a training program to become a family therapist. One of the assignments we were given was to talk with our parents to find out more information about their childhoods.

Despite the fact that I was a forty-something-year-old man, who was doing reasonably well in my personal and professional life, I approached the assignment with the anxiety of a gladiator going into the arena. Even as I write, I can still feel the same butterflies churning in my stomach at the very thought of having a conversation that might rock the family boat.

I decided to talk with my father first. He was by far the more dominant parent, and our adult relationship was often like walking on eggshells. I'm not blaming him. He was a very caring parent in many ways, but as far as our communicating, adult-to-adult, on a meaningful level, there was much to be desired on both our parts. Up to this point, we had never really talked about the underlying issues that caused our strained relationship; rather, we would usually argue about politics, people, religion, etc. I never thought of our family as dysfunctional, but as an adult child, it was unusual to spend extended time with the family without there being a major blowup.

We had our talk one summer when I was visiting for the Fourth of July holiday weekend. We were sitting around my father's pool having a drink before dinner. I casually started the conversation by saying, "You know, Dad, it's always puzzled me—I know Grandpa died of sclerosis of the liver, but Aunt Frances always vehemently denies that he was an alcoholic."

"Frances has always been in denial about Pa's drinking problem," he replied with a familiar tone that was his "put-down" voice.

I followed up by asking, "What do you think the reason for her denial is?"

He started by saying, "You know how emotional that Frances is. She just could never accept the fact that Pa was anything less than perfect." He hesitated for a moment and pensively went on to say, "She was the youngest of us five kids and the only girl; she was the apple of Pa's eye. I guess it's understandable that she couldn't think anything bad about him."

"That makes sense," I responded. I tried to ask as gently as I could, "How did his drinking affect you growing up as the middle child in the family?"

His frown and pursed lips communicated that he was obviously not very comfortable with the question, but, to his credit, he didn't dismiss it as I thought he might and instead answered, "I've really tried not to think much about it and usually would make excuses for the way he acted sometimes, but …"

He seemed to be choking up, and, when it appeared that he was regaining his composure, I asked, "Can you think of any examples of how he treated you when you were younger?"

"I haven't thought of this for years, but I remember even as a kid of six or seven, when I'd come home from playing with my friends after school, I'd go into the house through the back door to the kitchen. My mother would be preparing dinner, and I'd always ask her, 'Is Pa angry tonight?'"

I cautiously asked, "And if he was angry?"

"If he was angry, I did whatever I could to avoid him. I'd usually say a quick, 'Hi Pa' and go into to the bedroom that I shared with my brother Ed."

"And if he wasn't angry?"

He seemed to relax a little and replied, "What a difference! I could jump up on his lap, give him a hug, and he might show me some of his sketches he brought home from work. Or he might ask what I had been up to or how school was. I felt really safe."

It felt like I was taking a risk when I responded, "That must have been very difficult for you to never know how Grandpa would react."

For the first time in my life, I saw my father tear up. I didn't know what to say, so I just gave him a big hug.

My dad's crying was a real "Aha!" moment for me. It was the beginning of a more adult-to-adult relationship, as opposed to the parent-child relationship that we had had for years. There were still bumps in the road that would come up from time to time, but I really felt more understanding of where my father was coming from as the adult child of an alcoholic. I was able to deal more rationally with him when he would lapse into his more critical mode, and I was able to tell him it was not okay when he would put me down.

I've always been thankful that we had that talk. Not only did I get a better picture of what it was like for my Dad to grow up with the confusion of not knowing how his father would be on any given day, but it provided a glimpse of a side of my grandfather that I had never seen before. For me he had always been that kindly man who enjoyed a few beers every night at the kitchen table, sang German songs to me, and always asked at the dinner table, "Don, how ya making out?"

My grandmother had a sad but remarkable childhood. She was one of five children. Her mother died when she and her sister Nellie (that's right, Nellie Kelly), were, I think, seven and five years old. Her father put the two girls in an orphanage and raised the three boys. As I understood it, he didn't feel that he could be father and mother to the girls. I wish I had more information about the circumstances; I imagine it must have been difficult for him to give up his girls and for them to deal with feeling abandoned by their father and brothers. I have no idea if he ever kept in touch with my grandmother and Aunt Nellie. Like many emotionally laden events in our family, it was seldom discussed. My father's sister Frances was the Fausel family historian, but she died in 2004, so there is nobody left to answer the questions that have come up since I started writing about my family.

I do remember Aunt Frances telling me about what was probably an indicator of how my grandmother had been affected by growing up in an orphanage. After my grandfather died, Grandma lived with Frances, her husband Andy, and their four children. I'm not sure how it came up, but Frances mentioned how uncomfortable Grandma would become if she and Andy showed any signs of affection in front of her. She would usually say something like, "Oh you silly things, stop that mush!" I can see how Grandma's upbringing in the orphanage would have made it difficult to be comfortable with demonstrating affection, given that she most likely was not exposed to normal affection between couples. It made me think that one of our unwritten family rules was, "No mush at the airport." It wasn't posted on the refrigerator or recited at meals; I just intuitively picked it up from my parents. For the longest time, I remember that every time my parents would take me to the train station or airport, to go back to the seminary, we would all keep a stiff upper lip, even though we might be stifling tears. Over the years, we learned to express our feelings more genuinely.

Another example is that I remember when I would call home from Connecticut, at the end of the conversation I would quickly say, "Love you!" and just as quickly hang up. I don't know what I expected the response to be, but I wasn't about to wait to find out. Family therapists call that the intergenerational transmission process. That's where one generation passes behaviors on to the next generation. The good news is that we can learn to change those behaviors, and I did over time become more comfortable with saying "I love you" without hanging up. I liked that a lot better.

One thing I regret is that I didn't ask the questions that I have now, when I had the opportunity. But if I had asked either of my grandparents the questions I had, I suspect that they might have dismissed them without much thought. I can almost hear my grandmother saying, "Donald how do you expect me to remember that many years ago?" And that would have been that.

Here are a few of the questions I would have liked to have asked: How many years did you live in the orphanage? What was the orphanage like? Did the nuns run it? Were you and Aunt Nellie together in the same dormitory? Were you able to go to school while you were there? Where was the orphanage? Did your father or brothers ever visit? Did your father ever remarry? What ever happened to your three brothers? What are some of the happiest memories you have of the orphanage? What are some of the saddest? Did you have any special friends there? When you left, did you and Aunt Nellie leave together? How long after you left did you meet Grandpa? How did you meet him? So many questions that I'll never know the answers to! After reading an early draft of this chapter, one of my friends asked, "Why is it so important that you know the answers to these questions at this point in your life? You've managed to get along for all these years without knowing. What's the big deal?" I said, "That's a good question, I need to give it some more thought. Right this minute I don't know the answer, but thanks for asking the question."

Well, I gave the question more thought, and I'm still not sure what the answer is. I suspect that it has something to do with my growing older and having more time to wonder. Also, writing my memoir requires asking a lot of questions of myself and others. They are often questions I either avoided or never had the inclination to pursue. For me, part of the luxury of growing older is to be able to review my life and contemplate both the parts I can remember and those details where others can supply the missing pieces. It's like doing a jigsaw puzzle, where you can get help when you get stuck. Or there might be pieces of the jigsaw that are missing, and you'll never be able to complete it perfectly. But at least I know I tried.

Our Family Grows to Four

One of the biggest surprises of my young life was when my brother, Jim, was born. As was the norm for those days, no one ever told me he was even on the way. I didn't even notice that my mother was pregnant. If I wondered about her getting larger, I would have had no way of knowing that she was with child. At five years old, I knew nothing about where babies came from. It would be five more years before I got the birds and the bees' story from my neighbor, Louie C. What I do remember is that my father and I stayed with my grandparents while my mother was off giving birth to Jim. Any questions about her whereabouts or when we were going back home were shrugged off with a, "Oh, it won't be long" type of response. I didn't put it all together until after they brought Jim home from the Brady Maternity Hospital. I do remember having my treasured toy cars to play with on Grandma's oriental rug and using the intricate designs on the rug as streets to park and drive on. I'm not sure what I did all day long with my Grandma, but I know I looked forward to my father coming home every night after work.

Every night after supper, it was a ritual for my grandfather to leave to get his growler of beer at the neighborhood saloon. I suspect my memories of his nightly sojourns were from what my father told me and less from my own recollections. Apparently it had been a pattern with my grandfather from when my father was growing up and continued until he died. While my grandmother was washing the dishes, he would announce, "Frank [my grandmother's name was Mary Frances, but he always called her Frank], I'm going up to Yanas's to get a growler." Unless you're in your seventies, you probably don't know what a growler is. The word *growler* was very familiar to me, but I had never seen it in print. Just to make sure I had the right word, I Googled "a growler of beer." To my surprise, I got 338,000 hits in 0.09 seconds. By checking several of the sites, I learned more about a growler than I needed to know. The original growlers were galvanized metal pails, with lids. The origin of the term *growler* was perhaps my most interesting discovery. The father or grandfather would usually send one of the kids down to the tavern to fetch a pail of beer. If the kid was not careful and splashed some beer out of the pail, the old man was said to growl; therefore, the pail was named a growler. Isn't that interesting?

Welcome Home, James Austin Fausel

I remember the day my parents brought my brother, Jim, home from the hospital. He was born on December 22, 1934, so it must have been early in the new year that he officially joined the family. Uncle John and Aunt Liz were babysitting me when my parents brought him home. My mother was carrying something all bundled up in a blanket. "Here's your new brother!" she proudly announced. My cousins twice removed, Kate and Elizabeth, were also there for the big surprise, and they made a big fuss over him. I wasn't sure what to think. *Am I being replaced? Where did he come from? How much did he cost?* For several days after Jim arrived, I would check out this little redheaded baby in his crib. I had never seen a brand-new baby before, and I was amazed at how tiny his feet and hands were. So, after my little five-year-old mind considered my position from every angle, I finally decided, "He's no threat to me: he can't feed himself; he can't even walk or talk; he can't go to the potty on his own like me; he doesn't even have any teeth!" As I convinced myself that my place in the family was secure, I was able to go on with my life and not be upset about the attention Jim was getting as number two son. After all, I was number one son.

I will have more to say about my growing relationship with my brother Jim in future chapters. One thing I can say right now is that he had the quickest wit of any of us in the Fausel line. His wit surpassed any of my uncles or my father and certainly mine. His little zingers always made me laugh. Growing up he was just my kid brother; as an adult he was my valued close friend. I have other friends of whom I can say, "we are like brothers" but Jim *was* my brother.

My Mother's Motto: Silence Is Golden

The Irish of my parents' generation had a way of canonizing their mother after she died and went to heaven. It wasn't unusual to hear them refer to their mother in a way that they never referred to their father. "Oh, me sainted mother …!" after which they usually added, "May Gawd be good to her!" Or if they wanted to be emphatic, they'd add, "Jesus, Mary, and Joseph, she was indeed a saint." And if they were "in their cups" (an Irish euphemism for having had too much to drink) they might shed a tear or two. Well, in the case of my mother, I think it was an appropriate title. Not that she was perfect. But everyone loved Jane. Relatives, friends, and neighbors all loved Jane. I never heard anyone say a bad word about her. I remember Marge Port, her lifelong friend, telling me, "Your mother is a saint. The Lord is my witness, I've known her all these years and never, not once, was she mean to anyone. She could always see good in everyone. She believed that if you couldn't say something good about a person, you shouldn't say anything. And oh, how she loved to laugh. I remember back when we were working for the telephone company, she was a giggler. And 'Glory be to Gawd,' she was always available for any of us with a problem." That's quite an endorsement for sainthood.

My mother was basically a quiet person who always let my father take center stage, which he did without much encouragement. An example that stands out is that whenever we had an anniversary or birthday celebration at their favorite restaurant, after my father gave his prepared speech, the thirty or forty friends and relatives would chant, "Jane, Jane, speech, speech!" She would reluctantly stand and obviously embarrassed, shyly say, "Silence is golden." She'd immediately sit down to a round of applause. Her after-dinner speech became so predictable that "Silence is golden" became known as her motto.

When I think of my mother in those early days, I picture her wearing an apron. She always seemed to have an apron on. When she gave me a hug, I could smell the aroma of whatever she had been cooking for supper that was trapped in her apron. She was a good cook—nothing fancy, just plain meat and potatoes—but some of my favorite meals to this day are some of her specialties. Ham, mashed potatoes, and spinach seemed to fit together like apple pie and ice cream or bacon and eggs. Or pot roast, carrots, and boiled potatoes with gravy. Then there was her famous goulash. It really wasn't goulash, but her version of goulash. Ground beef with sliced onions and elbow noodles, covered with marinara sauce and bacon, and baked in the oven. It's still one of my favorites. I often make it when our grandchild, Alex, and nephew, Howard, come to our house for a Sunday dinner with their mothers. They love it. Or at least they say they do.

Although I remember my mother experimenting with pineapple upside-down cake and some fancy Jell-O dishes, or some new dish she learned at her bridge club, her all-time best dessert was what she called her "never fail cake." It was a simple, flat chocolate cake with vanilla frosting. It became our traditional birthday cake. I don't think I ever had a birthday party where we invited school friends over with presents, funny hats, gifts, and pin the tail on the donkey. Birthdays were strictly a family affair. Just the four of us and my mother's never fail cake, plus a present for the birthday boy.

I vividly recall one particular birthday—my eighth. Someone sent me a birthday card with a pin I could put on my shirt that simply had the number eight on it. I think I wore that eight-year-old pin on my shirt for the next two weeks. I remember my mother putting her arms around me and saying, "Eight years old, you're my big boy now." I also remember my father saying, "Well sport, you're eight years old, and I'm twenty-eight, how about that!" I thought, *Wow—twenty-eight—that's really old!*

My mother seemed to have this magical power of knowing how to locate everything that I couldn't find. "Mom, where's my blue sweater?" or "Mom, where's my baseball glove?" She might preface her response with one of her truisms (a nice word for a sarcastic remark) like, "If it had teeth, it would bite you!" or "You couldn't find your head if it wasn't tied to your neck." But she'd follow it up with, "Look in the bottom of the second drawer in the cabinet across from the bathroom." Or "Look on the back porch where you left it." And miraculously the item that once was lost was now found. I remember wondering, *How does she do that? Is it a power that all mothers have?*

She also had wise advice to dispense. One of these aphorisms that stands out is one she would give in the beginning of winter: "Don't put your tongue on the trolley tracks." I understood the consequences, but I never had the slightest inkling to even consider putting my tongue on the trolley tracks. Another was, "It's better to burp and bear the shame than not to burp and bear the pain." Perhaps that came from her McCarroll heritage, since most of her brothers had stomach problems. When my Uncle Austin would come to our house, before he'd even say hello, he'd often greeted my father with, "Geez, Ott, do you have any bicarb? My stomach's killing me." After mixing some baking soda with water, he'd be able to belch without shame. There's another list of sayings that just could be filed under, "As my mother used to say ..." I know she didn't have the corner on the market of these motherly maxims, so perhaps you heard some of them from your mother. "Whatever I say to you goes in one ear and out the other"; "Your eyes are bigger than your stomach"; "Don't make a pig of yourself"; "Don't smoke; it will stunt your growth"; "Don't cut off your nose to spite your face"; "Don't spit up in the air; it'll fall on your nose." Most of these I never understood. I hadn't considered "spitting up in the air" or "cutting off my nose." Perhaps the level of abstraction was beyond my comprehension at the time, but I never questioned my mother's wisdom.

Like most mothers in the 1930s, she was always there when we came home from school. There was no lunch room, let alone a free lunch, at St. Patrick's grammar school, so we came home for lunch to our peanut butter and jelly sandwich. After school there was usually a glass of milk and cookies waiting for us. I don't remember any conversation. I don't think there was a "How was your day?" or "What did you learn today?" But there was something comforting about cookies and milk and my mother's presence. It's hard for me to imagine how it would have been if both my parents worked outside the home or if my mother was a single parent and I was a "latchkey" kid. I'm not sure how I would have managed all that unsupervised time on my hands, though I suspect I would have adjusted. One factor that would have made it harder is that there was more of a stigma back then than there is today. Since the divorce rate is so much higher now, and there are so many more single-parent households today, there are an increasing number of families that require both parents to work to keep a roof over their heads and pay their bills. Today, you're almost an aberration if you grew up in a traditional two-parent, never divorced, two children and a dog nuclear family.

I think my nephew Jimmy was an exception to the "latchkey" kid syndrome. Both Jim and Diane worked. But in contrast to some of the horror stories you hear about latchkey kids, he made good use of his time. He watched the guy on television who taught painting landscapes, and the next thing you knew, he was painting landscapes. He'd watch the chef on a cooking show make Chicken Piccata and, sure enough, he'd cook a meal of Chicken Piccata. He always wanted to be an airline pilot. When he was young and I'd drive him someplace, he'd take the cigarette lighter from the dashboard and mimic an airline pilot welcoming the passengers aboard, "Ladies and gentlemen, this is your pilot Jim Fausel." He did become a pilot and flies for US Airways. His parents and I are very proud of his reaching his boyhood goal.

With one exception, my mother never had a paying job when I was growing up. My cousin Kate Reinfort's husband Charles (as an adult, he was always known to the family as Sunny) was drafted during World War II in 1943. They had twin daughters, Mary and Cathy. Since Kate was working as a secretary in a prestigious law firm, she needed someone to babysit. So, she would drop the twins off every day at our house, and my mother became their nanny. I know Kate paid her, but I have no idea how much. My mother always had cute little stories about the twins. The one that stands out was when they were learning their prayers. Cathy got very upset when my mother tried to teach her the Hail Mary. She insisted that the prayer should be "Hail Cathy full of grace" instead of "Hail Mary …" After all, she was the oldest.

Lest I overstate my mother's virtues, I should add that she was not always as understanding as I thought she should be. For example, I was a late bloomer in school. As I write this, I'm looking at my report card for the second quarter of the fourth grade; of eleven courses, I had a failing grade in three of them—52 in arithmetic, 58 in English, and 34 in spelling. In parochial schools, when your grade was below 75, the nuns emphasized your failure by writing the grade in red ink on your report card, so it wouldn't slip by your parents. Well, my mother had a fit. After she finished reading me the riot act, I felt like two cents. But I had figured out some time before how to win her over when she was angry with me. Between my tears, I managed to say, "I bet Aunt Helen wouldn't yell at Jean like that." To her credit, she didn't retort, "Well, Jean would never bring home such shameful grades." My guilt trip worked. She just came over and gave me a big hug and assured me that, "You can do better the next time." I heaved a sigh of relief and just hoped she would protect me from my father's reactions. He was the one who had to sign my report card, but interestingly I have no recollection of how my father responded.

I'm happy to report that, in the next quarter, I had a 92 in arithmetic, 85 in English, and a 91 in spelling. My average for the eleven classes was 90.5. I'm not sure how to account for my sudden surge in scholarship, but whatever it was, I was on my way to being a serious student. I never worried again about bringing home a poor report card again. Perhaps my mother's righteous anger worked.

The Mouse in the House

Speaking of anger, I can only remember one time that my parents had an argument, and, in the parlance of the 1930s, it was a humdinger. They may have argued behind closed doors, but this one reached into my bedroom. Here are the circumstances as best I can remember. My father used to enjoy going out with his brothers Ken and Ed to have a few beers on Fridays after work. Usually my aunts Helen and Agnes would come to our house to kibitz together. But on this particular Friday night, the "boys" were on their own. I'm not sure why my aunts weren't at our house, but apparently the later it got, the greater was the opportunity for my mother to build up her ire to a point where she dumped it all on my father, who might have had one too many beers. The yelling was so loud that it woke me up. I couldn't hear exactly what they were saying, but what I could pick up was clear enough for me to figure out that my mother was angry and scolding my father for staying out late drinking. It was like I was having a nightmare. I feared she was on the verge of kicking my father out of the house. Self-centered as I was, I began to wonder what was going to happen to me if my father left. Where would we get the money to live?

After ruminating over my fate as a fatherless child, I finally got the courage to get out of bed and cautiously make my way to the kitchen, where my father had retreated from my mother's assault. There I was in my flannel pajamas, holding my little "blankie," staring forlornly at my parents. Without my having to say a word, my mother, who was holding an attack broom, awkwardly started to explain, "You father and I have been chasing a mouse all over the house and can't seem to catch him." They seemed to sense my skepticism, and both came over to comfort me, assuring me that I needn't worry, that they would catch the agile rodent, and it was safe for me to go back to bed. I know I didn't say this, but thinking back, an appropriate response would have been what the kids say a lot today: "Whatever!" Well, whatever, I seemed to bring peace between my feuding parents, and it was the last time I ever heard them argue, let alone chase mice around the house. So ends the story of the Mouse in the House. This episode certainly didn't characterize their sixty years of marriage. As they grew older, it was apparent to me that they developed a solid love and companionship that I admired.

To this day, whenever I hear the song "When Irish Eyes are Smiling," I think of my mother. She died in 1989 in a nursing home from complications of Alzheimer's disease. She had been fading for almost three years. My brother and I were in Arizona, but we both visited her when we could. My father, however, hardly missed a day of seeing his "Janie." He often went to visit her on his lunch hour, since he was still working, and again after work. Even when she didn't recognize him anymore, he was still there to feed her and make sure she was comfortable. I can still see him trying to get her to eat or at least drink some Ensure. "Come on, Janie, just one more spoonful. Open your mouth, here comes the train. You look so beautiful today, just one more spoonful." Even though her memory had failed her, there was always a twinkle in her Irish eyes, as if she knew that her lifelong companion and the love of her life was there to watch over her. He was devastated when she died. He phoned me in Arizona. When I answered, I immediately knew there was something wrong. He started to talk and then there was a long pause as if he were composing himself. "Dad, are you okay?"

"It's all over. Your mother is gone."

Now *I* needed to compose myself. Even as I'm writing this, after nineteen years, my eyes are tearing up. Finally, I was able to say, "Dad, I'm so sorry. How are you doing?"

"I was there this morning after breakfast. She didn't eat anything. I was sitting next to her bed, holding her hand, and she opened those beautiful blue eyes and looked at me as though she recognized me. Then she closed her eyes. After another few minutes, she opened her eyes one more time, looked at me as if she were saying, 'Good-bye, Ott.' Then she was gone."

This was true love. To honor my sainted mother's memory, please join me in singing a chorus of "When Irish Eyes are Smiling."

When Irish eyes are smiling, sure'n it's like a morn in spring.
In the lilt of Irish laughter, you can hear the angels sing.
When Irish hearts are happy, all the world is bright and gay.
And when Irish eyes are smiling, sure they steal your heart
away.

The Brothers Fausel

When I think of my father, the first thing that comes to mind is his sense of humor. Whenever I'd bring new friends home, I'd introduce them to my father and then say, "Dad, say something funny!" and he would. After sampling his humor, my friends would usually say something like, "Gee, your dad is funny. Is he always that funny?" I'd reply with pride, "Yeah, he's a riot. Call the police!" Just a bit of the Fausel humor that comes from my DNA!

Often his humor had an edge and was at my expense, but it still was funny, and I couldn't help but laugh. "That Don, he's got more degrees than a thermometer, but he doesn't have any common sense." Or, one time when he picked me up at the airport, I had grown a Van Dyke beard while I was in Arizona. He took one look at my new appearance and ordered, "Hurry up, get in the car before any of my customers see you with me!" I knew he was kidding, but under that kidding was a message. "Get rid of the beard; I don't trust men with beards." I was getting tired of the beard anyway, but, contrary to orders, I didn't surrender it immediately. I waited a reasonable period of time before I removed it, just so he'd know I was an adult and made my own decisions. Of course I was thirty-something at the time.

Not only was Dad funny; all his brothers were funny. His sister could also be funny in her own quiet way. The whole family was funny. My Uncle Ken was a salesman for the Bowser Pump Company. Ken had to make periodic visits to his customers to see if they were interested in the latest type of gas pumps for their stations. He would often take me along on his trips to the north country to keep him company.

In between his meetings with customers, he had certain places he would routinely visit. He'd often visit a former speakeasy from the prohibition days between Glens Falls and Lake George. Unless you knew the speakeasy was there, you'd never have guessed there was anything but a run-down garage with some cars parked outside. We'd enter through this facade of a garage, go through a secret door, down a dozen or so steps, and end up in a poorly lighted, underground saloon. You'd swear you were back in the roaring twenties. All that was missing was a secret pass code like, "Harry sent me." Without Ken ordering, the bartender greeted him and brought him his drink. Ken bellied up to the bar, and he and Chet talked like two old friends, while I played the slot machine.

During my first three years in high school, my Uncle Ken and Aunt Helen, along with their daughter Jeanne, who was a year younger than I, invited me to join them for their two-week vacation at Lake George. Jean would usually bring a girlfriend along. I was smitten each summer with whoever her friend was. We spent the days swimming and fishing and the nights playing cards or going into town to cruise around the main drag or to see a movie. One movie we saw in the summer of 1944 that I'll never forget was *The Outlaw* with Jane Russell. The movies weren't rated as they are today, but the Catholic Church had its own rating system that was issued by the Legion of Decency. Not only did the Legion rate movies, but they required all Catholics to take a pledge in church every year not only that they would never go to a morally objectionable movie, but that they would never even go to a theater that showed them. Any movie that the church rated (C) was condemned, and it was a mortal sin to see it. Just another way of controlling our behavior! I Googled the Legion of Decency and guess what? I found that between 1934 when it was formed and 1975 when it went out of existence, it had condemned over fifty films, and one of them was *The Outlaw*.

One evening we went to Ticonderoga, New York, to see a movie. Uncle Ken dropped us off at the only movie theatre in the village. Jeanne and her friend Deanie wanted to see *The Outlaw,* so I just went along. I knew that the Legion of Decency was organizing boycotts to demonstrate that Catholics shouldn't see the movie under the pain of mortal sin and hoping they could keep people away. When I Googled *The Outlaw*, I found that there were several reasons for condemning it. The most blatant was the "shameless" display of Russell's ample assets (36 D).

Today, the movie wouldn't even be rated "R," let alone "X." Nevertheless, it was a mortal sin at that time, and I had to confess it or go to hell. Believe me, it wasn't worth going to hell for.

Moving on with the Fausel brothers, Uncle Chuck was my father's oldest brother. He was the black sheep of the family. When he divorced his wife, Barbara, divorce was not as fashionable as it is today. He was the only one in the family in his generation to get a divorce. Chuck worked for the local newspaper, but during the baseball season he was in charge of all the concession stands at Hawkins Stadium, the home of the Albany Senators in the Eastern League, a double "A" league. When I was thirteen, he got me a job selling scorecards at the main gate of the stadium. "Hey, get your scorecards here. Ya can't tell a player without a scorecard." I'd yell that over and over as the fans came pouring through the gate. I would get a penny for each scorecard I sold. On a good day, I might sell five hundred. Then, during the game, I'd sell peanuts. "Hey, get your fresh, roasted peanuts here. Only a nickel a half a dime, they must be good, they must be fine." I got pretty good at throwing the nickel bags of peanuts to customers in the middle of the stands.

Uncle Ed and Aunt Agnes had four children—Edward, who is about five years younger than I, Kenny, Patty, and Gerry. Ed was a very witty guy. My grandmother always used to refer to Uncle Ed as "poor Ed." He wasn't poor by any definition of "poor." He was just the last of the four "boys" to have a car. That qualified him as poor in her eyes.

My father was very close to his sister Frances. Not so much growing up, since she was his little sister, and she was twelve years younger. But as Frances grew up and was married and had children, their relationship changed. Frances had four children— Donna, Joyce, Linda, and Andrew (Drew). The youngest, Drew was almost twenty years younger than I, so I was more like an uncle than a cousin when he and his sisters were growing up. There were only two cousins on the Fausel side close enough to my age to hang out with—my cousins Jean and Joan. But as adults I've enjoyed spending time with all of them whenever I go back East.

Dad always called Frances's husband, Andy Nolan, Nolan. He never called him Andy. "That Nolan is a great guy." Or, "Nolan, can you come over and help me with my lawnmower? It's not working." He was very fond of Nolan. Tragically, Nolan died in his late forties of a heart attack. Dad became more like a father to what he called the "numerous Nolans." My father's role as surrogate dad was to go to all Drew's football or baseball games; to attend all their birthday parties; be there and take movies of all their first communions, confirmations, and graduations; give the girls away when they were married; and include them in all the Fausel family's activities.

Frances was also close to my mother. They were more like sisters. She would go with my parents on vacations after her children had grown up and was always invited to join them on holidays and other occasions. When my mother began to show the early symptoms of Alzheimer's disease, Frances was there to take care of her while my father was at work. Knowing she was living on a fixed income, Dad was always generous in paying her for her care-giving and housecleaning work, despite her objections.

World War II

Dad was doing well in the insurance business. By the late 1930s, he had accumulated a steady group of customers and was office manager and one of the associates at Howard B. Stark, Inc. On Friday nights in the summer, we would all pile into the 1929 Chevrolet and drive up to Warner's Lake, where we would meet Uncle Ken, Aunt Helen, and my cousin Jeanne and stay for the weekend. Dad became a good friend of the owner, Arnold Matice. He made a deal with him, bartering for our lodging and meals. He would tend bar for the weekend, and we would receive free room and board. I also had my first paying job at Matice's boathouse. I was in charge of collecting twenty-five cents from each bather who wanted to use the beach. In turn, I would give them a wicker basket in which to store their clothes and assign them to a dressing room, give them a numbered bracelet, and then store the basket on a shelf in the boathouse. On a good Sunday I could make two bucks.

Warner's Lake was a refuge for all of us during those hot and sticky Albany summers. The Lake, as we called it, was in the Helderberg Mountains but only about an hour's drive from Albany. We'd sing all the old songs to and from Albany and anxiously be prepared to beat one another yelling, "I see the lake first" as we rounded the final turn. Predictably, every time we reached a certain point on the Altamont Hill, our radiator would boil over and spurt rusty water all over the front of the car. We'd have to stop, let the radiator cool down, and refill it with several cans of water from our trunk. Our windshield usually had the residue of dry, rusted water when we arrived at the lake.

There were always a lot of other kids there to play with. While the adults sat and talked adult things, sitting in circles on the white Adirondack chairs on the front lawn, we would swim, go boating, take hikes, and play volleyball, softball, cards, whatever! It was at the lake that I received my second class in sex education. Bobbie Matice, her brother Richard, and Barbara Arute were keeping me company while I did my job at the boathouse. I had a crush on Barbara. She was from New Jersey, and her parents had a motorboat that they let me drive. We were all about the same age—preteen and early teens. I'm not sure how the subject came up, but they were surprised that I didn't know what they were talking about. I suspected it was about sex, but I wasn't sure. Finally, in an effort to enlighten me, Richard said, "You know?—Father, Uncle, Cousin Kate."

I still didn't know what they were talking about. Richard said more slowly and emphatically, "Father, Uncle, and Cousin Kate." I was still in the dark.

Bobbie came to my rescue. "Just pick out the first letter of each word."

I did, and I still wasn't sure what it meant, but I knowingly replied "Oh!" And I spelled out the "F" word. Can you imagine that? I was going into the eighth grade, and I had never heard the "F" word. It really wasn't until I went back to school that fall that I understood the conversation at the lake. I heard someone on the basketball court use it very forcefully to express their anger. Now I had to tell the priest in confession that I had used a dirty word. Thankfully, he didn't even ask me what the dirty word was.

Anyway, we liked Warner's Lake so much that we'd even go up there in the winter to play in the snow and go ice skating and tobogganing. One day that I will always remember was December 7, 1941. We were warming ourselves by the fireplace and listening to the radio in the living room of the main lodge with the Matice family when the program was interrupted, and the announcer informed us that the Japanese had bombed Pearl Harbor. I remember Arnold saying, "Where the hell is Pearl Harbor?" No one else seemed to know, but an immediate shroud came over the adults. I had no idea then how that announcement would change our lives.

It was another two and a half years before my father was drafted into the army. Up to 1943, men with children had been deferred. To me his going into the army was exciting. I'd be the only kid on my block whose father was going to fight the Nazis. It also gave me bragging rights in my sixth-grade class. My mother was not as excited. As the day got closer for him to leave, there were more frequent tears. April 13, 1944, the day he left for Fort Dix, New Jersey, was particularly difficult for her. After our hugs and good-byes, she, Jim, and I watched from our living room bay window as he walked with his little duffel bag to the end of the block to make his way to the Albany Armory on Washington Avenue to report for his induction instructions. He looked back once and waved at us. I can only imagine what was going through his mind. I have a hint of what it must have been like from reading Paul Grondalh's book, *Mayor Erastus Corning: Albany Icon, Albany Enigma,* when it was first published in 1997. My cousin Bob Brew sent me a copy, and the first thing I did was to look in the index to see whether my father was referenced. There were ten page references for Otto Fausel. I immediately read each one before I started the book.

From the Armory, they walked down Washington Avenue to the Union Train Station. Some of the inductees were accompanied by wives and children. In Grondalh's description, the display of emotions ranged from keeping a stiff upper lip to tears and sobbing. One of the men was so shaken that he was immobilized and unable to move without assistance. I suspect that my father was somewhere between the two extremes. Thankfully, back at 8 Judson Street, Aunt Liz came upstairs to comfort my mother. I had never seen her cry like she did that day.

The next morning, there was a picture in the *Albany Times Union* of the sixty or so inductees lined up, ready to board the train.

The main reason for the picture was that Erastus Corning II, the mayor of Albany, was one of the inductees. Erastus was first in line, and my father was right behind him. My father was looking directly into the camera as though he were the politician. An early letter from Fort Dix told us that he and Erastus and a few others played poker all the way to New Jersey. And that Erastus had told him he'd like to have my father join him at one of the largest insurance agencies in the city, Albany Associations, after the war was over. It seemed quite remote at the time, but this offer would eventually change the whole direction of his and our lives.

Dad spent the next two years at Fort Blanding, near Jacksonville, Florida. Since he had typing skills, he was assigned a desk job as company clerk. He rose to the rank of staff sergeant by the time he was discharged in April of 1946. This was a pretty cushy assignment of which he took full advantage. He was even able to sweet-talk his commanding officer into giving him the duty of escorting soldiers who had been caught AWOL back to New York for trial. The trips just happened to be around Christmas, so he was able to spend both Christmases with us back in Albany. I remember him showing me the sidearm that he was required to wear on the trips. He was quick to tell me he took the bullets out and kept them in his pocket, just in case his prisoners tried to gang up on him.

Many of his army buddies who left Albany with him were not as fortunate as he. The majority were sent overseas, including Erastus, who had a close call during the Battle of the Bulge. Several died, and others were disabled. One of Dad's best friends, Jake Carey, from lower Judson Street, came back as a paraplegic and spent the rest of his life in a wheelchair.

After the war ended, Dad was discharged, and he came home to his old job. Sure enough, not too long after he got home, Erastus called him and offered him a very attractive position. Dad agonized over his decision, but, to his credit, he told Erastus he felt an obligation to the Howard B. Stark agency, since they had paid all his commissions to my mother while he was in the army. Two

years later, Erastus called again, and this time my father thought
he had fulfilled the obligation, and he accepted a position as vice
president. For almost forty years, he and Erastus had a personal and
professional relationship. My father ran the business as executive
vice president and Erastus completed forty-two consecutive years as
mayor of Albany. His tenure as mayor of a major city is unsurpassed
in American political history. Erastus rarely went to his office at
Albany Associates, but he would call my father every morning
from his office at City Hall to talk about the business. Dad used to
joke about Erastus's daily greeting: "Otto, Erastus here!" My father
thought it sounded as though they were a vaudeville team. "Put
your hands together for Erastus and Otto!"

Dad was also part of Erastus's inner circle of friends who
accompanied him to his cabin in Maine every winter to ice fish during
the day and play poker for most of the night. It was a wonderful
opportunity for him to rub elbows and have a few drinks with
judges, senators, district attorneys, and other politicos. He used every
opportunity to drop a name or two with his friends and relatives.

I always thought he and Erastus had a peculiar but reciprocal
relationship. My father was a self-made man who had completed
only three years of high school and came from a humble family
background. Erastus, by contrast, was a patrician, a graduate of
Albany Boys Academy, a military school that he entered at age
eight; the Groton School, a private college preparatory boarding
school in Massachusetts, where other aristocratic families, like the
Roosevelts, the Harrimans, and the Peabodys, sent their sons; and
Yale, where he was a member of the secret Skull and Bones Society,
along with other famous alumni like George H. W. Bush, '48, and
George W. Bush, '68. His great-grandfather, Erastus Corning,
served as mayor of Albany from 1834 to 1836. His grandfather's
greatest accomplishment was founding what eventually became
the largest corporation in America at the time, the New York
Central Railroad. His father Edwin served as lieutenant governor
under Alfred Smith from 1926 to 1928, and his Uncle Parker
Corning was a U.S. congressman. Quite a pedigree!

Despite all his and generations of his family's accomplishments, Erastus was a very down-to-earth man. I remember the first time I met him, as a teenager. It was at his mother's home, the Upper Farm. The family had donated the Lower Farm to the Jesuits as a retreat house. What I remember most about the Upper Farm was that it had a swimming pool, a gardener's house, and thirteen bathrooms in the main residence. When my father introduced me, Erastus looked me straight in the eyes, shook my hand, and said, "I'm very, very, very glad to meet you, Don. Your father has told me many good things about you." Wow! Not "very," or "very, very," but "very, very, very glad" to meet me! Obviously I never forgot that greeting. Nor did I forget my last meeting with him in 1983, at the Albany Medical Center. He had lost forty pounds, had been bedridden for several months with oxygen tube in his nose, and was preparing to make what would be his last-ditch stand at University Hospital in Boston. As soon as my father and I walked into the room, he lit up and said, "Father Don, how are you? You don't mind if I call you Father Don? You'll always be Father Don to me." I responded, "Erastus, you'll always be Mr. Mayor to me and to four generations of Albanians." By that time I hadn't been a practicing priest for sixteen years, but I appreciated his feelings. Our visit was interrupted when Mario Cuomo came into the room to ask Erastus's blessing on his intention to run for governor of New York. We made a graceful exist.

The Great Organizer

In addition to my father's talent for his chosen profession, he was also the "go-to guy" for both the Fausel and McCarroll families, as well as his friends. Whether it was getting a family reunion together, delivering Christmas presents, providing transportation, celebrating the Fourth of July or Labor Day, or just organizing an impromptu dinner party, he was the man. He'd get on the phone, and, before you knew it, he had a dozen or more relatives or friends willing to join him and Mom at Veeder's restaurant for dinner that night. His New Year's Eve parties were an annual tradition for thirty or more celebrants. In addition to a great spread of food, there was plenty to drink. He'd prepare in advance a stack of records that were geared to keep everyone dancing. His underlying theory was that New Year's Eve was a time for dancing, not sitting around talking. Also, if you were dancing, you wouldn't be gossiping about somebody. As the guests arrived, they would be met by the familiar sound of the song "Hello, hello, hello, what a wonderful word hello …" This was followed by the lively music of the Philadelphia Mummers Band. By that time, most of the guests had arrived and he would play music more suitable for dancing. I got an e-mail from my cousin Walter McCarroll recently; it was on the occasion of what would have been my father's one hundredth birthday, had he lived. We had been corresponding about the first two chapters of my memoir and some of the memories he had. Veeder's restaurant came up, and Walt remarked, "Your dad was the party king, and if he were still alive, I know that Veeder's is where we would have celebrated his one hundredth birthday. Happy birthday, Otto!"

He and army buddy Adam Adelman were cofounders of the April 13 Club. The membership was made up of all those Albany veterans who were inducted on April 13, 1944. For over forty years, they had an annual dinner, which included wives, on the anniversary date and a clambake in the fall. The clambake was for the men only. One of the things that held the club together for so many years was that Erastus rarely missed an opportunity to be with his old army buddies. At my father's wake, a half a dozen came to pay their respects as a group. It was very touching.

Even when we lived on Judson Street, my father organized his first formal poker club. He called it the Mystic Knights of the Sea. If you ever listened to the Amos 'n' Andy show on the radio in the thirties or forties, I'm sure you remember some of the characters that made up the Lodge of the Mystic Knights of the Sea. In addition to Amos Brown and Andy Jones, there was George "the Kingfish" Stevens and his wife, Sapphire, as well as Lightning and Madame

Queen, to mention a few. The show was one of the most popular on radio. We'd listen to a fifteen-minute episode every night on a small plastic radio on a shelf in the kitchen that my father had made. When Dad started his card club, he gave everyone a name of one of the characters from the Amos 'n' Andy show. He, of course, was the Kingfish. In those days we weren't sensitive to the racial implications, but looking back, it certainly was a caricature of the African American community. The program had a short run on television, but CBS considered it too controversial because of the prolonged protest by the NAACP and other civil rights organizations.

Dad started another card club when he and Mom moved to Davis Avenue in 1952. That was their first move "uptown." As a World War II vet, he was eligible for a Veterans Administration home loan, so they left Cabbage Town and moved to the first home they owned. They were no longer stoop sitters; they actually had a back porch with jalousie windows, and a front and back lawn. By that time, I was in the seminary in Baltimore, and I remember him sending me a letter with a description of the new neighborhood and a room plan of the house. They were sure proud of that house, mortgage and all. As for the Jeffersons in the TV series, this was a real "Movin' on up ..." not to the east side but to the postwar suburbs.

Most of their new friends on Davis Avenue were also new homeowners in a new development. It was sort of a miniature Levittown, Long Island, in upstate New York. They quickly bonded with backyard barbecues and through sharing tools and lawnmowers and creating a kind of mutual help network. One of the first projects was helping one another turn their basements into game rooms. Five or six families were involved. One house at a time, they would all help tile the cement floors, cover the ceilings with acoustical tiles, put wood paneling on the walls, and build a bar. As each game room was finished, they'd celebrate with a party. My parents' game room was equipped with a dart board, portable poker table, and pool table.

Once the game room was completed, my father wrote the by-laws for a new card club: the "Every Other Saturday Night

TV Dinner and Card Club" (EOSNTVDCC). Several years ago, I discovered four years of the club's minutes. In addition to my parents, there were four couples in the club: my cousin twice removed Kate, and Sunny Reinfort, our neighbors Elmer and Marge Ragatzie, Larry and May Maranville, and another former Judson Street couple, Dee and Grant Harder. The minutes from the first meeting reported that my father gave every couple twenty shares of stock in EOSNTVDCC. He also assigned the officers and committee chairs. Sunny Reinfort was the vice president; Kate Reinfort was secretary; Elmer Ragatzie was treasurer; Marge Ragatzie was chair of the hospitality committee; Larry Maranville was chair of the annual dinner committee; May Maranville was chair of the sick committee; Dee Harder was chair of the Christmas committee; Grant Harder was chair of the recruitment committee; my mother was chair of the parade committee. Each office had a written job description, and there were rules for how the meetings would be conducted. After my father had assigned all the other positions, the only one left was president; my father was unanimously elected president.

Each meeting followed Robert's Rules plus Otto's Rules. At the beginning of the meeting, Kate would read the minutes from the previous meeting. Once the minutes were approved, he would ask for a report from each committee chair. If the chair had nothing to report, he would fine him or her a quarter, which would go into a kitty. For example, he would request a report from my mother's parade committee: "Madame Chairman, please give us your report for the parade committee." My mother would stand up and say, "Mr. President, we didn't have any parades since our last meeting." He would then fine her and ask for the next report. If anyone spoke without permission, he would fine them. By the end of the year, they'd have enough money in the kitty to have their annual dinner meeting.

After the meeting of the board adjourned, they would enjoy their TV dinners, after which the men played poker in the "game room," and the women played bridge in the kitchen.

A New Life for My Father

When Erastus died, Dad joined with his son Erastus III (Rasty), Lloyd Rodgers, and several other members of the former Albany Associates to form Corning & Associates, Inc. Dad maintained his position as executive vice president. He continued to provide service for his customers, some of whom were great, great, great-grandchildren of customers he had since his early days at Howard B. Stark, Inc., but he didn't have the same zest for the business. In 1988 my father and his colleagues Lloyd Rogers and Jerry Mineau took their "books of business" to Amsure Associates, Inc., and he and Lloyd were given vice presidents' positions along with benefit packages. For the next three years, he went to the office for a few hours a day, made telephone calls, and talked to his customers when their policies needed to be renewed but did not solicit new business. But Amsure was a place where he could hang his hat and feel that he was still useful.

In 1991 I was back in Albany during my summer vacation from Arizona State University, and one day he asked me to help him write a letter to his clients. I had my laptop computer with me, so I let him dictate to me the content and then made some minor changes to his text. Here is the letter he sent to his customers.

AMSURE ASSOCIATES, INC.
12 Computer Drive West
PO Box 1685
Albany, New York 12201

July 25, 1991

My dear loyal customers,

Today I woke up and realized I've been in the insurance business for over sixty years. Sixty three to be exact! I thought to myself, Otto, it's about time for you to retire. After all you'll be 83 on August 8 and I need to enjoy whatever time I have left. As you know I've been with Amsure for the last three years and at the end of this year, my *book of business* will be handled by my trusted colleagues Lloyd Rodger and Jerry Mineau. They will be available to you as I've always been.

I am grateful to all of you for the confidence you placed in me over the years. There are several families that have been with me since I first started in 1928. I've been fortunate to serve four generations of those families.

Amsure has provided me a very generous retirement package, which I appreciate. Between now and the end of the year, I will be available to answer any questions you might have.

Gratefully yours,

J. Otto Fausel
Vice President

In January of 1992, I received a phone call from my cousin Drew Nolan. A New York State trooper had picked Dad up in Thatcher Park in the Helderberg Mountains, lost and confused. It was a Sunday evening, and he had mistakenly thought he had to go to the office, even though he had retired. Once there, he had realized that the office wasn't open. He had started to go back home but lost his way and ended thirty miles from home. The troopers brought him to St. Peter's Hospital. That was a sad night.

I flew back and spent a few days helping Dad prepare to spend a couple of weeks with us in Arizona. Jim, his wife, Diane, and I had already discussed the possibility of his moving to Arizona permanently, but we thought we would ease him into the change.

When we got to Arizona, Dad lived with Jim, Diane, and their son, Jimmy. They had a nice space for him with his own bathroom, living area, bedroom, and Diane's gourmet cooking. Most weekends he would stay with me, but he began to become more confused. I remember one day the police called my office at the university and told me that they had found Dad in someone's garage and asked me to pick him up. He had crossed a six-lane road that was heavily traveled and managed to get to a house that had a garage that looked like Jim and Diane's. When I got there, he was having a nice chat with the kind people who understood his situation.

As good a caregiver as Diane was, we eventually had to hire a woman to be with him during the day. But at night he would often wake up my brother's family because he was confused. It became more and more evident to us that he needed a more structured environment.

My brother and I found a nice continuum of care facility called The Arbors. We made arrangements for him to be admitted into what they euphemistically called the "Memory Impaired" unit. It was very comfortable. There were about twelve residents in the unit, and he had a private room. There was no doubt that Alzheimer's had taken its toll on the memories we shared together, but at times there was a trace of the humor that was typical of the way he had lived for eighty-five years.

As I helped him unpack and settle in, I hoped that his characteristic humor would help him through this stage of life. I knew we were doing the right thing in moving him there, though I couldn't help but feel a great deal of sadness and guilt. I knew I wasn't abandoning him and that I would see him often, but just looking at him in surroundings that were so unfamiliar to him and sensing his feelings of helplessness and hopelessness brought tears to my eyes. But I guess that old rule of "no mush at the airport" was reactivated; I intuitively knew that to let out the floodgate of tears I was holding back would just make it more difficult for him. So I strategically brought up something to distract both of us.

"Dad, you might be able to help me with this couple I've been seeing in therapy. After all, you were married to Mom for sixty years. They're going through some tough times and are thinking of divorcing."

He handed me a gold medallion he had given my mother on their fiftieth wedding anniversary, which he had worn since she died. He said, "Read that!" On the back of the medallion there was an inscription that I read out loud: "To Jane, for Fifty Wonderful Years."

He looked at me thoughtfully and without missing a beat said, "Tell that couple that not all of those years were wonderful."

I thought to myself, *He's still got that sense of humor.*

We all visited him regularly and tried to make sure that one of us would be there every day. When he was up to it, I'd take him to church on Sundays and out to dinner. His favorite place was the Burger King not too far from The Arbors. Instead of having the Whopper, he'd have a junior Whopper, French fries, and a piece of their apple pie for dessert. He thought that was a great treat, better than a meal at a fancy restaurant.

He was at The Arbors for over six months and was doing pretty well until one night when I got a phone call from the hospital. He had fallen in the shower at The Arbors, and they brought him to the hospital with what they thought was a broken hip. I rushed to the hospital emergency room, and he was in a cubicle on a gurney. The first thing he said to me was, "This was the big one. I'm a goner."

We met with the doctor the next morning, and he suggested surgery. We agreed and signed a statement of no resuscitation if something went wrong during the operation. That was a hard decision. But he survived the surgery and was in the hospital for over a week. During that time he received physical therapy to determine whether he could go back to The Arbors or needed skilled nursing care. He gave it his best shot, but it became apparent to the staff that he would need skilled nursing care. This was another difficult decision for the family.

After he had been in the skilled nursing care facility for a little more than a month, I got a call from Jim telling me that Dad had passed away. I had been sick in bed with some type of flu or else I would have been there. When I got to the nursing care facility,

Jim, Diane, and Jimmy were all there. You know, it doesn't matter how old a parent is or how prepared you think you are for their death; it still takes you off balance. There are so many things that needed to be done; the real grieving often doesn't start at the time of the initial shock. At least that was the way it was for me. After we discussed what we needed to do to plan for Dad's funeral, I went home to a very vacant house.

The next couple of days were busy. We made the funeral arrangements for Phoenix and Albany. The funeral director in Phoenix prepared his body for the trip home, and we accompanied him on the flight. I reluctantly agreed to give one of the eulogies. I say "reluctantly" because I was afraid I would break down in the middle of my tribute to my father.

Relatives and friends paid their respects at the wake and funeral Mass at St. Catherine's of Siena Church. Even the bishop of Albany, Howard Hubbard, came to the wake. Another friend who was now a bishop—John Gavin Nolan—was in New York City but called the funeral home to express his condolences. At a least a dozen priests my brother and I knew were in attendance. When it was my turn to give the eulogy, the first thing I did was acknowledge their presence by saying, "After all these years, I still have a strong sense of *Fratres in unum*. That phrase was from a hymn we used to sing in the seminary. *'Ecce quam bonum, et quam jucundum, fratres, fratres in unum.'* Loosely translated, it means, 'Behold how good it is, how joyful it is to live as brothers in one.'" I then went on to explain that we had a tradition at all my father's birthday parties for me to write and sing a parody of an old camp song. And I had written some verses as part of the eulogy. The song was called "Bill Grogan's Goat." I instructed them that I would sing a line and they would sing the same line. I gave an example from the original song and asked that they repeat after me. They repeated each line after me, so I thought they had the idea. I went on with six verses of the parody I wrote for the service. Here are the first and last verses, to give you a taste of the level of the artistic quality.

Ode to Otto
We're here today, to celebrate,
A life that we all think was great.
For many years, he was on the go,
You spell his name, O-T-T-O.

Your memory will linger on,
And on and on, and on and on.
But now's the time, to say adieu,
Auf Wiedersehen! And we love you.

The song gave me more confidence that I wouldn't break down, and I expanded more seriously about my Dad's good qualities but did add one humorous story that fit the celebration. I recalled an incident that happened the last time I was home to celebrate Christmas in Albany. The previous Sunday at Mass, the pastor reminded everyone that if they wanted to get a seat for the Christmas High Mass, they better get there at least a half an hour early. Of course Dad and I got there an hour early. We walked into the church, and it was empty except for one family. That one family happened to be sitting right where he usually sat, the fourth row on the Gospel side of the altar. So, in we go, and Dad walks right up to where the family was sitting and asks them if they'd mind moving over. They looked a little puzzled as they took another look around the empty church, but the family of five graciously slid over in the pew so we could have our regular seats. Judging by the congregation's laughter, I knew they were thinking, "Yep, that's Otto!"

As I finished my eulogy, I saw Erastus Corning III in the back of the church representing his deceased father and family. I wondered if he was shocked by comparing this celebration with his father's more formal liturgy at the Episcopal Cathedral. I had a chance to talk to him at the cemetery, and he said, "That was a great tribute to a great man. I've never been to a funeral like that."

My McCarroll Roots

The family historian for my mother's side of our family is my cousin Jean Brew. She has meticulously and lovingly accumulated a six-generation genealogy of the McCarroll family, dating back to my great-great-grandparents, John and Mary. They were born in Ireland, Mary in 1790 and John in 1814. I would love to know the story behind the twenty-four-year age gap, especially since John married a much older woman, and I suspect that would have been unusual in the nineteenth century. Cousin Jean also wondered about the age gap. She felt frustrated at running into brick walls when she tried to get more information from the officials back in County Monaghan, Ireland. Even though they attempted to be helpful, they finally told her that the English had burned down the Catholic church, and all the records were destroyed. We'll probably never know why there was such a large gap in their ages. Another unsolved mystery.

My mother came from a family of eleven children. My father used to say, "Your mother's family was so large that her father needed to get a parade permit for them to go to church on Sunday." Unfortunately, only eight of the children survived tuberculosis and the flu epidemics of the early twentieth century. Both of Mom's parents died before I was born. My grandmother, Catherine or Kathryn Koons, my Aunt Liz's sister, was born in 1867 and died in 1923 at the age of fifty-six from tuberculosis. In the pictures I have of her in her later years, she looks like she was a much older woman. My grandfather, Austin McCarroll, was born in the same year as his wife but lived two years longer. He died of gangrene of the leg, which was the result of a long struggle with diabetes. Before he died, he had both of his legs removed as a result of the diabetes. From what I learned from my mother, one of her father's avocations was gambling. On the day he died, he was in the hospital but managed to get someone to play his lucky numbers, in an illegal numbers game called "policy." The story handed down to me is that he won.

I remember that my mother and Aunt Liz used to play the same game regularly. They would wrap fifteen or twenty-five cents in a small piece of paper with their numbers on it and give it to me to drop off at a little variety story on Clinton Avenue on my way to school. I had to check on my way back from school to see whether their numbers came out and to collect their winnings, which were infrequent. Once they won $15.00.

As with my Fausel grandparents, I wish I had had the opportunity to find out more about my McCarroll grandparents. I visited their graves in the cemetery when I was younger, and it was always a solemn experience to read their names on the brown granite gravestone and realize we never had the chance to meet.

The Brothers McCarroll

Of the six McCarroll brothers, five were alive through my early and mid-adulthood. Uncle Walter was born in 1891 and died in 1980 at the age of eight-nine. He married Mary Collins, who was born in Glens Falls, New York, in 1896 and died at the age of eight-six. When Uncle Walter was younger, he worked as a chauffeur for a wealthy family by the name of Reed at Lake Luzerne, New York. I remember Uncle Austin and his wife Marion taking me up to Lake Luzerne in his touring car to visit with his brother Walter's family. They had two boys, Billy and Walter. Billy was ten years older than I, and Walter has only recently admitted that he is three years older than I am. I remember having a lot of fun up there and can almost smell the scent of the pine needles around their house. I have fond memories of playing pitch and catch with a new baseball glove that my Uncle Austin gave me for my birthday. I amazed everyone, including myself, at how I could catch balls well above my head, by just putting the glove where I thought the ball would be. That's a silly thing to remember, when I can't even remember what I had for lunch yesterday. Now Aunt Mary's cakes, that's something to remember. She was a very sweet lady who baked wonderful, sweet desserts. Every Christmas, my father and I would visit with them when we'd drop off Christmas presents. Uncle Walter would get my father a glass of wine from a fancy decanter, and Aunt Mary would bring me a piece of her freshly baked chocolate cake. I always felt she had baked it just for me.

One of the first tragedies to affect my life occurred in 1939, when I found out that my cousin Billy drowned in Lake Luzerne. He was only nineteen years old. My Uncle Andy Brew and his wife Anna Mae, my mother's sister, had been to dinner at our house. After dinner, the men and I walked to Bleecker Stadium to watch a Twilight league baseball game. When we came back home, my mother and Aunt Anna Mae were sitting on the stoop waiting for us, obviously upset. Both of them had been crying. They were barely able to tell us that Billy had drowned that afternoon.

Billy's wake was at his home, as was the custom at that time. My mother prepared me for my first wake by telling me what to say Walter and Mary: "I'm very sorry for your loss." Hollow words, given the grief they were experiencing. I hope hearing these words from their nine-year-old nephew gave them some comfort. I followed the lead of the adults and knelt down on the prie-dieu, blessed myself, and said the funeral prayer I had learned from the nuns. "May his soul and the souls of all the faithful departed rest in peace." His face seemed very serene, but I was distracted by Billy's shoes. I've never forgotten them, and that was almost seventy years ago. They were wing tips, but a shade of brown that I had never seen before or seen since. I remember the lid of the whole casket was open, unlike today when the top half is open, and there are usually flowers on the lower lid.

The second oldest brother was Uncle Jack, who was born in 1894. I have less firsthand knowledge about him than any of the McCarroll brothers. I know from reading our genealogy and occasionally hearing other relatives talk about her that he was married to Lodeamia Smyth Van Dusen. But to me she was a mystery lady. I never met her, and I don't remember either her or Uncle Jack ever coming to any family gatherings. As far as I know, it wasn't because there was a big family feud and no one was talking to them; they just traveled in a different circle.

I did get to know Uncle Jack later in his life. He and Uncle Austin were both widowers and would hang out together. My father used to tell me that Jack was one of the best card sharks in the greater Albany area. He could deal each person four of a kind in draw poker and deal himself four aces. Everyone would build up the pot, thinking that four of whatever they had was a shoo-in, until Jack revealed that he had them all beat with his aces. At least that's what Dad said.

James McCarroll, known as Jimmy to all of us, except his wife, Marian Davis, who always called him James, was born in 1896. He was the family clown. In World War I, his assignment in the army was to entertain the troops. He could play the piano, the violin, and the drums, as well as sing. He was also a very funny guy. My mother told me that during the Great Depression the bank foreclosed on his house on Washington Avenue. If anyone would mention it, he'd reply in a Jimmy Durante staccato style, "They told me I lost my house. I told them they were nuts, I knew right where it was." Every time we drove by his former house, my mother would remind me of how her brother Jimmy coped with "losing" his house.

Uncle Jimmy was a very successful butcher since he opened his first market in 1921. Little did he know, eighty-seven years ago, that he was starting a dynasty of butchers! Over the years he moved from one location to another, but his last market was the classiest. He opened it in Delmar, New York, an affluent community that at the time was a suburb of Albany. He called it McCarroll's the Village Butcher. It was an upscale butcher's market where they served their customers coffee and snacks and samples, as well as the best of meats. His only son, Bud—Jimmy II, worked behind the counter with his dad, while mother Marion was the one who paid the bills and kept their accounts straight. The market closed in 1990, mainly because they were competing with the large supermarkets. But in 1995, Jimmy III and his wife

Christine opened a more upscale version than the first McCarroll's the Village Butcher.

In June 2008 I happened to be in Delmar and got lost. I stopped at Applebee's Mortuary to get directions to the cemetery where my parents are buried. I figured if anyone could give me directions to the cemetery it would be the undertaker. As I walked out of the mortuary, right across the street I saw a sign that said, McCarroll's the Village Butcher. It was like a miracle. I'd never have found it even if I had been looking for it. So, over I went. This was more than a butcher store; it was a combination deli, specialty foods, and fresh meals to bring home. I went over to the counter, where they were busily making sandwiches for the lunch crowd, and asked, "Are there any McCarrolls here?" Four hands went up. Christine wiped her hands on her apron and said, "Can I help you? I'm Chrissie McCarroll."

I said, "Well, I'm your cousin Don from Arizona." I had never met her before, so she went over to get her husband, Jimmy III. He came over, looking a little puzzled at first. He looked me over and said, "Well, there's a familiar face. You're Uncle Otto's son."

I said, "Yeah, and your Bud's son. You look just like your father."

"Yep, I'm the third generation of Jimmies. This is my wife, Chrissie."

In the meantime, their lovely daughter, Lauren, who was working the cash register, came over to meet her cousin once removed. It was quite a reunion.

I also learned that Jimmie III's son, Jimmie IV, was on his day off. Otherwise I would have met the whole next generation of Jimmie the butchers. I wouldn't be surprised if Lauren, who's married a Corrigan, thanks be to Gawd, a good Irish name, produces a Jimmy V to carry on the family tradition. What a family!

My Uncle Austin and Aunt Marion Lavery were my godparents. He was born in 1901 and she in 1902. Before they had Austin Jr., they treated me as if I were their child. I would spend several weeks with them each summer, and they really spoiled me. This might not sound like much, but every morning I'd have raspberries on my cereal. I had never seen a raspberry on Judson Street. As a youngster, I can't recall ever being in a restaurant with my parents until I was a teenager. But my godparents took me to restaurants where I could order whatever I wanted on the menu. The only thing I'd ever order when they took me out was a grilled cheese sandwich, a glass of chocolate milk, and a piece of blueberry pie for dessert. Even though they would try to get me to order something different, I would insist on my comfort food. To show you how much of a brat I was … one time they took me to a toy store. The story goes, I spotted a little red convertible car—you know the kind with pedals to make it go and a real steering wheel. I got in to pedal it around the store, and I wouldn't get out. They had to buy the car to get me out of it. Two of the salespeople carried me out in the car and put it in the back seat of Austin's car. I really don't remember that incident, but my mother told me about it when I was a few years older. I couldn't believe that I, good little boy that I was, was ever such a little monster. Shame on me!

One summer when I was visiting, Aunt Marion tripped and broke her ankle. The doctors discovered that, in addition to having a broken ankle, she was pregnant. My godparents were thrilled. I thought there was some connection between her breaking her ankle and being pregnant. What did I know!

Aunt Marion died in 1959, and, sadly, Austin Jr. died seven years later. He worked for the New York Power Company and was accidentally electrocuted when he came in contact with a live power line. Uncle Austin was devastated. For some years, he had had a premonition that his son was going to die before him. I'm not sure that anyone completely recovers from the loss of a child. But having recently lost his wife and now his only son was almost too much to bear.

To his credit, and with the help of my father and the comfort of his four grandchildren, he managed to deal with his grief for the last eleven years of his life. He became a closer part of our family. Sunday dinners, holidays, and even a trip to Arizona with my parents helped him cope. For the last few years of his life he lived at the Teresian, a nursing home for the elderly in Albany run by the Carmelite sisters. Every Sunday, my father would pick him up and bring him to our house for dinner. He still enjoyed his Manhattans.

When Aunt Marion died, Uncle Austin had the diamond from her engagement ring put in a setting with the diamond from a ring he had. As their only godchild, I now have that ring, which is a reminder of their kindness to that spoiled brat who wouldn't get out of the red toy car.

Uncle Vincent was born in 1903, just two years before my mother. His dear wife, Aunt Rita, was born in the same year. They had five children—Mary, who is only months younger than I; Rita, who married a classmate of mine from high school, Bill Byrne; Jean, who is still teaching kindergarten at age seventy-something; Joan, the youngest of the sisters, who moved to Florida decades ago; and Austin, the youngest of the family.

All the McCarroll brothers were pool sharks. Both Austin and Vincent had pool tables in the game rooms in their cellars. Most of them had diamond rings, even when they were so poor they "didn't have a pot to put a flower in." A diamond ring was almost as important as a customized pool cue. To flash that diamond ring when you embraced your pool cue was the mark of a real pool aficionado, i.e., a pool shark. They didn't play billiards; they played pocket pool, from eight ball to straight pool.

Mary, Rita, and Jean were all close to my age. At least we were all in high school at the same time. They went to the private Catholic girls' school, the Academy of the Holy Name, and I went to Christian Brothers Academy, a Catholic military school. I attended birthday parties at their house, and occasionally their family would join us at Warner's Lake. I remember Uncle Vincent taking long row boat rides by himself, coming back exhilarated and proclaiming in a feigned Shakespearean voice, "I was out on the lake communing with nature." I didn't know what communing meant, but he obviously enjoyed it.

Even though we were often geographically separated for long periods of time, the bond that we had as family always made it easy to pick up where we left off. When Uncle Vincent died in 1977, I was at the airport in Albany to fly back to Arizona. As I made my way to board my plane, I saw Mary and her husband, Art, coming down the steps from their flight from Chicago. We all stopped to exchange hugs, and I was able to express my condolences. Even though it was a brief reconnection, for me it was a very moving moment.

The Sisters McCarroll

My mother was the oldest of the three remaining McCarroll sisters. I have no idea how they got along growing up, but as adults they were very close. Right now, I'm looking at a picture from the Artgravure section of the *Knickerbocker News* dated March 20, 1931. The caption is "Baby Brigade." The article and picture take up three-quarters of the page. At the top of the page is a picture of eight women pushing their baby carriages down Central Avenue. It reads, "Young Albany believes in going buggy riding these sunny days as this scene demonstrated. The afternoon promenade is quite a social affair. Note the cordial cherubs greeting one another." Well, the cordial cherubs were, from left to right, "Mrs. Joseph Tommaney of 169 Second Street and son, Joseph Jr. [that was my Aunt Mary, but they only used the husband's first name to identify the wife in those days]; Mrs. Otto Fausel of 8 Judson Street." It goes on to identify the other six women in this twelve by five photo, but cousin Joe and I had top billing. As we should have! Aunt Mary and my mother were wearing flapper-style hats, eyes straight ahead, looking into the camera as though they were the proudest of the chorus line of new mothers. To top it off, the other kids were looking rather bored, while Joe and I were hamming it up for the camera. We both had smiles on our faces as we playfully grabbed one another's hands. It hardly seems that almost eight decades have passed since I made my first public appearance.

Before Anna May married, she lived with us on Judson Street. I have vague memories of her living with us. I know she had a job—she left after breakfast and came home for supper—but I have no idea about the details of her life. I do have hazy memories of my future uncle, Andrew L. Brew, coming courting, but they are just that—hazy.

One thing my cousin Jean McCarroll Black brings up is an expression Aunt Anna May used when all of us kids were together, and her first son Andy would "terrorize" the girl cousins. She would shout at him to "simmer down, Andy." After all these years, Jean still refers to Andy as "simmer down Andy." She might say, "Have you seen 'simmer down Andy' lately?" What a memory!

When I think about the McCarroll sisters, I often think of them as a trio: Anna May, Mary, and Jane. That's probably because during the Christmas holidays they did so much together. A pair of sisters would visit the third sister's house for the showing. The showing of the Christmas presents, that is. It's easy for me to picture my mother sitting on the floor with one leg under the other with all our presents stacked in front of her. She would display each one to the "ohs" and "ahas" of her sisters, re-box it, and go on to the next. They would have lunch and perhaps gossip or play cards. Often the husbands would join them after work for supper. The ritual would be repeated at each sister's house and was as much a part of the Christmas tradition as "Silent Night."

My cousin Joe was a year behind me at Christian Brothers Academy. Remember that annual boxing tournament I mentioned? Well, in the year that I won my division, Joe was one of my five opponents on the way to the championship. I don't remember the details of the three-round fight except that I won. After the fight, we walked back to his house where my mother had been spending the day with Aunt Mary. We had dinner when my father and Uncle Joe arrived. I don't think we even mentioned the boxing bout, and there were never any bad feelings.

As the McCarroll/Fausel families grew older, most of the parties moved to my parents' house. No matter where they were, for years the highlight of the evening was my Uncle John Dorn's renditions of several Irish songs. Officer John Patrick Dorn (JP), known to his colleagues in the police department as "Windy Dorn," was married to my grandmother's sister, Aunt Liz. JP was a character who could have come straight out of a Dickens novel. Or if he had had a white beard and a full head of hair, he could have passed as Santa Claus. He was bigger than life. As his nickname, Windy, suggests, he was a great storyteller and never at a loss for words. It was always hard "to get a word in edgewise," as my mother used to say, when JP was around. He loved to sing, especially Irish songs. No family get-together was complete until he sang his signature song, "The Mick Who Threw the Brick." I still can picture him when it was time for him to sing. His presence demanded the attention of everyone in attendance. With his suspenders holding up his pants below what some might describe as a beer belly, and all eyes riveted on him, he would fill the room with his baritone voice.

The family would usually end the party by everyone singing "I'll Take You Home Again, Kathleen" in honor of my mother's mother, Catherine McCarroll. Of course, Uncle John would lead us. May God be good to Uncle John and all our deceased relatives!

Reflections

In *Echoing Silence*, a book based on Thomas Merton's books, correspondence, and personal diaries, in which he often referred to writing as a vocation, it's clear that Merton saw writing as "a spiritual experience."[1]

Writing about my family and extended family in this chapter was indeed a spiritual experience for me. Whether the stories were joyful, frivolous, or sad, they had one common denominator for me—gratefulness. Someone said, "Remembering is like reliving." I found this to be true as I recalled the bonds I experienced growing up in a warm, joyful, safe, and stable environment. At times I felt the sadness of loss but also an overwhelming sense of gratitude for the good times we had that are always available in the deep and not-so-deep recesses of our memories. These feelings were reinforced recently when I spent a week back East with my relatives. I wish my wife had been able to join me, but she insisted that I go because she knows how important my relatives are to me. All of us over the years have had our joys and sorrows. As I mentioned earlier, I stayed at my cousin Rita's house as my home base. From the time I walked in the door, it was as if I had just seen her last week. We spent hours over breakfasts and dinners talking about the good times and the bad times and everything in between, including politics. She had lost her dear husband a year and a half before, but she is surrounded by her loving children and grandchildren, and fond memories of over fifty years that she and my friend and classmate Bill Byrne spent together with their family.

I spent two days with my cousin Bob Brew taking a nostalgic trip to Maine. Our destination was Ogunquit, where I used to spend time with my parents. Instead of taking the Massachusetts Turnpike, we took the scenic route through Whitehall, New York, Killington, Vermont, where I used to ski years ago, New Hampshire, finally having lunch in York, Maine, and continuing on to Ogunquit, where we stayed in a motel right on the beach for two days. We talked or laughed all the way up, even in the face of adversity, like not finding a place to park the car. I swear, all the tourist towns in Maine make their yearly revenue from parking meters.

When we got back to Albany, I visited with my cousin Walter and his lovely wife of over fifty years, Bella. You remember Walter—he's the cousin who always lied about his age but finally admitted he's eight-one. Bella and Walter have heroically dealt with Bella's fight against lymphoma for fourteen years.

I hadn't seen their four children since I've been in Arizona. Guess what? They're all grown up with families of their own. What a wonderful legacy for my oldest cousin and Bella! They proudly showed me a family portrait of their four grown children—Kathleen, Susan, Tom, and Dan—and their husbands and wives, and their grandchildren.

That evening I had dinner with my boyhood friend Father Peter G. Young at the Olive Garden in Albany. We go back so far, seeing him is always like getting together with a relative you haven't seen in a long time. We had a great dinner and brought one another up to date. I'm pretty up to date with what he's doing, since I get his quarterly newsletter, *Peter Young, Housing, Industries and Treatment.* That's his nonprofit organization, which offers programs in alcoholism and substance-abuse treatment, housing, and job training—what he describes as "The Glidepath to Recovery" system. He has rehabilitation programs all over the state of New York.

The next morning Rita and I met her son Vince and granddaughter Kelly (what a charmer) at Mass at their parish church. After Mass we went to the Cracker Barrel for a down-home breakfast. The morning was topped off by going back to Vince and Sherry's house to pay homage to the original pool table that Uncle Vincent had in his home for all those parties we had in his basement. The pool table must be a hundred years old, but Vince had it restored, and it's a treasure.

In the afternoon we went to visit my cousin Mary and her husband of over fifty years, Art White. Art is such a sweetheart, and he has had more than his share of health problems over the years. Right now he's bedridden, and Mary is his angel and caregiver. What a model of true love! We had a nice visit in Art's bedroom, and I learned something about Art that I never knew. He is part American Indian.

I also had the pleasure of meeting Mary and Art's son David and his wife, Twila. They recently left their jobs in Texas and moved to Albany to be close to David's parents. David is working at St. Peter's Hospital as a substance-abuse counselor, and his wife is working as curator of a museum in Schenectady. I hope David and Father Young can connect at some point.

That evening, after a few phone calls, we were able to get twelve of the cousins together for dinner. The Tommaneys were well represented with Mary Anne, Michael and Sandy, Jimmy, and Bob and Joan, who happened to be visiting from New Jersey. The Brews were represented by Jean and Bob and Terry and Martha. Then there were Rita and me. I think we all wished that we had more time to spend together. Let me propose a toast to all of us that my father always gave, "To the utmost."

I hope these reflections don't sound too much like a travelogue or remind you of an episode from that old radio soap opera *One Man's Family.* For me it was a spiritual experience that solidified what I already thought I knew about the ties that bind us together as family and to appreciate them even more. Even though you might not be a part of that family, I hope parts of it resonate with memories of your family and motivate you to explore your own roots.

Chapter 4
School Dazes

Kindergarten

My mother often repeated the story of my first day at St. Patrick's Institute (SPI), when I hung to her leg sobbing as she tried to abandon me with all those strangers. Apparently I wasn't the only one crying. There were a bunch of other budding scholars clinging to the legs of their respective mothers. Our teacher, Ms. Slattery, had her hands full trying to separate us from our mothers. We wanted no part of that strange place called kindergarten. Little did I know that it was the beginning of an educational journey that would last for the next twenty-two years.

I suspect it took a lot of cajoling for me to let go of my mother's leg, but obviously I did. According to my mother, there were just as many tears being shed by the mothers as the children. That was the gang that Ms. Slattery had to contend with on that first day of school and the rest of the year.

I have a class picture that helped me reconstruct the cast of characters that made up my kindergarten class of 1934. The picture was taken on the sidewalk in front of the convent of the Sisters of Mercy. There were seven girls sitting in the first row, in their freshly laundered dresses, their hands primly crossed on their laps and their legs crossed at their ankles, wearing Mary Jane shoes and ankle socks. Interestingly, there were sixteen boys lined up in two rows behind the girls. I'm not sure how to account for the disproportionate number of boys, but the odds seemed good to me.

Compared to the boys, the girls looked refined. The boys could have been characters from the cast for the *Little Rascals*, also known as *Our Gang Comedy*, a series of short comedy films that ran from 1922 through 1944. The series was about a group of poor neighborhood kids and the mischievous adventures they had together. The show was also picked up as reruns on TV. Some of you might remember some of the characters: Spanky, Alfalfa, Mary Ann, and Buckwheat, to mention a few.

Curriculum

As best I can recall, I didn't learn my ABCs or my numbers at home, so I was starting my school days from scratch. As I look back, it seems that for me kindergarten was more of a time to learn the social skills of getting along with my classmates than the skills of "readin' and 'ritin' and 'rithmetic." I have vague memories of playing with blocks, learning songs, and being taught that I had to share things with others. In 1990, when Robert Fulghum published his book *All I Really Need to Know I Learned in Kindergarten*,[1] I couldn't help but remember that some of my classmates didn't ever seem to learn those important lessons that Fulghum identifies as being essential for knowing how to live and what social skills we needed to develop to get along in whatever environment we found ourselves in. Most of us did learn our social skills under the watchful eye of Miss Slattery, but I'm not sure how much else we learned, besides our ABCs and numbers. That is the only academic accomplishment I can remember. It wasn't until I got into the first grade that I began to read. We were exposed to the *Dick and Jane* series. Remember, "Look, see Dick. See Dick run. Run, Dick, run." This must have been before phonics was introduced into the curriculum! Like many other things I learned in grammar school, I learned reading by rote. Just to make sure I had the correct spelling for rote, I looked it up my tattered 1950 edition of *Webster's Dictionary* and found the definition. Webster defines rote as "A fixed course or routine repetition of forms or phrases, often paying no attention to meaning." That certainly describes most of my early education. Just so we would recognize the word *run,* the next page with appropriate pictures quoted Jane urging Dick to run and see Sally. "Run, run. Run, Dick run. Run and see Sally." I'm actually not recalling the exact lines from the book. I got a copy from Amazon.com and reread each of the thirty-two pages. It was a trip into nostalgia. It brought me back to our kitchen table at 8 Judson Street with my mother hovering over me to make sure I was doing my reading homework and not listening to my favorite radio program, *Jack Armstrong, the All-American Boy.* Each page had one or more words that were repeated later on in the book. By the end of the thirty-two pages, we had a vocabulary of eighty-eight words. I counted them. I'm not sure if it took the whole year, a semester, or a quarter to finish the book, but I guess it worked because to this day I can recognize all the words I learned in the first grade.

Coming from a background of rote learning and a rather simple vocabulary, I was amazed several months ago when my wife and I visited her godson, Bill, and his wife, Amy, in California. They have a five-year-old son, Justin, who is in kindergarten. I could not believe what they are teaching kindergarteners today. He can read the newspaper, a restaurant menu, a regular book. Not books like *Fun with Dick and Jane,* which we started reading in the first grade, but much more sophisticated books. We were in a restaurant, and I noticed he was intently working on a card, checking things off with a pencil. It wasn't one of those coloring sheets that they give at McDonald's to keep the kids busy. He was actually responding to the questions on an adult evaluation questionnaire for the restaurant's records. I thought, well maybe this kid is just precocious, since both his parents are physicians. When I asked his mother what he was learning in kindergarten, it was beyond what I learned in third grade. When we got back to their house, she showed me the books he was reading and some of his daily schoolwork. Justin proudly read parts of a book he had been assigned. It was a science book. Although written in simple terms, it was really a book on cosmology. So, not only was he learning to read, he was learning about the universe. What a difference seventy-four years makes! I must confess I was a little envious of Justin's generation's kindergarten experiences. Not only were they not subjected to the rote learning that we were, but the content sure beat the life and times of Dick and Jane.

Arithmetic

Then there was arithmetic. It was not just reading we learned by rote. The times tables stand out! We learned each of the twelve times tables by the whole class reciting them out loud and in unison. I still remember my first-grade teacher, Sister Mary Agnes, right after we recited the "Pledge of Allegiance to the Flag" and our morning prayers, introducing us to the two times tables. She stood at the blackboard where she had written the tables and using her thirty-six-inch ruler to help the choir of first graders keep time. She started us off in a slow cadence that increased pace like a locomotive train as we went on:

2 x 1 = 2, 2 x 2 = 4, 2 x 3 = 6, all the way up to 2 x 12 = 24. As the months went on, we moved to each of the times tables. I did pretty well until we got to the six times tables and beyond. I had trouble remembering 6 x 7 = 42. So I would use my fingers to add six on to 6 x 6 = 36 to get to 42. I wonder if the advent of inexpensive calculators changed the way kids learn their times tables. I must ask my grandson.

Catechism

There was no class that was taught more by rote than our religion classes. To refresh my memory, I copied from the Internet the original Baltimore Catechism that we used from the first to the eighth grade. The catechism was divided into lessons. The first lesson was entitled "The Purpose of Man's Existence." Like all lessons in the catechism, its format was in questions and answers followed by a quote from Scripture to support the truth of the answer. Here are a few examples of the wisdom that we were exposed to. I'm sure it will be familiar to anyone who attended a Catholic grammar school:

1) Who made us?
   God made us.
   In the beginning, God created heaven and earth.
   (Genesis 1:1)
2) Who is God?
   God is the Supreme Being, infinitely perfect, who made all things and keeps them in existence.
   In him we live and more and have our being.
   (Acts 17:28)
3) Why did God make us?
   God made us to show forth His goodness and share with us His everlasting happiness in heaven.
   Eye has not seen nor ear heard, nor has it entered into the heart of man, what things God has prepared for those who live him. (I Corinthians 2:9)[3]

There you have it! Putting aside the archaic language, by the end of the lesson on "The Purpose of Man's Existence," we six- and seven-year-old first-graders had the answers to some of the most profound questions that many of us struggle with for most of our lives.

"Yes S'ter"

"Good morning, S'ter!" "Thank you, S'ter!" "Yes S'ter!" "No S'ter!" "I don't know S'ter!" I'm not sure whether all Catholic school students substituted "S'ter" for "Sister," but it was certainly the norm at St. Patrick's Institute (I'm not sure why they called it an institute instead of a school) to refer to the nuns as "S'ter." It wasn't meant to be disrespectful; it just seemed to flow more effortlessly from our lips. If the nuns were upset by it, they certainly would have let us know.

One comforting thing about SPI was you pretty much knew who your teachers would be for each grade from the time you entered kindergarten. Most of the teachers were nuns, which is not the case in many Catholic schools today. At SPI, six of the nine teachers I had were nuns. In addition to Miss Slattery, Miss Huba taught sixth grade and Miss Hart the seventh grade. There is something about most of my teachers that I remember very vividly after all these years. In different ways each one contributed, for better or worse, to the person I became in latter life.

First Grade, Sister Mary Agnes

I've already introduced you to Sister Mary Agnes, my first-grade teacher and the times table instructor. One other thing I remember about her class was that in the beginning of the year we all wore name tags so she could get to know our names. There were two other Donalds in our class, Donald Neville and Donald Klose. Imagine that—three Donalds in one class. My name tag read "Don F." To this day, when I'm writing a friend or relative I usually sign the letter Don F. I guess I don't want anyone to mix me up with Don N. or Don K.

Second Grade, Sister Mary Ann

Now, let me briefly recall what I remember about the others. Sister Mary Ann was my second-grade teacher. I remember the first day in her class as vividly as if it were yesterday. Our first assignment was to write our name and grade at the top of a fresh piece of paper in cursive letters, using the Palmer method of writing. We had already moved from printing. I carefully wrote my name on the left side of the paper and grade two on the right side. I can almost hear her swishing up and down the aisles, randomly checking on how well we could write cursive letters. When she got to my desk, she picked up my paper, looked at what I had written, and proceeded to tell the class what a dummy I was. If you remember, there was a slight difference in the Palmer method style of cursive for capital *G* and capital *S*. Holding my paper high enough for everyone to see, she proclaimed, "Look, class! Donald Fausel spelled 'Grade' with a capital *S*." Then she proceeded to walk up and down the aisles making sure everyone could see what an idiot I was. There were muffled giggles, and I held my head down, wishing I could disappear. I will talk about using shame as a motivator in a future chapter, but, to say the least, I felt ashamed.

Years later, at the reception for my ordination, Sister Ann came up to me for my blessing and introduced herself, "I'm Sister Mary Ann, your second-grade teacher. I bet you don't remember me." I had to bite my tongue not to bring up "the incident" at that time but I did have a chance to talk to her later. We had a nice chat, and I found out that it was her first year teaching, and she apologized profusely as I dispassionately recalled my first day in her class. I assured her that I had survived and was surprised that I had remembered it for over twenty years.

Third Grade, Sister Mary Christine

My third-grade teacher was Sister Mary Christine. I was one of her favorites, or "teacher's pets" as we were called. She often called me St. Aloysius and told me he was known for his purity and that I could be another St. Aloysius. I was flattered that she thought I could be a saint, but as a third grader I had no idea about what she meant by being pure. All I could relate to was the Ivory Soap ads on the radio. We always used Ivory Soap at 8 Judson Street. As a kid, I took a bath every Saturday night, whether I needed it or not. Since we didn't have a shower, my weekly bath was in our tub. I remember being fascinated by how Ivory Soap floated on the bath water and other soap sank. I asked my mother why we didn't use

Palmolive or any of the other soaps that advertised on the radio. Her answer was, "We use Ivory because it's pure. Like they used to say on the radio—99 and 44/100 percent pure." In my little third-grade mind, somehow I connected Ivory Soap pure with the pure Sister Christine thought I was. It took me years to figure out that she was talking about pure as in the Sixth Commandment. Even though I didn't understand what pure meant at the time, I did get the idea that she thought I was special, and I liked that.

There was one incident when I thought I could confide in her, but she disappointed me. Sister Stanislaus Mary, who was principal at the time, had issued an edict that cap guns would not be allowed in school. In one of the rare times that I blatantly broke the rules, I brought my cap gun to school. The word got out that the principal was waiting at the top of the stairs to search us as we came for our first class in the morning. She was an imposing figure, with her hands on her hips and her normal stern demeanor looking even sterner on gun collection day.

Before I reached the point of no return, I hid my cap gun by sliding it down my knickers where they ended at my knee. When it came my turn to be searched, she firmly asked me to empty my pockets. Seeing no evidence of a cap gun, she waved me on. When I got to my classroom, I was so excited that I had eluded discovery that I immediately told "my pal" Sister Christine how I had avoided detection. To my surprise, she held her hand out and said in a voice that seemed troubled, "All right, Donald, hand over your cap gun and bring it to Sister Stanislaus Mary." "Yes S'ter"! I said sheepishly. "Sorry S'ter." Her cold stare and silence was more devastating than any words she could have spoken. Not even a crocodile tear fazed her. Off I went to the principal's office for a verbal reprimand and a note to take home to my parents. My parents' reaction was predictable. I don't remember my sentence, but I do remember feeling guiltier than when I stole the pack of gum from Max's store. Looking back, the guilt I felt about the cap gun caper did not fit the crime. Even telling of my big-time disobedience in confession didn't help ease my guilty feeling.

Fourth Grade, Sister Mary Perpetua

I'm looking at my report card for the fourth grade. On the back of the card is a place for my teacher, Sister Mary Perpetua, to sign her name and for my father to sign his. I don't have any specific memories of Sister Perpetua, but the report card suggests I got off to a bad start for the first two quarters but finished strong with an average for all my classes of 90.5. What I never bothered to read before is the advice to parents on the back of the card above their signatures. Just to give you an idea of the paternalistic, superior position from which the school viewed parents, I'm going to provide several paragraphs of instructions.

TO PARENTS

The time after school up to supper should be given children for play. Sunlight and exercises at games will keep them healthy in soul and body.

Preparation of the next day's lessons should follow supper before the fatigue comes. Parents may help by hearing them recite but should give no special lessons as they have enough to do in meeting the requirements of their regular teacher.

Never permit them out of call after dark. Waywardness invariably starts with night street walking. Exact obedience in all things, and let parents be united in ever correction, the one never petting when the other punishes.

Send them to school every day. Truant playing in boys often begins with parents keeping them at home for some slight cause and even girls lose interest in their classes when torn from their studies. See that they are on time, for it is but a step from the tardy scholar to the truant.

Be sure they attend their religious duties on Sunday and have a prayer book or beads. On Confession Day see that they go at the time appointed for them and not at night, when they are in the way of grown people, besides contracting the habit of being out of doors after dark.

The Catholic School for which Priests, Religious teachers and people are sacrificing so much can affect the good intended only with the cooperation of parents. As you value your own and your children's salvation and temporal happiness, join us in the great work of preserving to God and America this generation.

The report cards were issued by the Diocesan Office of Education. So, it was not just St. Patrick's Institute parents who received this information. I realize that this was 1938 and that most parents were not as well educated as they are today, but, to put it mildly, the tone still seems a bit intrusive and insensitive. I'm sure whoever composed it and whoever approved it had the best of intentions. Not all the caveats are inappropriate or troublesome, but it certainly would not sit well with today's parents. Remember the book *I'm Okay—You're Okay*, by Thomas A. Harris? In his presentation of transactional analysis, he points out that it is more effective to communicate adult-to-adult than adult-to-child. Given the great respect our parents had for authority, apparently they didn't mind being talked to as children.

Reading the last sentence in the message to parents, I could not help but think of a motto that was imprinted on many Catholic buildings, *Pro Deo et Patria* (For God and Country). This was a generation that was mostly first- or second-generation immigrants who needed to prove to the Protestant establishment that they were patriotic despite being Roman Catholics.

Fifth Grade, Sister Mary Carmelita

Our fifth-grade teacher was Sister Mary Carmelita. Her nickname was Grandma. She looked as old as my Great-Grandmother Fausel, whom I described earlier. The one incident that stands out is when Sister Carmelita handed out the report cards at the end of the first quarter. To say the least, she was very disappointed with how most of the class did in the exams. She started by giving a lecture to the whole class on being responsible students, which ended up as a diatribe. The more she talked, the angrier she got. She called us all sorts of nasty names—*idiots* and *guttersnipes* are two of the words I can remember. Even though I didn't know what a guttersnipe was, it sounded pretty despicable. For a finale she climbed up on her desk and jumped off with a screeching scream. It was weird. I felt sorry for her and at the same time guilty for having been part of the group that could drive this poor woman to such histrionics. After she jumped, she tried to compose herself. She seemed embarrassed as she readjusted her habit with the little bit of dignity she could muster. Next, she picked up a list from her desk. She read a dozen names of students she wanted to see after school and then dismissed the class early. I was one of the chosen twelve who had to face her at the end of the day. More guilt! When we met with her, she was still angry, but she just gave us an assignment of extra homework that was due the next day. The unpleasant episode became the topic of conversations for months and was even brought up years later. "Remember the day when Grandma jumped off her desk screaming!"

Sixth Grade, Miss Gertrude Huba

What a change from Grandma! Our sixth-grade teacher was Miss Gertrude Huba. She was a knockout, as they used to say. I guess she was in her mid to late twenties. She could have passed for Hedy Lamarr. Remember her? Not only did Miss Huba look like a movie star, but she dressed like one. A pre-teenage boy's fantasy! She even wore tight sweaters that might have been considered "an occasion of sin." "Bless me father for I have sinned. I had impure thoughts about my teacher." More guilt!

Judging from the talk in the boys' bathroom, I wasn't the only one who had impure thoughts. It was not unusual to hear one of my classmates say something like, "Hey, did you see that sweater that Huba was wearing today? I'd love to get my hands on those knockers." I'm sure she would have been shocked if she knew what those little angels were saying behind her back. I really think she was quite innocent about the effect she was having on the guys. In contrast to her appearance, she talked like a nun. For example, I remember one spelling test where one of the words was "whistle." She said the word first and then used it in a sentence. "When the Blessed Mother hears a girl whistle, she cries." I've never forgotten that. I thought at the time it was a little odd for the Blessed Virgin to be concerned with girls whistling. From that time on, every time I heard a girl whistle, I thought of Miss Huba.

She definitely had no problems getting volunteers to clean the erasers after school. Then I knew what Sister Christine was talking about when she wanted me to be pure like St. Aloysius. I had no idea about Miss Huba's personal life. After the sixth grade, I don't think I ever saw her again. Even so, she remained part of my preadolescent fantasy life through grammar school and well into high school.

Seventh Grade, Miss Mary Hart

Before we even started the seventh grade, the eighth graders told us about Miss Hart's eccentricities. She was what they used to call a "maiden lady," probably in her late fifties or early sixties. She wore her hair in a bun and dressed as conservatively as Miss Huba dressed liberally. There were some former students who could imitate her high-pitched voice and her quirky body movements. One of the highlights they prepared us for was in geography class when she would teach us the difference between the diameter and the circumstance of the Earth. Each year she would bring in an orange as a prop. She would take a long pin out of her hair and insert it through the middle of the orange. We were prepared for what happened next. Just as we had been told, once the pin reached the other end, it predictably squirted juice on her dress. It didn't seem to bother her. She seemed pleased that she had been successful in providing us with a visual image of the earth's diameter. Despite our making fun of her behind her back, she was a good teacher. The seventh grade was the first time I received a 95 average for the year. My father rewarded me with a spiffy baseball mitt that was the envy of all the Judson Street Sluggers.

Eighth Grade, Sister Mary Genevieve

Finally, we reached the eighth grade and Sister Mary Genevieve. She was another elderly nun whose strands of gray hair peeked from the sides of the white wimple that covered her head and came around her chin and neck like a medieval crown. Unlike Sister Mary Carmelita she did not show signs of early dementia. She was soft-spoken and seemed always to be in control of the class without ranting and raving. She also enjoyed tapping into our creative potential. We had a number of seasonal plays that we put on for the rest of the school. I was in *A Christmas Carol.* I played the oldest of the Crachet children. When they brought in the Christmas goose at the end of the play, I had one line, "Oh what a goose, what a fine large goose, has there ever been such a goose before." This invoked muffled snickers from some of the eighth-grade boys.

Each year for graduation Sister Genevieve composed lyrics to the tune of a popular song. For the Class of 1943, she used the melody of the current hit, "Moonlight Becomes You." I still remember the first verse:

SPI Forty-three
By Sister Mary Genevieve

Schooldays are ending at dear SPI,
And out of the door we're wending our way.
Farewell to schoolmates, that we might never see,
SPI Forty-three.

It was hard to sing the farewell song with a straight face, but for Sister Genevieve, her annual good-bye song brought a tear to her eye.

Becoming a Teenager

During my nine years at SPI, I went from a five-year-old, struggling to hang on to my mother's leg, to a teenager, struggling to be independent, and feeling the effects of a surge of testosterone. I was ill prepared for both events. I never had the legendary talk with my father about the birds and the bees. As you may recall from chapter 2, I relied on my neighbor, who was a few years older than I, to learn about sex. Unfortunately, he was not well informed.

In researching testosterone for this section, I learned about its part in the changes I was experiencing—things I wished I had known at the time when I wondered what was happening to my body and moods. I also learned that it was not testosterone but the people we hung out with that probably had a more important part to play in determining how wayward we would be as teenagers. Not to mention the inability of the immature brain to assess risks properly. Luckily most of the guys I palled around with were pretty solid citizens. Even so, I wondered what was going on but didn't know who to ask. I would have been too embarrassed to ask my parents, and I learned that my peers were not as wise in these matters as they thought they were. I'm sure these factors contributed to the life decision I made in choosing a vocation.

Falling in Love

One of the euphoric parts of puberty was falling in love for the first time. My first love was Catherine Hayes. Let me give you some background on how we met. I was a member of the boy's basketball team that won the Catholic Youth Organization's championship for the city of Albany. We beat all our opponents. It was an elimination tournament, a minor version of the "March Madness" that happens every year in college basketball. We got a trophy and championship T-shirts. Even though we didn't have cheerleaders, there was a group of seventh- and eighth-grade girls who always showed up to root for us. Up to this point in my life, sports, especially basketball, was the love of my life. I even remember thinking that when I wasn't able to play basketball anymore, life would be over. I had earned my way onto the first string and, along with Jackie Spanbauer and Feet Lasch, was one of the major scorers. Once we won the championship and enjoyed our position of "big men on campus," our doting female fans had a party for us at one of the girls' homes. It was there that I first really met Catherine Hayes. I had seen her around school but never had the nerve to talk to her; I was too shy. I think I had a crush on her. Even though I was an upperclassman and a basketball star, I still didn't have any self-confidence around girls. Maybe this would be my big chance to talk to the girl of my dreams.

My First Kiss

After we had cake and ice cream and other goodies, it was time to play games. Any adults who were there stayed discreetly in the kitchen. Do you remember Post Office, Flashlight, and Spin the Bottle? I had never heard of them, but I was about to find out how to play. First, we were all paired up by drawing numbers from a hat. Guess who my partner was? That's right! Catherine Hayes. My heart was pounding. I thought she was the most beautiful girl in the world. Before the games started, we all found places to sit with our partner and chat. Catherine and I ended up counting the freckles on our arms to see who had the most. That was easy. I didn't know much about her, but I was smitten already. We were soon interrupted by someone getting up in the middle of the room and giving us the rules for Flashlight. The rules were simple: first, most of the lights were turned off. Then, whenever each couple was ready, you were to kiss your partner; the person with the flashlight would try to catch a couple kissing. If he or she did, then it would be their turn to take the flashlight. You couldn't turn the flashlight on the same couple more than once.

"Let's play Flashlight," Robert McCarthy, the custodian of the flashlight, yelled. My first kiss! Wouldn't you know, Robert McCarthy caught us in a romantic embrace. I had hardly begun to kiss her. Now I had to leave my beloved and take the flashlight and find another couple kissing. The game went on, and I never could get back to my partner. I had to wait until we played Post Office. Life wasn't fair.

When we arrived at school on Monday, Sister Mary Rosario, who was then the principal, called all the eighth-grade party boys to her office. As we arrived, the girls who had held the party were leaving her office. They walked passed us with their eyes to the floor, glancing up as if to say, "Are you in for it." As we went into the principal's room, there were no greetings. The seven or eight of us just lined up around her desk in a semicircle as she began her interrogation and tirade. I don't know where she got her information about the party and what went on, but by the way she went on and on, you would think we had all been at an orgy. It wasn't an information-gathering session; she was the prosecuting attorney, jury, and judge, and we were all guilty. I began to wonder if we had indeed done something really evil just by attending that party, let alone playing kissing games. I can't remember what our punishment was, but I never forgot the uncomfortable feelings I had just being part of the condemned. It was what I thought the Last Judgment would be like.

Apparently, the punishment to cure me of my evil ways didn't work. One day during class time, I wanted to see Catherine in the worst way, and I did something very uncharacteristic of me. I asked Sister Genevieve to excuse me to go the boys' room. Instead, I went across the hall, knocked on Miss Hart's door, and told her the principal wanted to see Catherine. When Catherine saw me in the corridor, she was really confused. I didn't really know what my next step was, so I asked her if she would like to go to the movies Saturday. She was so surprised and anxious that we might be "found out" in this elicit tryst, that she said yes and went right back to class. I looked forward to seeing her, but when I picked her up I didn't know what to talk about. Fortunately, she was a good talker, and we spent most of our time together watching the movie. Our next date was to go roller-skating. We met several of her girlfriends with their dates at the roller rink, so that took some of the pressure off me for witty conversation. I discovered that my major topic of conversation was sports. That came easily with the guys, but outside of sports talk, I didn't have much to talk about. I needed to learn to talk to girls and get over my tongue-tied shyness in their presence.

A few more awkward dates with Catherine and sad to say, we drifted apart when I graduated and went on to high school. I'm sure Sister Rosario would have thought that the good Lord had more important plans for both of us. Here's one other bit of information. Remember my mother's sorority pin from Tau Nu Sigma (Twenty Necking Sisters)? Well, at the height of our romance, I gave it to Catherine, without my mother knowing. I don't remember if I ever confessed that sinful act. I never asked for it back. I learned many years later that Catherine had become a nun in the order of the Little Sisters of the Poor. I wonder what she did with that Tau Nu Sigma pin.

Graduation day finally came. My whole extended family was there to mark my accomplishment. One of my fond memories of growing up as part of the Fausel/McCarroll clan was that whenever there was a wedding, graduation, or any important day in our lives, the family was there to celebrate with you. At my grammar school graduation, I remember my Uncle Ed waiting outside of St. Patrick's Church, where we held the ceremony. I sensed his pride as he read my diploma. "Donald Frederick, you were named after Grandpa. I'm sure he'd be proud of you." He then extended his hand to congratulate me and with the other hand stuffed a card in my pocket. "Where are you going to high school?" he asked. "We haven't discussed it yet." I became a little concerned, since I was soon to launch a new part of my life, and I didn't know which school I would be attending.

Christian Brothers Academy

There were three Catholic high schools in Albany: Cathedral, Vincentian, and Christian Brothers Academy (CBA). Of course I would go to a Catholic high school. That was a given. I'm not sure how I ended up at CBA, but I do know I didn't make the decision. It was my parents' decision. It was not a bad decision, and I might have chosen it myself had I been the decider. Still, it would have been nice to have had the opportunity to express my choice. Even, "How would you like to go to CBA?" But that was the way decisions were made in those days. The fact that a number of my grammar school classmates were going to CBA made it more appealing.

CBA was an all-boys military school, certified by the United States Armed Forces as a Junior Officers' Training Corps (JROTC) program. It had a Department of Military Science and Tactics, which had its own curriculum, books, and tests. We had four uniforms: the everyday uniform that was similar to a Marine's olive green uniform; a dress blue uniform with a jacket with three rows of brass buttons that we wore with blue pants with a gold stripe in the cold weather and white pants in the spring; and a white uniform for spring parades, proms, and graduation. We needed three hats as well—blue, white, and olive green. We also had to wear white gloves for parades and other events. I have no idea how my parents afforded the uniforms and tuition. At that time, I think the tuition was only $250 a year, but that was quite a piece of change in those days. Add to that the cost of the uniforms for the first year and you had a major expense that my parents had to handle.

Prior to starting academic classes, the plebes (freshmen) had to attend two-week training in the basics necessary to become a Jr. ROTC cadet. The training included: close-order drill for most of the mornings; mastering the obstacle course and listening to lectures on military science and tactics for a couple of excruciating hours in the afternoon. Thanks to the Internet, I was able to refresh my memory by looking up a definition for close-order drill and its purpose. Close-order drill is simply marching in formation. This we did from the first day we arrived until we graduated.

The obstacle course was much more strenuous than close-order drill. It included running, climbing, jumping, crawling, and balancing. Most of the activities were timed, and you had to complete each one in a specific time frame. I thought the drill instructors were picked because they scored high on their exam in sadism. They seemed to relish our repeating the most difficult tasks over and over. My nemesis was the ten-foot wall we had to scale. "Come on, Mister! Get your lazy butt over that wall." Not only was it physically challenging; the drill instructors' insensitive comments on my performance were enough to fracture my fragile teenage ego.

After we completed our "basic training," we were allowed to wear our uniform to the first day of classes. I was assigned to IB, one of the five freshmen homerooms. Our homeroom teacher was Brother Victor Dardis. In those days the brothers didn't use their family name; he was just Brother Victor. One of the first things he did after introducing himself was to appoint one of the class members as the class monitor. One of the responsibilities of the monitor was to give the order, "Class, attention!" when a teacher or officer walked into the room. We would all jump to attention next to our desks until we heard the order, "As you were." The monitor also started each class by invoking the name of the founder of the Christian Brothers, St. John Baptist de LaSalle. Once we heard the founder's name, the class would respond in unison, "Pray for us." Next, the monitor would say, "Live, Jesus, in our hearts." Our response: "Forever!" It's not surprising that I remember those prayers, also known as "ejaculations." They were repeated at least five times a day for four years. I still revert to "Live, Jesus, in our hearts" as a topic for meditation.

Every morning before classes began, each homeroom would have inspection. We all stood at attention by our desks as the officer of the day would go up and down each aisle and inspect every cadet from head to toe. You needed to have a haircut every two weeks; your shoes spit shined; a trained eye made sure your brass belt buckle was properly shined. If your appearance didn't fit the military code, you would get one or more demerits. For each demerit you had to walk around the flagpole for an hour with your rifle on your shoulder. "Donald good boy," the perfect cadet, only received five demerits in four years at CBA. That was when my rifle slipped out of my hand as I responded to the order of "parade rest." This happened in front of the whole cadet regiment, which was practicing for the midterm review at the Albany Armory. I can almost hear the voice of then retired Marine Colonel Bertrand T. Fay, the Commandant of Cadets, booming over the microphone from his vantage point in the balcony, "Give that cadet five demerits!" I sheepishly bent down and picked up my rifle, hoping no one could identify me. Thankfully, it was just a rehearsal for the actual event, when the armory would be filled with all our parents, relatives, and friends.

At the end of each school day, the Captain Adjutant would broadcast the orders for the following day. His voice was piped into all the classrooms.

"Now hear this, now hear this! Attention to orders, Headquarters Corps of Cadets, Christian Brothers Academy, Department of Military Science and Tactics, Albany, New York, February 22, 1944; company having the guard, "E"; officer of the day, Cadet Captain Richard Jones; uniform of the day, dress blues." He then would go on to announce the activities for the day and major events, e.g., "Saturday, February 24, football game, CBA vs. Albany High School; Cadet Regiment will assemble information at Beverwyck Park on Washington Avenue at 1300 to march to Bleecker Stadium; uniform—olive green."

Public events such as football game or Armistice Day or Memorial Day parades, when we marched as a regiment, always gave me a feeling of pride. Marching into Bleecker Stadium, over 500 cadets strong, with the band playing "The Marine's Hymn," gave me a lump in my throat. Of course I'd never have admitted that at the time to my fellow cadets, but I suspect that most of them felt the same way.

Hey, Mugssyyyy!

CBA was about two miles from my house on Judson Street. My regular routine was to stop at the house of my best friend, Muggsy McGraw, on the way to school. He lived a block from me on Clinton Avenue. I never rang his doorbell; I'd just holler his name, hey Mugssyyyy! One or two shouts, and he would appear at the front door, usually with his mother, Lillian, close behind, making sure he had everything he needed for school. Muggsy was a tough, well-built, Irish kid. He had a temper that could explode when you least expected it. I remember one morning after hearing me holler out my arrival, he came to the door with his hand wrapped in a bandage. His mother was not too happy with him as she practically pushed him out the door.

"What the hell happened to you?" I asked.

Still red in the face with anger, he responded, "Goddamn hair, it wouldn't stay down in the back, so I smashed the mirror with my fist." I knew enough not to ask any more questions. I only thought, *That's Muggsy for you!* Another time we were walking back from school. It was late fall, and light snow was beginning to cover the fading grass. We were having an argument—about what, I don't remember. I do remember calling him a dirty Jap (remember, this was during World War II). The next thing I remember was Muggsy throwing me a sucker punch and the both of us rolling around on the ground in our olive green CBA uniforms. When we got up, there was blood trickling down my cheek. Muggsy gave me his handkerchief, and that was the end of the fight. We walked in silence most of the way to his house. When I got home, my mother took one look at the gash under my left eye, and she took me over to Dr. Kircher's office for four stitches. Apparently she called Muggsy's mother because when I made my regular stop at his house to pick him up for school, Muggsy came out by himself. I said, "I had four stitches last night."

"Yeah, I know—sorry!" That was the end of that. It never came up again.

Academics

I'm looking at my weekly report card for the fourth quarter of my freshman year. We had six subjects: Religion, English, Mathematics, Latin, Science, and Civics. Every Monday we received grades in all six subjects. Our parents needed to sign our report card, and we had to bring it back to school the next day or receive a demerit. For the first week, my father signed under Parent's Signature and from then on, until he returned from the service two years later, my mother signed Mrs. J. Otto Fausel. Two things struck me as I looked at those signatures. One, my mother was a single parent during those very important adolescent years, when I needed a male role model more than at any other time in my adolescence. Two, granted that 1943 was before any serious feminist movement, by signing her name as Mrs. J. Otto Fausel, instead of Jane A. Fausel, was my mother signaling that her identity was tied to my father's name? Or was she just going along with the pre-feminist thinking? I suspect the latter, but it's another one of those questions I wish I had explored with my mother while I had the opportunity.

I did very well in all my classes that first year. In addition to our weekly report card, we received four quarterly cards. I was on the honor roll for two of those quarters and the merit roll for the other quarters. This merited a promotion to cadet corporal for my sophomore year. From the time my father left for the service, through my second and third years, my grades were at the merit level but they never matched my freshman year. I'm not sure whether it was because of my father's absence or just that I was in the midst of puberty.

Extracurricular

Basketball, baseball, football, and golf, in that order, were my major interests in life during my high school years. They even trumped girls! I did date several girls during my junior and senior years. The one who stands out was Jean Gervais. We did a lot of "necking" on her back porch when her parents weren't home. I never got beyond "second base" or to the "petting" stage as they used to say. Someone defined necking as "caresses above the neck" and petting as "caresses below." If I could believe the stories my peers told about their romantic episodes, I was a slow learner. Also, I guess Jean and I weren't going steady because I found out that she was seeing Bernie Keeler. Probably necking with him, too! I was crushed! I thought I was her one true love. Would I ever be able to trust a female again? We shall see!

Outside of the necking, I still was not that comfortable around girls. I recall routinely going to the Saturday night dances at the CYO center's gym. They had a live band that played all the popular songs of the days. I couldn't imagine anything more traumatic than asking a girl to dance and for her to say no. Perhaps my fear of rejection was deep-seated or perhaps it was because I wasn't that good a dancer. I just knew one dance step. Remember, this was the era of the "jitterbug" and the one step that I had mastered was for a slow dance. I called it the "one-two slide step." I had to wait until they played a slow dance before I could muster up the courage to ask a girl to dance. I would start off at one side of the gym, do the one-two slide step all the way up to the end of floor, turn left, go to the opposite side, and back to where I started. I had covered the whole court with the same step. That was my dancing repertoire. It's a wonder anyone wanted to dance with me.

After the dance, I'd usually go with my friend Ted Caldes to the Boulevard Café on Central Avenue and order a piece of strawberry short cake and a glass of milk. That was a big Saturday night for us. Ted was a handsome young man, of Greek origin, and an all-city shortstop for Albany High School. I thought maybe if I hung out with him, the girls would be fighting to get at our table. Nope, it didn't work, but we had a lot of common interests to talk about besides sports. He was very interested in the Catholic church and always would bring up topics that taxed my ability to provide a reasonable answer. He brought up subjects that gave me pause to think and not just parrot what I had learned in catechism. I was not surprised, later on, when I found out that he became a lawyer.

I did well in sports and made the freshman basketball team and the freshman baseball team and played intramural football for my homeroom. Basketball was my favorite. I was even asked by Brother Robert to suit up with the Junior Varsity for several games. This was a real honor for a freshman. Brother Robert put me in as a forward toward the end of the first game, and I scored two baskets and a foul point. Wow! This made up for my ineptitude on the dance floor.

The freshman baseball team was coached by Brother Victor. Muggsy McGraw and I competed for the catcher's position. He had a better arm for throwing out runners trying to steal second base. I ended up sitting on the bench for most of our games or being used as a right fielder and pinch hitter. I decided there and then that I was going to focus on basketball. I made the junior varsity team in my sophomore year and the varsity in my junior year.

Each year I developed new moves and wondered how I had ever played the year before. While I was focusing my energies on basketball, my skills on the dance floor remained at the one-two slide step level. I wonder if, I focused as much time on dancing as I did on basketball, would my life had gone in a different direction. As I realized later in life, any guy who could dance well was always popular with the ladies.

When not practicing at CBA, I spent most of my leisure time at the Catholic Youth Center, which, as you may recall, was just around the corner from 8 Judson Street. I even got a part-time job there on weekends refereeing four or five games a day for the Catholic Youth Organization (CYO) Junior League. Increasingly, this became my second home and sports, my primary interest.

My father was discharged from the army during the fall of my senior year. While he was away, I wrote him regularly, keeping him up to date about my school activities. Now things were back to normal. My father didn't waste any time getting back to work; we had our regular family dinners for four, and both he and my mother seemed very relieved that the war was over, and we were an intact family again. Every night my father would ask me about school and how I was doing in trying out for the varsity basketball team. I liked that, even though he might not have been able to figure that out by my obscure answers.

I was spending long hours at the CBA gym, trying to impress the new coach, Chuck Yund. I think he was just out of college, and this was his first head coaching job. Even before the formal season started, he would play half-court three on three games with us every day after class. By the time the official "tryouts" for the team started, he knew most of us returning varsity players pretty well. I slowly became aware that I might not make the team, even though I had made it as a junior with Coach Bill Bainor. It became apparent that if you were a senior and you didn't make the starting team, you'd be cut from the roster. Coach Jund wanted to use the slots on the second team for juniors so he could groom them for the following season. Over the period of several weeks he kept cutting five or six players a week by putting a list of those who were still in the running on his office door. I made it to the last cut. I will never forget the sinking feeling in my stomach as we all gathered around his door to check the list, and I saw that my name was missing. I felt like a complete failure. Those who made the list did a good job of checking their emotions so they wouldn't make the others feel bad. It was hard for me to sincerely congratulate anyone, since I was in a state of shock.

After supper I was sitting on the couch pretending I was reading the paper. My father came over and asked, "How's the basketball star doing?"

I casually responded, as if it didn't make much difference to me, "I was cut from the team."

My father didn't know what to say. In an effort to comfort me, he put his arm on my shoulder and said something inane like,

"Well, that will give you more time to do other things." I had a strong sense that he was feeling my pain and did the best he could to communicate that to me.

I threw myself into my job at the CYO. I gradually was given more responsibilities in planning the city-wide programs, coaching, refereeing, umpiring, and running the day-to-day after-school programs for the kids. I don't think I went to see one CBA basketball game that year. Life does go on.

My Calling

One of my heroes when I was a teenager was Father Harry B. Hines. He was a Catholic priest who was the director of the Catholic Youth Organization for the Diocese of Albany. He must have been in his early fifties when I first met him. He was a big-framed man with a charismatic personality. His disheveled mop of salt-and-pepper hair on his six-foot, three-inch frame made him stand out in a crowd of his fellow priests.

As I mentioned, the CYO Center was around the corner from our house. I practically grew up there. It was where I learned to play basketball, pool, ping pong, and developed my one-two slide step for the Saturday night teen dances.

Father Hines's office was in the CYO Center. Of the hundreds of days I interacted with him, one day stands out. I was a senior in high school, and he and his secretary, Mary Burke, and I were in his office. She was efficiently folding a stack of letters to stuff in envelopes. Mary was a very attractive, single Irish woman with jet-black hair, which she wore in a Maureen O'Hara style that was popular in the late forties. She had started working for Father Hines the year she graduated from high school and had been his right hand for at least ten years.

On this particular day, Father Hines and I had just finished our work on the spring baseball schedule. He relaxed in his executive chair and out of the clear blue asked, "What are you going to do when you graduate next month?"

A little off guard, I very tentatively answered, "I've been thinking about going to Siena College."

"That's a good school. What are you going to major in?"

Again I cautiously responded, "Well, I've been thinking about social work. Someone told me that the need for social workers is going to increase in the next ten years."

There was a pause in the conversation, and he continued, "Social work? Did you ever think about becoming a priest?"

"Well, I thought about it, but I never believed I had a vocation."

After just a few seconds hesitation, he announced, "Well, let's see about that." Mary was still stuffing envelopes, pretending she wasn't listening to the conversation.

Father Hines broke into his typical take-charge voice and said, "I'm going to make an appointment for you to see Monsignor Rooney."

Monsignor Rooney was the Chancellor of the diocese. Before I knew it, Father Hines was firing an order at Mary Burke. "Mary, get Ray Rooney on the phone."

I'm thinking, *What's going on here? Is this how you know you have a calling to the priesthood? All it takes is a call to Ray Rooney?*

In a few minutes, Mary reported, "Father, Monsignor Rooney is on the line." As Father Hines reached for the phone, Mary looked at me, rolled her eyes, and shrugged her shoulders as if she were saying, "That's HBH for you!"

"Ray, Harry Hines here. How ya doing, my friend? Yeah, this is a busy time for me, too." Getting right down to business, he continued, "Listen Ray, I have a young man here in my office who's thinking about becoming a priest."

I'm thinking, *God, he's talking about me. I thought I told him I was thinking about going to Siena.*

"Yeah, that's right. He's been working part-time for me for the last few years. He practically runs the place. Very bright, talented, and comes from a good Catholic family. Can you talk to him about his vocation? Great, I'll let him know. Listen, we have to get out on the links when we both have some free time. Thanks, Ray!"

He turned to me to tell me the "good news": "Well, he can see you next week." Without any further discussion, he picked up his *New York Times* and started reading. My head was spinning. "Wow! They must think I'm eligible to be a member of their club. I can be like Bing Crosby in the movie *The Bells of St. Mary's* or Spencer Tracy in *Boys Town*." To say the least, I was flattered. I began to convince myself that this must be how you know you have a vocation; this is the calling I've heard about—it must be the will of God.

That fall there was no Siena College for me; I was off to St. Thomas Seminary in Bloomfield, Connecticut, with everything I owned in a footlocker. So much for a self-directed life!

Camp Tekakwitha

Before I left for the seminary, I spent my last summer at Camp Tekakwitha, a boy's camp on Lake Luzerne. The camp was sponsored by the CYO. This was my second summer as a counselor. I was the only counselor back from the previous year, so, with the blessing of Father Hinds, I was appointed head counselor by Father Hart, the camp director. This was a great opportunity for me to develop leadership skills on the job. Father Hart left most of the details of running the programs to me. I loved it. The other counselors were my age, and a few were older, so at times it was a little awkward for me to walk the fine line between being "one of the guys" and their supervisor at the same time.

I did all the scheduling and assigning of tasks and oversaw the everyday operation of the camp. Looking back, I should have been a little reticent to take on those responsibilities, but, for some unknown reason, I had the confidence to rise to the occasion. Looking back, I probably should have said no, but Father Hart apparently thought I was capable, so once again I relied on an authority figure to make decisions for me. Shades of Father Hinds!

Reflections

As I reflected on my life as a Catholic schoolboy, I had the advantage of a perspective of five decades. I was reminded of one of my favorite quotes from Albert Einstein: "Unthinking respect for authority is the greatest enemy of truth." When I recalled Einstein's words, I thought he might have been describing me and how docilely I integrated what I was taught during my formative years—particularly, what I learned about the prescribed beliefs that I accepted from church authorities. I had such great respect or fear for the authority of the good nuns, brothers, and priests that I embraced whatever they taught me as "the truth." For years, it never occurred to me to challenge the beliefs that they passed on to me in my religious upbringing.

I learned to have that respect for authority from my family. It was not something that my mother and father preached, but I was very aware of the esteem that my parents had for our religious "superiors." It either just rubbed off on me or it was in my DNA. It might have been a little bit of both. I observed early on the great deference that my parents showed for priests. My father's otherwise strong, often aggressive manner of communicating with others would melt in the presence of one of my teachers or one of the parish priests. It was almost as if he became a child again. It was also obvious by the way my mother would cower when Father Donavan made a routine home visit to our house. It was as if Jesus himself had popped in to pay us a call. It was not all that surprising that, as a child and well into adulthood, I never got beyond regurgitating what I had memorized in class so I could do well on exams and get my parents' approval. I'm not blaming anyone for my not being more critical in my thinking. No one ever said to me in so many words, "Donald, you are not allowed to challenge any of the doctrines of the church, or you'll go directly to hell." True, my teachers and parents didn't just pass on the content of their beliefs; they passed on a way of thinking, an attitude they had about authority and their beliefs. To paraphrase G. K. Chesterton, "My church right or wrong" was how their views on religion came across to me. It's close to a definition of "prescribed beliefs." Or, in the words of Tennyson, in his poem, *The Charge of the Light Brigade*, "Ours is not to reason why, ours is to do or die."

The more I thought about my early "indoctrination" to religion, the more I realized how I came to the conclusion as child that I was expected to accept the doctrines I was taught without having any doubts.

Shame, Guilt, and Perfectionism

The pain, shame, fear, and guilt that I often felt because I thought I had committed a sin that would bring me eternal damnation and torture was based on an image of God who was a jealous God, who was obsessed with his own power and majesty and quick to take offense. This was the God that I grew up with; this was the God I learned to fear more than love. So much of what I learned was based on guilt and shame. Add a touch of perfectionism, and you had the core of my religious training. At an early age, I was introduced to a God who was an angry God, a punishing God, a God who demanded perfection, a God who was more concerned with my being obedient than with my spiritual growth. As Bishop Gregory Robinson wrote, "Obedience on its own does not bring growth."[2]

I approached the issue of a loving versus an angry God, like other spiritual/religious issues I was struggling with in my personal life, from my role as an academic and as a therapist in my private practice. At the same time that I reconsidered the beliefs I was taught, I began to do research and give lectures and workshops on the effects that the concept of the God of my youth—that God of blind beliefs—had on me and others. I began to see the negative impact these images of God were having on the clients I was working with in my therapy practice. I'm not suggesting that this was a simple black-and-white situation, but it became even more apparent to me that guilt, shame, and perfectionism were part of the underlying dynamics. I found the same symptoms in several groups of helping professionals who were referred by their respective professional organizations to therapy groups I was leading for professionals addicted to drugs or alcohol.

Years later I realized that I needed to differentiate between guilt that comes from our conscience and, in Freudian terms, the guilt that comes from the superego. The guilt that comes from our superego says, "I feel guilty, therefore I am guilty" while the guilt that comes from our conscience says, "I am guilty, therefore I feel guilty." I remember one client who felt guilty if he saw some broken glass in the street and did not stop to pick it up. His rationale for feeling guilty was, a car might run over the glass, have a tire blowout, someone could be killed, and it would be his fault because he hadn't picked up the glass. He felt guilty; therefore, in his eyes, he was guilty.

One of the workshops I developed and offered at least a dozen times was entitled, *Be Ye Perfect: Mission Impossible.* By that time I had realized that the need to be perfect was something we could aim for, but we didn't need to feel guilty because we were not able to achieve it. To give an example of how perfectionism was ingrained in me, I remember that, at a very early age, my mother brought me to Sam, the barber, for a haircut. I must have been no more than five, because I was too small to sit in the barber's chair without a booster seat. As Sam was cutting my hair, I recall thinking, *I need to sit perfectly still and do whatever Sam tells me to do. Don't move an inch one way or the other. I bet he'll be so impressed that he'll tell his family about the perfect little five-year-old whose hair he cut today.* Can you imagine that! I'm sure I must have been prepared for being the perfect customer. Those behaviors and expectations became part of who I was— the family hero. Remember from chapter 3 that my father was an adult child of an alcoholic (AcoA)? There is an adage that captures the intergenerational transmission process that Ernie Larson describes:

> What you live you learn.
> What you learn you practice.
> What you practice you become.
> What you become has consequences.[3]

The author had that right, and I certainly learned my lesson well!

My father never took on the excessive drinking behaviors that he had learned from his father, but he did learn and practice some of the other characteristics that are associated with alcoholism—what they call in AA being a "dry drunk":

- the need to control
- the need for perfectionism
- an overdeveloped sense of responsibility
- the fear of expressing feelings (don't feel; don't talk about feelings; don't trust)
- inappropriate guilt feelings
- tendency to view issues in terms of black-and-white
- self criticism and criticism of others[4]

These and other characteristics listed in the reference above should not be taken as an indictment but as a listing. Perhaps I chose these particular characteristics from the long list because it was apparent to me that these are the ones that were passed on to me. I feel grateful that, over the years, I had the good fortune to be able to work on these issues, as I tried to show in chapter 3 by describing how I began the healing process with my father by finding out more about his relationship with his father. The good news is that, since these are learned behaviors, we can learn new and more functional behaviors. We are not doomed to pass them on to the next generation.

Chapter 5
The Seminary Years

As the time to depart for the seminary came closer, I became more apprehensive about leaving home, my family and friends, the CYO, and everything that was familiar to me. I had a lot of second thoughts about the seminary, but I didn't mention them to anyone; after all, Father Hinds and Monsignor Rooney had endorsed my calling. I knew my parents were proud of my going to the seminary, but they never pushed me one way or the other. They didn't question my motives or whether I was sure I could live a celibate life and give up having a family or bring up anything about their being grandparents. They tried to maintain a very neutral position. Although they never verbalized their thoughts or feelings about my choice, I had the impression that their position was that they would support whatever I wanted to do.

Outside of going to summer camp, this would be the first time I had ever left home for any extended period of time. I felt homesick before I even left home. I could identify with those campers who got so homesick that their parents had to bring them back home after a couple of days at camp. I realized I would be back for the Thanksgiving and Christmas vacations, but three months seemed like a long time.

As I prepared for my departure , I had to buy a black suit and tie, a black overcoat, a black fedora hat, and a black cassock. The cassock is that ankle-length garment that buttons from the neck to the ankles. Looking back, all the black attire sounds a little morbid, but I never questioned—why black? It was just another uniform to set us aside from those who weren't chosen. I did wonder why I was chosen from all the members of the graduating class of CBA, 1947. I felt humbled by that mystery, especially since I could think of dozens of my classmates who would have been more "worthy" than I.

We received a list from the seminary of items that we needed to bring. I remember my mother being confused when she read the list. She rushed downstairs to tell Aunt Liz that I needed to bring my own bed and that it had to be comfortable. Actually, the list suggested bringing a bed comforter, not a comfortable bed. We never had a comforter for any of our beds on Judson Street, so she immediately assumed they wanted me to bring a comfortable bed. As a matter of fact, as I thought back to holiday gatherings, when we'd pile our coats on the hosts' bed, I couldn't think of any of our relatives or friends who had comforters on their beds. They were doing well if they had a chenille bedspread.

When my father came home from work and read the list, he straightened us out. We all had a good laugh, knowing that we wouldn't have to cart my bed to Connecticut. He remarked that a bed comforter probably marked one of the differences between the "lace curtain Irish" and the "shanty Irish."

The day of my exodus finally arrived. I had said my good-byes to kith and kin and was off for the new adventure. We followed the unwritten family rule, "No mush at the airport," even though we were not flying but going in our "new" car. A year before, my father had purchased a secondhand 1938 Hudson Terraplane. This was a big step up from our 1929 Chevrolet. We were moving on up to the "lace curtain Irish" class.

We packed up the Terraplane with all my earthly belongings, including my newly acquired bed comforter, and off we went.

There was no Massachusetts Turnpike then, so we took the scenic Route 7 through all those inviting New England towns like Lenox, Lee, Great Barrington, Sheffield, and on to Bloomfield, Connecticut. Even though it took longer to get there, it was a much more relaxed way to travel than on a six-lane superhighway. As usual, when we took a long trip by car, my father and I sang most of the way. It was a legitimate way not to talk about our feelings, but, at the same time, it was a family activity that we enjoyed. We had a repertoire of old favorites that we could always rely on. My mother sat in the backseat and would request some of her favorites, like "Tell Me Why," "Daisy," "Doodle Do," and other songs from the "good old days." I remember my father asking, "When we're gone, who's going to keep the old songs alive?" I didn't have an answer for him, so we just kept *Doodle Doing* on to the seminary.

Bloomfield is about three miles from Hartford. My new address would be 467 Bloomfield Avenue. As we turned onto Bloomfield Avenue, I could feel the butterflies in my stomach. We passed through an upscale neighborhood with elegant houses on both sides of the road. I learned later that Katherine Hepburn's mother lived in one of them. How about that! I'd come a long way from 8 Judson Street.

As we rounded a curve in the road, a gothic tower appeared in the distance that we thought must be St. Thomas Seminary. The butterflies intensified their dance in my stomach. As we approached the tower, sure enough, the sign reading St. Thomas Seminary proclaimed my address for the next two years. There was no turning back now.

The main seminary building was a stately structure on a slight knoll above eighty acres of woodland. It was indeed impressive, but at this point it was also rather intimidating. The long driveway to reach the main building was reminiscent of movies where the estate of a super-wealthy nobleperson was at the end of a long, winding road. When we reached the main building, there was a line of cars with young men in black suits unpacking their cars.

Judging from their interactions with one another, it seemed like quite a few of them were returning from the previous year and didn't seem too welcoming to newcomers. Perhaps my assessment of my new surroundings was just a matter of my own insecurity, but encountering what seemed to be an established clique didn't help my comfort level.

After checking in at the office to obtain my room number, my father and I managed to get my footlocker up to the second floor. To say the least, my room was rather spartan. There was a single bed for my bed comforter, a bureau, a closet, and one desk and straight-back chair. A washroom with showers and a row of sinks for washing and shaving were at the end of the floor. There was another room across from the washroom that housed the toilets, or as they were called in the seminary, the "jakes." Of all the synonyms for toilet—the john, lavatory, rest room, water closet, WC, the men's or ladies' room, powder room, comfort station, etc.—try as I might, I couldn't find any reference for jakes. You didn't have to be at St. Thomas long to figure out what the jakes were. Without an explanation, just one person saying, "I have to go to the jakes!" or "Where are the jakes?" and you could immediately translate the local lingo into your native tongue.

My parents helped me unpack, and my mother made my not-so-comfortable bed with my bed comforter. By the time we explored the facilities and grounds and were all impressed with my new home, it was time for my parents to head back to 8 Judson Street. There were reassurances that they would visit on the next monthly visitor's day (sounds like a prison), hugs for my mother, and a hearty handshake with my father, but no tears. We all kept that unspoken rule of keeping a stiff upper lip.

I watched the Hudson Terraplane and my parents fade into the distance until I found myself standing alone, not knowing a soul. Now what? The schedule provided showed that I had two hours before dinner, then chapel and lights out at nine o'clock. I decided to seek refuge back in my cell—I mean, room.

New Friends

On my way to my room, I exchanged passing greetings with some other seminarians and their families who were busily moving their belongings into their new lodgings. They seemed friendly enough but understandably focused on getting settled in their rooms. I hesitated to offer my assistance until I saw a heavy fellow with elderly parents struggling with boxes, luggage, and the rest of his personal effects in bags. They stopped me to ask for directions. The son greeted me with an engaging smile and said, "Hi, I'm Everett O'Keefe from Cherry Valley, Massachusetts, and this is my mother, Blanche, and my father, Richard." They put their baggage down and gave me a warm, New England welcome.

Using my new name, I replied, "I'm Fred Fausel from Albany, New York." By the way, I had decided to part my name in the middle like my father, J. Otto Fausel. For the next two years I became D. Frederick Fausel. I'm not sure why. But why not? I was starting a new life, so why not a new name? Besides, I liked "Fred." It was my grandfather's name, and I thought that Fred Fausel had a ring to it that fit me better than Donald. It soon evolved into Freddie or Uncle Fred. Everyone pronounced my last name Fosell with the accent on the last syllable. At home I was Don or Donald, but in Connecticut I was Freddie Fosell. Perhaps I was a little schizophrenic, or I just wanted to use a name that I liked better than Donald. But as Sigmund Freud supposedly said, "Sometimes a cigar is just a cigar."

Back to the O'Keefes! After Everett's parents left, he and I were no longer alone in a foreign environment. Little did I know that this chance meeting on our first day at St. Thomas would become a lifelong friendship for me and Everett (a.k.a. Heavy Evie). Our families also became fast friends over the years. We visited with the O'Keefes in Cherry Valley and they visited with us, in Albany. They were like our extended family.

Bells, Bells, Bells

Before we knew it, the bell for dinner sounded, and we made our way to the refectory. Interesting name for the dining room! I never gave much thought as to why they called it the refectory but was enlightened when I Googled it and found it was from the late Latin word *refectorium*, which dates back to the fifteenth century and was defined as a dining hall. After all these years, I finally knew why they called it the refectory instead of the "mess hall" or just plain "dining room."

Everett and I were assigned seats at separate tables. So, I was alone again. But not for long! There were nine seminarians at each table. Every table was presided over by a second-year college man, who sat at the head of the table and was the first one served. Our table was a mixture of "newbies" and veterans. The veterans at the table were helpful in sharing their experiences and what we could expect for the next few days. They gave us tips on faculty members (which ones were tough and who were the easy marks); pointed out the big men on campus; and in general gave us the lay of the land. Despite my misgivings, I was already beginning to feel more comfortable in my new surroundings.

After dinner we had fifteen minutes before chapel. A couple of the veterans introduced us to the "butt grounds"—the only place on campus where it was okay to smoke. Even though I didn't smoke, it was a meeting place for smokers and nonsmokers in the days when we didn't know about "secondhand smoke." A bell summoned us to chapel, and I was told by a new classmate named Fitz that I was in for a treat. Even though I couldn't imagine what sort of treat we would have in the chapel, Fitz wasn't wrong.

We were ushered to our seats in the chapel by the sacristans, who had a list of the student body; the students who were in the first four years of high school occupied the pews in the front of the chapel, and the students in the first two years of college—the class of 1951 (that was us) and the class of 1950—filled the rest of the chapel in order of seniority.

After some preliminary logistical information from the dean of discipline (an ominous title that smacks of the Inquisition, though this individual was a rather benign man), Father James Conefrey introduced the main attraction, the rector, Right Reverend Monsignor Raymond G. La Fontaine. He made his entrance in his full monsignor regalia. The purpose of his talk was to welcome us to the seminary. He proceeded to entertain us for a half an hour. I thought this was one of the funniest men I'd ever listened to. He didn't need a laugh track; he had us virtually rolling in the aisles with one "one-liner" after another. I was becoming more and more convinced that I was going to like it here.

After Benediction and night prayers and some time for individual devotions, the bell rang again, and it was time to go to our rooms. The "Grand Silence" had begun. Another term borrowed from the monastic tradition. It basically meant that after night prayers in the chapel until grace was said before breakfast, there was no talking at all. It seemed strange to see over four hundred energetic, active, young men making their way from the chapel to their rooms or in the corridors between classes in silence. Strange indeed, but after a while I welcomed the monastic like silence, which gave me the opportunity to connect with a peaceful source of all energy.

Before I knew it, I was awakened the next morning by the bell and someone knocking on my door, intrusively chanting "*Benedicamus Domino*" (Let us praise the Lord). Even though I was startled by this abrupt awakening, I was prepared for my response, *Deo Gratias*! (Thanks to God!). With that prayer on my lips, I made my way to the washroom with my shaving kit, washcloth, soap, and towel. There were at least two dozen sinks to choose from. Everyone was seriously shaving, brushing their teeth, or washing their faces. All in silence, of course! No horsing around or trying to agitate your neighbor. It was not like the locker room at CBA.

At 6:00 AM a second bell rang, and it was down to the chapel for morning prayers, meditation, and Mass. By 7:30 AM another bell, and we were on our way to breakfast. Back to clean our rooms at 8:00 AM, and another bell rang at 8:30 AM, summoning us to our first class of the day, Latin with Father John L. Sullivan. He had the driest sense of humor of any of the faculty and an ability to use his wit to interest us in the study of Latin. The bell again announced the end of his class and that we had ten minutes to get to the next class, French with Father Daley. His nickname was Père Daley because he taught French, and *père* is the French word for father. When they hired another Father Daley to teach chemistry, the students nicknamed him Apples Daley. Why Apples Daley? Well, since we had a Père (Pear) Daley, an Apple Daley seemed to fit. Père and Apple Daily were a peach of a pair. (Seminary humor.) Apple Daley's class followed Père Daley's class and, after spending three hours in class in the morning, the bell called us to lunch.

At 1:30 PM we had physics with Monsignor La Fontain. His humor made physics interesting to me, even though it could be cutting. His class was taught in a stadium-type lab with a place for demonstrations where a desk would usually be. One time he caught me peering over the top of my new glasses, and he called this to the class's attention by saying, "Okay Grandpa, what's the answer?" I didn't even know the question. When it was apparent that I hadn't been paying attention, he got a laugh from the class by saying, "Go back to sleep, Grandpa." For a few weeks, everyone called me Grandpa.

The last class of the day was English literature with Father Thomas Stack, affectionately known as "Tombo." He was responsible for my lifelong love of reading, especially the classics. One of the first novelists he introduced us to was a Norwegian woman, Sigrid Undset, who won the Nobel Prize for Literature in 1928. At forty-six, she was one of the youngest authors and only the third woman to receive that honor. And to Undset goes the distinction of being the only Catholic novelist of either gender in the last century to receive that award. I became so immersed in her book *Kristin Lavransdatter* and her re-creations of medieval life, that when one of the characters in the novel died, I unconsciously found myself praying for him at Mass the next morning.

As much as I enjoyed Tombo's class, the ever-present bell would ring, and it was time for recreation, which I loved even more. Depending on the season, there were intramural teams in touch football, basketball, or baseball. Also, St. Thomas was represented in a community college league in basketball and baseball, with varsity and junior varsity teams. More about that later.

After recreation and a shower, it was time for dinner. After dinner there was just enough time to get to the butt grounds for a short break, followed by chapel, night prayers, and again the bell for the Grand Silence, and the final bell for lights out. Perhaps you've noticed that our lives were ruled by bells. I didn't think about it at the time, but as I was writing this, I thought that Edgar Allen Poe might have written his poem "The Bells" a hundred years earlier in 1849 with us in mind.

"The Bells" and Poe's last poem, "Annabel Lee," are two of my favorite Poe poems. Here's a brief selection from "The Bells" that puts the seminary bells in a different perspective. I'm sure many of you will remember these ageless words.

> To the tintinnabulation that so musically wells
> From the bells, bells, bells, bells,
> Bells, bells, bells-
> From the jingling and the tinkling of the bells.
> To the tintinnabulation that so musically wells.

Tintinnabulation is one of my favorite words. It's been over sixty years since one of my instructors told our class that tintinnabulation was a good example of the figure of speech onomatopoeia. I've never even saw either of those words in print since then. Nor have I had a chance to use either tintinnabulation or onomatopoeia, so I just wanted to throw them in while I had the chance.

This was a normal day at St. Thomas. What I intend to do now, is to point out some highlights of my St. Thomas years. First, here is some general information about minor seminaries in the forties and fifties.

The Minor Seminary

St. Thomas was typical of the many minor seminaries throughout the United States in pre-Vatican II. Minor seminaries offered four years of high school and two years of college. The high school included both boarding students and "day hops." Albany didn't have a minor seminary of its own at that time, so they sent all their seminarians either to St. Andrews in Rochester or to St. Thomas. I found out a few days after classes started that there were three other new students from the Albany Diocese—Mark Touchette from White Plains, John Dee from Troy, and Jim Kelly from Green Island. They called us the "Albanians." Although there were representatives from Massachusetts, New Hampshire, South Carolina, Vermont, and Brooklyn, the majority of the seminarians were from every nook and cranny of the Nutmeg State. Even though we were outnumbered by five to one, it didn't take long for us to blend into what our class chose as its motto, *Fratres in Unum*. This is a phrase from Psalm 132: "*Ecce quam bonum et quam iucundum habitare fratres in unum.*" Translated, "How good and how enjoyable it is when brothers live in unity." I felt that I was part of an extended family.

The Blue and White of Old St. Thomas

I took to the seminary as the proverbial duck to water. The camaraderie with a bunch of guys who were like-minded; the liturgy and the Gregorian chant; the sports and the feeling that I had a purpose for my life made a perfect fit for me. I loved it!

As captain of the varsity basketball team, I had the opportunity to set the score straight (at least in my own mind) with Chuck

Yund, the CBA basketball coach who cut me from the team. The basketball league that we played in was equivalent to a college junior varsity league. So, I would have been a college sophomore playing against teams, like U Conn, Fairfield University, and the University of Bridgeport.

In addition to sports I also had major roles in our first- and second-year class productions. It's hard to believe now, but our first year's production was a minstrel show. Blackface and all! I was one of the four "end men," along with Ace Shea, Mark Tuchette, and Evie O'Keefe. I was Mr. Snowball and sang "If You Knew Susie," an Eddie Cantor song. I want to apologize for my insensitivity to racial issues in the forties. It's sad to remember that it was not unusual at that time for even Catholic parishes to have minstrel shows to raise money. Blackface was not considered racially offensive in the 1940s. White men smearing their faces black and imitating African-Americans had been common on American stages since the 1830s and was just one form of the coarse humor that most racial and ethnic groups were subjected to at that time. We've come a long way!

The second year I did a Sid Caesar routine, where I contrasted an English and French soldier going into battle. My second routine was a monologue of an Italian immigrant, Tony Pocaglupi, attending his first baseball game. More politically incorrect caricatures! The problem was, I was good at it. The local parish priest, who was in attendance, asked whether I would do those two routines in his annual parish show. And I did! They loved me in Bloomfield.

Looking back, my stage personae helped me conquer a minor stage fright that I had. Assuming another character seemed to give me confidence to be more comfortable in my own shoes. I remember one incident in speech class that I think contributed to my stage fright. Father John Byrnes was the instructor. I was the first one whom he called on to give a five-minute prepared speech before the class. This was before my "thespian" days. I could feel myself choking up as I approached the podium. After I finished my presentation, I waited for his feedback. I thought I had managed to mask my anxiety fairly well and felt confident. I was surprised when he chose to embarrass me in front of the whole class.

His first words, spoken in a supercilious tone that he had mastered over the years, were: "Well, Mr. Fausel, you have a voice so high that only a dog can hear it." The whole class burst out in laughter that made me want to evaporate there and then.

He continued by rhetorically asking, "What are we going to do with you? Let me see! What I want you to do is a simple exercise. When you're on the campus, yell as loud as you can 'Ship Ahoy!' ten times in a row and ask your classmates to let you know when your voice is at a lower pitch." That was his prescription. He didn't point out any positives in my presentation. As others had their turn during the rest of the semester, I soon realized that his style made every presenter feel like the laughingstock and that he got laughs at others' expense.

Rather than go into more details about my "happy days" in Bloomfield, let me just quote from our yearbook, *Stella Matutina*. Each of the graduates had a picture and mini- biography of his time at St. Thomas. Here is mine as it appeared in the yearbook.

Donald F. Fausel

8 Judson Street   *Albany, New York*

As we look back upon our years of St. Thomas's history, "Freddie" Fausel shines as a fine example of sportsmanship and leadership. His excellence in sports has earned for him various positions on St. Thomas teams, ranging from pitcher for the intramural softball team to captain of the Varsity Basketball Team. Many will remember Fred as a loyal promoter for the Meershaum Bowl Pipe Society, an offshoot of the "PA'ers." This Sid Caesar comedian was another of the numerous contributors to our successful Junior and Senior shows. "Uncle Fred's" witty and masterful performance as master of ceremonies at our senior banquet will long be remembered by us, as well as his enthusiasm as the chairman of the Mission Society. Such an abundance of activities and abilities assure our Fred of victory in all life's endeavors.

It sounds a little bit like a eulogy. If you read all of the sixty-four bios of the graduates of 1951, you'd think that we had assembled a class of the greatest guys on the planet. As I look back, I think one of my best friends, Bob Mulvee, who later became a bishop, wrote mine.

Graduation day came, and I proudly walked down the aisle to the strains of *Pomp and Circumstance* to receive my Associate of Arts degree. The class of 1951 posed for a group picture and a last rendition of our alma mater:

> The blue and white of old St. Thomas
> The blue and white of STS
> Loyalty to you we promise
> Love for you lives in our every breath
> And whatever fate befalls you,
> We'll be ever at your side.
> Years from now we proudly boast boys,
> The fame of STS will never die.

Corny as the song's sentiment seems today, it brought a tear to my eye. I was really going to miss the friends I had made at St. Thomas, and I am happy to say I still have maintained relationships with a number of my classmates. Just the other day, my wife and I had dinner with my good friend Pat Healy and his wife, Sandy. Pat was from Bridgeport, Connecticut, from a large, Irish Catholic family. Even after fifty-eight years since our graduation and both of us leaving the active ministry, we still enjoy talking about the good old days.

Summertime

From the first year of St. Thomas until our class was ordained, we spent six weeks of our eight-week summer vacation at the villa on Brandt Lake in Horicon, New York. As the town's brochure describes it, "Brandt Lake is five miles of crystal clear liquid joy.

Snugly surrounded by glacial mountains in the Adirondacks ... it is an unspoiled jewel of the Adirondacks." What it doesn't mention is that the Diocese of Albany had two summer camps there—Camp Gibbons for the minor seminarians and Camp St. Isaac Jogues for the major seminarians. Bishop Gibbons, who studied at the American College in Rome for his four years of theology, adapted the Roman system where the seminarians would spend summers at a villa. As minor seminarians, we occupied the buildings that were formerly a camp for boys. Once we completed our two years in the minor seminary, we moved up the hill to Camp Isaac Jogues. The lodgings were less "luxurious"—more like barracks than cabins—but I don't remember anyone complaining.

The bishop had two purposes in sending us to camp for the summer: to guard us from the evils of the outside world and for the major seminarians to teach catechism to the children from the local communities. Every day, buses would bring children for a combination of religious training and fun and games. At noon the buses returned to take their precious cargo back to their homes. My classmates at St. Thomas used to tease us Albanians for having to be protected in "the hot houses of the villa" and suggested that the bishop needed to keep us under his protective care so we would avoid occasions of sin.

The minor seminarians didn't get to teach catechism but spent three hours each morning in a Latin class with a Jesuit from Fordham, Father McGurty, conjugating verbs, declining nouns, and translating Cicero, Caesar, and Horace. The afternoons we had to ourselves, swimming, playing volleyball and softball, and preparing for the annual play for the benefit of the Horicon Volunteer Fire Department. My job, along with my good friend Roger Buckley, was to write, direct, and usually star in an original musical show that the seminarians would perform for the public. Roger and I usually did a song and dance routine. The one I remember most clearly was based on the legendary vaudevillian team of Gallagher and Shean from the 1920s. They loved us in Horicon.

The Major Seminary

After graduating from St. Thomas, we anxiously awaited our letter of assignment to the major seminary where we would study for the next six years; that would include two more years of college and four years of theology. There were a number of seminaries where the Diocese of Albany sent its seminarians to study. One of us would go to study at the American College in Rome, another to Catholic University in Washington DC, another to St. Mary's Seminary and University in Baltimore, and the rest to St. Bernard's in Rochester, St. Bonaventure's in Olean, New York, Dunwoody in the Diocese of New York, and Our Lady of Angels at Niagara University. We all received our assignment letters while at the villa. It was a memorable "mail call." We made a little ceremony of opening the official letter from the diocese and announcing our appointment, which was greeted by cheers and embraces from those who were already studying there. If you had aspirations of becoming a bishop, your hope was for the American College in Rome. By the time it was my turn to open the letter that would have a major effect on my future; Clem Handron had already been awarded the Roman prize. I wasn't really hoping for Rome, so I wasn't disappointed. My preference was really for one of the New York seminaries. I carefully opened the envelope only to find out that I would be going to Baltimore. Ray Butts, who was in his last year at St. Mary's, took me under his wing to help prepare me for living just north of the Mason-Dixon Line.

The more I found out about St. Mary's, the more I liked it. It was founded in 1791 and was the first Catholic seminary in the United States. In 1805 it was chartered as a civil university in Maryland, and in 1822 Pope Pius VII established the seminary as the country's first pontifical university with the right to grant degrees in the name of the Holy See. I could say I was moving uptown because the original building that housed the first two years of philosophy was on Paca Street in the heart of the Baltimore ghetto. After Paca Street, four years of theology at Roland Park; this really was uptown.

The Paca Street seminary was genuinely awesome. Its halls were hallowed with decades of seminarians' prayers and devotions. It was celebrating its 160th anniversary when I entered in 1951. The prayer hall where we said our morning and evening prayers and met for meditation and spiritual presentations had been the room where the three Plenary Councils of Baltimore were held. The walls were covered with bigger-than-life pictures of bishops and archbishops of the nineteenth century—icons like Archbishop Spalding and the future cardinal and native Baltimorean James Gibbons. I remember praying that their spirits could seep into me by some type of osmosis. I was overwhelmed with the feeling that I would be praying in the same chapel where they prayed and said Mass. It brought out some unrealistic, romantic, adolescent feelings in me that I had never experienced before. By the way, the third Plenary Council of Baltimore was presided over by then Archbishop Gibbons. The Council was responsible for the Baltimore Catechism, which I mentioned before as having had a strong influence on my life.

Our rooms were indeed austere. I felt as though I had been taken back in time to the eighteenth century when I saw the basin with a large pitcher that would be my one place to wash, shave, brush my teeth, and freshen up. If I wanted hot water, I had to bring my pitcher to the end of the hall, to the bathroom with a sink that accommodated about thirty seminarians. I can't remember there being any showers. What most of us would do was to fill up our pitchers the night before so we could be ready for a cold "birdbath" in the morning. Some would get hot water from the bathroom in the morning and bring it back to their rooms for a not-so-smooth shave. I was lucky: I had an electric razor.

Despite the austerity, there was a certain asceticism just being in this holy place. I remember walking through the halls after night prayers and thinking, *Lord, let me become a holy priest, like so many hundreds of seminarians who walked these halls before.* I felt a great serenity that I had never experienced before. Even as I'm writing this, I took time out to meditate and recapture those feelings of serenity I had then and to be thankful for the tranquility I have now.

A number of my friends from St. Thomas had been assigned there, so it wasn't like starting all over again. Basically there were two major groups: the St. Thomasites and the St. Charlesites. St. Charles was a minor seminary in Maryland run by the Sulpician fathers, the same order that ran St. Mary's. In the beginning we pretty much stuck together with our old friends from the minor seminary, but it didn't take long for the cliques to break up. Sports were the major leveler. Teams were made up of St. Thomasites and St. Charlesites. I was introduced to handball by one of my new friends from St. Charles.

The Philosophers

We continued with our liberal arts education and our major in philosophy. In first-year philosophy we took an introduction to philosophy course taught by Father Jimmy Minnahan, SS, a cherubic little Irishman, who was very entertaining but only expected us to regurgitate what our text had to say. Father Carlton Sage taught us the history of philosophy. His name suggests a scholarly person, which he was, but he often got so deep in his own thought that it didn't come through to most of us; then there was epistemology, which someone called the "Grape Nuts" of philosophy; it basically asks the question, Can the mind know? I'm not sure who taught it, but I didn't appreciate the importance of the content at the time, though somehow I passed the course. We had a class in sociology, where the instructor read from the textbook in class. We all agreed that we could have skipped the class and just read the book. The biology class was taught by Father Acock, an eccentric older gent, as we called the Sulpician fathers (the Gentlemen of San Sulpice). His entire exam would be one question. For example, he would announce that the question for the final exam was, "The amoeba?" He'd then pass out blue books and expect us to fill one or two books. I did enjoy the lab, where we had to dissect mice and frogs and watch fruit flies multiply in a jar.

Looking back, I realize that our classes looked good on paper but, with few exceptions, relied on our simply memorizing material that the instructor fed us. I can still remember the definition of philosophy that I had to parrot back in Latin on an exam. *Philosophia est scientia omnia rerum per ultimus causa.* (Philosophy is the science of all things through their ultimate causes.) But I had no appreciation of the real meaning of the definition.

The second-year courses were equally disappointing. I remember writing home to my parents that I was taking courses in cosmology, psychology, ethics, and the philosophy of education to impress them how difficult the second year was; but we still weren't being taught the basics of critical thinking. I wasn't aware of that at the time and just went along with the expectations of the learned faculty. As at St. Thomas, the sports, the camaraderie with so many great guys, and being in such a spiritual atmosphere helped me through the two years at 600 North Paca Street.

St. Mary's at Roland Park

When I entered St. Mary's Seminary at Roland Park in 1953, it was strictly for the four years of theology leading up to ordination. It has since added an *Ecumenical Institute of Theology* and a *Center for Continuing Formation for Priests.* The "new" St. Mary's was built in 1929 (the same year that I was born) on a forty-acre campus surrounded by woodlands to the south and west. A long, winding drive lined with large oaks and elms leads to the main entrance. The building itself is made of limestone with terrazzo floors and oak paneling in a major interior room.

Arriving at 5400 Roland Park for the first time was like a homecoming. In addition to all my friends from Paca Street, there were seminarians from all over the country, who easily blended into our growing circle of *Fratres in Unum.* I remember that first day before we officially started the seminary routine.

After I unpacked, I played a doubles tennis game with two of the Paca Street gang and Jim Montgomery, from the Diocese of Washington DC. Jim had been captain of Mount St. Mary's basketball team before deciding to become a priest. He was to be a fierce competitor in all sports at St. Mary's. I found out some years ago that he had become a monsignor, and his claim to fame was baptizing one of Lyndon Johnson's daughters.

Once again, we first-year theologians were "newbies" entering the world of theology. For the next four years, we had courses in moral and dogmatic theology, Scripture, and ethics, along with one or two elective courses. There were several noted scholars who taught us, but again, looking back at the methods of teaching, they were not designed for us to critically evaluate what we were being taught. Every class I had at St. Mary's was a lecture. There was virtually no interaction between the instructor and the students or between the students in the classroom. Each classroom was set up with a mini-stage and a lectern. The professor would enter the class, say a prayer to the Holy Spirit, ascend to the lectern, put his notes on the lectern, and proceed to lecture us for the next hour and a half.

I have a pretty good memory, but I don't remember our asking any questions or the professor encouraging questions. Perhaps others learned that way—by passively listening and taking copious notes—but unfortunately it was not the best way for me to integrate the important information that was being presented. Oh, I passed the examinations and even earned two degrees, an STB (Bachelor in Sacred Theology) and an STL (Licentiate in Sacred Theology) cum laude. The STL meant I was licensed to teach theology.

In addition to taking extra classes for the STL, I had to write a dissertation. My topic was, "The Moral Obligation for a Catholic Education." To support my thesis, I used the encyclicals of the popes and canon law. Using those sources, I predictably made a strong case for making Catholic education a moral obligation for the laity. I never took other research resources or family problems into consideration—things like the cost for a family to educate their children or other realities that families face. I just followed the party line. I remember meeting with my faculty mentor only twice, once when he approved the topic and when I turned in my magnum opus of over 120 pages for him to evaluate. I never received any feedback, but I must have passed because several years ago I checked with the St. Mary's library and, sure enough, my dissertation is still on file. I'd love to get a copy. I suspect I would be shocked and embarrassed by my uncritical thinking in 1957.

It was only in my post-seminary education at Fordham and Columbia Universities that I learned to think critically and to challenge what was being taught. Remember, my time at St. Mary's was pre-Vatican II, and I know seminary training has changed quite a bit. It was almost fifty years since I had been back to Baltimore, so I decided to find out for myself. In 2006 I went back to Baltimore to present a paper on globalization at a conference. My hotel was only blocks away from Paca Street. After the conference was over, I walked up to Paca Street, hoping to spend some time roaming through the halls of the seminary and revisiting fond memories of my two years there. Much to my surprise and dismay, when I reached Mother Seton's house, which had been next to the seminary, lo and behold, there was no seminary. No one had told me they had torn it down in 1969. The only thing that remained was the chapel, which had been designated a National Historic Landmark in 1971. I went into the chapel, where a retreat was being held. So, after saying a prayer, I silently slipped away.

I decided to visit Roland Park. After a half-hour taxi ride, I was happy to see that my alma mater was still standing, as tall and elegant as I remembered it. I went to the front door, and it was locked. I rang the bell a number of times, and no one answered. I walked all around the building, and it was like a ghost town. After trying every door, I finally saw someone getting out of his car and heading toward the delivery door. I followed him in, explaining that I was an alumnus, and he didn't question me. It was so quiet it was spooky. I arrived at the main floor where the classrooms and chapel were, and still nobody was around. The classrooms seemed less formal the way the chairs were arranged and without the platform and lectern. Perhaps the classes were more interactive.

I made my way to the chapel, where I had spent so many hours during my four-year stay. There was a plaque on one of the pews, which stated that Pope John Paul II had prayed there. Although I didn't agree with many of decisions he made during his twenty-five year reign, I thought he was a holy man. I knelt down in the spot where he had prayed and basked in my feelings of serenity. I finished my prayer and made my way up to the third floor where my old room was. As I was walking toward the room, a man in his late sixties wearing shorts and a T-shirt confronted me by asking, "Can I help you?" in a rather harsh tone. I later found out that he was the rector of the seminary.

I replied, "I'm an alumnus and was just looking for my old room." He immediately changed to a much gentler tone. We had a friendly talk as I asked about former faculty and the Baltimore alumni. I learned that he had started at the seminary a few years after I left and had been the rector for the last dozen years. I thought to myself, *We would never have seen the rector in shorts and a T-shirt when I was a seminarian*. I asked him where everyone was and he told me he had given everyone the weekend off, and the priests and seminarians would be returning soon. Wow! Things had really changed. He invited me to have lunch in the refectory and apologized for not being able to join me. We said our good-byes, and I found my way to the refectory or, as it was now labeled, the dining room. It was the same room but a completely different environment than the one I knew in the 1950s. It was set up for a buffet meals that had no particular time schedule. Seminarians could just walk in any time they wanted, grab something to eat, and either eat there or bring it back to their rooms. What's that quote from Cicero I mentioned earlier, "Oh, the changed times, oh, the changed customs!"

There were a few seminarians eating and chatting. I grabbed a sandwich and some chips and asked them whether I could join them. I explained why I was there and my history with St. Mary's and my time in the ministry. They had so many questions about me that I hardly had time to find out much about them. Their questions focused on my leaving the active ministry and why, and how I had been accepted after leaving. I did have a chance to ask them about life in the seminary today and, to say the least; it was drastically different than when I was there. The rigidity of the schedule had changed, for one thing, and it seemed as though they were being treated more like adults with more choices to make on their own. Best of all, they had opportunities in class to discuss and interact with the professor, rather than being lectured at. We exchanged e-mail addresses, and I did hear from two of the students for a while, but we gradually drifted apart.

Our Rector

For my four years at Roland Park, our rector was the Very Reverend James Laubacker, SS, who was indeed a very spiritual and compassionate man. Although his outward demeanor was stern, he was a surprisingly nice guy. I had the opportunity to get to know him when I was appointed an infirmarian in my third year of theology. There were three other infirmarians, and we had the responsibility of caring for anyone who had some illness or injury. There was a nurse who supervised us, but we were the ones who dispensed pills, gave enemas, bandaged wounds, took temperatures, and were available in the infirmary to listen to any health problems. There were perks. We sat at a special table in the refectory and got the leftover bacon and eggs from the professors' table, while everyone else was eating Purina. Also, we didn't have to take turns serving meals.

When I was a fourth-year theologian, I was appointed head infirmarian, and one of my responsibilities was to report to the rector every morning about the community's health. In the beginning, I'd approach his chambers with some timidity. I'd knock on the door and hear an invitation to "enter." There he was, every day, sitting behind a huge mahogany desk, in a huge room, and I would be standing there reporting how many seminarians were confined to their rooms, etc. As time went on, these sessions would often extend to talking about how I was doing in class, my family, or what was going on in the world. I felt very privileged to have that sort of relationship with the rector, who I felt was a model of holiness and at the same time very human. When I checked out the school's Web site, I found they had dedicated the prayer hall in his memory by naming it Laubacker Hall. Given all the years he had presided there and spoken to us on spiritual topics, I thought that was very appropriate.

Holy Orders

Before you could be ordained a priest, there were certain milestones you had to pass. There were the five minor orders and the three major orders ending with ordination as a priest. Although it wasn't one of the orders, the first step was tonsure, from the Latin word *tondere,* meaning to shear. This was a ritual in which the bishop would take a small snip of hair from the back of your head as a symbol of your giving yourself to divine service. Several weeks before being tonsured, you awaited a knock on the door from one of the priests to let you know whether you were going to be tonsured. This occurred early in the fall of second theology. I was relieved to hear the good news that I would be tonsured.

The minor orders were porter, lector, exorcist, cantor, and acolyte. The same procedure was followed for each order. They were awarded two at a time. I remember writing my parents that I was now an exorcist and had the power to drive out evil spirits. My father, in his usual style of double messages, wrote back that it was quite an honor, and I should start on myself.

I had to make a major decision before becoming a sub-deacon. When you were ordained a sub-deacon, you had to take the vow of celibacy. I struggled with this decision to the point that I didn't know whether I could handle it. I had a very narrow of view of celibacy. I tended to look at it as just fighting off sexual temptations—impure thoughts or actions. I never looked at it from the vantage point of giving up the right to have a family and all that entails. The impure thoughts and actions were seldom an issue when I was in the safe confines of the seminary, but they would emerge when I was home on vacation. I would confess my sins to a parish priest, Father Stramitis, who didn't speak English well. He would give me a routine penance of "three times Our Fathers, three times Hail Marys," and I would go back to the seminary for another semester of confessing venial sins to my confessor.

Several weeks before the ordination to the sub-deaconate, I went to one of the Sulpician priests who was known for his piety. It was rumored that he had been physically impaired when he performed an exorcism on a woman in Hawaii. I confessed to him that I was struggling with impure thoughts and actions and that I had serious concerns about taking the vow of celibacy. He listened careful to my concerns but didn't ask me to go into details nor did he ask any questions. He calmly told me that it was not unusual to have these doubts before taking a vow of celibacy but that once I was ordained this wouldn't be a problem. I had the impression that I wasn't the first one who had come to him with this dilemma. I felt reassured by his response and went out of confession feeling more confident. I wish that he or my regular confessor had explored the charism of celibacy in more depth. With their advice, I went on to be ordained a sub-deacon. At that time I didn't realize that celibacy was a gift and that not everyone is given that gift. The question of mandatory celibacy versus voluntary celibacy never came up.

In one of my daily visits with Father Laubacker, I told him I had been thinking about becoming a Sulpician and asked his advice. He was very supportive and emphasized my qualities of leadership and my potential to be a scholar. After all, I had earned an STB and was working on my STL. These were all positive signs of my having what it took to teach in a seminary and continue doing research. He told me that I would have to ask my bishop in Albany to release me for this special work and suggested that I continue to pray over it. Years later, I wondered whether my choice of being a Sulpician was an escape to the sheltering walls of the seminary, where I thought I wouldn't have the temptations I would in a parish.

In addition to celibacy, the other obligation that being a sub-deacon entailed was to pray the Liturgy of the Hours, often called the Breviary or the Divine Office or simply the Office every day. The Breviary follows the hours of the day from morning prayers to evening and night prayers that the monks chant. Each day is different, depending on the liturgical time of the year. It includes psalms and canticles and extracts from Scripture. At that time it was in Latin and took about an hour and fifteen minutes to complete. Ideally, it would be best to distribute the "hours," saying morning prayers upon awakening and Vespers in the evening. More often than not, I would end up at the end of the day reading the whole hour and fifteen minutes at one time. After the novelty of reading the Breviary wore off, it became more of an obligation than a time of prayer.

During my last summer at the villa, I approached the bishop of Albany, William A. Scully, to release me to join the Sulpicians. He was most gracious and explained how he believed each diocese had a responsibility to release a priest who wanted to teach future priests.

I spent most of the last year in the seminary working on my dissertation and preparing for an oral exam for the STL degree. The oral exam was in Latin before a panel of three faculty members. This was one of the most stressful half hours I ever experienced. Each professor questioned me on moral and dogmatic theology and Scripture. As I sit here writing this, my use of Latin has diminished in the last fifty-five years to translating signs on buildings or *E pluribus unum* on coins. I have no idea how

I managed to carry on a conversation in Latin, let alone answer scholarly question adequately.

Ecce Quam Bonum

My brother, Jim, drove from Albany in my 1956 Chevrolet to take me home for my ordination. My father and mother had given me the car as an ordination present. That was before they knew I was going to be a Sulpician and wouldn't need a car. There was a ritual that the seminarians had to see off everyone leaving for ordination. The whole student body formed a gauntlet that I had to go through to get to my car. There I was at the top of the gauntlet, with my new straw hat and black suit and Roman collar as they began to sing. This was the moment I had dreamed about for the last eight years. With tears in both eyes, I somehow made my way to the car, shaking hands like a politician. When I finally reached the car, I said to my brother, "Home, James!" and he replied, "Yes, boss!" and we were off to Albany.

Reflections

As late as last week, a new acquaintance who discovered I had spent eight years in the seminary, asked if I would do it again if I had the chance. I've been asked variations of that question a number of times over the years. The question is a little more complicated than it seems. We all know that hindsight is 20/20. So, knowing what I do now, my answer would be an emphatic, "No!" But if I were able to put myself back in the vantage or disadvantage point of the forties and fifties, when priests were on pedestals and the culture that I grew up in valued their wisdom, the answer would most likely still be "Yes!" I have never regretted the time I spent in the seminary or the priesthood. I believe I made a positive contribution to many lives. I don't feel it robbed me of my youth or was solely to blame for every problem I had later in my life as I tried to grow up by making up for "lost time."

Whatever anger I might have felt, I think I learned to channel it through a workshop I did for a number of years. The title of the workshop was "Anger is as Anger Does!" As the title of the workshop suggests, feeling angry is normal and healthy. Learning to express anger appropriately is difficult for most of us. If we don't learn to handle anger, it can turn into depression, guilt, or anxiety, if not dealt with positively.

The anger workshop examined the many faces of anger, violence, depression, and manipulation and offered specific guidelines for learning healthy ways of expressing anger and dealing with other people's anger when it is directed at us. In retrospect, I think I intuitively taught that workshop to learn for myself how to deal with my own anger as much as to help other people with their anger.

I never felt there was a conspiracy to retard my growth. The time that I grew up in was just that—the time I grew up in. Neither I nor anyone else could have controlled that; it was just an accident of time, just as my age is an accident of time. Would I have liked to have grown up in post–Vatican II? Of course! Would I have liked to have been introduced to critical thinking earlier in my life? Of course! Would I have liked to have had more clear choices than I thought I did? Of course! But that was then and now is now. To fantasize otherwise is tantamount to saying, "I wish they had computers when I was a seminarian." Or "I wish I had grown up in San Diego in a home on the Pacific Ocean." There is something to that old saying about "playing the hand we're dealt."

In many ways I was encouraged as I talked to the seminarians at St. Mary's when I visited with them in 2006. They had the opportunity in class and small groups to discuss among themselves and with their professor issues that would influence their lives as priests—not just the negative parts of celibacy but discerning whether they had the gift of celibacy and how they could make it a positive force in their lives as priests. In other ways, I was discouraged. They seemed to be more conservative than I assumed they would be. I guess I wished that they had more of the spirit of Pope John XXIII than Pope John Paul II. My hope is that they eventually move more to the center. Perhaps they will, after going down some dead-end paths as I did.

I am grateful for the path I followed. I might have gone down some dead-ends that turned out to be agonizing, but in the long run they brought me, by circuitous routes, to where I am today.

Chapter 6
The New Priest

After eight years in the seminary, ordination day—June 1, 1957—had finally arrived. My hopes and dreams, along with those of ten other seminarians from the Diocese of Albany and four Franciscans were to be fulfilled. I remember waking up early that morning in the rectory of my home parish feeling as if I were dreaming. "Where am I?" "What am I doing in this strange bedroom?" I slowly came back to reality. This was indeed *the day!* After a quick shower and shave, I knelt down at the prie-dieu in my room to say the morning prayers from the Breviary and to meditate. I had already decided on the topic for meditation. It was a quotation on the role and responsibilities of a priest, written by a Dominican priest, Father Jean-Baptiste Lacordarie , who lived in the nineteenth century:

Thou Art a Priest Forever

To live in the midst of the world with no desire for its pleasures; to be a member of every family, yet belonging to none; to share all sufferings; to penetrate all secrets, to heal all wounds; to go daily from men to God to offer Him their homage and petitions; to return from God to men to bring them His pardon and hope; to have a heart of fire for charity and a heart of bronze for chastity; to bless and to be blest forever. O God, what a life, and it is yours, O Priest of Jesus Christ!

This was a source of meditation that I had used often in the last few years in the seminary. It always instilled in me a sense of gratitude for God having chosen me to be a priest. But as I reflected on the text that morning, the expectations became overwhelming, and I wondered how I could ever meet them. I consoled myself with what I thought my spiritual director might have said: "They are high goals for anyone to achieve, but they are just that—goals—and no one can meet them all the time; we just need to ask for God's help. None of us is perfect. We just try to do the best we can." I wasn't completely satisfied with my imagined spiritual director's knee-jerk reaction. I had a quote from St. Paul on a holy card in my Breviary that seemed to recognize the humanness that we all share. It read:

A priest is a man chosen from among his fellow men and made a representative of men in their dealings with God, that he may offer gifts and sacrifices for sins. Who can feel for them that are ignorant and that err: since he himself is also subject to weakness ... Nor does any man take the honor to himself, but he who is called by GOD.

St. Paul's acknowledgment that the priest himself is subject to ignorance, error, and weakness was much more consoling than my made-up spiritual director's advice. As I look back now at Father Lacordarie's expectations for a priest, in addition to being unrealistic, it inspired me much later on to offer yet another workshop entitled, *Be Ye Perfect: Mission Impossible.* The workshop examined the part that unrealistic expectations play in our emotional and spiritual lives and how we can deal with our need to be perfect. I have a theory that "perfectionism" underlies practically every other problem that we have in life, from addictions to fear of commitments in interpersonal relationships. I need to remind myself of that more often.

I'm not sure how I got to the cathedral for the ordination ceremony, but I joined my fellow *ordinandi* (an ominous Latin word for "those about to be ordained") at a packed cathedral. As we walked in a procession down the aisle to the thunderous welcome of the cathedral's huge pipe organ, I spotted my family in the first pews of that august church. Pride was written all over their faces, as they picked me out of the *ordinandi,* carrying our vestments, which the bishop would soon authorize us to wear, I gave my father a wink, and I could tell by the expression on his face that he was about to break that old family rule of "no mush at the airport."

Ordination Day and First Mass

A month before ordination, friends and relatives received a formal invitation. I have kept a copy of it for all these fifty-two years. It read:

The Reverend Donald Frederick Fausel
son of
Mr. and Mrs. J. Otto Fausel
Joyfully announces his
Ordination to the Holy Priesthood
to be conferred by his Excellency
The Most Reverend William A. Scully, DD.
Bishop of Albany
on Saturday, the first of June
Nineteen hundred and fifty-seven
In the Cathedral of the Immaculate Conception
and with his family
cordially invites you to offer with him his
First Solemn Mass

Sunday, the second of June
at twelve o'clock
Saint Catherine of Siena's Church
Albany, New York

Reception, Sunday Afternoon
From three until six o'clock
Saint Catherine's of Siena Parish Hall

I can't remember where I got the format for the invitation, but it looks a lot like a wedding invitation, without a spouse. I also have a photo album that my cousin and CBA classmate, Bill Byrne, created for my ordination, first Mass, and reception. He was an amateur photographer, and the album is a memorial to his skills. I hadn't looked at it for some time, but as I prepared for this chapter, it brought back many happy memories. There are over forty 8 x 10 black-and-white pictures that he assembled in the album, which, except for the fact that the album cover is not white, and the content is different, looks very much like a bride's wedding album. I'm not really sure of the significance of the similarity of the invitations and the album to a wedding. Perhaps there isn't any. What I do know? I appreciated it at the time and again as I revisited those happy days after over fifty years.

In addition to the pictures of my being ordained and saying my first Mass, there are so many pictures of friends and relatives on both sides of the family who have since died. I'm looking at one picture in the atrium of St. Catherine's grammar school where my grandmother, my Aunt May, Mrs. Tommaney, my Uncle Joe's mother, and my father's sister Frances are sitting on a couch under a sign that reads, Cross only at Corners! Then there is a cluster of the youngest cousins, who are now in their sixties—my cousin Bob Brew and Terry Brew, Mary Anne and Michael Tommaney, all dressed in their Sunday best and posing very maturely for the camera. There are small groups of relatives waiting for the meal to be served. My Aunt Anna Mae and Uncle Andy Brew look so young, with their dark hair, in contrast to the silver hair they had in later years. Those pictures are a perpetual gift. Thank you, Bill!

Then there are also the pictures of long lines of guests waiting to receive my first blessing. They ranged from Mayor Erastus Corning II to the maintenance man for the parish. I must have given my first blessing over five hundred times. Each person knelt at the prie-dieu, and I pronounced the words in Latin, "May the blessing of the most omnipotent Lord, Father, Son, and Holy Spirit, descend upon you and remain forever." I remember feeling very humbled by the deference people were showing me but very much aware that the high esteem that I was accorded was not because I was Donald F. Fausel, but because of their belief that an indelible mark of priest had been imprinted on my soul by ordination: "Thou art a Priest Forever, According to the Order of Melchizedek." Yes, Melchizedek, the "priest of God Most High," known to us in the Old Testament and referred to in the Dead Sea Scrolls. The awesome power of the priest is forever. Even though an individual priest might lose his right to function as a priest, he is a priest forever, and in cases of emergency could still absolve sins or administer the healing power of the "last rites" to a dying person.

Summer Assignment

Since I would not start my first teaching experience until September at St. Joseph's College, a minor seminary for the Archdiocese of San Francisco, I received a summer appointment at St. John the Baptist's Church in Schenectady, New York. The parish was in Old Town Schenectady, a charming section of the city that dated back to Colonial times. I was welcomed there by the pastor, Father Denny Dillon, a white-haired, rotund Irish gentleman from the "old sod." He was a great guy, but he never sat down and gave me a list of my responsibilities. Besides saying Mass, hearing confessions, and visiting the sick, I wasn't sure what my job description included. The parish had a grammar school, but since it was summertime, that wasn't an option. Imagine that! All the years I spent in the seminary, and we never had a class that prepared us for the day-to-day work of a parish priest. Luckily the other two assistant pastors, Johnny Maxim and Joe Delaney, provided on-the-job training. For the first couple of weeks I followed them around on their visits to parishioners who were in the Ellis Hospital or bringing communion to the sick in their homes; visited the County Home that was in the parish; and took my turn being on duty for any walk-ins who wanted to arrange for a baptism or wedding, provide food packages for the poor, or obtain rent for an out-of-work parishioner, etc. Occasionally, someone would come in with a personal or marriage problem that I didn't feel equipped to answer. I just used my intuitive listening skills, which I found out years later when I was being trained in counseling was often all people needed—someone to listen to them and not necessarily give them advice.

I also got to see for the first time what it was really like to live in a parish house. The other two assistant pastors were about ten years older than I. They made it clear that I didn't have to call them "Father," although it felt awkward at first. I always called the pastor "Father" in deference to his age and position.

I soon found that it was a ritual to meet in Johnny Maxim's room for cocktails before lunch and dinner. There were often priest visitors from nearby parishes who joined the Maxim happy hour. Johnny was in charge of mixing the martinis. His formula included a splash of vermouth in a shaker of gin. When I became a sub-deacon, I was required by the diocese to take a pledge for ten years not to drink alcohol. So, as my new colleagues were getting a buzz on at least twice a day, I was sipping on my lemonade.

In contrast to the happy hours, dinner time was always formal. We all wore cassocks, and Father Dillon would preside at the head of the table. He'd carve the roast and pass it around to the rest of us. He had a little bell to summon the cook when we needed more mashed potatoes or when it was time for her to take the dishes off the table and serve coffee and dessert. I always felt like the "poor little rich boy" at breakfast when I was the only one at the table, and I had the power of the bell.

During the summer I received three textbooks from the rector of St. Joseph's College, Father James "Beansie" Campbell, for the classes I would be teaching in the fall: ancient and medieval history, religion, and English grammar. I had my work cut out for me if I wanted to stay ahead of the classes they chose for me to teach. I took one look at the English text and saw that it had several chapters on diagramming sentences. I had never really learned the complexities of diagramming sentences in grammar school or high school, but I was soon to become an expert diagrammer. I don't think I had ever had a class in ancient and medieval history, so that was going to take up a good part of my leisure time in Schenectady. The one course that I thought I had a good grounding in was religion, but I learned more about a modern approach to Scripture by reading the text than I had in the seminary. I might be exaggerating a little but not very much.

Toward the end of the summer, I got together with a couple of my married high school buddies for a sort of going away party. My old friend Muggsy McGraw was there, and he took me aside and proceeded to take his prerogative, as someone who had known me most of my life, to give me some sage advice. "You know Fausel, you got your ass in a tub of butter. Three meals a day and no heavy lifting! Plus you got instant security and instant status in the community. Don't blow it, buddy!" I knew he had had a few drinks over the course of the evening, but I was a little surprised by his candor and even more surprised with his assessment of how the priest is viewed by some hardworking folks, who saw us as an elite class and who had things much easier than they could ever hope for. I kept to myself my own clichés about how we sacrifice so much to be priests, but frequently over the years recalled his words, as well as the deep feeling he had for anyone in the clerical class.

Go West, Young Man, Go West!

My summer assignment was coming to an end, and again I found myself saying good-bye to friends and relatives, but this time I would be moving across the country to Mountain View, California. To my surprise, we broke the old "no mush at the airport" by starting our good-byes several days in the advance. My parents, Jim, and I were able to awkwardly express our real feelings about my leaving, rather than pretend life was not changing. My father even wondered out loud whether I was moving so far from "home" just to get away from him. Of course he used his usual humor, but his feelings were still apparent. I tried to assure him that I had had no idea that I would be assigned in California and would have preferred to be back East.

The fact that Jim was also starting the minor seminary in Canada made the empty nest syndrome even more of a reality for my parents. Feelings and tears were shed at home so we didn't have to wait for the airport.

This would be my first airplane trip. As I walked up the steps to board the plane, I looked back like a politician to wave good-bye to my family. I thought, *for me it is a new and exciting experience, but for them it means going home to start a new phase of their lives.* I said a prayer that we would all do well.

I had to change planes in New York City and found myself on a four-prop plane sitting in the middle of several platoons of Canadian troops in their wool uniforms. For the next thirteen hours, I thought I was in hell or at least purgatory. Apparently they had orders not to take their jackets off, which contributed to a not-too-fragrant environment in the plane. This was my last cross-country flight on a prop plane. My flight back East in 1959 would be on a brand-new jet, and it only took five hours to fly coast to coast.

When I disembarked from the plane in San Francisco, I could see two gentlemen in Roman collars waiting for me. Fathers John Olivier and Gene Strain gave me a warm male welcome with firm handshakes and a pat on the back. I recall having dinner at the airport, but what stands out most of all is my disappointment when the waiter brought the shrimp cocktail I ordered. I had expected to sink my teeth into jumbo East Coast shrimp, but instead what I got was those tiny bay shrimp of which you need a half a dozen to equal one "real" shrimp. Of course, gentleman that I was, I didn't mention my disappointment. I don't remember anything about what I had for the rest of the meal, but fortunately there was nothing disappointing about my new colleagues. Father John, call me Jack, taught college Latin and Gregorian chant. Father Gene, call me Sarge, taught mostly high school courses. I think his nickname came from his abrupt way of getting students' attention. After a little chitchat about my trip out West, they gave me a mini-orientation to St. Joseph's—the students and the faculty. They painted a very positive picture of what I had to look forward to.

By the time we got down the peninsula to St. Joe's, it was already close to 11:00 PM, and I had no idea of the beauty that awaited me in the morning. My handlers brought me up to my room on the third floor. Wow! What a difference from the seminary rooms I had occupied for the last eight years. This was a suite, with a study, an executive desk and chair, separate bedroom, private bath and shower, a full-size bed, and even a bed comforter. Each floor had a faculty member to mentor thirty or forty students. I wasn't sure what my responsibilities would be, but I looked forward to meeting my mentees.

The next morning when I looked out my bedroom window, I thought I was in paradise. I had never seen a real palm tree or a eucalyptus tree. I'd come a long way from upstate New York.

We had a week before the students arrived. This gave me time to learn what was expected of me and to get to know the cast of characters on the faculty. And there was a cast of characters. Perhaps I still viewed the faculty as if I were a seminarian and couldn't completely grasp that I was now one of "them."

To mention just a few of the faculty, starting at the top, the rector, James "Beansie" Campbell, reminded me of a character out of a Dickens novel, with a round face and a body to match. He was a very gentle and fair man who had the respect of the faculty. I'm not sure if that's how the students viewed him, but he always treated me with respect. Then there was Father William O'Connor, known to the students as "Willie." He was my confessor and also the bursar for the community. He looked like a good wind would blow him over, and even though he must have been in his seventies, he had a full head of jet-black hair. Since the Sulpicians didn't get a salary, whenever we wanted to go out for dinner or to a movie, we had to ask the bursar for money. He wouldn't delve in detail into our plans, but he would go to his little cash box and carefully count out whatever he thought we would need for our night on the town.

The dean of discipline was Jack "the Cat" Canfield. The students called him the Cat because they thought he spent all his time slithering around the halls of St. Joe's hoping to find someone breaking a rule. The rumor was that he never slept. I got to know him as a colleague, and he wasn't anything like his reputation. He invited me to take a trip during the first Christmas vacation on the famous Pacific Coast Highway, which runs from San Francisco to Los Angeles. It's not the fastest way to travel, but it's one of the most scenic drives in the country. The crashing waves, the rocky cliffs, the curves in the road that open up new, breathtaking vistas at every turn, made the trip an unforgettable experience. We didn't go all the way to Los Angeles, but we did get as far as Morro Bay. On the way we visited Big Sur, the Hearst San Simeon mansion, Carmel by the Sea, and Monterey Bay. I have the old, faded 35 mm prints to help bring back the beauty of my trip with the Cat.

In reviewing that trip, I began to wonder if Jack the Cat didn't have devious reasons for inviting me as his traveling companion. He had a prewar blue Ford convertible that he had been working on for some time. This might have been its test run. What he hadn't told me was that periodically something would cause the motor to stall, and I would end up having to push the car until

Jack got it running again. One time I managed to get the car to a top of small incline and had to chase it to catch up and jump back in on the run. All in all, it was a great trip despite the push and run episodes.

There were two places where I informally met my new colleagues. One was in the Faculty Room and the other in kitchen after hours. After dinner every night we gravitated to the Faculty Room to watch *Paladin: Have Gun Will Travel* on a twenty-inch black-and-white TV. It was there that I first met Father Joseph Riddlemoser. He was a very distinguished man with a mane of pure white hair. He extended his hand to me as if he expected me to kiss his ring. "I am Father Joseph Riddlemoser. You may call me Father." I wasn't sure if he was kidding or not. "Joe," as the students called him, was a legend at St. Joe's when I arrived. He started teaching on 1926 and retired in 1970, over four decades later. I have that information from a reliable source. A former student, Bill Wall, has been the class historian for many years. Among other pieces he circulated was "A Day in My Life at Saint Joseph's College (Seminary) 1958." This was a day-by-day, hour-by-hour, thirteen-page, single-spaced memoir of his first year at St. Joe's. More references later from Bill (known by his colleagues as #294, his St. Joe's laundry number).

The other place where many of the faculty gathered after hours was a small kitchen with a refrigerator filled with beer and snacks. I was invited to stop by any time. I consulted with my confessor about the pledge not to drink alcoholic beverages. His interpretation was that because it was taken under duress, as a condition for ordination, it was not valid if I felt in any way forced to take the pledge. Much later I wondered if that same reasoning could also apply to mandatory celibacy.

So, with that assurance from Willie O'Connor, I felt free to have a beer with the boys. I didn't make a habit of it, but it was a relaxing atmosphere in which to meet more of my new colleagues. There's nothing like solving all the problems of the world over a bottle of Bud. Every once in a while, four or five of us would get in the company car and go out to a pizza place called Me and Ed's on the El Camino Real and indulge our appetite for one of the best pizzas I've ever had.

One of my favorites was Father Rock. He was an older gent who at one time had been rector of St. Joe's. The students called him "Pop Rock." He was a great lover of classical music. I remember he invited me to listen to his new Hi Fi set that some students had put together from a Heath Kit. When he found out I didn't have a radio, he gave me a tabletop radio. Now I really was in paradise.

By the time the students arrived on September 14, 1957 (Bill Wall), I had spent some time with the entire faculty and felt quite comfortable in my new surroundings. One of my responsibilities as the youngest faculty member was to sit in the confessional while the rector said the main morning Mass, just in case any of the students wanted to go confession. I would assist with communion and then say Mass on the main altar after the rector finished. The students would stay until the breakfast bell rang, and as soon as it did, all three hundred would rise and march off to breakfast even if I were in the middle of the consecration. It never made much sense, but it was another example of the power of the bells.

My First Classes

My teaching schedule was three classes a day, five days a week. We had class on Saturday since we had a free day during the week. My first class was English grammar at 10:30 AM. That gave me time to work on those sentence diagrams, grammar rules, quizzes, tests, and correcting papers. Even though I didn't have a choice in the courses, I soon felt confident in teaching English grammar and could diagram the most complex sentences with the best of them. That would be useful for the rest of my teaching and writing career.

My next class was at 2:30 PM when I met with the history scholars. I soon found that I enjoyed history and didn't mind the extra preparation. From that point, history became one of my lifelong interests. Rather than just read the course textbook, I read everything on ancient and medieval history that I could get my hands on. I guess I took to heart the oft-quoted wisdom of George Santayana, who writes, in *The Life of Reason,* "Those who cannot remember the past are condemned to repeat it."[1] Even today, I'd choose an historical novel or biography for pure reading pleasure.

I tried to make this class as interesting as possible. I remember that the first assignment I gave was to write an essay on "I Was a Teenage Cave Boy." There were some exceptional papers. For first-year high school students, they demonstrated vivid imaginations grounded in the little information they had, plus they seemed to enjoy the assignment. I was surprised at the number of students who volunteered to read their papers in front of the class.

To help engage the class, I divided them into two armies, the Spartans and the Athenians. I randomly assigned each student a rank, ranging from general to private. Each week we had an oral quiz. Both "armies" could get points for answering questions correctly and lose points for an incorrect answer. They had time to discuss their answers, with the highest officers leading the discussions. They would keep track of their points for the semester. It turned out to be a lively rivalry that helped keep their interest and, I hope, an interest in history.

My last class for the day was religion, at 3:30 PM. This was right before recreation, so the troops were usually chomping at the bit to get out onto the sports fields. I wish I could remember the title of the text because it was rather avant-garde for a pre-Vatican II religion textbook. One example I remember very clearly was a chapter on the *Epic of Gilgamesh.* Gilgamesh was king in the land between the Tigris and Euphrates rivers in the second and third millennia, BCE. He is described as part god and part man. Briefly, one of the characters the king encounters in his travels is a guy by the very memorable name of Utanapishtim, who would be comparable to Noah in the Old Testament. Like Noah, Utanapishtim is instructed to build an ark to prepare for a great flood. The details are even similar. "It was to measure 120 cubits on a side, six decks dividing it into seven levels, all measured to a height of 120 cubits, with nine compartments inside."[2] Rather than taking pairs of each animal, Utanapishtim was directed to take seeds of life from everywhere and load them onto the ark. Another similarity was that Utanapishtim sent doves forth when the flood had subsided to see whether they were near land. And sure enough, the dove brought back a small twig from a tree. My point is that the story in the Old Testament about Noah and the great flood was not original; it was a familiar story among most of the countries in Mesopotamia to illustrate a point, not necessarily to report on an historical fact. The people of the time recognized this, as they gathered around the bonfire to listen to a narrator repeat one of their favorite stories and be comforted by their god's loving care to see their ancestors through the flood. For me, who had four years of Scripture in the major seminary, this interpretation was a revelation. Not that I believed that every word in the Bible was to be taken literally, but it offered empirical evidence that Noah was not the only Noah, and that was okay. The message that the allegory—or, if you prefer, the parable— conveyed was more important than the story itself. The historical fact is that we didn't have the corner on the market on Noah, even though "the Bible told us so." This stimulated a lot of discussion in my first-year religion class.

Study Halls

In addition to the five classes the students had each class day, they also had three and a half hours of study hall (Bill Wall). The first study hall was at 8:00 AM, before the first class. The other three hours were between classes in the morning and afternoon. There were two study halls for the high school students. Each study hall would have one of the priests to mentor the 150 students working at their assigned desks. The junior priests usually had more mentoring responsibilities. You were there like the cop on the corner as a reminder that any "fooling around" would mean a punishment. The main punishment was being required to write out "lines" in the dictionary. A minor infraction, like talking to your neighbor without permission, might mean twenty-five lines, and a major violation, like causing a disruption in the study hall, could mean one hundred lines or more. I always thought it was a waste of time to write lines from the dictionary as a punishment, but that's the way it was at St. Joe's in the late fifties. The system was not teaching the students any self-discipline or mastery over their own domain. It was like a cat and mouse game. As I walked around the study hall moving my lips as if I were reading my Breviary, I had to give the impression that I had eyes in the back of my head to catch someone talking. I never found the game of "gotcha" very satisfying.

Meals

There was an hour for lunch. After all, we weren't sadists. The priests sat up on a raised platform to eat a slightly different meal than the students. I think the students thought it was to have a good view of their behavior as young gentlemen. But it was the last thing on my mind. I just wanted to enjoy a good meal and chat with my colleagues, even though most of the meals were "silent" meals, where one of the senior or junior students would read out loud from a podium in the refectory. The books did not necessarily have a religious theme, but it gave the students an opportunity to practice speaking in public.

Although the faculty got better meals than the students, my source, Bill Wall, reported that the student meals weren't all that bad. They were prepared by an order of French Canadian nuns, who also did laundry, cleaning, etc. I'm sure one of the many reasons there are hardly any minor seminaries today is that there are not enough nuns ready, willing, and able to provide those services, and it would cost a fortune to pay lay staff to do what the nuns did.

One thing I do remember about the meals was that we always had our salad at the end of the meal, whereas we Americans dive into our salads at the beginning. I found out that this is a French tradition. The Sulpicians originated in France and apparently brought that tradition with them. The rationale for having salad at the end of the meal is that it is good for your digestion. Pass that along to your gourmet friends.

Recreation

Okay, so here it is now, 4:30 PM, and it's finally time for recreation. Remember, the students had been up for prayers and Mass since 6:00 AM; attended five classes and three and a half hours of study hall with only time out for breakfast and lunch; this was a very demanding day. My three classes and one study hall was a piece of cake in comparison. But in their great wisdom, the designers of the schedule recognized that old adage, "All work and no play …" This applies to all of us but especially to teenage boys who are going through the early stages of puberty, with all its testosterone changes and energies that needed to be dissipated. You can take just so many cold showers! I doubt that the founding fathers ever talked in terms of dissipating testosterone. Whatever their rationale was, no one would disagree that physical activity was an important part of the curriculum. The intramural sports program was very well organized. There were four teams on the high school side—the Bears, Trojans, Indians, and Ramblers (Bill Wall). Each team had four divisions—the Peanuts, Frosh, Juniors, and Seniors. They played softball in the fall, basketball in the winter, and baseball in the spring. The competition was fierce, and the concrete rewards not much more than knowing you had been able to hold your own with your peers.

While the students were competing in the sport of the day, some of the faculty would watch, and some of us would play tennis or go to the pool to relax. I remember writing back home boasting that I had been swimming in the middle of March on St. Patrick's Day. My father was still shoveling snow from his driveway.

Class Walks

Another avenue for releasing some of the pent-up energies that accompany adolescence was class walks. There were two kinds of class walks—the monthly class walk and "the" class walk. Every Thursday was a day without classes. Each Thursday, the students who wanted to walk to town would have to sign up a group of twenty to twenty-five students and get a faculty person to agree to accompany the group into the nearby town of Los Altos and the El Rancho shopping center. According to Bill Wall, the round-trip took between two and two and a half hours. Since I was the youngest "gent," I was often asked by the students to be their chaperone (a rather archaic word, but it's defined as "somebody who accompanies and supervises a group of young people") for these walks. I always agreed to go, even though I thought the whole idea of the students needing to be monitored outside the seminary walls was old-fashioned. I felt like a mother hen protecting her flock from harm's way. Was it a matter of trust? Were we afraid the students might sneak off and purchase a copy of a sports magazine or, worse yet, see Elvis wiggling his hips on a TV screen?

The annual class walk was an all-day excursion that was one of the highlights of the year. I was asked by the class leaders to accompany (sounds better than chaperone) the class on their May 1958 walk. I wasn't sure whether or not to be flattered by the invitation.

According to Bill Wall, the class had already been reduced from 107 at the beginning of the academic year to 85. The picnic grounds at Steven Creek Dam were where we would spend the day. It was about a mile and a half one way. Bill goes into great detail about the barbecuing, playing "water slaughter" in the pool with a soccer ball, softball, hiking, etc. I don't know how I kept track of everyone. Apparently I didn't, because he tells the story of several of his classmates who escaped from the picnic grounds and then hitched a ride back in a truck just as the group was getting ready to leave. This and the fact that they "found" two full cans of beer was news to me. Perhaps they gave me the honor of leading them on the walk because they could count on me to not be so vigilant in monitoring their comings and goings. It appears that they had that right.

At the end of the year, the rector called me in to give me an evaluation of my "freshman year." I was pleased that it was very positive, and I would be coming back for the 1958–59 academic year. He also told me that the provincial of the Sulpicians would like me to go the Catholic University in Washington for summer school to start working on a graduate degree in counseling. It wasn't an order, but it also wasn't a choice. No one had asked me what I wanted to study, but coincidentally it was an area of study I felt would be useful and in which I had been interested in for some time.

My brother, Jim, and my good friend Pete Young drove out from Albany to take me back for the summer. They stayed a few days and witnessed the end of the year good-byes. Jim mentioned that it reminded him of the end of summer camp, with all the good-byes and displays of bonding that were evidenced by the students' feeble attempts to cover up any feelings by poking and jabbing one another. I guess they had learned my old family rule of "no mush at the airport."

We had a great trip home, much of it on Route 66 and other two-lane highways. There were relatively few superhighways compared to what we have today. This was just at the beginning of the Federal-Aid Highway Act of 1956 under the leadership of President Eisenhower. The federal government paid for 90 percent of over 41,000 miles of highway. One stretch of road stands out. We were approaching Bakersfield, California. I was driving, Pete was in the passenger's seat, and my brother was in the backseat taking movie pictures with my father's camera, when all of a sudden, from the middle of nowhere, we heard a siren blaring behind us and saw a swirling red light beckoning us to pull over. We obediently did. Out stepped a stereotype of a redneck sheriff, sunglasses and all. He was not too happy with my brother filming him, along with the scenic background. Before we knew it, we were following him back to the sheriff's office in Bakersfield. Once we got there, he sat down behind his desk, put his feet up, and asked, "Well, boys what was the big hurry?" He really didn't want to know. Before we could answer, he gave us a choice. "You all can come back next Monday and let the magistrate decide, or you can pay the sixty-dollar fine right now!" It was really a "take it or leave it" offer, so we scraped up the sixty dollars and carefully made our way out of Bakersfield.

There was one other thing that stands out. In a gas station men's room, washing up after taking care of business, I spotted a dispenser of prophylactics on the wall. I decided this was a good chance for me to engage in some social action. With all the best intentions, I took a piece of soap and plugged up the slot where you paid for your purchase. To this day I cannot believe what I did. How dare I violate other people's rights because I believed I was preventing sinful behavior? More likely I was probably responsible for the birth of more than one unwanted baby.

Summer School

I had about a week at home before packing up again and driving to Washington DC to start summer school. I had a chance to get together with friends and relatives and some of my ordination classmates. We exchanged stories about our first year as priests and our ministries. Although some of them were teaching religion in high schools, it was a lot different than my full-time teaching in the seminary. They also had responsibilities in a parish and seemed to be finding more satisfaction as parish priests. For the first time, I began to question seriously whether I wanted to spend the rest of my life as a Sulpician. As I thought of some of my colleagues at St. Joe's who had spent their whole lives teaching Latin I, it seemed that it would get very boring. I knew it was a noble vocation to teach future priests, and I had enjoyed the first year—but would my mind become numb after a few years?

I realized that one of my fears was the fear of boredom. I put the thoughts aside, knowing I had a couple of more years before I had to make the big decision.

The one thing that I hadn't noticed before I went to California was that practically all my relatives and most of my friends called me Father Don. It made some sense for my younger cousins to call me Father Don, but my older cousins and my uncles and aunts, whom I always called Uncle Austin or Aunt Liz, now called me Father Don. I knew it was out of respect for the office, but it just didn't feel right. Even my parents, when referring to me in the third person, would say things like, "Father Don would love to get together with you before he goes to Washington." It just shows how deeply rooted esteem for the priesthood was in Catholic culture at that time.

I had two summer sessions of five weeks each to earn twelve semester credits toward a degree. So I packed up the Chevy, armed with a map, and started off for a new experience. When I got to the city of Washington, I wished I had a navigator to get me to Catholic University. Now this is a true story. Catholic University was usually referred to as CU. I was stopped at a red light, completely confused, when four young women pulled up next to me in a convertible with the top down. Without thinking, I rolled down my window and hollered, "How do I get to CU?" As they pulled away as fast as they could, and I sat there in my Roman collar, I gradually realized they must have thought I was some sort of pervert, using a pathetic line to try to pick them up.

With a little help from a Washington police officer, I finally made it to the Sulpicians' House of Study, which was a residence house right on the campus of CU. I checked in and was assigned a room and given directions about meals, curfew, and other house rules. I was just glad I made it there and had bed and board for the next ten weeks. The room was a throwback to my days as a student. Even so, I remember thinking there was a certain feeling of protection knowing I would be safeguarded from the outside world.

The next morning I went down to the basement to say Mass. There must have been twenty makeshift altars for the residents.

It seemed very strange to be saying Mass as an individual, with twenty other priests in their own world. This was pre-Vatican II, and concelebration wasn't an option. To celebrate Mass as community would have made much more sense than each individual doing his private celebration. Plus, it would have been much more practical.

At breakfast I met several other candidates whom I knew from St. Mary's who were candidates to become Sulpicians. Kevin Brassell from Rhode Island had been a good friend of mine, and we were in a couple of classes together that summer. This had to be one of the hottest summers in Washington's history. And there was no air conditioning in the Sulpician House or in most of the classrooms at CU! Plus, we had to wear our black cassocks to class and to meals! Since most of our classes were in the morning, Kevin and I joined a group of several others who had discovered that the only place in the city where you could cool off was at a movie theater. Remember how in the early days of air-conditioning, the theaters would have big banners on the marquis proclaiming, KOOL AIR CONDITIONING? We spent many afternoons in the coolest places in town. It didn't matter what the movie was, as long as we could cool off.

Despite the heat, I was developing what would be a lifelong interest in psychology and mental health. I took classes in personality theory, communications 101, human behavior and the social environment, and a basic statistics class and a research class. These were academic areas that we never were exposed to in the seminary. I found the courses helpful in my personal life, as they forced me to look at my own choices and be a little more introspective. I could see how the content could be useful for priests in any type of ministry where they were often in the trenches dealing with psychological problems as well as spiritual issues.

California, Here I Come

After summer school I spent four or five days in Albany; with trips to Lake George and Saratoga Lake, I was feeling more like a human being again. The weather was perfect, and I didn't have to take refuge in the movies to stay cool.

Back I went to Mountain View for my second year. Two newly ordained Sulpician candidates joined the faculty. Brian McKane and Pete Caligari had both been ordained at St. Patrick's at Menlo Park, California, another Sulpician major seminary. Brian and I became great tennis competitors and played every chance we got. Pete was a six-foot-three, athletically built guy from a family of several priests. He shared the third floor with me, and we both had responsibilities for mentoring half the students on the floor. I remember one Saturday morning I was in my room while the students were preparing their rooms for inspection, and I heard a loud rendition of what I learned was the Kingston Trio singing "Tom Dooley." Out I went to see who the culprit was. As I got to the other end of hall, Pete had his tape machine in the hall, and there were a bunch of students gathered around singing along with him and the Kingston Trio. This was 1958, the early days of a folk music revival. I didn't know that yet, because all I listened to was classical stations. At that time I thought the Kingston Trio was some sort of a cult that we had to stifle, at least in the seminary. I discreetly suggested to Pete that he might want to check with Jack Canfield to see whether it was okay to play popular music in the hallways. After all, the students couldn't even have a radio. If a student were caught with one, he could be expelled on the spot. Ironically, in the next couple of years I became a great fan of folk music. I even remember going to a Kingston Trio concert in the late seventies in Arizona, and I can't count the number of times I paid good money to see my favorites, Peter, Paul and Mary, perform. That was all part of my transformation.

I was assigned the same classes that I had taught the previous year. This meant that I didn't have to spend as much time to keep one lesson ahead of the students. I was also assigned the position as infirmarian, probably because of my experience at St. Mary's. Nurse Betty was our full-time nurse, and I had two college students to assist me. Sick call was every evening after supper. I had to be there to push pills, take temperatures, bandage bruises, etc. Wouldn't you know that was the year of the great flu epidemic and, before the administration decided that we had to send the entire student body home, I had to make dozens of "house calls" every evening. Bill Wall has a whole article on the epidemic. Despite the epidemic, I thoroughly enjoyed that year at St. Joe's. I have nothing but happy memories. Toward the end of the year, I got my assignment from the Provincial to go to Fordham University in the Bronx, New York, to continue my work on my master's degree in counseling. I don't know why they didn't send me back to CU, but I never questioned the assignment. I received a second letter assigning me to Solitude in Baltimore for the fall. I better explain Solitude. It is not as bad as it sounds. The Sulpician system is that after a candidate completes two years of teaching, he is assigned to eight months of Solitude. The program is much like the Tertiary that the Jesuits serve once they have taught in one of their high schools for two years. The title Solitude is deceiving because it gives the impression that I was going to some sort of a hermitage all by myself. Actually, I would be with seven other candidates

Before I leave my recollections about St. Joe's, I want to bring you up to the twenty-first century and my reconnection with some of the students from forty-seven years ago.

Alumni Day April 29, 2006

Sometime in the fall of 2005 I got a surprise call from one of my former students at St. Joseph's College/Seminary. Remember, it had been forty-six years since I left there.

"Hi, I'm John Flynn. You might not remember me, but I was a student at St. Joe's when you taught there in 1958."

"John Flynn, of course I remember you. How did you find out my phone number?"

"I Googled you!"

Of course, I thought. How else, in these days of advanced technology! We chatted a little bit, and it turned out he was going to be in Phoenix the following week and wondered if we could get together for dinner. We made arrangements to meet in the lobby of his hotel. He warned me not to look for the freckle-faced, red-haired kid I might remember; he had been told he looked more like Terry Bradshaw. Anyway, we met, and, sure enough, all his freckles had faded, along with his hair. We drove to Tempe, Arizona, to Monte's Steak House and had a great dinner. He brought me up to date with a lot of his classmates. The flow of our conversation was so smooth; it was almost like the four decades had not passed. John connected me with a list-serve of his former classmates, and before long I had heard from at least a dozen of them. Bill Wall, whom I have mentioned several times, suggested I might want to go to the Annual Alumni Day. I thought it was a great idea and looked forward to stepping back in time and seeing some familiar faces. Actually, none of our faces were that familiar, since we had all aged over the years.

Bill met me at my motel in Palo Alto. We had a great lunch at the Fish Market Restaurant right near my motel. After lunch, we piled into his little red sports car, and off we went on a trip into nostalgia. Bill took me out to where St. Joe's used to be before the Loma Prieta earthquake of 1989. How sad! Where the seminary once proudly stood was now a development of upper-class houses. We toured what we could of the old grounds, with Bill pointing out, "That's where the baseball diamond used to be," or, "Let's walk down here to see the Old Grotto." Old memories came popping into my mind. We even went up to the Maryknoll residence on the hill, where the Maryknoll students and faculty lived. Fortunately, it wasn't touched by the earthquake.

Bill jogged my memory again by taking me down to the picnic area at Stevens Creek Canyon where I had chaperoned his class on their first class walk in May 1958. As he pointed out the parameters of the territory I had to monitor, I thought it was no wonder that several of the more adventuresome students had slipped beyond my vigilant view to find a store where they could purchase some beer and blemish my reputation as a dependable guardian of youth.

The next afternoon Bill picked me up to take me to the St. Patrick's Seminary at Menlo Park, where we would celebrate the twenty-fifth anniversary of the Alumni Association. We arrived at St. Pat's a couple of hours early to meet with eight members of the same class and enjoy some cold drinks, reminisce about the old days, and solve some of the problems in the current church.

Mass was celebrated at 4:00 PM in a full chapel, followed by a social hour and a banquet-type dinner. I was introduced by Frank Brady, the master of ceremonies, as former faculty member "Don Freddie Fausel." After the banquet I met with dozens of former students and faculty. This was a real treat. I was surprised that so many of them remembered me and had stories to prove it.

What impressed me the most with the class that started with me in 1957 was that they still have such a strong bond with one another and fond memories of their time at St. Joe's. Even though the majority of them were never ordained, they still projected the feeling of *Fratres in Unum*.

Fordham University

Fordham is a Jesuit college with a campus at Rose Hill and three other sites in the New York City area. The campus at Rose Hill is an oasis in the middle of the hubbub that is the Bronx. The stately, majestic Gothic architecture provides a serene atmosphere that is enhanced by the well-kept grounds and landscaping. The campus has a special dormitory for priests and religious. The good news was that in contrast to the rooms at CU, those at Fordham were air-conditioned. This meant I could spend more time on my studies and less time staying cool in the Lowe's movie theaters.

I was glad I was not back in Washington, not just because of a more livable climate, but the learning environment was more to my liking at Fordham. I continued with more advanced classes in psychology/counseling and began to explore a number of different types of therapy. Each of the classes was usually structured with a mini-lecture by the prof, but the major portion of the class time was devoted to interaction between the instructor and the class, and with other students when we broke into small, task-oriented groups. Incredible as it seems now, for the first time in my academic studies I began to think critically rather than blindly accepting what the instructor taught. Critical thinking was what had been missing in my worldview for all these years. I had been too conditioned and too eager to accept ipso facto what those in authority told me was the truth, without using my God-given reason. Critical thinking was my epiphany, my "aha" moment, my leap of understanding of what had been missing in how I processed and acquired knowledge. This was indeed an awesome realization, equivalent to a spiritual or religious awakening.

I also had the opportunity at Fordham, much more so than at CU, to spend time with my fellow students, most of whom were not clerics. This was another eye-opener. I found that I enjoyed our casual conversation over coffee or lunch. Two of the female students invited me to their apartment for dinner. Not only was it a treat to enjoy a home-cooked meal, but I was there not as Father Don but as a fellow student. We enjoyed many common interests not only in our studies but also in the changes that needed to be made in the church. This gave me a whole different perspective about what young Catholics were really thinking about the church. Before these very harmless, casual talks, I actually didn't remember ever having an adult conversation with any woman who was not a relative. For a man approaching thirty, that could be a record. Talk about being a late developer! Summer session ended all too quickly, and before I knew it, I was packing to go to Solitude.

Solitude

Eight candidates arrived in early September 1959 at what had been a mansion, on the property of St. Mary's Seminary, reportedly owned by one of the nephews of the legendary Napoleon Bonaparte.

Remember Father Jimmy Laubacker, the former rector of St. Mary's? He was now the spiritual director of Solitude. Addison

Wright, whom I knew from St. Thomas, and six others, from St. Patrick's in Menlo Park, California, made up our group. After we settled in, Father Laubacker got us all together and went over the schedule. The first ten days would be a silent retreat. I won't go into an hour-by-hour breakdown of our schedule. But after the ten days of retreat, the regular schedule was even more demanding.

For Mass we paired off with one another, first to offer Mass and then to serve it. Meals were all "silent meals," except on major feast days or when we had visitors. The mornings were divided into time to work on writing meditations and sermons and a group session with Father Laubacker, where he spoke on different schools of spirituality. The afternoons were divided into time for spiritual reading, praying the rosary together, a short recreation period long enough to play a set of tennis or one-on-one basketball—then more time for meditation or writing. We had no input into the program but had some latitude on the content of our meditations, readings, and writing. After supper we had an hour and a half of recreation. It was during those times that I learned to play bridge. Often it was the only thing that I had to look forward to. It was a gloomy day when I couldn't get a foursome together for a hand of bridge.

With all the time I had for self-assessment, and with the knowledge I had recently acquired about human behavior in summer school, I was beginning to doubt more and more whether I was cut out to be a Sulpician. It wasn't that I hadn't found my two years at St. Joe's enriching and enjoyable, but I kept projecting myself twenty and thirty years into the future, and my fear of boredom kept coming up again and again. I was also beginning to question the lack of choices I had been given by the Sulpicians in planning for my future. Perhaps it was because I hadn't been assertive enough when I was given assignments, but, as I experienced it, I was like a soldier being assigned by his superiors to wherever they thought he was needed. I realized that, even if I went back to my diocese, my choices would not necessarily be part of the process but that I needed to take more responsibility for my future.

I spent a number of private sessions seeking advice from Father Laubacker. I never had the sense that he was attempting to tell me what I should do. To his credit, I found him to be a good listener who would clarify misinformation that I had, give me his perspective of how the system worked, and then turn it back to me. It was quite clear that I would be "the decider." I had the impression that he had taken one of those communication classes from the counseling program. For example, he listened carefully to my concerns about not having any input in going to St. Joe's; not being asked about what classes I would teach; and being sent to two different universities for summer school to be trained in a field that I coincidentally happened to like but had not been consulted about whether it was something I was interested in studying. He acknowledged that he could understand how that might be upsetting but went on to explain that that often happens to candidates unless they have expressed a passionate interest in a particular discipline. He assured me that since I had developed a strong interest in psychology he was sure that would be taken into consideration. At that time the only psychology course in the curriculum in the major seminary was a general course. I was not interested in teaching the general course; I was more interested in actually practicing counseling/psychology or teaching a course that would be helpful for priests going into the ministry. He agreed that that would be a useful course but wasn't sure how it would fit with all the other required courses.

Finally, in February, I told Father Laubacker that I wanted to go back to my home diocese. I know he was disappointed, but again, to his credit, he did not try to pull a Father Hines on me. At this point in my life, it wouldn't have worked. At twenty-nine, I was beginning to take more responsibility for my life. A little late, but nevertheless I might finally be growing up.

Father Laubacker made sure that I had a chance to say my good-byes to all my colleagues. It was not a clandestine, middle-of-the-night departure. I had already informed the bishop's office and had an appointment arranged. I would now see what life held in store for me outside the protective seminary walls.

Reflections

One of the issues that I hadn't discussed with Father Laubacker was my growing concern about my motives for wanting to become a Sulpician in the first place—what I referred to earlier about my having taken refuge in the seminary as a dysfunctional way of dealing with my fear of not being able to remain celibate if I wasn't protected behind the seminary "walls." I'm not sure how conscious that motive might have been, but, as I learned in my courses at CU and Fordham, no matter what theory I applied, from Freud to Jung, I would have fallen somewhere between preadolescence and adolescence in my psychosexual development.

I was beginning to spend an inordinate amount of energy suppressing my sexual desires and fantasies, especially when I was interacting with appealing women on a day-to-day basis at summer school. I got to the point that I doubted my ability to live a celibate life. I had confessed these fears to a Jesuit priest at Fordham. I can only remember his first name, Father George. He was an older gentleman who gave me the impression that I wasn't the first priest who had expressed these doubts. I had several meetings with him to discuss my dilemma. I guess I must have felt more comfortable talking to him about my doubts and fears about living a celibate life than I did with Father Laubacker, since Father George really didn't know me, and I felt more anonymous. I must admit before I put my cards on the table that I expected him to react by saying something like, "Well this is a hell of a time to bring this up. You had eight years in the seminary to figure that out. Why now?" Thankfully, he didn't, and he gave me a chance to give him some of the reasons why I thought I had gotten this far before dealing with the issue. I reviewed my conversation with different confessors over the years and what I thought was poor advice, and he just listened silently. He was very nonjudgmental. He acknowledged that I wasn't blaming this on anyone else but recognized the impact the culture I had grown up in had had on me. He suggested that I was unintentionally groomed to be a people-pleaser and that I had learned my lessons well. I was able to open up much more to him because his approach was so different from that of the priest at St. Mary's who told me the "temptations" would change when I was ordained.

Father George asked me about my spiritual life. I had to admit that outside of saying Mass every day and routinely reading my Breviary, I had abandoned daily meditation, morning and evening prayers, the rosary, and spiritual reading. Without being intrusive, he asked whether I was interested in Ignatian spirituality. He shared several books with me that we discussed. This was helpful because I had first experienced Ignatian spirituality on a retreat at the Shrine of the North American Martyrs at Auriesville, New York, where the early Jesuit missionaries were martyred. Although I was familiar with Franciscan, Dominican, Benedictine, and Carmelite spirituality, I found I was more attracted to Ignatian spirituality. I liked the way the spiritual exercises were structured to fit the needs of individual participants.

There were other issues that I had to deal with, but I had gained some degree of confidence from working with Father George. Some of the issues overlapped with my doubts about motivation. I recalled an incident that occurred during one of my visits to Albany between St. Joe's and summer school. I was filling in at a local parish, performing Masses during the weekend. After Mass they had coffee and doughnuts for the parishioners. I was enjoying my doughnut when a woman whom I never met came up to me and said something close to, "Oh, Father, I understand your brother will be ordained in a couple of years. Your mother must be so proud. Just think, there'll be two priests in the family! How blessed she is. She'll never lose her two boys." She was one of those gushy, "pew duster" church women, so I didn't pay too much to what she had just said. I simply acknowledged her with a nod as I finished my doughnut and moved on. Later I thought of what she had said and have thought of it often since, especially the part about "She'll never lose her two boys." I know that in some cultures, "My son the doctor or my son the lawyer" is a sign of family pride, but in no way is it connected to not losing your son. I've said before that neither of my parents ever put pressure on me to be a priest, but there was always that not-so-subtle respect that they always showed for priests. I wondered how much of their unspoken wishes I had absorbed and how much it might have influenced my choice to be ordained.

One of the other issues I was struggling with at the time was the dogma of God punishing us to suffer eternal torment in hell for any unforgiven mortal sin. From the time I was in grammar school, that never made sense to me, but I never challenged the good nuns or priests. I didn't obsess over it, but, from time to time, the issue would arise, and I could never seem to justify a loving God punishing one of his children for all eternity. For example, I knew that the church taught that giving in to impure thoughts was a mortal sin. I also knew how hard I struggled to put impure thoughts out of my head. I often didn't win the battle. If I died before I was able to confess my sins, according to what I was taught, I was a goner for all eternity, no matter how often I was successful in not giving in to temptation. I know there are ways of getting around those interpretations, but they seemed like casuistry. I did not believe that we should have to go through subtle, sophisticated, and sometimes deceptive arguments and reasoning to arrive at a solution to a moral issue.

A follow-up question was, how could I be perfectly happy in heaven when billions of people are being punished with eternal torture in hell for whatever mortal sin they had committed? Not just for impure thoughts but for any mortal sin. When the church changed the rule about not eating meat on Friday, I wondered about all those poor souls who were guilty of that particular mortal sin. Did the church release them?

It wasn't until much later in my life that I felt comfortable with relying on the primacy of conscience. I will explain the process in greater depth in chapter 8, when I describe how I learned to deal with these issues, as well as others, after Vatican II.

Chapter 7
Back Home Again

My relatives and friends were delighted that I had come to my senses and was back home where I belonged. Most of them never understood what the Sulpicians were all about and why I couldn't be a priest in the Albany Diocese. It was nice to feel welcomed.

I called the chancery, the building where all the diocesan business is transacted, to confirm my appointment with Bishop Scully and got "the Chief," Monsignor James Hart, who was now the bishop's secretary. Along with his other responsibilities, he took care of the bishop's appointments and schedule. He was an old friend from my Brandt Lake days when we competed as pitchers in our summer softball league. He picked up the phone with a friendly, "Hello Otto. Glad to have you back!" As long as I knew him, he had always called me by my father's first name, another one of my aliases. That a.k.a. dated back to the seventh grade, when the parish priest called on me in class, thinking my father would surely have named me Otto. The name Otto stuck with me through ordination, just as Freddie did in Connecticut. No wonder I was having such a hard time trying to discover my identity.

After a brief update on the last few years of my life as a Sulpician and reminiscing about a few pitchers' battles we had, the Chief confirmed my appointment with the bishop and added that he was looking forward to seeing me. I thought to myself, *it's always good to have a friend at court.*

Bishop William A. Scully had succeeded the thirty-five-year reign of Bishop Edmund F. Gibbons. He had been bishop of Albany for three years when he ordained my class in 1957. He was a "New York boy" and many thought he had higher aspirations than Albany. He frequently went back to "the city" to visit with his friends and relatives. He moved the bishop's residence in Albany from an old, drab mansion to a new, bright mansion in a new section of the city. Many resented the money spent on the new residency and attributed it to his New York City taste. The few times I met with him I found him to be very charming but always conscious of his position as bishop.

At that time the chancery was located in a stately, three-story house that had been donated to the diocese. The bishop's office would have been appropriate for the CEO of a large corporation. Monsignor Hart ushered me into the office and introduced me as if we had never met before. After we chatted about my last two years teaching in California, we got down to the business at hand. I was impressed with his commitment to release priests to the Sulpicians. He seemed to have a high regard for the work they did.

He started with, "Well, Father Fausel! I have a problem in Green Island." Outside of my classmate from St. Thomas, Jim Kelly, who grew up there, I wasn't sure if I even knew where Green Island was. "You see, the pastor, Father LeFebvre, needs time to recover from an operation and will be living with his sister for a couple of months in Troy. I need someone to fill in for him as temporary administrator of the parish. So, I was hoping you could help out." I obediently responded like a good soldier, "Yes, your Excellency!" without giving it a second thought.

He sort of mumbled, "Good, good!" Then he said, "Now there is one more thing I want you to consider. You don't need to give me an answer right now. This would be a more permanent assignment. Father Elmer Donnelly, the director of Catholic Charities in

Schenectady, has had some health problems. They're not urgent, but he wants someone to replace him as director. Now this would require you to get a master's degree in social work. You've been recommended by Father Sise, the diocesan director of Catholic Charities, and several other people whose judgment I trust. If this is something you're interested in, we'd make the arrangements at Fordham University's School of Social Work. So, think it over, maybe talk to Father Sise, and let me know in a couple of weeks."

My head was spinning. I was very happy to see that he was not ordering me to go to Fordham but was giving me a clear choice. I told him that before I went into the seminary I had considered going to Siena College to study social work. I didn't know much about the master's program, but I had spent the summer at Fordham, and that had been a good experience. He wasn't one for chitchat. It was apparent that he was satisfied that we had completed our business. I picked up on his cue and thanked him for his time, since I knew there were other people waiting to see him. On the way out, I passed the Chief's desk, and he gave me one of those knowing winks that conveyed that he was already in the know on my appointments and had probably added his two cents about Catholic Charities.

I had dinner that evening with my parents. In some ways it felt as though I had never left. I wondered if they noticed anything different about me but didn't ask. All I know is that they were happy I was back home. Since I had last been home, they had moved uptown to New Scotland Avenue to a brand-new tri-level house with a swimming pool, a family room, a dining room, an office for my father, three bedrooms, a front lawn that had required my father to purchase a sit-down lawn mower, and a backyard that bordered on a wooded area. My father had indeed done well in the insurance business.

The next morning, after I got the directions from my father to Green Island, I was off to an exciting new challenge. There were only a little over two thousand people on Green Island and one Catholic Church. I arrived there and was met by the housekeeper, a Mrs. Toomey, please call me Grace. She was a widow who had been with Father LeFebvre for over twelve years. As my mother would say, she was pleasingly plump. Like many of the women of the day she always wore an apron. As she showed me around the rectory, it was obvious she spent a lot of time cleaning. She informed me that lunch would be at noon and confessions at 4:00 PM. That didn't sound like too heavy a schedule, nor did the rest of the week. Two masses on Sunday, office hours by appointment, and monthly meetings of three parish groups—the men's Holy Name Society, the Women's Rosary Society, and a teen's group. All these meetings were in the evening, so I guessed I was going to have a lot of time on my hands during the day. There were no hospitals to visit on "the Island," as they called it, no jails or homes for the aged, just home visits to the sick. I really had to figure out how I was going to spend my time. Again, they didn't have a class in the seminary on the differences between a busy urban parish and a parish in the smallest town in the state of New York.

I arrived for lunch at noon on the dot to a delicious bowl of soup and some fancy sandwiches. I immediately knew that Grace and I were going to get along well. There I sat at the head of the dining room table, with a fresh white tablecloth, real silverware, and cloth napkins. Grace had explained that when I was ready for dessert, I should just press the buzzer under the carpet to summon her. Now this was really uptown, for a small town—no bells to ring but a buzzer to buzz. Not what I would have expected on "the Island."

I settled in very nicely to living in a small town. Of course the Island was only across the Hudson River from Cohoes, Troy, and Albany. It wasn't like I was out in the boonies. I found that the folks weren't much different from anyplace else; they had the same problems and the same hopes for their families and were anxious to be part of their community of worship.

I must admit that it was a little lonely being in the rectory all by myself. It was different than living in a community like St. Joe's, where you could just go down to the faculty room or to the kitchen and chat with your colleagues over a cold beer.

I was just settling into my new responsibilities when I received a call from the Chief to let me know that the bishop wanted to talk to me. He indicated that it was about another issue—not Fordham. The Chief was cozy like that; he'd give you a hint but wouldn't go any further.

This was another surprise! The bishop started his conversation by telling me that Father Dick Denine, the director of Marian Lodge, the diocesan camp for girls, was very sick and needed an assistant for the summer. I'm not quoting him verbatim, but his words went something like this: "I know that you were head counselor at Camp Tekakwitha, and you were a leader among your peers at Camps Gibbons and Jogues. I also know you're young to be given a position at a girls' camp, but I'm sure your experience with the Sulpicians has given you a spiritual background that will make up for your youth. So, I'm hoping you'll consider the position." I probably should have said, "Thank you, your Excellency, for your confidence, but right now I'm struggling with my own sexuality and am having doubts about being able to live a celibate life. I'm afraid that being in that environment might not be helpful. It would almost be like putting me in an occasion of sin. So, I respectfully decline the appointment."

Of course I didn't say that; I obsequiously replied, "Thank you, your Excellency, for your confidence. I would be happy to assist Father Denine."

He seemed pleased and, after all, that was my job as a "people-pleaser," especially pleasing those in authority. I had learned that skill early on and had apparently learned it well. "Yes, S'ter," "Yes, Father" tripped so easily from my lips, it wasn't difficult to substitute "Yes, Bishop."

"Fine, I'm sure you'll handle yourself well. Oh, by the way, have you given more thought to getting your master's degree at Fordham?"

"I have, your Excellency, and I've talked to Father Sise as you suggested. He was very encouraging, and I value his opinion. I'm also excited about the work that Catholic Charities does and would be happy to accept the assignment." This is a very close reconstruction of our conversation. Reading it now, I have several thoughts. *Is this guy for real (meaning me) or is he so eager to please he's willing to put what's best for him aside to please his superior?* But it wasn't all that black and white. I was being honest about my excitement about working at Catholic Charities, but I just didn't like the "butt kissing" way I expressed it.

I wonder, *if I had stayed in the Sulpicians how the bishop would ever have managed to fill in all the gaps in the diocese without me.*

I did attempt to visit Father Denine at St. Peter's Hospital, but the nurse told me he wasn't strong enough to have visitors. Two days later, he died. I received another call to come to the chancery! I suspected the bishop realized that it might be okay for me to be assistant director under the watchful eye of Father Denine, but he wasn't sure about my being the director on my own with a staff of thirty young women and 160 campers. I was wrong. He wanted to let me know personally that he would like me to be director of Marian Lodge, and he would relieve me of my duties at Green Island to give me time to prepare for the opening of the camp in June. Between now and then I would be in residence at St. Peter's Church in Saratoga; my only duty there would be to say Mass on Sundays. The rest of my time I needed to devote to recruiting a staff, marketing the camp in all the diocesan schools, ordering nonperishable food for the first month, and making sure the physical plant was ready for the campers. Oh, I also had to find out where the twenty head of horses were wintered and order hay for the summer. I think that merited being released from my duties on the Island.

I was soon to find out that Pyramid Lake was a jewel, with its own island for camping trips, mountains to climb, and evergreen trees and blue skies everywhere you looked. This was to be my summer home for the next four years. How lucky could I get!

Before I left the bishop's office, he told me that he tried to get up there several times during the summer, as if he were putting me on notice that he might stop in at any time. That didn't faze me, since I felt I had just gotten a dream assignment.

The Chief had some concrete information for me. He gave me the names of the winter caretakers, Mary and Joe Murphy. Mary was the full-time postmistress at the small post office in Paradox, New York, where the camp was situated. Her husband, Joe, was the handyman who took care of the maintenance of the camp year round.

Marian Lodge, 1961–64

I hadn't been on Green Island long enough to establish any strong attachments. I had been planning a bus trip with a group of teenagers from the parish to the amusement park at Saratoga Lake, but that never materialized. I felt like the "bad shepherd," leaving my little flock, but I recognized that I had a major job to complete in a short period of time.

I checked in with the pastor, Father Dan Burns, at St. Peter's in Saratoga and had lunch with him and the two assistant pastors, Jerry Tierney and Joe DiMaggio. That's right, Joe DiMaggio. I knew both Joe and Jerry from several years at Brandt Lake. Joe was ordained a year ahead of me and Jerry a year after. I was glad to find out that everyone realized I wouldn't be of much help until we pulled up stakes after the summer camping season.

My first task was to go up to Paradox, New York, to meet with Mary and Joe Murphy. They had been with Father Denine for a number of years. After we exchanged greetings, the first thing Mary told me was that they had not received their check for the last couple of months. I told her I had just received the checkbook and that as soon as I got to the bank to sign the card, I'd get their checks to them.

Joe and Mary must have been in their sixties. In addition to being the postmistress, Mary had a one-pump gas station and serviced the camp vehicles along with her other customers. Joe drove me into the camp in one of our trucks. It was a good mile from the post office. The road wasn't paved, but for a dirt road it wasn't bad and contributed to one's sense of leaving civilization and going into the wilderness. Joe had a very bad limp and wore a colostomy bag, neither of which seemed to slow him down as he showed me around the grounds. He explained that he had had to interrupt his painting in the main lodge to meet me. Father Denine had asked him to have the painting complete by the beginning of the season, and it would be done. Joe wasn't a painter by trade, nor was he an electrician or a plumber; he was just an all around good handyman. I told him I came from a long line of non-handymen, so I was glad to have him to rely on. He seemed relieved because, as I learned later, he and Mary weren't sure if their new "boss" would have his own people, and they would lose a good chunk of their income.

Before I left, I got the address of the farm where the camp's horses were being wintered. It was just outside the town of Ticonderoga, about eight miles from Paradox. The owner of the ranch was Floyd. He reminded me of Gabby Hayes, Roy Rogers's old sidekick, chewing tobacco and all. After introductions he made it clear that Father Dinine had always paid him on time. They didn't have any written agreement, but the flat fee was $700 for wintering the horses. Seemed reasonable to me, but what did I know? He made me think I was getting a bargain when he told me he would only charge fifty cents a bale for hay during the summer.

He took me out in back where the horses were running free in his spacious fields. He informed me that they were just losing their winter coats and were all as healthy as could be. They sure looked healthy to me. He pointed out one horse and told me, "See that horse, that's Suzy, Father Denine's favorite. Make sure those stable boys take good care of her." Stable boys? Where do you get stable boys? Something else I had to put on my "to do list." Floyd and I made arrangements for him to deliver the twenty horses just before camp opened and to include the first shipment of hay. I felt like a real horse trader.

Recruitment

Louise Knight, a longtime friend of Father Denine's and former head of staff at Marian Lodge for many years, got in touch with me not too long after his funeral. She offered to meet with me to help me get oriented to my new job. We met for several hours, and she was a wealth of information. Our meeting was not long after my visit with the Murphy's and Floyd, so at least I had the lay of the land. Louise was never married and was retired from teaching but had a passion for seeing Marian Lodge continue the momentum that she and Father Denine had started. Like a good student, I kept copious notes on every word she spoke. Perhaps the most important thing she suggested was that I get in touch with Bobbie Carr, who had been the head-of-staff for the last several years. Louise had already talked to her and knew that she was interested in returning and would be helpful in contacting former staff. Recruiting staff was at the top of my agenda, and it was a great relief to know where to start. I thanked Louise profusely, and she offered to meet with me any time she could be of help. I thought, *What a great person!* Sadly, there would be no next meeting. Less than a week later, I attended her funeral. She had died of a heart attack. Even though I hardly knew Father Denine and Louise, I was impressed with their commitment to Marian Lodge, and I was very touched by their deaths. I felt that I had a responsibility to move their legacy at Marian Lodge forward.

I met Bobbie Carr and several other former staff members at the reception after Louise's burial and felt confident that I could count on them for support. Bobbie taught in the Troy school system during the school year and had replaced Louise when she retired from Marian Lodge several years ago. She volunteered to help me with the staff recruitment, contact the nurse, and even locate the stable boys. That was a great relief. Despite the tragic events of the last few weeks, I felt less stress knowing I had support from veteran "Marian Lodgers."

I blocked off several afternoons to interview possible counselors from the College of St. Rose in Albany. Bobbie Carr was a great help with the interviews and adding her assessment of the candidates. I thought it was important for her to be involved, since she would have the most contact with the staff and knew far better than I the mix of skills needed for a program for counselors in a girl's camp. Each day we interviewed at least twelve candidates for about a half hour each. We also had other candidates from out of state whom Bobbie interviewed by phone and mail.

The Horse and Pony Show

Armed with a slide show of Marian Lodge pictures that Bobbie and several former counselors put together, plus a routine that would rival a professional PR presentation, off I went on my 1960 diocesan tour to recruit campers from eight to sixteen years of age. I pushed the horseback riding program, synchronized swimming, arts and crafts, fencing, boating, and being part of a lifelong sorority. First I warmed up the audience with some camp songs from my Camp Tekakwitha background and then some funny stories using some routines from my Brandt Lake repertoire and shows from the seminary. There were usually some girls at each school who had been to Marian Lodge, and I played on their loyalty to the camp. My goal was to recruit 160 campers from over fifty grammar schools. I had approximately two months until the first of the four two-week sessions opened in June. Mission accomplished.

In between my gigs promoting the camp, I was able to cajole Rose O'Malley into being our chef. She was a great cook who had been the head chef at Cathedral Academy for years and had attended my ordination as a friend of the family. She and I sat down for an afternoon and ordered all the nonperishable food from the Marinville Brothers that we would need for the summer. Rose reminded me that we would need six "kitchen girls" to help her. I hadn't figured out a detailed budget, but using my eighth-grade arithmetic, I calculated that since the fee for each camper was $60 for each two-week session, if we had 160 campers at $60 each, we'd take in $9600 per session times four sessions, totaling $38,400. I figured we could afford six kitchen girls. Then there were the two stable boys, who would have been willing to work for room and board just to be around the horses and 160 girls. I almost forgot the nurse, who luckily was willing to return for her third year. Things were shaping up.

A Time for Heavy Lifting

Two weeks before camp was scheduled to open, my old friends from CBA, Kenny Tunney and Pete Young, both now seminarians, drove with me in a packed station wagon to help open up the camp from its long winter's rest. The two stable boys, John Bink and Mike McGraft, joined us. John had been a stable boy the year before and was in between jobs, and Mike was a Siena sophomore who wasn't all that familiar with horses but needed a summer job. We did our own cooking or went out for meals. Our schedule was Mass in the morning at 7:00 AM, and, outside of stopping for meals, we often worked up until 10:00 PM. The counselors and the rest of the staff came the next week for their orientation and to make sure the cabins they were assigned to would be clean and ready for the campers. It was nice to have Rose O'Malley for our meals.

It had been a while since I had done any heavy lifting, but contrary to what Muggsy McGraw had told me, heavy lifting was part of my job description. Whether it was getting the canoes and rowboats out of the boathouse, setting up the swimming areas, getting the stables cleaned for the horses, stocking the basement with all the nonperishable food from Marinville Brothers, or checking the septic tanks, I was one of the "boys." After a hard day of trying to hold up my end, I'd hit the mattress at about 10:30 PM and be asleep in five minutes.

The director's "cabin" was a converted two-car garage that I found out I would be sharing with one of Father Dinine's friends from the College of St. Rose, Monsignor John Collins. He had taught at St. Rose's for years and spent his summers at Marian Lodge. He was in his early seventies and just assumed that he would continue as if his old friend Dick were still there. In deference to his age and position, I couldn't tell him to stay home in his parish in

Rensselaer because the quarters were a little tight. I guessed he knew that, so I gracefully welcomed him back for the summer. He arrived with several boxes of books, his fishing gear, and a case of Cutty Sark scotch. He was a kindly man, who seemed content just to be back at camp. He really didn't interfere with my job; he did a little fishing, a little reading, a little drinking, and never missed a meal.

It's Showtime

What a difference two weeks makes. Even though I could hardly get the smell of creosote off me, after painting miles of rails, we met our goal of 160 campers, and the camp was just as spiffy as a convent. The staff was lined up in their Marian Lodge T-shirts ready to assist parents and campers, and I wore my best cassock and welcoming smile. The only complaint we received was from a few parents who thought the parking lot was too far from where they had to drag their kids' luggage, but the complaints were made in good humor, knowing we couldn't do anything about that.

In those days we didn't accept credit cards, mainly because most people didn't own one, so they either paid by check or cash. I already had my plan to take the deposit to the bank in Ticonderoga early Monday morning in our old dump truck, just in case some robbers were planning to ambush our Marian Lodge station wagon. I had John Bink, who looked like he might have been a fullback in the NFL, ride shotgun as a further safeguard.

Once the parents had said their tearful good-byes and left their offspring in our care, we had the first of Rose O'Malley's great meals, a pep talk by me, and a few rounds of two of their favorite camp songs, "If You're Happy and You Know It, Clap Your Hands" and the camp song, "The Blue and White of Marian Lodge." We then went to the chapel for Benediction. I must admit I was moved, at the end of Benediction, when everyone sang the hymn "Holy God We Praise Thy Name." It was the beginning of an unforgettable eight weeks.

Rise and Shine!

At seven the next morning the huge bell in front of the main lodge summoned us all to Mass. Cabin by cabin, from the youngest campers on up, they made their way to the chapel, under the watchful eye of their counselors. At the time, all priests said Mass with their backs to the faithful. Even from that disadvantaged view of the campers I suspected that some of them were not all awake. But they were at least present.

After Mass we all made our way to the dining hall for breakfast. There was a head table that the administrative staff and I occupied. After I said grace, there was no doubt that the campers were awake and ready for fun. No sooner than they had all said "Amen" at the end of grace, someone started another of their favorite camp songs, "My name is John Johnson, I come from Wisconsin. I work in the lumber yard there, Yah, Yah!" And so on and so on! The singing went on until breakfast was served. Bobbie Carr turned to me and asked, "Do you think you can get used to this? It's a daily routine!" I assumed it was a rhetorical question but even so, I responded, "Pass the coffee, please!"Actually, I really enjoyed the energy that the campers showed, plus I loved to sing.

After breakfast and time to tidy up their cabins, the campers joined their assigned groups for the day's programs. I was amazed how smoothly five or six different activities could be going on at one time and all well supervised. There was volleyball competition for the senior campers; a beginners swimming class in the cove; practice for synchronized swimming at another roped-off area; a group going off for arts and crafts; and eighteen campers every hour heading for the stables for English riding lessons. Each of the riding groups had been divided according to the information they had provided about their riding experience. At the end of each month, we had a horse show with competition according to age and skill level. The only thing I had to do was pass out the ribbons for each competition.

The Bishop's First Visit

I received a call from the Chief that the bishop planned to visit that day. I thanked him for the heads-up and told him we were having a horse show today. They arrived in time for lunch in a brand-new Buick that the Chief chauffeured. They enjoyed both the lunch and the lively singing. I gave the bishop my job of awarding the blue, red, and white ribbons. It was almost as though we had planned the day to impress him, but it was just another day at Marian Lodge.

Before he left, he pulled me aside and told me that Father Donnelly was doing fairly well and wouldn't need relief from his Catholic Charities job at this point, so we could hold off Fordham for another year. He would like me to go back to St. Peter's in Saratoga Springs after camp was over and, for the fall semester, teach some religious classes in the high school and in the spring start preparing for Marian Lodge. It was more of a suggestion than an order but it didn't seem I had much of a choice. Luckily, I was very happy to go back to St. Peter's and teach, along with the parish work, for the fall semester.

While he was there I showed the bishop the converted garage that Monsignor Collins and I shared. He was obviously surprised at the living conditions and told me we had to talk about what possibilities we had to build a better living quarters for the director. I told him I had been thinking about several buildings and how we could finance them. He seemed pleased that I was taking the initiative and asked Monsignor Hart to make a note for us to discuss this the next time he came up.

Evening Programs and Special Events

Not only were the days packed full of activities, but every night we had a different program. They ranged from campfires to movies to religious pageants; and there were armature nights, where different cabins presented skits, and individuals showed off their singing, dancing, and even stand-up comedy routines. All of this required preparation, and there was time set aside during the day for practice. It was always very competitive between cabins, and there were always awards for the winners. Yes, "Marian Lodge has talent!"

Then there were special events days. The one I enjoyed the most was "Carnival Day." I never ceased to be impressed with the creativeness and spirit of cooperation the campers and counselors put into this event. Each cabin would have a booth, usually with a barker to attract "customers" to games of skill and chances to win prizes.

The final campfire was always a tearjerker. After telling some spooky stories and recalling fond memories of the last two weeks together, we could always count on the "Campfire Song" to put everyone in the mood to come back the next summer. It was more powerful than "Auld Lang Syne."

The Campfire Song
Each campfire brings a new-a-new,
The flames of friendships true-a-who,
The joys we had in knowing you,
Will last the whole year through-a-who!
And as the embers glow away,
We wish that we could ever stay,
But we all know that we can't stay.
We'll come again another day.

Hugs and tears were contagious, from the most sophisticated teenagers to the smallest eight-year-olds. Promises to write and to be at the Christmas reunion at the College of St. Rose in December were exchanged between tears and sobs. How could they not come back next summer?

The Edifice Complex

I learned in psychology that Freud developed a concept that he called the Oedipus complex. His theory was related to the relationship between a son and mother. I have a new one: the

Edifice complex, related to someone who has an obsessive need to construct buildings. I think I had a touch of it.

Before I mentioned anything to the bishop about building plans, I had several meetings with the owner of Young Brothers, the local lumber company, about some possibilities of logging during the winter months for enough lumber for three buildings—a cabin for the director; a cabin for the nurse and the infirmary, and a cabin to house thirty campers and three counselors with a fireplace and a room for play on rainy days; plus his cost for doing the actual building. A major stipulation was that the logging had to be done on the farthest point of the 800 acres, where it would not be visible from the camp grounds and that the cost of reforestation by planting seedlings would be the responsibility of Young Brothers. That seemed like a good deal: the logging would pay for the three buildings, and the environment would not be marred by ugly bald spots in the forests.

I even became an amateur architect by providing a rough design for the three buildings. The director's cabin would have a small kitchen, a living room with a fireplace, two bedrooms, a bathroom, and, most important, a screened-in porch that looked out on beautiful Pyramid Lake. The infirmary would have living quarters for the nurse, an examination room, and two rooms that would accommodate six campers if the nurse needed to keep an eye on them. With some input from the counselors, the campers' cabin would be for the younger campers and would have built-in double-decker bunks beds and two separate rooms for counselors, plus a playroom. The bishop's lawyers looked over the preliminary agreement and put it in lawyer language, and we were all set. The logging would begin when the snow lay on the ground, and the construction would begin as soon as the snow had melted.

Closing Camp for the Winter

I knew the bishop was pleased with my plans and negotiations with the Young Brothers and the way I had managed the camp that summer. He responded very much like my father. Neither of them gave much acknowledgment for my accomplishments. I would usually find out from my father's friends how proud he was of any of my achievements. Like, "Your father was sure proud of your getting your degree cum laude; you'd think he earned it himself." The bishop visited the camp several more times that summer, but when we'd talk about the construction, it was as if he and his lawyers had had the idea to put the deal together. If it wasn't for the Chief, I wouldn't have had any idea that the bishop had told Father Burns in Saratoga, "Keep your eyes on that boy; he's a shaker and a mover."

One thing I never told the bishop, and I planned to put in the annual financial report under "miscellaneous" was a bill for having the septic tanks cleaned. A couple of fly-by-night septic tank cleaners had stopped by the camp, and gave me an estimate for cleaning all the septic tanks. There was one huge tank near the main lodge and eight others throughout the camp. The tank near the main lodge measured eight feet deep, four feet wide, and six feet in length, and it hadn't been emptied in several years. They had given me an estimate of a cent and a half per pound for the waste. Well, that seemed reasonable to me. I had no idea of how many pounds of waste had accumulated over the years. When they brought me the bill of over $4,000, I almost had a stroke. I had no idea of how I could challenge the bill. All I knew was it was a lot of crap! I bargained them down $500, but that was the best I could do. If the bishop ever called me on the $3500 for the miscellaneous item, I didn't know if he would still have thought I was a "shaker and mover."

Closing the camp wasn't as bad as opening it. We had the same crew as we did for the opening, but they were anxious to get back to the city, so they worked a little harder and faster. It only took a week for us to put things back as we found them. On our "to do list" was to get the horses back to Ticonderoga, turn the water off for the winter, put the boats and canoes back in the boathouse, make sure all the cabins and the chapel were secure, and close the stables. I drove Mike and John back in the camp station wagon, and we sang most of the way back. It was going to take a while to get the camp out of our individual systems.

All things considered, I think we had a great first season. I certainly learned a lot. For an unhandy guy, I could unplug a toilet with the best of them. I was pleased with my administrative and leadership skills, which I never knew I had. Seeing that 200 people were fed three times a day, entertained, and kept safe—I definitely had not learned that in the seminary. But most important, I had a great time. It made up for all those summers on Judson Street when my parents couldn't afford to send me to camp.

Reflections

My office was in the Main Lodge; it had a large porch overlooking the lake. This was the same building where the dining room, kitchen, and large "family room" were. There were several classic Adirondack chairs on the porch that, except for all the traffic going by, would have been a perfect place to sit and meditate. Nevertheless, I would often sit out there to relax. Frequently, one or more of the counselors would join me just to chat. As the summer went on, I became more and more comfortable talking with staff about topics ranging from politics to religion, as well as everyday problems they might be having with their boyfriends or parents. As you might recall from the last chapter, it was only the previous summer at Fordham that I had begun to deal with my delayed development in interacting normally with women. I began to realize that after all those years of being isolated from natural interpersonal interactions with women, I found that I enjoyed their company and that I felt guilty for this simple and natural enjoyment. Hard to believe? Well, looking back, it's hard for me to believe that I was so indoctrinated that even mentioning my reactions in writing reactivated those old feelings of guilt.

There were several women whose company I enjoyed more than others. One was Lauri. She was a veteran of many years at

Marian Lodge and was part of the administrative staff. She had graduated from the College of St. Rose and was in her last year at Albany Law School. In addition to enjoying her company, I was physically attracted to her. She had short, blonde hair, sparkling blue eyes, a great smile, a quick wit, and a challenging mind, not to mention a shapely body. Did I just refer to her body? I don't think I could have done that back in 1960. This was the type of behavior that led to impure thoughts; and impure thoughts lead to impure actions. Giving in to impure thoughts could give you a ticket straight to hell, without passing Go and collecting $200. At least that's what I was taught and what I had accepted.

Lauri was a young, intelligent, and well-educated Catholic woman. In one of our conversations, Pope John XXIII's name came up and, like many Catholics I knew, she thought he was a refreshing change from his predecessor of happy memory, the aristocratic Pius XII, who had reigned for nineteen years on the throne of Peter. At first I was surprised that Lauri knew that in January 1959 Pope John XXIII had announced his intention to convene an Ecumenical Council in 1962 and that there were commissions already preparing documents for the Council to consider. She and a small group of her "sisters" had a discussion group, and they anxiously awaited Vatican Council II. It had been one of their recent and ongoing topics. Her first question to me was, "I wonder how many women will be in attendance at the Vatican Council?" All I could say was, "Good question!" Judging from the enthusiasm with which she expressed her question, I already had a good idea of some of the topics in which she would be most interested.

Even as I was looking forward to the next time I would have a chance to talk more with Lauri, I found myself reviewing what I had learned in preparing for my First Holy Communion— especially the final line in the Act of Contrition, which reads, "I firmly resolve, with the help of Thy grace, to sin no more, and to avoid the near occasion of sin." I asked myself whether the attraction I felt for Lauri was an "occasion of sin." If it was, did I have to avoid all contact with her? Or did I first have to see if I actually acted out those "impure thoughts" that were going through my mind about becoming intimate with her before she could be officially declared an "occasion of sin"? I wondered what she would think if she knew I was even considering her to be an occasion of sin. In Alcoholics Anonymous, I know they would call that "stinkin thinkin"! We had learned as children that an occasion of sin was, "Any person, place, or thing that of its nature or because of human frailty can lead one to do wrong, thereby committing sin." I probably got full credit on my exam for parroting that back in my blue book. But I was having a difficult enough time at age thirty-one getting my mind around this concept.

I don't mean for this to be a catechism lesson, but for those of you who didn't have the nuns in Catholic grammar school, or even if you did, think of it as a refresher course. The catechism made it even more complicated by identifying two types of "occasions of sin": remote and proximate (near). It's remote if the danger it poses is very slight. It's proximate if the danger is "certain or probable." Someone once told me that the best way to think of a near occasion of sin is to treat it as the moral equivalent of a physical danger. Just as we know we should stay alert when we're walking through a bad part of town at night, we need to be aware of the moral threats around us. We need to be honest about our own weaknesses and actively avoid situations in which we're likely to give in to them. I still didn't think of Lauri as a moral threat just because I felt attracted to her. I had no idea of whether or not I was likely to give in to my fear of becoming physically involved with her, since I'd never been in that situation before, so for the time being I made the judgment that it was just a remote occasion of sin, unless I found out otherwise. Even back then, I didn't think life should be so legalistically complicated. We shall see what we shall see.

I had a new appreciation for penitents who came to me in confessional with similar dilemmas and wanted me to make their decision for them. Perhaps I had been too quick in giving them my opinion, when it would have been more appropriate for me to remind them to follow their conscience. Was I the decider or were they? Even though I could intellectually accept the primacy of conscience, it would take some years before I could emotionally accept it. I still had to deal with the guilt from my shame-based background that was so deeply instilled in me. I looked at this as another point in my transformation from having prescribed beliefs as a child to a more responsible adult faith. I don't think Jesus ever intended our just being human to be an occasion of sin.

There were many other enjoyable interactions with Lauri and other women throughout the summer. It wasn't that I didn't struggle with my conscience. Was I giving in to the occasion of sin by having impure thoughts or was this just a normal physical reaction to a woman I was very attracted to? I always had recourse to confession. Every week I drove into Schroon Lake about six miles from the camp to confess my sins to the old pastor in the village. I had the impression that he thought I was verging on being scrupulous. I would say, "Bless me father for I have sinned …" and proceed to tell him my list of sins. "I'm not sure if I broke my vow of celibacy by having impure thoughts about a woman that I work with."

"Well, if you're not sure it's a sin, you don't have to confess it. Is there anything else?" I thought if he just flipped it off like that, then it couldn't have been a sin. I knew that I needed to get beyond leaving it up to authority to determine whether or not I had sinned, and I had a long way to go before I could rely on my own conscience, but for now, I was where I was. I never saw Lauri after camp closed that summer. I continued to fantasize about what could have been, but I left Marian Lodge that August realizing that I had a lot more work to do on my sexuality if I were to remain a celibate priest.

Grandpa and Grandma Fausel

Grandma McCarroll

Grandpa McCarroll

Family of three

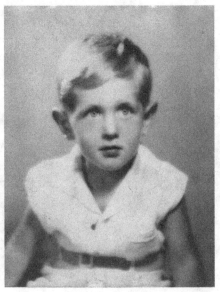

Donald 1932

Kindergarten class 1934

Donald with baby Jim

Donald the Altar Boy

Jim's first communion, Don's confirmation with Uncle John

Christian Brothers Academy Cadet Fausel 1947

Dad's induction Into Army 1943
Behind Mayor Erastus Corning II

St. Thomas Seminary Basketball team 1951 (Don is #3)

St. Thomas Seminary, Seminarians 1950.
I'm holding the basketball

Vaudeville Team Fausel & Braselle St Mary's Seminar 1955

First Mass, St. Catherine's Church, June 1957

Father Fausel and family

Staff, Marian Lodge Camp for Girls, 1962

Dad's 75th birthday, 1983

Wedding Day January 1, 1995

Don's 70th birthday, November 1989

Jim & Don at 70th birthday

The Emperor and Empress on sabbatical, China, 1996

Chapter 8
The Turbulent 1960s

B efore looking at the 1960s, it would be helpful to remember the eight years under President Eisenhower. We all liked Ike; even if we were Democrats, we still liked Ike. Eisenhower's presidency occurred during a relatively benign time in our country's history. Some viewed him as a "do nothing" president, others as a kindly grandfather who liked to play golf. Neither of these perceptions was entirely correct except for his loving to play golf, but his campaign slogan, "I like Ike," still prevailed. But as the poet, prophet, and songwriter Bob Dylan reminded us, "The Times They Are A-Changin"! I believe that John F. Kennedy made it clear in his inaugural address in 1961 when he said:

> Let the word go forth from this time and place, to friend and foe alike, that the torch has been passed to a new generation of Americans—born in this century tempered by war, disciplined by a hard and bitter peace, proud of our ancient heritage—and unwilling to witness or permit the slow undoing of those human rights to which this nation has always been committed ... [1]

I suspect that President Kennedy did not imagine just how his clarion call would need to be applied to our enemies within as well as those countries that were not our friends and wished us harm.

What I intend to do in this chapter, is to recall with you my memories of some of those major events that took place during the sixties; what I was doing at the time; how it affected me as I was struggling with my own issues with the church; and how the 1960s continue to affect us today. I don't intend this to be a sociological treatise—just one man's viewpoint.

I will try to follow a chronological time frame, but many of the major events, like the Vietnam War, lasted through and beyond the sixties, while the assassination of President John F. Kennedy happened on a specific day, though the effects of his death lasted for decades.

Back to St. Peter's in Saratoga

My first day back at St. Peter's, Father Burns gave me two assignments. One was to teach three religion classes a day at the parish high school. The three classes required three different preparations since they included sophomores, juniors, and seniors. That was more than I bargained for, but it was just for the fall semester. The other was to be chaplain of the Newman Club at Skidmore College. Skidmore was a small, women's liberal arts college with only 2,400 students. It wasn't part of the elite "Seven Sisters" colleges, which was to women's colleges what the Ivy League was to men's colleges, but I think it thought it was equal. It was very expensive and at that time restrictive in its admissions procedures. It helped your chances of being accepted if your mother and grandmother were alumnae. I thought it was ironic that I should be chaplain at an all women's college when I was also director of an all girl's camp. It was like a conspiracy to test my resolve to be celibate.

Newman Clubs are located at most major non-Catholic colleges and universities, and they are designed to bolster the faith of Catholic students, in lieu of the Catholic atmosphere at Catholic colleges. The Newman Club at Skidmore wasn't very large, since there were relatively few Catholic students. The larger clubs had a full-time chaplain and often had their own chapel and offices and very active student bodies. We had a meeting once a month on campus to discuss a current religious topic of interest, and students could make appointments with me at St. Peter's. We did participate in several state meetings and one national meeting in New York City. There were several thousand students at that meeting, and it generated a spark of interest in the six students I drove to New York City in the Marian Lodge station wagon. There were several special meetings for chaplains, where some of the more experienced chaplains shared what they found helpful in attracting more students to their meetings. I found these meetings very helpful.

A Skidmore student who had been attending our meetings called the rectory to make an appointment to talk to me about breaking up with her boyfriend. Her name was Anna, an attractive, blonde young student, who I thought was quite flirtatious. She'd often stay after the meetings to ask questions. Once she suggested we have a cup of coffee so we could talk more. I said, "No, perhaps another time." As soon as I said it, I thought it was a mistake.

When the time came for her appointment, I was dressed very professionally in my cassock. I opened the door to the room where she was waiting and she looked like one of my fantasies. She wore a tight cashmere sweater with a short skirt and high socks and was sitting in a provocative way on a couch for couples. I immediately took my seat behind the desk to make sure she got the message, "This is a business meeting." Before she could say anything, I said, "How can I help you, Anna?"—hoping this would set the tone for our meeting. Our conversation went something like this: "I have this stupid, idiot boyfriend that I'm trying to get rid of. All he wants is sex; he hasn't got a brain in his head. After listening and talking to you after our meetings, I keep thinking, *This is the kind of man I want. He treats me like an adult.* I enjoy talking to you."

Oh, oh! I wasn't prepared for this. My male ego liked what I was hearing, but my conscience was overwhelmed with guilt for perhaps having given her a double message, the "maybe another time!"

I did my best to reassure her that she had a lot going for her and that I was impressed with how she was handling her breakup with her boyfriend. After listening more about her problems with her boyfriend, I offered to refer her to a therapist who could help her get over this bump in the road. I made it clear that I was not the one who could help her. She seemed to accept her need for counseling, and seemed to understand the boundaries of my role as chaplain of the Newman Club. I had the impression that she might be confusing my interest in her as a romantic interest. It was a good lesson for me and, I hope, for Anna.

Besides teaching and working with the Newman Club, and the regular parish work at St. Peter's. I found that I had a gift for visiting the sick at home or in the hospital. I think I got more out of those visits than they did. I admired the strength and faith they had, even in the worst of situations. I remember one young boy, Joey, who had leukemia. He always brightened up my day when I visited with him. I first met him at the Albany Medical Center, where he was being treated for acute lymphoblastic leukemia (ALL). He was eleven years old. The first time I walked into his room he gave me a big, "Hi, Father, how'd you know I was here?"

"I have secret spies at all the hospitals, and when one of our parishioners checks in, they let me know."

"Are they angels?"

"I can't let you know that; otherwise it wouldn't be a secret."

"Hey, how you like my haircut?" pointing to his bald head, which brought out the color of his beautiful blue eyes.

"On you it looks good!"

"I want to be an altar boy when I get better and have hair again."

"I think I can help you with that. You know you'll have to learn Latin."

"Can you help me with that?"

"You bet! Only if you do what the doctors and nurses tell you to do. Next time I'll bring you a book with everything you'll need to know."

"Great!"

"Would you like me to bring you communion next time I come?

"Sure! I made my first communion."

"I knew that!"

"How'd you know that?" He looked at me as if he already knew the answer.

"It's just another one of my secrets!"

"Yeah, I know, if you tell me it wouldn't be a secret."

For the first few visits we didn't directly talk about his cancer—we worked on his Latin lessons, and I would share letters from his classmates. He always seemed surprised that they remembered him. I knew he had other people to talk with about his fears and sadness that he wasn't back in school, so, unless he brought some of his feelings up, I didn't. I had a sense that he would be comfortable talking to me. My job was to make our visits just as normal as possible.

Joey learned his Latin in record time. I gave him a certificate that he was officially an altar boy. He proudly showed it to all the nurses

Some of you might remember how difficult it was to learn the original Latin response to the priest's prayers. If not, let me give you a small example.

Priest: *Introibo ad altare Dei.* (I will go to the Altar of God.)
Server: At that time the server, symbolically representing the people, responded, *Ad Deum qui laetificat juventutem meam.* (To God who gives joy to my youth.)

Every time we practiced that response, I would have to hold back tears—it wasn't clear to me how God was giving joy to Joey's youth. But Joey seemed to have his own secret resources. I could see his satisfaction as he mastered each Latin phrase and became a certified altar boy.

During the time Joey was a patient in the hospital I also became close to his family and became part of their support system. He had a younger brother, Bobby, who was feeling a little jealous because of all the attention Joey was receiving and felt guilty about feeling that way. I think it was helpful for me just to normalize his feelings and give him a little extra attention. I didn't have any pat answers for his parents' question of "Why Joey?" I just tried to patiently listen and recognize that it was a question that had been asked for generations, without a satisfactory answer. I often felt impotent when I was in those situations and figured my best response was to be honest. If I had an answer besides trite, knee-jerk reactions, I certainly would have shared it with them and the rest of the world.

When Joey came home after being discharged, with his oncologist prescribing no more treatments for the time being, the family invited me for dinner. I felt like part of their family in a very special way, and for the first time I felt I was experiencing the "joy of Joey's youth" as well as the joy that his family was feeling.

After several months at home, when Joey was strong enough, he served Mass for me at St. Peter's. As I'm writing this, I'm waiting for my car to be serviced at the dealership. Sitting in the lounge, I'm feeling that same joy that I felt with Joey and his family just by remembering their happiness as they saw Joey kneeling at the altar dressed in a cassock and surplice, responding in Latin to my prayers and not missing a phrase. We were all just as proud as punch, as my mother used to say, but Joey was the proudest of all.

I kept in touch with the family for a couple of years after I moved to Arizona. After a while our main connection was Christmas cards, and gradually we lost touch. I regret that. Wow! Joey would be fifty-seven now!

The Birth Control Pill and the Sexual Revolution

It was in May of 1960 when I read in the news that the Food and Drug Administration had approved a new birth control pill. It would eventually be known as "the Pill." It was reported on page seventy-eight of the *New York Times,* so initially it didn't attract much attention. But before long, the pill would be credited and blamed for the sexual revolution and the change in sexual morals. Although not all scholars or journalists agreed that the pill had that much impact on the cultural change that had started decades before when Alfred Kinsey published his 1948 book, *Sexuality and the Human Male.* Kinsey explicitly stated "that premarital sex among women, the yardstick used to define existence of a sexual revolution, was rising in the 1940s and had remained flat since the 1920s."[2] U.S. Census Bureau statistics on "premarital pregnancy and vital statistics on single motherhood between 1940 and 1960 point to the unexpected conclusion that there was more sexual activity during those decades than Americans were willing to admit."[3]

Whether or not the pill was responsible for the sexual revolution doesn't minimize its importance. It made artificial contraception easier and more available to millions of women. As many women believed, it helped to even the playing field. Clare Boothe Luce, former congresswoman, playwright, editor, and ambassador to Italy, remarked when asked to make a statement about the pill's potential for women's rights, "The modern women is at last free as a man is free, to dispose of her body, to earn her living, to pursue improvement of her mind, and to try a successful career."[4]

Forty-five years later, 2005, "more people had taken the pill than any other prescribed medicine in the world."[5] In the 1960s, "it was welcomed by a generation mired in social upheaval, from civil rights battles and the Vietnam War."[6] I didn't realize this, but when the pill was introduced in 1960, pharmacists were only allowed to prescribe it to married women. Maybe I shouldn't have been surprised because at that time single women weren't eligible for credit cards, and birth control was a crime in Connecticut.[7]

In my conversations with parishioners at St. Peter's, it was obvious that they hoped the commission that John XXIII had appointed to review the church's position on artificial forms of birth control would at least modify the current teaching of the church. Many of them were struggling with raising the children they had and thought they should have the right to decide about what was appropriate for their family. They believed that they, not someone in Rome, who knew nothing about their situation, should be responsible for making decisions about how many children they could cope with. Most of the people I spoke to were college graduates, and were not as compliant in accepting Rome's position as their parents might have been. They were familiar with the positions that many reputable theologians took on the need for change and to "bring the church into the twentieth century." When Pope John XXIII died and Pope Paul VI chose to restructure the commission, there was a small flicker of hope for change. There was more hope that the Vatican Council II, which would include all the bishops, would have a better chance to open the windows and doors of the church to let fresh air in, as Pope John XXIII had envisioned. I will devote much of the next chapter to assessing the dynamics of the Pope's Commission on Birth Control and Pope Paul VI's response in his encyclical *Humanis Vitae.*

From Marian Lodge to Fordham University

My second summer at Marion Lodge was much more comfortable, with the new cabin for the director, I had more privacy on my screened-in porch and in my private bedroom. We used the converted garage for a storage room. Monsignor Collins was back with his case of scotch, books, and fishing pole. He commandeered "his space" next to the fireplace in a comfortable chair where he could read and sip scotch. He seemed to be very content. The new cabin for the younger campers and the nurse's office and infirmary were all stained and ready for the beginning of the season.

Many of the same counselors were back this year, and that made it easier for everyone. One of the new counselors, Miss Sue B. (the campers called all the counselors Miss and their first name), was a Skidmore student who was very adept at horsemanship and became the head of our riding program. She was a delight, with large, dark brown eyes and a smile that made her that much more attractive. She decided she wanted to transfer from Skidmore to Marymount College in Tarrytown, New York, so she would be in a Catholic environment. She also asked me to prepare her to be baptized a Catholic. I gave her instruction and baptized her, and a few years later I was the celebrant at her marriage.

Over the past forty plus years, we've kept our long-distance relationship intact, with the exceptions of some gaps when we lost touch. Most recently she called to wish me a happy birthday. I've always been happy to receive her calls, but I was particularly touched that she remembered my eightieth birthday. It's like a voice from the past that is always with you. Her call prompted me to check out a book she coauthored, *Straight Talk about Breast Cancer*. I Googled her and discovered that her book had received five stars from reviewers. That's the highest rating a book can receive. Somehow, I wasn't surprised. As a very compassionate and spiritual person, plus being a dermatologist and a cancer survivor, she had all the qualities and credentials to write a book that would be helpful to women facing the emotional, physical, and spiritual shock of being diagnosed with breast cancer. Bless you, Dr. Sue B.

Another of the new staff was our first African-American counselor, Miss Jackie, who was from New York City. She had a very engaging personality and fit right into the program. Also, Miss Cricket joined us from the University of New York at Albany. The campers called her Cricket because she looked just like a television character in a popular TV show. Cricket had the potential to be a star. She was petite, with long, brown hair, parted in the middle, which was a very popular style at the time. She looked like a "flower child" that you might see in Berkeley or Woodstock. She was typical of a model sixties girl. She Googled me a few years ago; she was living in New York City, was a successful author of plays, and was happily married. I was happy to hear from her and to know she was doing so well.

Cricket had been recruited by Miss Maureen, a College of St. Rose student, or Rosebud, as they were called, who had been at camp the previous year. In addition to being a very attractive Irish Coleen, she had the best sense of humor of any of the staff. She also recruited Miss Janie, a native of Troy, who was attending college at Marquette University and was a high school friend of Miss Maureen. They were all favorites of the campers and I must say of mine.

Miss Cricket started taking lessons to be baptized. I would meet with her in my office for an hour every day and go over the catechism with her. She was bright and not only asked good questions, but had learned to think critically. We planned a baptism ceremony for the fall when, we hoped, many of the counselors could attend.

In the middle of the summer, I received a letter from the bishop confirming my appointment to study social work at Fordham and advising me that I would have to take a day off to go to Fordham for a personal interview within the next two weeks. So, off I went in the camp station wagon to New York City. At that time the Fordham Graduate School of Social Work was housed in an elegant brownstone on Thirty-Eighth Street in the middle of Manhattan.

My first problem in "the city" was finding a place to park. I drove around and around the block, my frustration building with each turn. Finally, someone pulled out just as I passed his spot. At last, I was about to back into the vacant spot when, much to my chagrin, some New Yorker pulled into "my space." I was furious, but what could I do? I had my Roman collar on, which usually is a plus for getting a parking space, but apparently not in New York City. Another fifteen minutes, and I finally got a parking place. It was a couple of blocks from the school, and I was getting concerned that I was going to be late for my appointment. And Fausels are never late! To make matters worse, it was a hot, muggy day in New York City, and I was sweating bullets to get there on time.

I finally made it to the office of the interviewer, Ms. Social Worker, and had to wait for twenty minutes before I was escorted into her office. There she was, sitting behind her desk, the stereotype of a social worker in the 1960s. Her hair was tied in a bun at the back of her head; she was dressed prim and proper in a social worker–type dress. Rather than apologizing for keeping me waiting or introducing herself, she looked at me intensely, and the first words out of her mouth were, "How do you deal with anger?" That took me off balance, which I suspected was her intention. I hemmed and hawed until I came out with the brilliant answer, "I guess I don't handle it very well."

She looked at me a little less intensely and responded, "That's a pretty good answer. It seems very honest, but it doesn't tell me how you handle your anger."

I then went into my parking story. She listened attentively and threw in a few questions or comments: "Sounds like you were really mad. But when you walked in here you seemed calm. How did you calm yourself down?"

"I'm not sure. I think I used a technique I learned in a class I took at Catholic University a couple of summers ago. It's "self-talk." I told myself, *Not everyone is always going to be considerate. Most people are.* That seems to calm me down when I run across impolite people."

She switched gears and threw me off balance again. "Are you angry at me because of the type of questions I'm asking you?"

I thought for a few seconds and tentatively replied, "I suppose I am!"

"Suppose?"

"No, I know I am!"

"Because?"

I was getting irritated with this woman, and I responded, "First of all, I don't see the purpose of the questions you're asking. I thought I came here to find out more about the program and how I might get credit for courses I've already had. Also, I'm not sure how appropriate these questions are. I feel like I'm being interrogated or in a therapy session. And it's beginning to annoy me." I felt relieved just getting that off my chest.

"Well, that was an honest response. Actually, one of my purposes in asking this type of question is just to see how you actually handle anger. We could talk about anger all day, but that would be on a cognitive level. If you're going to be working with clients in the real world, a lot of them will be hostile, and you'll need to work with them in a professional way even if they piss you off. By the way, do you think because you're a priest and this is a Catholic school, we'll treat you any differently?"

"That hadn't even entered my mind. I don't expect to be treated differently than any of my classmates." That must have satisfied her, and she began to ask the type of questions that I expected—questions about my background and experience in the field of social work as a nonprofessional. And she gave me an opportunity to ask questions about the curriculum. I was particularly interested in the types of internships that would be available. The interview ended on a friendly note. I must have done okay because in a couple of weeks I received a letter of acceptance. That was forty-eight years ago, and I have never forgotten that interview, which could have changed the course of the rest of my life.

Back to Marian Lodge

It wasn't until I got to the Tappan Zee Bridge, which connects Nyack, New York, and Tarrytown in Westchester County, that I said to myself, *Self, stop all this awfulizing and beating yourself up about the interview.* I was laying so many "I should haves" on myself that I almost convinced myself that they'd never accept me. I finally realized that there was nothing I could do about it now, so I gave myself instructions to *chill out,* as we used to say. It worked for a while and then I'd find myself thinking that, if I wasn't accepted at Fordham, it probably meant I wouldn't become director of Catholic Charities in Schenectady, and I'd spend my next ten years in a little parish in North Creek, New York. There I was catastrophizing again! Then I thought, *That wouldn't be so bad.* I liked all those little towns in the Adirondacks—Chestertown,

Warrensburg, Lake George Village, Bolton Landing. As a matter of fact, the more I thought about it, the more I liked it. I told myself, *Enough already, you're "shoulding" all over yourself!* I guess I did learn something from Alfred Ellis!

It was about halfway through the camping season when I got back from my interview. I hadn't been obsessing about it that much, perhaps because time had been occupied with the camp. Or maybe my self-talk worked. When I received the letter of acceptance from Fordham, I was happy but not overjoyed. I didn't want to lose face, but in the words of Doris Day, I had convinced myself *Que Sera Sera*!

St. Patrick's Home for the Aged

The diocese had made arrangements for me to live at St. Patrick's Home for the Aged in the Van Cortland Park section of the Bronx. St. Patrick's was run by the Carmelite Sisters. In addition to the chaplain's room, they had two extra rooms, which were available for any priest from Albany doing graduate work in New York City. Their Mother House was in Germantown, New York, which was in the Albany Diocese, which might have accounted for their generosity.

I found out that an old friend, Father John Gavin Nolan, was working on his PhD in history at Fordham and that he would be occupying one of the rooms and I the other. I packed a couple of bags and was on my way for a new experience. Since Albany was only a two-hour drive to the Bronx on the New York Thruway, and I would be going back to help out at different parishes on most weekends, I didn't need to bring too many of my possessions.

I remember being shown by one of the nuns to my room and introduced to the chaplain, a semiretired New York priest, Monsignor James Reardon, whose room was right next to mine. As my McCarroll relatives might say, "He was as Irish as Patty's Pig." I told him I was from Albany and was a friend of John Nolan. He looked me over and with a twinkle in his eyes said,

"Oh, another one of those 'apple knockers' from upstate." This is the gist of a conversation that I've never forgotten.

I responded in kind, "That's me—an apple knocker from upstate who's here to get me an education."

"You're not from that hick town that Nolan's from—ah, ah, Macdonaldville?"

"No, he's from Mechanicville; I'm from Albany."

"Oh, a big-city boy!"

"Well, Albany is the capital of the state. Listen, has Father Nolan been around yet?"

"Oh no, he's at the six-day bicycle race at Madison Square Garden in 'the city.' He goes every year."

"Really, do you know when he'll be back?"

"No, he stays there for the whole six days. He packs some sandwiches and cookies. He loves it."

I stood there with my mouth open. I couldn't imagine anyone being such a fan, but apparently Nolan was. After all, a monsignor told me so! To my embarrassment, I found out the next morning that he was giving the new boy a line that in fishing lingo would be, "I fell for it hook, line, and sinker." He and Nolan had a good laugh at my expense. I guess I *was* an upstate apple knocker.

Graduate School of Social Service

When I entered Fordham in 1961, there were over one hundred accredited graduate schools of social work in the United States. Fordham ranked in the top twenty. Even though Fordham is a Catholic university, run by the Jesuits, there was only one Jesuit priest on the faculty in the social work program, and he taught a course in ethics.

The orientation and registration went well. Since I had some graduate credits, they waived nine credit hours, and I was able to sign up for more administrative courses. I had a chance to meet some of my future classmates. There was a good mix of midcareer students and younger students fresh out of their bachelor's programs. I couldn't help but notice that most of the women were not the typical social worker type that I mentioned before. No social work shoes or prim dresses; they were dressed more in the sixties styles.

There was another Catholic priest in my class, Patrick Carney from the Archdiocese of New York. He was ordained the same year that I was. My initial impression was that he was rather stiff—not a hair out of place, cuff links in his starched shirt, and a suit that probably came from Brooks Brothers. It didn't take me long to change my mind. The old adage, "You can't tell a book by its Brooks Brothers suit, I mean by its cover," was right again.

We also found out about our first year internship. I would be with a unit of five other students in the Queens Welfare Center 53 in Long Island City, New York, just across from Manhattan on the 59th Street Bridge. Patrick Carney was one of the other students, along with Peter, an energetic young man just out of college. I saw him some years later at a conference, and he had spent his career in the army mental health corps, rising to the rank of full colonel. He was ready to retire from the service and intended to teach at some university. Patricia was a buxom, brunette young woman from Manhattan who had several years of social work practice after college and was a step ahead of Patrick and me. Sophia was a veteran of many years of working in the field. She had emigrated from Yugoslavia and had spent most of her career in the states. George was from New Jersey and was relatively new to the field. He later went on to become a dean, at Rutgers' school of social work, I believe.

Our practice supervisor was an employee of the Welfare Department for decades. We all called her Mrs. M. The agency gave her time to work with the students because training master's students is part of the responsibility that every social service agency has to the profession. We were fortunate to have Mrs. M. She was an experienced, capable, impartial, and insightful judge of potential social workers. I suspect she was approaching retirement age, but she never lost her enthusiasm for her work or her passion for helping to mold each student in a very unobtrusive way. She was an excellent role model. She not only "talked the talk but walked the walk" as they say in the twelve-step programs.

Each of us had a desk in a huge room that used to be a warehouse. To give you an idea of how large the room was, there were 406 desks crowded three feet from one another. There were no partitions between our desks, which gave us very little privacy. By the way, we were in the Zebra Unit. I was 403 Z. I wasn't the lowest on the totem pole. Carney often kidded me, since he outranked me; he was 402 Z.

Our student group had a meeting room where we went over our cases and got input from Mrs. M. and from our colleagues. Each of us would have individual meetings once a week with Mrs. M. She would go over our process recordings, which we had to do on each case, and she would give us feedback. A process recording is used by students and new social workers. It includes not just factual information on the client but any feelings you have as you interview them. That allows your supervisor to see if there are issues you need to work on that are interfering with the helping process. Mrs. M. would review the process recording and underline in red what needed to be deleted for the agency records. She would then discuss any feelings from the original recording that were problems. We would then record what was needed for official records.

I can clearly remember my first clients. Francisco, his wife Rosa, and their baby were on public welfare because Francisco had agoraphobia and couldn't leave the house, not just to go out to work but for any reason at all. He would try to venture outside their apartment, but as soon as he got to the elevator, he would break out in cold sweats and retreat to his apartment. The following is the beginning of my process recording; the parts that are italicized would be deleted by Mrs. M. before I recorded for agency records. It went something like this:

On 10-25-61, I visited the Flores family in their apartment in the LaGuardia Housing Project in Jamaica, New York. Present for the visit were: Francisco, father, age twenty-one; Rosa, mother, age eighteen; and Rico, son, age seven months. *Their housing project covered over four blocks with eight high-rise apartment buildings. When I got to the apartment complex, I felt intimidated by the clusters of residents, mostly African-Americans and Puerto Ricans, hanging out looking suspiciously at the stranger carrying a briefcase. They seemed to be talking about me. They definitely knew I didn't belong on their turf. I didn't understand Spanish, but several of the hanger-outers directed some comments my way that seemed to amuse his friends. I made my way to the Flores's apartment without stopping to chitchat.*

Rosa made her way to the door carrying baby Rico. Francisco remained sitting on the couch, not acknowledging my presence. I had called ahead to make the appointment and basically told them I wanted to see if there were ways I could help them get back on their feet. *I don't know what I expected, but they both seemed so young to be parents. Their one-bedroom apartment was furnished rather shabbily. Besides the couch there was a small TV that looked like it had been passed on to them, a small kitchen table, and an overstuffed, worn-out lounge chair.* We focused mainly on Rico and how well and friendly he was. I asked about doctors' visits, and Rosa readily gave me information about Rico's doctor, how often she visited with him, and how happy she was to hear him tell her how well Rico was doing. She went on to tell me that she was breastfeeding him because she read an article in a magazine that said it was good for babies, and her doctor encouraged her. I gave her positive feedback on her care for what was best for the baby.

I tried to engage Francisco in the conversation. He pulled out a cigarette and slowly began to tell me what a hopeless case he was. He went on to talk about how disgusted he was with himself for not being able to go outside so he could get a job and support his family. I acknowledged that that must be a lousy feeling but said that, if we put our heads together, we should be able to come up with some solutions. I got more information about when he was not feeling so lousy and what was different then. He agreed that between now and the next time we met, he would give that more thought, and we would discuss what he discovered.

There was much more in the interview but this is just to give you an idea of what a process recording is. For example, the cultural differences for me as a "white boy" who needed to confront my feelings about the environment my clients were living in and my obvious discomfort in being in a situation that was foreign to me. Mrs. M. was most interested in discussing whether I thought I had established an initial relationship with Francisco and Rosa and, if not, what I could do differently in our next visit, and what our plan and goals would be for future visits.

Mrs. M. was very skilled in helping me look at my own feelings that might interfere with the helping process. This helped me in my personal life as well as professionally. She helped me realize that I had as much, if not more, to learn about myself as I did about the skills of applying theory to practice. I guess it all goes back to Plato's dictum, "Learn to know thyself" (428 BC–348 BC).

Pat Carney was living in a parish in Yonkers, New York. Since he had to pass through the Bronx, he volunteered to pick me up on the two days a week we had to go to Long Island City. I really appreciated his offer, especially since he was a native New Yorker and should know his way around the city. I was sure that I would get lost on my own. I guess I overestimated Pat's knowledge of the city outside of Manhattan. The first day of our internship, we went over the 59th Street Bridge, toward Long Island City, he took a turn at the end of the bridge, and we ended up on the bottom level of the bridge and drove right back to Manhattan. That was the last time that happened.

Pat turned out to be a pretty good guy, once I got to know him. He knew all the gossip about the clergy in the archdiocese and thrived on clerical stories. He had great expectations of how Vatican II would renew the church, and that was often a topic of our conversations. I relied on him to keep me up to date. We both had high hopes that the Commission on Birth Control that Paul

VI had reinstated would change the teaching of the Church to allow other types of birth control besides abstinence and Natural Family Planning (NFP). Both of us had firsthand knowledge of the burden the present restrictions were putting on good Catholic families. I was pleasantly surprised by how liberal Pat was on contraception but also many of the other issues the Council would be considering. Actually, the Council never made any decisions on birth control but left it to the Commission on Birth Control.

We were both optimistic that the Council would re-evaluate celibacy as a requirement for ordination and would permit priests to marry and would seriously consider women be able to be ordained as priests. I think we were a little naive.

The Class of 1963

The MSW program is a two-year, sixty-credit-hour program. The classes in the social work program were even more interactive than at summer school and certainly more interactive and required more critical thinking than the seminary courses. In the MSW classes, we broke up into small groups to work on topics we would have to present to the class for more discussion. Depending on the class, the topic might be, the philosophical issues underlying the right to universal health care; or comparing Freud's and Jung's approaches to therapy; or techniques for working with resistant clients. In the beginning, I used to wonder what the instructors were getting paid for, since we were doing all the work. They would contribute to the discussions but very infrequently would they give anything that even looked like a lecture, except in statistics. I very quickly saw their rationale and recognized that it was a much better way to learn than what I had experienced in the seminary.

I enjoyed the interaction with my classmates. One particular student, Linda B., I really looked forward to seeing. She was in two of my classes—Social Policy and Human Behavior in the Social Environment. From the first time I met her at the orientation, I found her very attractive and engaging. She was blonde, very bright, with a model-like figure; a recent graduate of an exclusive Catholic women's college in Connecticut; had worked two years in a child welfare agency doing adoptive studies before coming to Fordham; had a great sense of humor and a smile to go with it. She and I were in two work groups that required meetings outside of class. Several times our team met at her apartment, which she shared with Maria, a graduate student in education from Puerto Rico. The team would work for two or three hours, go out for a hamburger at a neighborhood tavern, and come back to her apartment to wrap things up. Sometimes I'd stay for a while and chat with Linda. We shared so many interests. It wasn't like my high school days when I never knew what to talk about with the girls in my class. I guess I was finally maturing. Better late than never!

I had told Linda and Marie about my housemate, John Gavin Nolan, and what a character he was, and at some point they invited us both for dinner. We played bridge after dinner, and he had us in stitches. He didn't tell jokes; he could just take a situation and bring out the humor in it. He was one of the funniest guys I ever met. He looked like one of the Kennedys and drew a crowd wherever he went. He had no inhibitions.

Here's an example of the type of situation he could turn into a circus. He and I were down in Greenwich Village, walking around, checking out the hippies, when he saw a guy on the corner giving a political speech but unable to attract a crowd. Nolan walked right up to him and started a debate that immediately drew a crowd that kept growing. I don't remember what they were arguing about, but at one point he had Nolan in a corner, and I thought he had stumped him. Not for long. Nolan looked him straight in the eye and said, "Have you ever read the Henderson Report?" The guy looked at him and said, "What's the Henderson Report?" Nolan indignantly replied, "If you haven't read the Henderson Report, we haven't anything to talk about!" and walked away to the applause of the street audience.

I asked him, "John, what the hell is the Henderson Report?"

"I don't know, I just made it up. He had me, and I wasn't going to let him win." That was typical. His quick wit and Irish sense of humor usually got a belly laugh out of me.

Several times Linda invited us to house parties, and Nolan was the entertainment, and I was the second banana. We had a song and dance routine that we called the "Priestly Brothers." Our signature song was, "When It's Apple Blossom Time in East Orange, New Jersey, We'll Make a Peach of a Pear." They loved us in Manhattan.

Other times Nolan would say, "Call up your friend Linda, and see if she and Maria want to play bridge." More often than not, they would, and we'd scoot on down to Manhattan from the Bronx for an enjoyable evening of bridge and laughs.

Things went from there to my inviting Linda to a movie or to go down to O. Henry's Steak House in the Village for dinner. I knew our relationship was gradually changing, but I convinced myself that there was nothing wrong with that; we were just friends. We enjoyed one another's company, and there was no sexual activity. One night after studying for an exam together (just like two high school kids), when I was ready to go home, Linda said out of the clear blue, "You know, I love you!" Wow! My knees got weak! *How do I handle this?* I didn't put that much thought into it; I just embraced her and kissed her. After that, we sat on the couch cuddling and gazing at each other as if we really were two teenagers. I felt euphoric! This was bliss. This was ecstasy. It must be love. We both agreed that we had a lot to talk about, but before I left there was more hugging and kissing, and I said, "You know, I love you!" I thought this was the real thing. It wasn't like talking on the phone to my parents and saying, "Love you!" and hanging up fast. Eventually I left for the Bronx. Driving home I kept thinking, *This can't be wrong.* Cognitively and emotionally it just seemed right. I didn't even feel guilty. *If the church doesn't change the rules on celibacy, then I'll change.* From that point, I intuitively knew that I was not meant to be celibate.

When I got back to St. Patrick's, I called Linda, and we talked for another hour. Neither of us had any regrets about our expression of love. We talked more about what would happen if the church didn't change its position and allow optional celibacy. I was quite clear that I would prefer to remain as a priest, mainly to preach the social gospel, but that if push came to shove, I would ask for a dispensation, and we'd be married. I didn't need to be a priest to practice social justice and the beatitudes. These were not issues that I hadn't spent time thinking about before learning that Linda and I loved each other. I had been thinking about those issues for some years. I just needed motivation to put those thoughts into action. Maybe I was being swept along on the waves of the antiauthoritarian attitudes of the sixties.

The next morning when I saw Nolan at breakfast, his first words were not "Good morning" but "Where the hell were you last night? You didn't get home until after 1:00 AM!" I told him that Linda and I were studying for a test, which was true. He looked at me rather skeptically and said, "Listen buddy, you better be careful. I've watched the way you two look at one another, and you might just find yourself in big trouble." I was a little miffed with his keeping track of my comings and goings, but I graciously thanked him for his concern and assured him that Linda and I were just friends. I did confess that when they changed the rules on celibacy and allowed married priests, I would like to pursue our relationship beyond friendship. His response was a sarcastic "Keep dreaming, buddy!"

Linda and I had a wonderful three months. We didn't pursue our relationship beyond the hugging and kissing stage, but we continued to see each other almost every day for dinners, movies, etc. She continued to invite Nolan and me for bridge. We continued to discuss our expectations for Vatican II and the alternatives. I even bought her a gold necklace with a medal that read, "I love you more today than yesterday, but not as much as tomorrow." She gave me her college ring. It was almost like we were engaged. It was a very joyful time for both of us. Then the bubble burst!

I've never forgotten the shock. It was on a weekend. Monsignor Joe Ryan, later to be archbishop of Alaska, was Nolan's and my "houseguest" at St. Patrick's. Joe was Secretary of the Catholic Near East Association and reported directly to the pope. He had an office in New York City and Lebanon. The three of us often went out to dinner or a Broadway show when Joe was in town. I had been an altar boy at his first mass at our home parish. Through my seminary years, he always maintained contact with me and was very supportive. I had hoped to spend a little time with them during the weekend.

I received a call from Linda, and she was crying. When she was able to calm herself down, she told me what was going on. Remember now, this was 1962 and having a relationship with a priest could be a major scandal, no matter what the couple's intentions were. In Linda's exuberance over how happy she was, she had written a letter to one of her college girlfriends and told her about our relationship and how we hoped to be able to get married. Apparently, her friend was so upset that she went to her parish priest to ask for his advice. He told her that she had an obligation to tell Linda's parents about how this ne'er-do-well priest at Fordham was seducing their daughter. When her parents heard that news, her mother immediately came from Connecticut to rescue her. Her mother wanted to arrange a meeting with me to put an end to our relationship. Linda was devastated. The pressure from her parents was so intense that she couldn't think straight. I agreed to meet with her mother at the lobby of the Biltmore Hotel in Manhattan. She would be standing under the famous clock holding a book that I had let Linda borrow. Looking back, the clandestine arrangements seemed weird, verging on laughable, but at the time it was heartbreaking.

I met Linda's mother at the prescribed time under the clock at the Biltmore, and she invited me up to her room. I had hoped to be able to convince her that I loved Linda, and we were looking forward to the church changing the rules on married priests, and if not, I would get a dispensation. She didn't buy that. When we got to her room, she proceeded to tell me what would happen if I didn't stop seeing her daughter immediately. She would go to the bishop of Albany and report my behavior. I asked her how Linda felt about that. She mellowed a bit and said, "Linda cares for you very much. But she'll do what we tell her."

She went on to tell me that Linda's father would be coming from Connecticut the next day, and he wanted to see me. In the meantime they didn't want me to communicate with Linda. It was obvious that I wouldn't get anywhere by trying to plead my case against celibacy any further. I didn't have the sense that she or her husband was vindictive; they were just trying to protect their daughter from ruining her life because of an impulsive, immature decision that they thought would be disastrous. It contradicted everything that they believed in, and she was their only child. I agreed to meet with her husband on the following day.

When I got back to St. Patrick's, Joe Ryan thought I had been avoiding him and insisted I go out to dinner with him and Nolan. Rather than sit in my room and ruminate about my dilemma, I decided to go. After our regular two VO Manhattans, I was feeling less sorry for myself, but I knew alcohol was not the answer. I needed to talk to Nolan when we got home. I passed on having a nightcap, and when I heard Nolan's door close, I knocked to see if he had time to talk with me. I told him where I had been that afternoon and about the meeting the next day. After he got in his, "I knew something was going on! You can't fool old Gav!" he settled in and got serious. He asked me what I wanted to do. I told him I really loved Linda and did want to marry her, but not under these conditions. I had hoped there would be some change in the celibacy rules after Vatican II, or else I could get a dispensation. His reply was the familiar, "You're dreaming, buddy, that's not going to happen."

I thought about what he said and responded, "I don't want to do it their way. I feel like it would be a 'shotgun' wedding! Plus, there are a lot of practical things to consider. Like finishing our MSWs so we'd have opportunities for jobs."

"Okay, then this is what we'll do. I'll go with you, and I'll swear to them that I'll make sure that you and Linda don't have any contact." And that's what we did. When we arrived at their room at the Biltmore, Nolan took over. He first assured the parents that Linda and I didn't have a sexual relationship beyond exchanges of signs of affection. That there was a love between us that he thought we both realized didn't have much chance of lasting under these circumstances. He pledged that he would personally see that Linda and Father Fausel broke off any relationship.

The father, a very street-smart and successful businessman, listened very carefully, looked at me as if I were a serial rapist, and said very clearly, "Son, I own a gun, and if you ever contact my daughter, I'll use it." He then took a holy card from his wallet. The card had a picture of the Blessed Mother and the prayer, the *Memorare*. Again, he looked at me straight in the eye and said, "Take this prayer, and read it every day." I took it but didn't agree to read it every day.

We said our good-byes and left the room. As soon as we got down the corridor from their room, Nolan looked at me and began to laugh. I kept saying, "John, it isn't funny, it isn't funny, stop it!"

He replied, "I know, but I can't stop laughing." By the time we got to the elevator, he was able to control himself. But on the way down, he'd try unsuccessfully to stifle a laugh, and I'd give him an elbow in the ribs. I'm not sure why, but I began to laugh as I looked at him bent over in the corner of the elevator. The laughter was just one more thing I had to feel guilty for. By the time we got back to St. Patrick's, Joe Ryan was furious that we had invited him for the weekend and then left him there by himself. Nolan came up with a semi-reasonable explanation, and Joe was appeased by a pre-dinner VO Manhattan.

It was only a couple of weeks before final exams, so there weren't many opportunities to run into Linda except in large groups. I kept my promise not to contact her, but it wasn't easy. She didn't contact me, either. I wish there had been some way to bring closure between us, but I think we both understood that, under the circumstances, we would be hurting more people than just the two of us, and neither of us wanted that. Nevertheless, I was devastated by the way things ended. This was the first time I had ever experienced a loss like this. I spent many sleepless nights. A lot of those country-and-western songs made sense for the first time. I even thought that if no one else had written a country-and-western song called "Tears on My Pillow," I would write one. When I started writing this section, out of curiosity I Googled "Tears on My Pillow," and, sure enough, in 1958 Little Anthony and the Imperials had a record by the same title. I don't mean to minimize my sadness with an attempt at humor, but that was the way my family usually handled emotional situations. I was beginning to learn some new ways of handling grief.

The next year Linda didn't come back to Fordham. I heard from some of her friends that she had transferred to the University of Connecticut. I felt guilty about that and wished I could have let her know how I felt. I did find out a few years later at a conference that she got her MSW and was working in as a clinical social worker. That was good news.

Reflections

While I was writing my story about Linda and me, it reactivated many of the sad feelings that accompanied our broken relationship. At the time, nothing that was going on in the world mattered to me except my own grief. Now, forty-six years later, Linda would be seventy-two, and I'm now eighty and I still feel traces of guilt. I wonder if this was really love or whether it was my immaturity acting out. At the advice of my therapist, I did a great deal of meditation and research on love. I still have the notes I took, plus more recent references. There are many new categories for types of love, but, for the most part, I relied on the ones I used forty-six years ago.

Again, not to be pedantic, but bear with me. I found it helpful to review my notes. The most basic typology of love is divided into three sorts of feelings:

1) Eros, which is based on strong feelings toward another, which usually occurs in the first stages of romantic love. I wondered if our relationship would have lasted for a much longer time than three months if it hadn't been for the Biltmore meeting. I'd like to think so. Eros is probably what most people mean when they say, "I'm in love." It can range all the way from warm, fuzzy feelings about someone to strong, sensual passion and a variety of sexual activities. Most specialists in relationships believe that the eros type of love is not stable until it is tested by hardships, and when one of the couple loses those "head in the clouds" feelings, they think they have fallen out of love and the relationship ends.

2) Philos or Philia type of love is based on friendship between two people. In my readings, the majority of the experts on relationships agree that lovers who start out by being friends first, before engaging in sexual activities, usually have relationships that last longer. The basis for this is that friendships are the foundation for a successful relationship.

3) Then there is Agape. This is unconditional love. It can include sexual love, but it is more like charity. Companionship is a major component of agape. It is an unselfish love, and there is a good balance of giving and taking. With agape, we are often more concerned with the needs of our loved one than we are with our own needs, and the other way around. I had one relationship with a very attractive, accomplished woman that was strictly a friendship for almost seven years. We enjoyed one another's company: dinners, movies, tennis, discussing books, going to parties together as a couple, but I have no idea why there wasn't any sexual activity involved. It was a good relationship but was missing some of the components of a more balanced relationship.

Erich Fromm

One of the books that helped me at the time and, like all classics, is still applicable today, was written in 1956. It's a book I've recommended to students, clients, friends, and dozens of people in between. It is Erich Fromm's *The Art of Loving*. The fiftieth edition was published in 2006. As the title indicates, Fromm believed that love is an art. It's not something you fall in and out of. It demands the same mastery as any of the other forms of art. The expressions "fall in love" or "fall out of love" always seemed strange to me. It sounded as if love was an accident. One day you're walking along the street, and you trip and fall in love or out of love.

I'd like to review with you several segments from Fromm's book that I found helpful at the time I was dealing with my separation from Linda, as well as other separations in my life. The impact of Fromm's wisdom took more than one broken relationship to sink in. To look at just two or three statements from Fromm's book certainly does not do justice to his book. The fiftieth anniversary edition is only 123 pages long but has two added sections: "Meet Erich Fromm"; "Love in the Life of Erich Fromm," by Rainer Funk, which provides an insight into Erich Fromm the man and for me a better understanding of the loves of my own life.

In this first reference, Fromm talks about unity and how various pursuits don't produce unity—not our work, which is not interpersonal; not the unity achieved in "orgiastic fusion" which is only transitory; and not the unity achieved by conformity, which is only pseudo-unity. He believed that the only answer lies in the achievement of interpersonal union, of fusion with another person in love.[8]

This quotation is one I'm sure I had read before, but its importance never dawned on me: "This desire for interpersonal fusion is the most powerful striving in man. It is the most fundamental passion; it is the force which keeps the human race together, the clan, the family, society … Without love, humanity could not exist for a day."[9]

The other quote by Fromm, which is probably his most famous, is, "In love the paradox occurs that two beings become one and yet remain two … Immature love says: 'I love you because I need you.' Mature love says 'I need you because I love you.' We are only capable of knowing and caring for the other if we are also capable of understanding, caring, and knowing ourselves."[10] I wondered if my love for Linda and others in my life existed because I needed them rather than needing them because I loved them? I also realized that I needed to care and know myself better before I could know and care for anyone else. I recognized that this was an ongoing process and that I had much more work to do before I could answer these questions.

Until I found my soul mate later in life, I discovered that I probably had ranged between eros, philia, and agape with prior relationships. When I met and married Jane, I knew I had finally gotten it right. I will speak more about our relationship later, but for now let me say that our relationship is a mature love, that at our time of life it is more agape and philia with a focus on companionship and true friendship, as well as the interpersonal fusion that Fromm identified.

I would like to mention one more thing about Fromm the man. The section in the fiftieth anniversary edition of *The Art of Loving* where a colleague of his gives an account of "Love in the Life of Erich Fromm" is both surprising and, at second thought, inspiring. Surprising in the sense that he was married and divorced once; had a seven-year affair with Karen Horney, his colleague and competitor; married again, to Henny Gurland, whom he nursed through a painful type of arthritis before she eventually committed suicide; and married Annis Freeman, who became his lifelong partner and who developed breast cancer, which they both lived with for over twenty years. My initial surprise was that my hero was a human person, who struggled with relationships like most of us. But as I read more about his relationships and how he lived his book, I was inspired by the words of his colleague, Rainer Funk, who knew him as well as anyone and wrote:

When I was Fromm's assistant in Locarno in the 1970s, again and again I became witness to Fromm's unusual

ability to love ... Above all, however, one could see this
in his love for Annis, when he kissed her for instance in
the elevator, said good-bye to her, how he spoke with her,
how he looked at her and touched her, Fromm's ability to
love is still alive in his book *The Art of Loving.*"[11]

This says more about the man than any words I could possibly
write.

Limerence

They say you teach what you want to learn. That certainly has
been true for me over the years. In this case it was for me to learn
more about what I was doing wrong in my pursuit of love. I was
able to find in my archives an article written by Marie Dillon,
a reporter for the *Arizona Republic,* about a workshop I would
be presenting at the Franciscan Renewal Center in Scottsdale,
Arizona. The title of the article was "You're Not Sick—but It's
Not Love Either." The article was composed from an interview
I gave the reporter. As I reread the article, I thought I had said
some smart things that were worth sharing. Most of the content
for the workshop came from well-grounded research, but a good
portion was from my own experiences.

Ms. Dillon started the article by quoting the lyrics of a popular
song, "You're Not Sick, You're Just in Love." Some of you might
remember the song, which was written by Irving Berlin in 1950
for the show *Call Me Madame.*

She goes on to quote me: "It might feel like love, and if you're
lucky it might someday be love. But if you can't sleep, can't eat,
can't do anything but think about that one certain person, then
you're really aren't sick, you're in 'Limerence.' The term was coined
by Dr. Dorothy Tennov, a psychologist who compiled fourteen
years of research into a book, *Love and Limerence: The Experience
of Being in Love.* According to Tennov, 'Limerence is a one-sided
emotional state in which one's thoughts center around and are

affected by a single individual. Often referred to as being 'in love', but not to be confused with the real thing."[12]

Since I had been on both sides of the "one-sided emotional state", Tennov's book appealed to me immediately. Ms. Dillon went on to quote me again: "'I wouldn't say it's always unhealthy, but when people don't learn from the experience, or when they make some major decisions (like getting married) while in a limerent state, it can be problematic. Some people go through a series of limerent relationships and get to a point where they feel bad about themselves. Never figuring out why their relationships don't work,' Fausel said.

"'Also, you might meet an appropriate partner but you're waiting for that euphoric feeling to happen again. You still have that Hollywood image of love and might pass over a perfectly good person, just because there are no immediate ecstatic feelings,' he said.

"'I really think people sometimes confuse limerence with the love that's necessary to sustain an ongoing, meaningful interpersonal relationship,' Fausel added."

Ms. Dillon asked, "How do you prevent limerence from getting out of hand?"

"'There are no easy answers, but keeping a journal of your thoughts might help you realize if you're in limerence. Also if you can think of only good qualities that the limerent object (LO) has and no bad qualities, that should be a red flag. Once you recognize that it is limerence, it's a lot easier to handle,' he said.

"'The limerent object, on the other hand, has an obligation to be candid if he or she doesn't intend to return the affection. They have to eliminate hope, undercut it,' Fausel said. 'They can't even offer friendship, because that's a hope, a glimmer, a foot in the door. It really is not fair to give double messages,' he said."

In the process of reviewing what love is and isn't, it occurred to me that, given Fromm's position that "interpersonal fusion" is so important, with the sheltered life that I, along with most pre-Vatican II seminarians, lived during those years of indoctrination, how could I have been expected to make a mature, rational decision to live a life of celibacy for the rest of my life? If you wanted to be a Catholic priest, you had to be a celibate priest. The sad part was that I was never adequately prepared to be a celibate. Judging from the large number of ordained priests who left a ministry they loved because of mandatory celibacy, I apparently was not alone.

I don't mean this to be an *apologia pro vita mea* or an attempt not to take responsibility for my decisions. I needed to explore the whole concept of celibacy in the context of love, rather than whether or not I could live without having sex in thought, word, or deed. I needed to find a view of celibacy that looked at it positively, rather than negatively, before I could make a mature decision. After reading at least half a dozen books and many more articles on celibacy for this reflection, I could look at celibacy from a more balanced perspective. My concern now is mandatory celibacy. I knew the pros and cons for mandatory celibacy; there is no question about celibacy not being a divine law, but a church law and that it could therefore be changed by the church; or that Saint Peter himself was married; or that the law forbidding clergy to marry was finally handed down at the Second Lateran Council in 1139 AD. This is just factual information. I believe that if the church is to survive, we need to develop a more positive view of celibacy and make it optional.

In chapter 10 I will discuss mandatory celibacy in more detail. I will spare you a thorough review of the literature and suggest for our purposes focusing on an author who has written four books on the priesthood. The author is Father Donald Cozzens, PhD, currently a professor of religious studies at John Carroll University and previously president-rector of St. Mary Seminary and Graduate School of Theology in Wickliffe, Ohio. In addition to his latest book on celibacy, *Freeing Celibacy*, 2006, he wrote two other books that focused on the priesthood and celibacy: *The Changing Face of the Priesthood* and *Sacred Silence and the Crisis in the Church*. I highly recommend all of his books.

Chapter 9
Turning Points

The turning points described in this chapter all took place in the 1960s. They include events in my own life and in the life of the Catholic Church and society in general. The assassinations of the Kennedy brothers and The Rev. Martin Luther King Jr. paralyzed the whole country and had an impact on the rest of the world. The Vietnam War polarized our country and led to Lyndon Johnson making it clear that he would not seek or accept his party's nomination for president. Despite the high hopes many had for Vatican II, forty-four years later some eminent theologians are asking the question, "Vatican II: Did Anything Happen?"[1] Perhaps one of the most dramatic and damaging turning points for the church was Pope Paul VI's encyclical *Humanae Vitae*, which dismissed the majority vote of the Commission on Birth Control to change the church's teaching. This and other decisions by the church's hierarchy had an effect not just on my life but on the credibility that the faithful had for their leaders.

Second Year at Fordham

The academic year went relatively smoothly. I made a promise to myself to avoid any serious relationships with any of my women classmates. I also realized it would have been very difficult if Linda had come back for her second year. I wasn't sure how I would have handled that. I thought of her often during the summer when I was at Marian Lodge, and being back in the familiar environs at school didn't help with my obsessive thoughts. I tried to avoid places we used to hang out—the restaurants, the Bitter End in Greenwich Village, Lowe's movie theaters—since these just intensified my thoughts of her. This time I had the sense to talk to Nolan when I was wavering and tempted to contact her, and he always knew what to say. He was so empathetic; I had the suspicion that he might have had similar experiences when he was a younger priest.

One bit of advice Nolan gave me that I have always been thankful for was his suggestion that I see Brother Mark Egan, an Irish Christian Brother and professor of psychology at Iona College in New Rochelle, New York. He became both my therapist and spiritual director. Brother Mark was a very low-key gentleman. He had a great sense of humor and was very non-prescriptive in his therapy. I liked that. It made me feel that I was in charge of my own destiny, and he was my guide. Sometimes we met in the Iona school's cafeteria over coffee, sometimes just walking around the beautiful campus, and other times in his office. He always seemed to have time for me, which I appreciated. He was even accessible for a phone call or would make the half-hour trips to the Bronx, and we'd have dinner at Stella D'Oro's, a great Italian restaurant that was just a few blocks from St. Patrick's Home for the Aged. Those times we usually ended up talking about politics, the Vietnam War, the church, or sports. He was helpful in my making a decision about whether to stay in the church as a priest or be laicized. One sad note: I had lost track of Brother Mark after I moved to Arizona. I Googled him to see if he was still at Iona and found out that, sadly, he had died in 1979 at the age of fifty-eight. I regret not having kept in touch with him; he was not only an excellent mentor but a good friend. May he rest in peace.

My internship for the second year was at St. Vincent's on the Hudson in Westchester County. It was a private hospital for the mentally ill. Another Fordham student, Dick O'Brien, also had his internship there. Dick was a midcareer social worker who had worked as a parole agent for years and had the opportunity to take advantage of an agency scholarship to get his MSW. Again I was fortunate; he lived in the Bronx and offered to pick me up so we could carpool to St. Vincent's. During our commutes, we got to know one another and enjoy each other's company. I learned a lot from Dick about working with involuntary clients. Plus, we were both Yankee fans and saw several games at Yankee Stadium, which was only three stops on the subway from where I lived.

Our supervisor, Barbara Jones, was a veteran clinical social worker. She was trained in psychoanalytic therapy and was very much into that model. Although we had briefly studied Freud and his followers in several of our classes, Fordham took a more eclectic approach to therapies, and this often caused conflict between Barbara and us. But it gave us an opportunity to learn Freud in more depth. Given some of the clients we were working with, the newer approaches like Gestalt, Rogerian therapy, and various brief therapies did not seem appropriate for working with the seriously mentally ill. For example, I remember the first client Barbara assigned me. Her name was Frances, and she was an eighteen-year-old woman who had been hospitalized for several months and diagnosed as a catatonic schizophrenic; she was pretty much non-communicative with any of the staff.

Before I met with her I read up on catatonics and found that catatonic schizophrenia is one of several types of schizophrenia, a mental illness in which reality is interpreted abnormally (psychosis). Barbara told me that if I raised Frances's arm above her head, she would keep it there until someone lowered it. This is the most extreme type of catatonic behavior. Fortunately, catatonic schizophrenia is rare today because of improved treatment and the availability of new drugs. With effective treatment, including talk therapy, the patient can manage the symptoms of the disease and work toward a healthier life.

No pun intended, but I was shocked to hear that Frances had undergone a series of electroconvulsive therapy (ECT) treatments. As students, part of our training was to observe patients undergoing what seemed to be a brutal treatment. ECT is a procedure in which electric currents are passed through the brain, deliberately triggering a seizure. The procedure can change the brain chemistry and alleviate symptoms of mental illness. The treatment remains controversial. Although it is still used today—less frequently and with more safeguards—much of the stigma attached to ECT is based on early treatments, which used much higher doses of electricity and were administered without anesthesia. These procedures often caused severe memory loss and, in some cases, death. It was easy to spot a patient who had been through the treatment; they usually had a zombielike gait and looked like they were in a trance.

Watching a patient being given an ETC treatment was not a pleasant experience. A patient was strapped down on a table, and the doctor would put what looked like a wooden stick in their mouth so they wouldn't swallow their tongue when the electric current passed through their brain. When the current was administered, the whole body would jerk up and down, almost as if the patient were being electrocuted.

When Barbara first brought me to meet Frances in her room, all that was going through my mind was her having had to go through what seemed to me, as an observer, a very primitive procedure. Frances, a very attractive young woman, was sitting in a chair, with a vacuous look on her face, staring out her window on a beautiful fall day.

Barbara introduced me. "Good morning Frances, I want you to meet Father Fausel. He will be your new therapist."

Barbara had already warned me not to offer my hand or to reach out to her in any way. So I softly said, "Hi, Frances, it's nice to meet you. I hope we can get to know one another." She didn't respond one way or another, just continued to gaze out the window. Barbara said she would leave us alone and quietly exited the room. For the next forty-five minutes, we just sat there. Occasionally, I would make a remark about the nice day or her pretty blouse, but there was no response. Before leaving, I did as Barbara suggested. I said to Frances, "I'll be back tomorrow at the same time," then made my exit. Barbara's rationale was that if I said the same thing every time and followed through, it would build up trust in Frances.

After showing up four or five times, I finally got a surprised response from Frances. When I entered her room, she didn't respond to my greeting. She was staring at her hands, which she had in front of her, palms up. After five or ten minutes, she broke her silence by saying in an agitated voice, "I'm afraid what these hands can do." I responded in my best Rogerian voice, "What they can do?"

Frances answered, "I'm afraid they might kill someone."

I wasn't sure what to say, so I just said, "Do you want to share more with me?"

Her immediate answer was, "No!"

I stayed the usual forty-five more minutes with her in silence and then told her that I would be back the next day at the usual time and if she wanted to, we could talk more about her fear of what her hands could do. I knew from what Barbara had told me that Frances had been molested by her stepfather when she was fourteen, and her mother had pressed charges and divorced him. My plan was to gain her confidence to the point where she was willing to tell me about the traumatic experience without my pushing her before she was ready to talk about it.

When I returned the next day, she acknowledged my presence with what was almost a glimmer of a smile. I teased her by asking, "Was that a smile I saw? It made me think you were glad to see me." She replied with a more generous smile. And for the first time she had eye contact with me. I thought it might be time to suggest our going outside for a walk instead of being cooped up inside. It was a beautiful fall day, so I asked if she'd like to take a walk outside and enjoy the foliage. She replied with another smile, and off we went. We walked side by side around the beautiful campus. If I took a deep breath and inhaled the fresh fragrances of the fall day, Frances would do the same. She surprised me again when she said, "That's delicious!"

"We'll have to do this more often!" I said. She took another deep breath and agreed by nodding her head and smiling. We sat on a bench in the shade in silence. I had a difficult time dealing with silences in conversations but was learning to give the patient an opportunity to fill in the gap if they chose to. After about twenty minutes of sitting in silence, Frances said, "It's time for me to get back to my room. Will you be back to see me tomorrow?"

"Same time, same place!"

From that time on, Frances slowly opened up more and more. Sometimes she would chose to be silent for part of a session, but it was almost as if she was testing me to see if I still accepted her even when she was quiet. As the semester went on, she gradually shared with me the molestation by her stepfather and how scared she was of him and how much she hated him. After several sessions of allowing her to vent her anger, I focused more on her mother and how much she must have loved her to divorce her stepfather and bring charges against him. She didn't buy that initially, but after several more conversations about her mother, she seemed to be more willing to look at what she had done for her. Frances began to see her mother more positively, and eventually I had several joint sessions with Frances and her mother.

Barbara told me that Frances was now participating in group activities and that she had progressed enough to be released from the hospital for outpatient treatment in Yonkers, where she and her mother and sisters lived. When I saw Frances, she was delighted that she was going home and gave me the news with a big, unexpected hug.

Each of the interns had to present a case before staff, psychiatrists, psychologists, therapists, and psychiatric nurses. I chose to present Frances for my presentation. Not that I was taking credit for her progress, but it was a part of our team effort. During my months with Frances, there was regular consultation and advice from all the team members. That was one of the things that I liked about working at St. Vincent's. We were involved in all staff meetings and meetings with the primary team that was working with our patients.

Here's one little incident that didn't involve patients directly. I was waiting for the elevator door to open, and when it did, there was my former English and speech teacher from St. Thomas Seminary, John Byrnes. He was ready to disembark along with another priest. I was dressed in a medical coat with my Roman collar underneath. He looked at me as if he had seen a ghost and stammered, "Well, Freddie Fausel, what are *you* doing here?" I was just as shocked to see him and was surprised that he recognized me after eleven years. I countered with, "I'm an intern here! What are *you* doing here?" Again, he stammered, "We're here to visit Father X, poor fellow isn't well. It might be nice if you could visit with him."

I told him I'd talk to my supervisor before I did. Father X might be embarrassed to see a former student here on the staff. He changed the subject and asked me about what I'd been doing with myself since I left St. Thomas. I gave him a quick resumé, and we parted, with his telling me he'd look me up when he came to visit again. As far as I know, he never did.

I found out later that Father X had been picked up by the police in the men's room at the Hartford train station, where he was trying pick up young boys for sex. I felt bad for Father X. There were always rumors that he was gay, but he seemed like a pretty decent guy to me.

I admired Father Byrnes for his loyalty to Father X, but as I was writing about this incident, I wondered whether Father X had gone back to teach at the seminary after he was released from the hospital, or whether he was assigned to a parish where he would have an opportunity to prey on young altar boys. After all, this was the sixties, and that was the way most priests who took sexual advantage of young boys were handled by their superiors. It brought to mind how the bishops handled the 2002 sexual scandal of pedophiliac priests, moving priest pedophiles from parish to parish without informing the parishioners that their new priest was a sex offender, not just living in their parishes but having direct contact with young children. To make matters worse, many of the bishops did everything they could to cover up the scandal rather than protect the innocent children. Most of the cover-ups were festering during the 1960s before they became fodder for the press in the early 2000s. Even then, many of the bishops kept on hiding behind lawyers to protect the priest pedophiles and defend against the growing lack of trust in their integrity among the faithful, instead of protecting the innocent children.

Another thing that kept me busy the second year was the thesis we were required to write as part of our graduation requirements. The thesis was a major research paper, which was similar to a doctoral dissertation but didn't require an oral exam. I wrote on the benefits of camping in child development. I was able to support what I had learned in my experience at Marian Lodge with the latest research. I wish I had known when I first took over as director what I learned from the research. I never had a clue that there was that much academic research on camping.

"Lord, Make Me Pure, but Not Yet!"

Unless you're familiar with the writings of St. Augustine of Hippo, you probably would never have guessed that the title for this section is a quote from his book, now known as *The Confessions of St. Augustine*, written between the years AD 397 and 398. I'm not sure if St. Augustine meant this prayer for me, but 1,568 years later, it definitely resonated with me when I first read it and reread it. I didn't consciously take it as license to live a noncelibate life, but in the back of my mind it was comforting to know that someone with the stature of St. Augustine could empathize with the problems I was having living a celibate life. I guess my prayer would have been, *Lord make me pure by changing the church's law on mandatory celibacy—as soon as you can.* Part of me knew that wasn't going to happen in my lifetime, but another part hoped that it would.

I had kept the promise I made to myself at the beginning of the academic year that my classmates were out of bounds for close personal relationships. That didn't mean that I didn't have temptations to pursue female company. Continuing to repress those temptations came to a head on my birthday. I was feeling sorry for myself. Despite all the blessings I had in my life, I kept coming back to the depressing thought that I would live the rest of my life by myself. I had received birthday cards from relatives and friends, but they didn't make up for the void in my life. I bought a copy of the *Village Voice* because they always had ads for singles parties on the weekend. They were held in people's apartments, and the host charged a minimum fee to attend. I decided I would go to one that Friday.

After reading a number of ads describing the different parties, I chose one that read as though it would attract an interesting group of singles with similar interests. The ad specified college graduates. I wasn't consciously going there to meet a sex partner but just to have a good time on my birthday with what I hoped would be a congenial group and perhaps to connect with one particular, special person.

The address was on the Upper East Side of Manhattan, which at that time was a coveted address. After parking my car a few blocks away from the high-rise, I had second thoughts but convinced myself that it would be a new experience, and I made my way to the party. The host's apartment was on the seventeenth floor. As soon as I got off the elevator, I saw a line of people waiting to pay their fee. It was only a short wait before I paid my five dollars and got my name tag from the hostess. I don't remember her name, but she was very welcoming and pointed out the punch bowl and snacks and encouraged me to just mix in with the crowd: "We're all strangers looking to meet new friends." I thanked her, took the felt pen, and wrote Don F. on the "HI I'M …" name tag.

I guess I must have looked lost because a very attractive woman in her mid-thirties came up to me and said, "Hi, I'm Jeanne. Is this your first time at one of these parties?" I replied, "Is it that obvious?" She went on to tell me that she attended one or two parties a month. "It's better than hanging out at bars." I agreed with her, and she continued the conversation by asking me what I did for a living. I told her that I was a full-time master's student at Fordham and was doing an internship at St. Vincent's Hospital in Westchester County. She told me that she was a buyer for one of the major department stores in Manhattan and that the reason she went to these parties was to meet someone who made about the same salary as she did so that after they were married they could invest one salary and live off the other. That way, they would have a nice little retirement fund or money for trips while they were still young. I told her unenthusiastically that that wasn't a bad idea, and I had never thought of it. It was at that point that she started looking around the room and excused herself by saying I might want to get something to drink, and she recommended the snacks.

There must have been thirty-five or forty singles there, and it seemed like some had already coupled up in a corner or on the balcony or some other cozy spot. As I made my way to the punch bowl, I spotted another attractive "thirty-something" woman. As I reached the bowl, she said, "Can I buy you a drink, handsome?" I responded like someone I heard in the movies, "You sure can, gorgeous!" As I looked at her name tag I said, "I mean, Irene!" She had a beautiful smile and a regal look about her with dark hair and Eastern European features, and best of all, she didn't get into financial issues like the woman in my previous encounter. There was an immediate connection. After I got my drink and a little plate of snacks, she suggested that we commandeer a corner on a couch and get to know one another. I thought that was a great idea and willingly followed her to a small couch with a lot of pillows, which made it easy for us to claim it as our own.

Her first question was, "What does the *F* on your name tag stand for?" I told her "Fausel" and then the story about there being two other Dons in my first-grade class etc., which I shared with you earlier. We had a wonderful conversation. She had a great sense of humor that made me laugh out loud. There was nothing pretentious about her; she taught English at one of the community colleges in Manhattan; was divorced, but it was not bitter divorce; wanted to meet someone who was Jewish (I thought "oh, oh") but that wasn't a major qualification except to satisfy her parents. She was curious about what I was doing at St. Vincent's and the usual social history that you share on a first "date." After about a half an hour of chatting, she said, "I know a little German *Hofbrauhaus* in the neighborhood. Why don't we go there for some good German beer and dance to the umpa band?"

"Sounds like a good idea to me!" And off we went. The name of the place was Peter's Hofbrauhaus. They had a lively Friday-night crowd. It wasn't the easiest place to carry on a conversation, with the three-piece German band blasting away; every few songs they encouraged the audience to sing along, but we managed to have bits and pieces of a conversation, while joining in with the singing and an occasional dance. It must have been after 1:00 AM when we left. On the way home, Irene said, "I'm going to visit with some friends in New Jersey tomorrow and come home on Sunday. They have this cute little cottage just minutes from the beach. Are you interested?" Without hesitating, I answered with an unconditional "Yes!"

"Great!" was her reply. She explained that she would ask me to come up for a cup of coffee, but it was late and she didn't want to disturb her roommate.

"No problem, I'll look forward to seeing you tomorrow." She gave no verbal response, just a passionate kiss and hug.

On my way home to the Bronx, I began to think, *Maybe I should talk with Nolan or Brother Mark?* I finally made up my mind with a resolute statement to myself, *I'm going to celebrate my thirty-third birthday by enjoying the beach and the company of a new friend.*

I picked up Irene in the morning as arranged. She had prepared a picnic basket with a bottle of wine for the hosts and a thermos of hot coffee for our trip across the Hudson River to New Jersey.

The day was a little chilly and overcast, but Irene was a ray of sunshine on this drab day.

We got to the shore about 10:00 AM. The sun was trying to come out, but it wouldn't be a day for swimming. Irene introduced me to her friends: George, who was a lawyer for New York City, and Ann, who was a nurse at St. Vincent's Hospital in downtown Manhattan. They had prepared a late breakfast, which we ate out on their patio. Ann and I had mutual colleagues, since both St. Vincent hospitals were under the same management, and Ann had done a rotation there as part of her training and still kept in touch with several of the nurses. They seemed to be a very happily married couple who enjoyed one another, their jobs, and their friends. After breakfast we bundled up in our windbreakers and went down to the beach. Just the smell of the saltwater and the sound of the waves coming in to the shore made up for not being able to swim. In the afternoon, Irene and I went to the small town to shop for the ingredients for supper. It was a quaint little beach town that reminded me of Cape Cod.

Irene and Ann did a great job in the kitchen preparing the salad, vegetables, and some snacks while George and I prepared the steaks on the patio. I remember thinking, *This isn't any different from my parents entertaining in Albany.* Supper was just as congenial as the other meals, and after we all joined in the dishwashing and cleaning up, George lighted a fire in the fireplace, and we played bridge until it was time to go to bed.

I had wondered about the sleeping arrangements, but apparently they had been decided, which was okay with me. It was a joy to wake up in the morning with Irene's smiling face looking at me. If there had been some guarantee that married life with Irene would be like this, I think I would have mailed my papers to the Vatican for a dispensation from celibacy on Monday. Of course I knew that I was just fantasizing, but I didn't want to come back to reality. "Lord, not yet!"

After a very quiet Sunday reading the *Times,* walking on the beach, and just hanging out, we left for Manhattan, as it was getting dark. We had a quiet ride back; Irene had her head on my shoulder and was in and out of sleep. I guess we both had had too much fresh sea air and good food. I told her I really liked Ann and George and appreciated their hospitality. She said that Ann was her best friend since school and that both she and George really liked me. She went on to say jokingly that my only negative was that I was not a nice Jewish boy. She envied Ann, who was Jewish but whose family had no problem in accepting George, who was not. She went back to sleep, and I realized that my fantasy life of having found the perfect woman for me might already be in trouble.

When I called her the next day, I could tell immediately that there was trouble in River City. She started by telling me how much she liked me and enjoyed my company but (oh, oh!) her mother had phoned her earlier, and the first thing she had asked was, "Who was that young man you spent the weekend with?" and then, "Is he Jewish?" Irene knew she was going to face the religious issue sooner or later, so she told her mother what a nice person I was—but that I wasn't Jewish; I was a Catholic. She said there was a long pause on the phone with her mother just repeating "*Oy, oy, oy!*" She tried to mimic her mother's exact reactions, which went something like this. "*Oy!* What do you think your poor father is going to say? A rabbi's daughter keeping company with a non-Jew, when there are so many nice Jewish boys available! *Oy, vey!* You'll break your father's heart!"

I told Irene that I could understand her mother's reaction; it wasn't too different from that of other ethnic/religious groups who use guilt to control their adult children. I knew from experience because I had been dealing with it for years. In an attempt to keep things light, I shared with her that a Catholic friend of mine claimed his mother had the East Coast franchise on guilt. I asked her if we could talk about this more in person. She agreed to meet me after work Monday at a little pub near her apartment.

That evening we met at a small Italian restaurant near her apartment. We both ordered a drink and something to eat. There wasn't much conversation during our meal. It was like we were two different people from the day before. Irene finally broke the silence by saying, "I was so happy the last few days. I really thought I would have the chutzpah to stand up to my parents. But if my mother was so unhappy about us, I can imagine what my father's reaction would be. He'd probably disown me if he thought it was serious." I just held her hand, and we were both close to tears. I finally moved to her side of the table and just held her.

When we both calmed down, I told her I was not just a good Catholic boy but that I was also a priest. She looked a little shocked but in some ways impressed. I told her that, up to this point, I didn't think it was that important—until I heard that her father was a rabbi. I wanted her to know that I did have plans to leave the priesthood if the church didn't make changes about celibacy.

We both agreed that we had a lot to think about and that we should not do anything rash like say there was no hope for us to be together. I suggested that we should not see one another for a couple of weeks and then reconnect to discuss what decisions we thought were best for both of us. We agreed that we would get together to discuss what conclusions we had reached. I couldn't believe we were both being so reasonable when obviously we had such strong feelings for one another. We parted with a warm embrace and a gentle kiss.

A week or so later I received a letter from Irene. She expressed her warm feelings for me again and how painful it was for her to write this letter. Her father had predictably threatened to disown her if she didn't end her relationship with that "shkutz" (a derogatory term for a non-Jewish male). His exact words were, "You will no longer be my daughter!" I did write back and expressed my sadness but also my understanding. I added that if things changed she should let me know. We had discussed her favorite movie, *Casablanca*, so, to add a little humor, I ended with, "We'll always have New Jersey!" I never heard from her! It's hard to believe she would be seventy-seven years old now. I hope she has had as wonderful a life as I've had—so far!

Graduation and Back to the Albany Diocese

That spring I received my MSW degree. My parents came for the graduation ceremony at Fordham. It was held outside on the Rose Hill Campus in the Bronx. I remember that the main speaker was Sargent Shriver, husband of Eunice Kennedy and brother-in-law of John F. Kennedy, who appointed him to be the first director of the Peace Corps. I don't remember much of the content, but it was inspiring. His focus was to encourage graduates to devote their lives to service at whatever level suited them.

I packed up again, said good-bye to Monsignor Reardon and the good nuns at St. Patrick's Home for the Aged, and was off to Albany for a few days off before I reported for my new assignment as director of Catholic Charities at the Schenectady office. I had also been assigned to be in residence at St. Columbia's Church. I arrived there the same day as the new pastor, Father X, an Irish priest who had spent the last fifteen years in a small parish in the northern part of the diocese. There was another assistant priest there, Bill Esmond, whom I had known in the seminary and at Brandt Lake. My duties there were supposed to be minimal, since my major responsibility was Catholic Charities.

The office for Catholic Charities was on Union Street in Schenectady in a converted two-story family home. The name was eventually changed from Catholic Charities to Catholic Family Services. We offered foster care and adoption services, family and individual counseling, and temporary help with financial assistance. Ms. Nina Rose was the supervisor for the five counselors. She had been there for over ten years and was disappointed when I was appointed director right out of graduate school, though in those days, the directors of Catholic Charities were always priests. I picked up on her disappointment and had a conference with her. We were able to iron out some of her feelings. I admitted that it didn't seem right for me to be director when she had so many years of experience and assured her that I would not interfere with her supervisory role and would focus mainly on relations with the community and other social service agencies, working with the board, and fund-raising. I also told her that I would like to meet with the staff for a half an hour each week to see what I could do to support their work. Ms. Rose and I started off more in step and developed a good working relationship.

I spent the first few weeks meeting with other executive directors from Jewish Family Services, Family Services of Schenectady, the Mental Health Organization, the Commission on Human Rights, and the United Way. All these meetings were for what today we would call networking. It paid off, because within the year I was appointed to the Commission on Human Rights, the board of the United Way, and the Mental Health Organization. Plus, I was invited to make presentations at churches, annual meetings, etc.

I was really enjoying my new job. I saw it as an opportunity to have an impact on the community and contribute to change in the social service delivery system. I knew I eventually was going to leave the active ministry, but in the meantime I thought I had an obligation to pay the diocese back for the cost of my professional education. I believed that I could do this by preaching the social gospel and using my position in the community to work for social change both locally and nationally. My sermons and involvement in the community were always focused on the disenfranchised and about peace and justice. I never preached about infallibility, birth control, masturbation, or any other topic with which my conscience could not agree. I no longer automatically took prescribed beliefs for granted.

Civil Rights and the Assassinations in the 1960s

There are only a small number of major national events that I can remember as clearly as the assassination of the Kennedys or Martin Luther King. After all these years, I remember: Pearl Harbor, the death of Franklin D. Roosevelt, Victory in Europe Day, and victory in Japan during World War II.

If you ask anyone old enough to remember where they were when they learned that President Kennedy was shot, they most likely would be able to tell you the details of where they were, who they were with, etc. I know I can. It was my thirty-fourth birthday, November 22, 1963. I was having lunch at Wolfert's Roost Country Club in Albany. It was an executive meeting of the four directors of the offices of Catholic Charities for the Albany Diocese; John R. Sise, director of the diocesan office; Richard Downs, director of the Albany office; George O'Brien, director of the Troy office, and me. I can even remember what I had for lunch. It was Friday, and the church had not yet changed its rule of no meat on Fridays, so of course we all had salmon. I don't think that was a great penance for any of us. We were finishing our dessert when someone came in tears, shouting, "The President's been shot!" The four of us immediately got up to go into the bar to watch the news report on TV. There was a crowd trying to get near enough to the TV to see what the latest news on his condition was. We were all in a state of shock. We waited until Walter Cronkite made the announcement that President Kennedy had been pronounced dead at 1:00 PM CST. I had very little information about Vice President Johnson, but my first thought was, "Oh no, not Lyndon Johnson!" A crack of gunfire and America changed forever. We'd never know how history would have differed if President Kennedy had lived to complete his promising presidency.

That weekend, after saying an early Mass on Sunday, I spent most of the day glued to the TV at my parents' house. My father and I didn't even leave the TV for lunch. My mother, bless her heart, brought it to the living room, so we didn't miss a minute of the coverage. My father and I both watched in disbelief as Jack Ruby, a Dallas strip-club owner, shot the suspect, Lee Harvey Oswald, on national TV. I still can hear my father yelling, "Jane, Jane, come in here, you'll never believe what happened!"

The struggle for civil rights covered a good part of the 1960s. Sadly, an another shot rang out on April 4, 1968, killing one of the most visible leaders of the movement, Rev. Martin Luther King Jr. He was standing on the balcony of his room at the Lorraine Motel in Memphis, Tennessee, when he was felled by a sniper's bullet. He had come to Memphis to support the sanitation workers' strike. After a long history of grievances, on February 12, thirteen hundred African-American sanitation workers went on strike in response to an incident in which twenty-two black workers were sent home without pay, in bad weather, while all the white workers remained on the job.[2]

On the evening before his death, Dr. King delivered one of his most famous speeches, "I've Been to the Mountaintop." In that speech he seemed very resigned, knowing in his heart that he had done everything he could to change society but that he might not be with his followers when his goals of justice, equality, and civil rights were reached. Ironically, the Nobel Peace prize recipient, the proponent of peaceful means for change, died a violent death. I remember watching on TV with sadness when many blacks took to the streets across the country in a massive wave of riots. Their actions would not have been condoned by Dr. King, but certainly he would have understood them. Ironically, the man who had spent the last thirteen years of his life, from the Montgomery bus boycott to the Memphis sanitation strikes, preaching peace and his vision of a better world for all, a more equitable world for all, would not be physically there to experience it, but his message that "We Shall Overcome" and his life's work are still inspiring generation after generation.

In speaking to a group right after the assassination, Robert F. Kennedy said these words about Dr. King, which, prophetically, could just as easily been applied to his own life: "Martin Luther King dedicated his life to love and to justice for his fellow human beings and he died for those efforts." He then suggested to his audience that we have two choices: "[W]e can be filled with bitterness, with hatred and a desire for revenge … [o]r we can make an effort, as Martin Luther King did, to understand and to comprehend and to replace that violence, that bloodshed that has spread across our land with an effort to understand with compassion and love."[3]

Two months later, Senator Robert F. Kennedy's blood flowed on the floor of the kitchen of the Ambassador Hotel in California. He had just won the California Democratic primary, gave an inspiring speech to his supporters, gave the victory sign, and left the hotel's Embassy Room's ballroom. When he reached the kitchen, Sirhan Sirhan was waiting with his .22 caliber revolver to put three bullets in Kennedy's body, a fatal one in his head. As Kennedy lay wounded on the kitchen floor, Juan Romero, a busboy, cradled the senator's head and placed a rosary in his hand. Kennedy asked Romero, "Is everybody safe, okay?" and Romero responded, "Yes, yes, everything is okay." How ironic that RFK, a man who came from a patrician background, who devoted his adult life to helping the less fortunate attain justice and civil rights, was asking about others as he was lying on the floor in a pool of his own blood, dying. Writing about these violent acts against our country's leaders, I couldn't help thinking, "What kind of country are we living in?" I realize it is a gut reaction and doesn't take into consideration all we have to be thankful for living in the United States, but it was my reaction. Having said that, I will never forget the moving words his brother, Senator Edward Kennedy, spoke at Bobby's eulogy. Holding back tears, he solemnly intoned the last paragraph of his eulogy:

> My brother need not be idealized, or enlarged in death beyond what he was in life; to be remembered simply as a good and decent man, who saw wrong and tried to right it, saw suffering and tried to heal it, saw war and tried to stop it. Those of us who loved him and who take him to his rest today, pray that what he was to us and what he wished for others will someday come to pass for the entire world. As he said many times, in many parts of this nation, to those he touched and who sought to touch him: "Some men see things as they are and say why. I dream things that never were and say why not."[4]

The death of Robert F. Kennedy was indeed the death of a dream. If there was one reason RFK was a candidate for president, it was to end the war in Vietnam. The antiwar movement was not yet a significant factor. However, with Martin Luther King Jr. and RFK having joined forces to speak out against the war, their support had the potential to make it a much stronger factor in American politics. We'll never know for sure! We will never know if the history books would have been written differently. Would a Kennedy administration have been able to avoid an extended presence of American troops in Vietnam and the 58,168 names on the Vietnam Memorial in Washington DC? Or would a Kennedy administration ever have allowed the war to build up to over 500,000 American troops? We'll never know!

The Vietnam War

I first heard of a Vietnam War when I was in the seminary in Baltimore in 1954. I kept hearing about Dien Bien Phu and the French having an extended battle there with the Vietminh. I didn't pay as much attention as I wish I had. I did learn that the Vietminh were the Vietnam Revolutionary League established by Ho Chi Minh, a name that would become more familiar. I remember when the Vietminh forces surrounded the French defensive complex at Dien Bien Phu with as many as 70,000 soldiers. I'd listen nightly to the reports on TV and radio. The fighting went on for fifty-six days as the Vietminh pushed the French forces back until they only occupied a small part of Dien Bien Phu. In 1954 the French surrendered after suffering casualties of 7,000 men and 11,000 of their soldiers were taken as prisoners.

After the drama of the battle at Dien Bien Phu was over, I lost interest in what was going on in Vietnam until I started reading in the press that President Kennedy had begun sending "military advisors" to South Vietnam early in his presidency. At the same time, he proved himself a master of "brinkmanship" by calling

Khrushchev's bluff in the Cuban Missile Crisis. This and the Kennedy administration's concern about Vietnam being a key player in the Middle East brought tensions to the highest point yet in the Cold War. Soon after the Cuban crisis, in 1962, Kennedy established the Military Assistance Command of Vietnam (MACV), which was to train the South Vietnamese army.[5]

This seemed unthreatening enough, but as the decade proceeded, we would find out differently. I obviously don't have the space to cover this time period in any depth, but I would like to point out some of the highlights that had a dramatic impact on us, both during the war and for years after it ended.

After Lyndon Johnson became president, he maintained a moderate policy on troop deployment until 1964, when two Navy destroyers in the Gulf of Tonkin reported that North Vietnamese gunboats had attacked them unprovoked. The report incensed the American people and Congress. Johnson requested that Congress pass the Gulf of Tonkin Resolution, which they did, by a large majority. Basically this gave the president a resolution that was considered a declaration of war in every way except for the name. Even though there were questions about the veracity of the report, bombing runs were ordered soon after the incident. Although the escalation of troops was deferred until after the 1964 elections, by 1965, just ten months after the Resolution, 75,000 troops were in Vietnam. By 1966 200,000 troops had been dispatched, and by the end of 1968 the number had reached 500,000.[6]

Despite numerous setbacks, the Johnson administration claimed to be making headway. Those of us who watched the news and were part of the antiwar movement became increasingly doubtful that we were being told the truth. I can clearly remember students chanting over and over, "Hey, Hey, LBJ, how many kids did you kill today?" There were increasing numbers of demonstrations on college campus all over the country. Groups like the Students for a Democratic Society (SDS) organized rallies against the Vietnam draft and encouraged students to burn their draft cards publically.

In Schenectady, I joined the Clergy and Laity Concerned about Vietnam (CALCAV). One of the major events our local group sponsored was having Fathers Dan and Philip Berrigan, two activist priests who were leaders in the antiwar movement, come to Schenectady and conduct an all day "teach-in" at one of the local church auditoriums. They drew a packed house and were received with great enthusiasm. Their presence gave a boost to our local organization. I felt honored to be on a panel with Dan Berrigan. The publicity led to several radio interviews with me and a rabbi and a Protestant minister.

The impact of the antiwar movement was so politically persuasive that even when the Vietcong launched the Tet Offensive in 1968, in which they attacked twenty-seven different U.S. military bases at the same time, General Westmoreland's request for 200,000 more troops was denied. The Tet Offensive turned millions of Americans against the war and split the Democratic Party into antiwar and pro-war factions.[7]

The My Lai massacre and cover-up was another disastrous, unfortunate event that stands out clearly in my mind. I needed to refresh my memory with more research, but my feelings were clear. I never thought our government was capable of committing such an atrocity and then spending over a year trying to cover it up. I know I was not the only one who felt so let down. Five hundred unarmed Vietnamese civilians, including women and children, were killed by a company of U.S. soldiers who were frustrated by their inability to find any Vietcong in their search-and-destroy mission. The massacre happened in 1968 but did not become public until 1969. The commander of the company, a Lieutenant Calley, was eventually sentenced to life in prison for war crimes and murder but was released in 1971 because the perception was that he was a scapegoat.[8]

I was curious about what William Calley was doing today, forty years after he was convicted, so I Googled him. Interestingly, I found that for the first time in all these years he spoke publically about My Lai at a luncheon of the Kiwanis Club in Columbus,

Georgia, on August 19, 2009, just when I was writing about My Lai. In responding to questions after his brief talk he expressed remorse: "I feel remorse for the Vietnamese who were killed, for their families, and for the American soldiers involved and their families. I am very sorry."[9] In answering other questions, he would usually respond by falling back on the phrase, "I was following orders." To me it brought back one of the possible titles that I originally thought of for my memoir, *My Country, My Church, Right or Wrong!*

When Richard M. Nixon took over as president, he did little to heal the country from the angst of the Johnson years and the years of discontent because of lack of transparency and outright lies to the American people. After all his campaign promises, the war and a series of deceits by the Nixon administration lingered on until President Ford called the war "finished" in 1974.[10] During the time that Nixon served as president, from 1969 to August 9, 1974, when he resigned because of fear of impeachment, the country had to endure the Watergate trials, and more deceptions about the war; as well as the tragedy on May 4, 1970, when the Ohio National Guard fired into a crowd of university demonstrators, killing four and wounding nine students, which triggered a nationwide student strike that forced hundreds of colleges and universities to close.[11] By that time I was in Arizona and had joined the antiwar movement at Arizona State University.

Add to that tragedy the exposure of the years of deceit that were published in the *New York Times* in June 1971 as the *Pentagon Papers.* I had the pleasure of briefly meeting and chatting with Daniel Ellsberg, the author of the *Papers,* in 2006 at a conference in Baltimore where we both were presenting papers. I found him— one of the most famous "whistleblowers" of all time—to be a very humble and sincere person. Not everyone in his position would have put his job on the line, along with a possible jail sentence. I suspect that many of you remember that he was the one who copied 7,000 pages of documents clearly showing that government officials had lied about Vietnam under previous U.S. presidents from Truman to Nixon, all of whom, except for Ford, had authorized a number of covert actions that increased the U.S. involvement in Vietnam without the knowledge of the American people. The publication of the *Papers* caused outrage, not just with the common citizen but with the Congress. If you would like to know more about the *Pentagon Papers*, the Nixon administration's efforts to stifle their circulation, and the aftermath of their publication, I would highly recommend Ellsberg's revealing book written in 2002, *Secrets: A Memoir of Vietnam and the Pentagon Papers.* [12]

The Vietnam War was always with us. Magazines, newspapers, and TV news programs wouldn't let us get too far away from the carnage of our troops and the Vietnam people. There were very few nights where the war wasn't in our living rooms with clips of wounded or dead soldiers in body bags, the bombing of innocent civilians, or Agent Orange being dropped on or near villages to deny the enemy cover and concealment by defoliating trees and shrubbery.

Although the product was effective in defoliating large areas where the Vietcong were hiding, there were chemicals in Agent Orange that were believed to be harmful to humans. Veterans, and even their children have been treated by the VA for a variety of illnesses, including non-Hodgkin's lymphoma, multiple myeloma, respiratory cancers, and a number of other potentially fatal diseases.[13] The war lives on!

Vatican Council II

Amidst all the turmoil of the 1960s, fifty years ago, much to the surprise of most of the world, and without conferring with the cardinals, the seventy-six-year-old Pope John XXIII, announced his intention of holding an Ecumenical Council. For three years, the world's bishops prepared, reviewed, or revised documents for debate at the Council. Vatican Council II met in four sessions from 1962 to 1965.[14] It included over 2,600 Catholic bishops from around the world with 240 from the United States. This

Council had more observers from other religions and non-Catholic denominations and lay observers than any other Council.[15]

The Council had five defining goals: 1) to elaborate a positive relationship between Catholicism and the modern world; unlike other Councils, it was not out to condemn the Enlightenment; 2) to abandon the harsh denunciation (anathemas) used in previous Councils; 3) to affirm the fundamental human right to religious liberty; 4) to reform Catholic spirituality; 5) to affirm that fundamental truths were taught by religions other than Roman Catholicism. At the request of Pope John XXIII, the spirit of Vatican II was to be more pastoral, and the rhetoric was to be more conciliatory and was to avoid the usual controversial language and critical statements directed toward other religious bodies or governments.[16] For me and many of my colleagues, this was not only refreshing to read but renewed our hope that major changes would be made.

After four years of debates, revisions, and compromises by the Council's fathers, sixteen documents were approved and promulgated by Pope Paul VI. The four Constitutions were: 1) *Dei Verbum* (Dogmatic Constitution on Divine Revelation); 2) *Lumen Gentium* (Dogmatic Constitution on the Church); 3) *Gaudium et Spes* (Constitution on the Church in the Modern World); and 4) *Sacrosantum Concilium* (Constitution on the Sacred Liturgy). There were also nine Decrees and three Declarations.

I will discuss in the Reflection section of this chapter two documents that are relevant to the "Primacy of Conscience"— the Constitution *Lumen Gentium* and the Declaration *Dignitatis Humanae.*

The Commission on Birth Control and *Humanae Vitae*

One of the items that I had hoped would be discussed at the Council, artificial birth control, was withdrawn from the agenda by Pope John XXIII at the suggestion of one of his confidants, Cardinal Suenens. The cardinal thought the document needed more in-depth attention than the draft he had reviewed. His assessment was that it was just a rehash of the Encyclical of Pius XII, *Casti Connubii,* on marriage. The pope took his advice and appointed a Commission that worked concurrently but separately from the Council.[17]

Pope John XXIII's death on June 3, 1963, and the election of his successor, Paul VI, temporarily halted the work on the Council session scheduled for that year. The new pope reinstated the Commission on Birth Control. The work of the Council wouldn't be completely evaluated for years and the Commission's work would be evaluated almost immediately, when the encyclical was promulgated. The encyclical, *Humanae Vitae,* received instantaneous attention from the media, theologians, and the laity when it was promulgated in 1968, two years after the Commission sent it to the pope; it seemed to have more importance than Council documents.[18]

When the Commission was first formed by John XXIII, it was made up of two Jesuits, one Dominican, and three academics. In 1964 nine new members, mostly clerics and academics, were added. In 1965 thirty-nine members, including Pat and Patty Crowley, the founders of the Christian Family Movement (CFM), and three other couples were appointed to the Commission by Paul VI. This seemed to augur well for change in the church's position on birth control. In 1966 fourteen cardinals and bishops were added to the Commission.

During the period of time the Commission was meeting, I was finishing my master's degree in social work at Fordham and, toward the end of the Commission's deliberations, I was director of Catholic Charities in Schenectady. While I was at Fordham, I was more focused on completing my coursework and thesis, but once I got to Schenectady, I experienced birth control as a very real problem for the couples I worked with. I was in residency in several different parishes during that time and was involved with couples who were struggling with the church's position that only the so-called "rhythm" method, or abstinence, was an acceptable form of birth control. These were devout Catholic couples—real people, not statistics—who had tried the rhythm method, and it didn't work for them. At the same time I was reading a number of respected theologians who were suggesting that the only humane resolution was to let folks follow their own consciences in choosing what was right for them. As a confessor, I tried to follow the advice that St. Alphonsus Ligori, the founder of the Redemptorist religious order, gave to confessors. He counseled them, when dealing with marital couples who had sex even when procreation was not their goal, not to pry too intently into their marital sexual relations. This was his attempt to temper the severe forms of the Augustinian position that marital sex was only for procreation.

I got to a point that in the confessional when someone would say, "I practiced artificial birth control six times," I would just ask, "If you sinned, are you sorry?" Sometimes they would say something like "Father, I guess I'm sorry, but I can't say that I have a firm purpose of amendment. I can't promise that I won't do it again." They would often go into their reasons for using birth control methods not condoned by the church. I'd usually say something like, "Look, right now, at this minute, you are sorry if you offended God, right?"

"Well, yes!"

"So if you walked outside the church, it's possible that you might get hit by a bus, right?"

"I suppose so."

"So, as long as you are sorry right here and now, that's all I need to know." I realized that it wasn't solving their problem, but I felt it was a legitimate response to their dilemma. They were being honest with me, and I felt I could give them absolution.

Another direct connection I had with couples who were trying to live by the church's doctrines was through the Christian Family Movement. I was asked by several of these groups in Schenectady to be their chaplain. CFM was a lay movement started in the forties in Chicago by devout Catholic couples who wanted to contribute to social change in their community and in the world.

It soon became a national movement. Often, the couples in the groups I met with would bring up the issue of birth control and ask about the possibility of the Commission voting to change the rules. Again, these were good Catholic couples who were struggling to bring up a family and at the same time trying hard to conform to a teaching of the church that they didn't agree with. It sounds corny, but I could feel their pain.

As more and more rumors leaked from the Commission, couples expressed optimism, thinking that the church would actually listen to their struggles. Listening to couples in my parish was enlightening for me. I became more convinced that the church had to recognize the pain that these good people were struggling with and make reasonable changes in their current teaching.

The Commission held its final meetings during the last two weeks in May and the first week of June 1966. One of the weeks they planned was a pastoral week where the laypeople would have an opportunity to express their positions and feelings on birth control as married members, representing "the sense of the faithful."

Patty Crowley came well prepared with information she had collected from surveys from CFM members and reputable demographers. She was particularly impressive in describing the negative effects that the "rhythm" method had on women. Another laywoman was just as effective in her presentation. She was more personal. She described herself as a woman who had been married for seventeen years and had had five children, three miscarriages, and a hysterectomy. After establishing her credentials to speak to the Commission, she went on to describe the true meaning of sexuality in a Christian life. She described the conjugal act as a total gift of body and soul to the loved one, "a gift of pleasure and of psychological fulfillment."[19] I suspect that many of the hierarchy present, with their fancy titles, educational backgrounds, and medieval vestments, received a powerful lesson in sex education. There's no way I can do justice to the powerful impact these faithful Christian women had as they described how it was in the real world, not just for themselves but for the many women they represented. If you're interested in reading a very moving report of their testimony, I would strongly suggest your reading pages 102–108, in Robert McClory's book *Turning Point*.[20] In addition to his accurate and scholarly report of the inside story of the Commission of Papal Birth Control, his thesis is that *Humanae Vitae* is "the" turning point in the life of the church. After reviewing a number of research projects and studies written over the forty-one years since the promulgation of *Humanae Vitae*, I would have to agree with McClory's conclusions.

There have been dozens of reports measuring the impact that the encyclical had on the faithful. To give a couple of examples that are typical of the majority of the surveys, the *New York Times* published a poll eighteen years after the *Humanae Vitae* was promulgated, showing that 70 percent of adult Catholics used artificial birth control and 80 percent said one could disagree with the pope on birth control and still be a good Catholic; in 1991 a Gallup poll found that 87 percent of Catholics believed the church should permit couples to make their own decisions based on their consciences.[18] In my opinion, this is *sensus fidelium*, speaking but being ignored by the hierarchy. It's the hierarchy not listening to the lowerarchy.

It was not just the negative consequences of the encyclical that was problematic but the high-handed process that was used by the minority of the Commission to change the playing field. Before the final vote was taken, the rules were changed, and the only voting members on the Commission of over seventy members would be the sixteen bishops and cardinals named by the pope, most of whom only attended the last plenary meeting.[20] All the other participants were no longer technically members of the Commission but were considered "experts." This unexplained procedural change was a major concern for many advocates for change, especially because the change in membership was surmised to have been initiated by the archconservative Cardinal Alfredo Octavianni, the aged head of the Congregation for the Doctrine of the Faith and confidant to the pope. He was well aware that the vote of the entire seventy members of the Commission would be embarrassingly in favor of change. If I had spent all those years working on the Commission under the impression that I was a voting member, I would have been a little miffed at losing my vote. I suppose I should have known better, but it was behavior I would expect more from the Mafia than the Holy See. In the language of my old Judson Street neighborhood, it sounds like "dirty pool."

Despite the timing of this unusual procedure, the reports from the majority and minority, the voting process proceeded. There were three major papers that were presented at the final meetings of the Commission: 1) a minority report, written by an American theologian, Rev. John Ford, an ally of Cardinal Octavianni, who spoke passionately for maintaining the current teaching of the church as articulated in *Casti Connubii,* the 1930 encyclical of Pope Pius XI on Christian marriage; 2) the majority rebuttal, the *Summary Document on the Morality of Birth Control*, which denied that *Casti Connubii* was an infallible doctrine; 3) the majority report, *Responsible Parenthood*.[21]

There was further discussion about whether they would send a minority and majority report to the pope. Recognizing that they would never reach a unanimous position, the Commission agreed to send one official position representing the majority position to Pope Paul.

There were three questions for the bishops to vote on: 1) was contraception intrinsically evil? The vote was nine bishops "yes," three "no." 2) Was contraception, as defined in the majority report, in basic continuity with tradition and the declarations of the magisterium? Nine bishops voted "yes," five "no," and one abstained. 3) Should the magisterium speak on this question as soon as possible? Fourteen bishops voted "yes," and one "no." The majority of the bishops and cardinals gave their assent to the majority report.[22]

I will include more about the aftermath of the pope's decision, which was against the majority report, in the next chapter, but for now, let me point out that two years after the pope received the report—in 1968—Paul VI promulgated the *Humanae Vitae*. So much for "as soon as possible"! To me it was like the pope saying, "Let us sit down together and discuss birth control, but we'll do it my way, I'm the 'decider.'" But of course the church is not a democracy, and we should learn to expect Rome to continue to act like the absolute monarchy that it has become. At least now I know why it took Paul VI two years to approve my dispensation from the priesthood, which I sent him in 1968. He must have been busy making up his mind about the encyclical. Seriously, if you would like to know all the details about the decision-making of the Commission, again I would recommend McClory's book. It's fascinating and infuriating. Especially, Appendix I, pages 171–187,[23] where he has included the complete text of *Responsible Parenthood*, the majority report of the Birth Control Commission.

Reflections

In recalling Vatican II, I remember being excited about the possibilities of positive changes in the church. It was almost like an Obama, "Yes, we can, yes, we can" spirit that was giving us hope. I was particularly impressed with the pastoral language the documents used, in contrast to the finger-pointing, name-calling, strident style of past Councils. Reading Robert Blair Kaiser's reports for *Time* magazine and his book *Clerical Error*, in which he describes many of the Council's participants, who attended his weekly house parties, I felt as if I knew many of the major players personally.

As far as content goes, I appreciated that several of the documents that I mentioned before, *Lumen Gentium*, the Dogmatic Constitution on the Church and the Declaration on Religious Freedom, *Dignitas Humana*, addressed the important issues of the primacy of conscience and the *sensus fidelium* (the sense of the faithful) which had been considered as an important part of the magisterium.

What I intend to do in these reflections is to share with you some thoughts that I have on what I think are some underlying issues on the primacy of conscience and the *sensus fidelium*.

I mentioned a while back that I've been meeting for the last ten years twice a month with a group of men and women who discuss books, articles, and DVDs, and we call ourselves "the Seekers." I've realized that I was a seeker for many years before I started to meet with the group. Participating with the Seekers has been an enormous help in my journey toward truth, a journey that is a lifelong mission. I regret that over the years I have often lost my way and strayed off the path of seeking truth. When I did, there was never much doubt that I was off track and needed to make some adjustment in my behavior. There were other times when I needed to revaluate what I had learned but took for granted just because the source was an authority. I learned that I needed to follow a responsible path; I needed to listen to my conscience.

Conscience is not some type of a Jiminy Cricket voice that was given to Pinocchio by the Blue Fairy as his official conscience. It's much more complicated than that. Just so we can be on the same page, without being too pedantic, I'd like to share some of the research that I did to clarify in my own mind the church's teachings on conscience and the *sensus fidelium*. Although it was not directly addressed in the Council documents, I found that I also needed to clarify infallibility as it relates to the other concepts.

I will start with a quote from Pope John Paul II that describes the process a seeker goes through to arrive at a "good" conscience. "In order to have a 'good' conscience, persons must seek the truth and make judgments in accordance with that same truth."[24] The pope is assuming that we have checked out the major source for developing an informed conscience—the magisterium, which includes the "teaching church" and the "believing church" (*sensus fidelium*). The believing church was intended to have a consultative role to ensure the truth of the doctrines of the magisterium. The content of the teaching church is made up of the Scriptures and traditions ranging from the teachings of the early fathers of the church, and all twenty-one Ecumenical Councils from the Council of Nicaea in 325, when Emperor Constantine made the church the official church of Rome, and it went from a church that followed Jesus' teachings to one that enforced required beliefs. This is not an exhaustive list of what is included in the magisterium, but it gives an idea of how extensive this information has become during the 1,640 years between the first and last Ecumenical Councils. I doubt that anyone is expected to review each document in the magisterium to have an informed conscience. That is one reason for the publication of the Catechism of the Catholic Church (CCC).

The second edition of the Catechism was promulgated in 1997 with an apostolic letter from Pope John Paul II. The aim of the Catechism is to present a synthesis of the essential doctrine of the church in both faith and morals in light of Vatican II and the whole tradition of the church: "It's the principle source of the church's magisterium."[25] It is where all the prescribed beliefs are. This document is a far cry from the little blue-covered Baltimore Catechism that many of us studied throughout our days in Catholic grammar school. The Catechism of the Catholic Church is a model for bishops' conferences throughout the world to use to develop their own national catechisms.

The teachings of the church on conscience can be found in Article 6, items 1777 through 1802 of the Catechism. Item 1778 defines conscience as "a judgment of reason whereby the human person recognizes the moral quality of a concrete act ... In all he says or does, man is obliged to follow faithfully what he knows to be just and right." It's quite clear that our judgment and reason is the key to figuring out what is right and wrong. We are not expected simply to accept automatically what the magisterium views as right or wrong (prescribed beliefs); we are given the responsibility (responsible faith) to use our God-given gift of reason to make our own decisions even when they are at odds with the magisterium. The Catechism envisions the development of our conscience as a lifelong task, which is assisted by the Holy Spirit. One concern that I have with the relying on the magisterium is that even though it covers a great deal of material from the "teaching church," it's difficult to find clear statements of what the "believing church" has contributed to the magisterium. I believe this is an important factor. We've already seen how the "teaching church" dismissed the vote of the laypeople who were members of the Commission on Birth Control. I've always had the suspicion that they were just there as window dressing and that Cardinal Octavianni never took them seriously. I suspect he had a secret plan to make sure that the only ones who would vote would be the bishops and cardinals.

Reading the Venerable John Henry Newman and many other theologians since his time reassured me of the importance of the participation of the believing church in contributing to the contents of the magisterium. The fact that there are many examples of teachings in the magisterium that are just downright wrong and need to be corrected gave me more cause to take another look at the need for the believing church to be taken more seriously. One blatant example that stands out is the "Syllabus of Errors," promulgated by Pope Pius IX in 1862.[26] He identifies eighty statements that he condemns. Many of those statements, especially those that concern science and religion, have not stood the test of time. To say the least, there are statements in the Syllabus that are an embarrassment for the church in the third millennium, especially since Pius IX was the pope who lobbied the doctrine of infallibility through the first Vatican Council.

Aside from those teachings that are simply wrong, the future Cardinal Newman's main concern is with the lack of inclusiveness in the teaching of the magisterium, which minimizes the voice of the "believing church."[27] In an essay entitled *On Consulting the Faithful in Matters of Doctrine,* he described the role of the *sensus fidelium* (the sense of the faithful) in relation to the magisterium in unambiguous words:

> Consulting the people is not to be regarded as just a friendly gesture on the part of the pope and bishops.

Consultation is something the laity have a right to expect. Their view may serve at times as a needed witness of the truth of a revealed doctrine.[28]

Newman also warned what the consequence was for not paying attention to the believing church. He is quoted in a book edited by John Coulson, *On Consulting the Faithful:* "When she (the teaching church) cuts off the faithful from the study of divine doctrines, and requires them a *fides implicita* (blind faith or unquestioning trust) in her word, which in the educated class will terminate in indifference, and in the poor superstition."[29]

In putting such a strong emphasis on the sense of the faithful, it almost sounds like Cardinal Newman had some sort of democratic structure in mind to replace the absolute monarchy of Rome, with all its trappings and power over the people.

Primacy of Conscience

Because of the loss of confidence in the magisterium experienced by many members of the believing church in recent years, it is acutely urgent for members or lapsed members to understand the concept of the primacy of conscience. Primacy of conscience is deeply embedded in our Western moral tradition and is often charged with leading to relativism and exaggerated autonomy in morals. In an article in the *Australian Journal of Theology* on the principle of the primacy of conscience, Brian Lewis points out that according to this principle "One must follow the sure judgment of conscience even when through no fault of its own it is mistaken."[29]

Lewis goes on to recognize that it is often claimed that the primacy of conscience is responsible for a shift to relativism in morals and a skewed independence of an increasing number of people today. He acknowledges that many, including Catholics, believe that they are entitled to make up their own minds on faith and morals without reference to outside authority as long as they do not compromise others' rights. Lewis does not see these people as espousing a "do your own thing " posture, and he is equally clear that:

- the primacy of conscience does not mean, nor has it ever meant, liberation from objective truth.
- no objective formula of truth or moral law coming from outside can take the place of conscience because it is through the mediation of conscience that one perceives and acknowledges the divine law.
- because it is an exercise of human reason, conscience is fragile and fallible and can lead to errors of judgment.
- in all of our activities, one is bound to follow one's conscience.

There are numerous documents that I could use to support Lewis's position, but I just intend to refer to a couple of statements that clearly reinforce the concept of the primacy of conscience. St. Thomas More, who some have hailed as the patron saint of conscience, said at his trial for not giving in to Henry VIII's demand that he sign a statement of allegiance: "You must understand that, in things touching conscience, every person is bound to respect his conscience more than any other thing in the world."[30] These were strong words for someone who was going to be executed for the stand he took in defying the king.

To add just one more voice that supports the primacy of conscience, here is a statement made by then Joseph Ratzinger (now Pope Benedict XVI) in which he eloquently expressed the church's understanding of the primacy of conscience. At that time, in 1968, he served as Chair of Dogmatic Theology at the University of Tubinger.

Above the pope as an expression of the binding claim of church authority stands one's own conscience, which has to be obeyed first of all, if need be against the demands of church authority.[31]

It seems clear to me that in the opinion of the current pope a well-formed conscience trumps the magisterium. That's why I believe it is so important to arrive at an informed conscience, whether or not we agree with a particular teaching of the magisterium. That is the essence of a responsible faith.

The next chapter examines the post-Vatican II church. It will focus on some of the issues that the Council didn't cover, including infallibility, mandated celibacy for the priesthood, and women's issues, including women serving as priest.

Chapter 10
Life in Post-Vatican II

Even though my work with Catholic Charities was rewarding, like many others who had high expectations for Vatican II, I was disappointed but not surprised that the Council fathers had not addressed the issues in which I was most interested. At that time there seemed to be a very remote possibility that Rome would make changes in the near future regarding mandatory celibacy or women being able to be ordained. After over forty years, I am more convinced than ever that the hierarchically structured church needs to change to a more democratic structure. To do this, the church needs to be more serious about implementing the documents of Vatican II, especially as they related to the role of the laity and recognizing that the Vatican does not have the corner of the market on truth.

Vatican II ended in 1965, and I set a date for myself to apply for a dispensation by 1967. In 1964 I had moved my residence from St. Columbia's Church in Schenectady to the Dominican Retreat and Conference Center in Schenectady. The reason for the move was that the pastor at St. Columbia's had a drinking problem, and I couldn't manage my work at Catholic Charities and at the parish at the same time.

To give you an example, Father Mac (not his real name) would disappear for a week or more at a time. More often than not, we would get a phone call from a police precinct in New York City and the captain, usually with a touch of a brogue, would say something like, "This is Captain O'Leary from Precinct 49 in Manhattan; do you have a Father Mac stationed at your church?"

"Yes, we do. Is he okay?"

"Well, we picked him up at a hotel down near the Bowery, and he was drunk as a skunk and didn't have the money to pay for his room. We have him here now, but we don't want to press charges. Can you send someone to come down and pick him up?"

"Yes, we can. Will tomorrow be okay?"

"Yeah! Listen, this poor guy needs some professional help. Our records show that this ain't the first time he's been picked up. You know what I mean?'

"I do, Captain, and I appreciate your letting us know."

Picking up the pastor in New York City meant that either Bill Esmond or I would have to drive to New York and bring him back to Schenectady—a total of about 350 miles—and it was not a pleasant trip. Having made the trip, I know; I just don't mean the time and miles. Father Mac would have sobered up when we arrived at the police precinct, and from the time he got in the car till the time we reached Schenectady he was either apologizing profusely or crying or both. It was sad to see a man in his early sixties with such self-hate. He was not a bad man, by any means. When he wasn't drinking, he was a pleasure to be with, but when he was under the influence, he was a completely different person. His anger with himself was directed at Bill or me. It was taking a toll on all of us, including the parishioners, who would complain about smelling alcohol on his breath. I couldn't handle both a parish and Catholic Charities. When Bill, who was senior to me, wasn't available, I had to make the trip. After the last episode, Bill and I discussed the situation, and I volunteered to speak to Monsignor Hart, the bishop's secretary, to alert him to the situation. We both felt a little guilty about "turning him in," but we thought that it would be in everybody's best interest.

I got an appointment to speak to Monsignor Hart at the chancery office and expressed my concern for Father Mac and his need for professional help and also my need to have a residency that didn't demand as much time as St. Columbia's. Monsignor Hart assured me that we had done the right thing, and he would take care of arrangements for Father Mac to receive help. He also told me that he had just the place for me to live. The Dominican Retreat and Conference Center in Schenectady needed a chaplain for the nuns, and all I would have to do was to say Mass for them every morning. That was a relief. I really was beginning to feel pulled in two different directions.

The Retreat Center was ideal. It was only about two miles from my office. I was impressed when Sister Jean Marie showed me my living quarters in a converted windmill. There were three rooms, one on top of the other. The first floor was a living room with a kitchenette, just in case I wanted to prepare a meal; the second floor was a study; and there was a spacious bedroom on the third floor. Plus, it was secluded—on a beautiful campus where retreats, days of recollection, and conferences were held. Every morning after Mass, which was held in the convent, only a short walk from the windmill, I would go to the dining room, where one of the nuns would serve me breakfast. Living in the windmill, I felt like Thomas Merton, who was given permission by his abbot at Gethsemane to live by himself in a small hermitage on the grounds of the monastery. For him it was an opportunity to live like a hermit and do his writing, meditation, and study. It gave me the opportunity to focus on Catholic Charities and my social-change activities in the community.

Positive Social Change

Remember, back in an earlier chapter when Father Hinds asked me what I intended to do when I graduated from CBA? I told him I was thinking about going to Siena College to study social work. I only had a vague idea about what a social worker did, but

I did know that there was no requirement for mandatory celibacy. I found out much later that I was probably meant to be a social worker because there was a lot of overlap in what social workers and priests did. Of course there were also many obvious differences. In Schenectady most of what I did was social work and working toward social change; I was a change agent. When I was in my role as a priest, I was administering the sacraments, preparing and giving sermons, preparing adults for marriage or baptism, ministering to the sick, etc. As a social worker I was administering Catholic Charities—raising money by writing grants, soliciting funds from corporations and foundations, representing the agency on a number of community boards, etc. Following are a few examples of my role as a social worker/priest.

One of the more exciting and creative programs that came out of President Lyndon B. Johnson's so-called War on Poverty was the Economic Opportunity Act (EOA) of 1964. The purpose of this act was to mobilize human and financial resources of the nation to combat poverty.[1] There were a number of programs that EOA introduced; perhaps the best-known is Head Start. The program is for children three to five years old. It enriches a child's learning experience and prepares him or her for kindergarten and continued success in school. Services include nutrition, health and mental health information, parent involvement opportunities, and support services. Perhaps the reason it is still in existence after over forty-four years is its demonstrated success rate. There are a number of anecdotal and empirical studies suggesting that one of the major factors in its success is the fact that it involves parents as volunteers in the program, recognizing that they are a key component in their children's educational success. A recent article, "U.S. Education Milestone: 25 Million Success Stories for Head Start Program," bears witness to the program's success.[2]

Another of my favorite programs was the Community Action Program (CAP). I remember very clearly the day when Schenectady received CAP money to start a CAP program. Each community that received the money had to follow the guidelines handed down from the Office of Economic Opportunity. One of the most innovative requirements was the idea of "maximum feasible participation." This meant that the governing board had to be made up of three groups of equal numbers from the community. The first group was the "poor" people; they would have equal representation with local government officials and civic leaders. Each group would elect its own members to serve on the CAP governing board. There was a series of meetings in which each group held its own meetings to select its members. After much deliberation within each group, nine recognized neighborhood leaders, nine local officials, and nine civic leaders from mostly social service agencies were elected. I was elected as a civic leader. After each group chose its members, the board of twenty-seven members met briefly to elect a temporary chairperson and decide on a name for the organization. We chose the title Schenectady Community Action Program, Inc. (SCAP) for our not-for-profit organization, funded by OEO.

There were meetings several times a week for the first several months. A number of standing committees were formed, and a timetable for completing our tasks was established. I was on several committees, but the most important one, in my eyes, was the personnel committee, whose first responsibility was selecting an executive director for SCAP. There were many discussions about whether we should choose an indigenous person from the community or a professional with experience in community organizing. We finally agreed that we would seek a professional with experience in organizing, and if he or she happened to be an indigenous person, that would be a bonus.

The personnel committee narrowed the pool of applicants for the position of executive director down to three and presented its selections to the board. After much discussion about the qualifications of the finalists, the board chose Mike Nardallio. Mike had a master's degree in social work and had worked for the state of New York and the Albany office of Catholic Charities. I remembered him from high school as a tough football player from Schuyler High School. One of the things that stood out in the hiring process was the salary for the position. It was $13,000. Some of the representatives on the board from the neighborhood organizations thought that was a little high. I thought it was a little high, too. I was making $6,800 as director of Catholic Charities. In those days I thought anyone making over $10,000 was rich. But I recognized that to be competitive we needed to offer a tempting salary.

One of the things with which we had to struggle in the beginning was to make sure that we followed the requirement of "maximum feasible participation." In the early meetings the professionals and civic leaders seem to dominate. The indigenous leaders seemed a little intimidated by the other two groups. The chairperson made efforts to facilitate their participating more, without much success. Finally, we decided that it would be helpful for all of us to spend a day on retreat with a professional facilitator to work on participating equally. Although it was awkward in the beginning of the retreat for folks to be candid, the facilitator provided a series of exercises that helped, and, by the end of the day, he joked that he thought he had created a monster—there were was so many indigenous folk participating. We ended the day with a cocktail party and dinner that also contributed to solidifying the group.

I mentioned in passing in the last chapter my involvement with the antiwar group, Clergy and Laity Concerned about Vietnam (CALCAV). What I didn't mention was the opposition from some of my brother priests and parishioners to my taking a stance for peace. Their position was that the church—and particularly clergy—had no business being involved in political movements. I didn't have any problem with those who expressed their beliefs to me publicly or privately, but I did have a problem with anonymous phone calls and letters accusing me of being a Communist or questioning the legitimacy of my birth.

Looking back on the sixties and the attitudes of some of the hierarchy, which they freely expressed, while just as freely

trying to suppress others' freedom of speech, I was not surprised
when my research turned up a report about Catholics' support
for the war. It claimed that liberal Protestants and Jewish clergy
urged negotiations while conservative clergy, including the
Roman Catholic hierarchy and Evangelicals, openly or tacitly
supported the war effort. The report quoted Cardinal Spellman,
vicar of the Catholics in the U.S. military, remarking in 1965, "I
support everything it [the United States] does ... My country,
may it always be right. Right or wrong, my country."[3] Now we
know where most of the hierarchy and clergy were getting their
marching orders from. No wonder that the rank and file sitting
in the pews were so supportive of the Vietnam War.

Another issue related to the war that brought down more heat from
the right on members of Clergy and Laity Concerned about Vietnam
was the issuing in October 1967 of a "Statement on Conscience
and Conscription," in which we endorsed the right to oppose this
particular war alone, not all wars. The statement went on to say
we would publicly counsel all who in conscience could not serve,
to refuse service by nonviolent means.[4] Within a matter of weeks,
thirteen hundred clergymen had signed the statement. As a result
of the national and local publicity the statement on conscience and
conscription generated and my being identified in the community as
a member, I had a half a dozen young men contact me for counsel.

Since Catholics were not ordinarily conscientious objectors
with regard to every war, they had to make a case why they could
rely on their consciences for this particular war. The answer was
based on the primacy of conscience. I found the young men
whom I counseled to be very sincere, well informed, and resolute
in their stance as to why they couldn't serve in a combat position
in Vietnam. They had struggled with their consciences to come to
this conclusion. They were not cowards. They loved their country.
But they did not believe, with Francis Cardinal Spellman, "My
country, right or wrong." They just did not believe that this war
was a just war. They were willing to serve as medics or in some
other noncombat position but not to fight against Vietnam.

I was asked to be part of a panel on a local radio station with a rabbi and a professor from Union College to discuss the rights of young men who chose to follow their consciences. Apparently I said something that riled some veterans of World War II. I received a call from Monsignor Hart at the chancery wondering what I was up to. He mentioned in a friendly way that the bishop had received a number of letters complaining about my position on the war in Vietnam and my giving aid and comfort to the enemy. I explained that the position of CALCAV was not against all wars but just the Vietnam War. He informed me that the bishop had no problem with my expressing my views peacefully but just wanted him to give me a call to make sure I wasn't planning to do anything too radical. I assured him that we were a peaceful organization and not Communists. He closed the conversation with, "Well, don't do anything I wouldn't do." I responded, "Tell the bishop I'm keeping good company."

The following year, after I had already left to study at Columbia, the Berrigan brothers and seven other demonstrators broke into the draft board office in Catonsville, Maryland, and burned the draft records. The Berrigans and their fellow demonstrators were tried in a very public trial, convicted, and imprisoned for their actions. Father Dan Berrigan spent four months as a fugitive from the FBI after his conviction. He was captured and sent to prison for eighteen months.[5] I wondered how the bishop would have felt about the Catonsville nine?

A New Start

In 1967 I made an appointment to see the auxiliary bishop of the diocese, Bishop Edward McGinn. Bishop Scully had retired because of poor health, and Bishop McGinn was his temporary replacement. The purpose of my meeting was to inform him that I planned to leave the priesthood. I had known Bishop McGinn since I was in the seminary but had never had an opportunity to talk to him in any depth. I would run into him at meetings, and he was always very cordial and would ask how I was doing or remark about my assignments, but that was it. To say the least, I was a little nervous about the meeting, having no idea how he would react. I guess I was still intimidated by anyone in a position of authority.

After some preliminary chitchat, I got down to business. I told him that I wanted to apply for a papal dispensation to leave the priesthood. He looked at me a little sadly and verbally expressed his surprise. He went on to tell me that he had heard such good things about my work in Catholic Charities, he thought I would have a very promising career (I never thought of being a priest as a career) in the church. He asked why I wanted a dispensation. As best I can remember, my reply went something like this: "As hard as I've tried, I'm finding it very difficult to lead a celibate life. What looked easy when I was eighteen became more complex and difficult as I got older. When I said 'yes' to celibacy, I think I had a very immature and limited idea of what celibacy entailed. I never saw it in the full context of having a family. I like being a priest very much, but I often feel like a hypocrite. If it wasn't for mandatory celibacy, we probably wouldn't be having this conversation. There are other issues besides celibacy, but I can live with them." I thought I was talking too much, so I stopped. He waited for what seemed like several minutes before asking, "Have you discussed this with anyone?"

I confidently replied, "Yes, Bishop, with a number of people: my confessor, other priests, my therapist, a lay friend, retreat masters, and I've prayed over it for a number of years."

Again he was a little pensive. I expected him to come up with some pat answer, but he seemed very understanding when he replied, "My sense is that you've given this serious thought, and you sought good advice. I know you are well aware that this is a serious matter, so I would like you to do one more thing before I feel comfortable enough to pursue a dispensation. I ask that you consult with Father Owen Bennett at St. Anthony's on the Hudson. He's a very fair person who will take a neutral position and not try to talk you out of your decision. He'll just ask questions."

I immediately responded that I would. As I left, he said, "Your bishop will be praying for you."

At my meeting, Father Bennett was very supportive. After listening to my story and asking some questions, he reinforced my decision. He made one suggestion, which he made clear was just that—an idea to think about. He suggested, "You might want to think about asking the bishop for a two-year leave of absence to work on your doctoral degree if you have any doubts. I know you have agonized over this decision, and you also said you want to work on your doctoral degree, so this might be an alternative. If the bishop agrees, and if, at the end of the two years, you decided that you don't want to leave, he would have a priest with a doctorate or at least an ABD. If you still wanted to get a dispensation, then you could go ahead with your plans, and you would still have your degree, or close to it. Unless there is some urgency to get the dispensation right away, it sounds like a win-win situation." He asked if it was okay with me for him to report back to the bishop the content of our discussion. I told him it was okay with me, and I would think about the alternative he suggested.

When I spoke to the bishop, he told me that Father Bennett was impressed with how I had struggled with my decision. He agreed that if I wasn't able to live a celibate life, it would be best for me to leave. The bishop said that he agreed with Father Bennett's alternative, and that if I even had the slightest doubt, he would agree to grant me a leave of absence for two years to work on my doctorate and pay my monthly salary, not as director of Catholic Charities, but as an associate pastor. At that time, it happened to be $166.66 per month I was never sure how they arrived at that figure, but in 1967, with room and board included, it seemed more than fair to me. He also told me that, unless I decided otherwise, I would be a priest in good standing for the next two years. I told him I couldn't guarantee that I could remain celibate during that time but that I would do the best I could—and I meant that. He came back with a phrase I hadn't heard in years, "Angels can do no more." We both agreed with the alternative for two years, and there were no written or signed papers. As I left, he gave me a blessing and repeated his promise that he would be praying for me.

I applied to three doctoral programs: Columbia University in New York, the Heller School of Social Work at Brandeis University in Massachusetts, and Bryn Mawr College in Pennsylvania. They were three of the top schools of social work, and I wanted to stay in the East.

At Columbia I was interviewed by two of the icons in social work education, Al Kahn and Florence Hollis. Both of them were prolific writers, Kahn in social policy and planning and Hollis in clinical social work. They were both interested in my assessment of the Community Action Program in Schenectady, and I felt very comfortable about sharing my experience and evaluation. A week or so after my interview, I received a letter of acceptance to Columbia. It included a stipend of $3,600 per semester from the National Institute of Mental Health. I wrote to cancel my upcoming interview at Bryn Mawr and since I also had interviewed at Brandeis I wrote Dean Schottland to thank him for the time he had spent with me and for his kindness.

I had the summer to prepare for Columbia and bring closure in my work with Catholic Charities and the community. There were several going-away parties, an article in the *Schenectady Gazette* describing my accomplishments and future plans, and dozens of heartwarming cards wishing me well. Although my parents understood that I would be on a leave of absence and that I might get a dispensation from the priesthood, their hopes and prayers were that I would not leave the priesthood. To their credit, they didn't try to influence me directly to stay in the priesthood, just as they hadn't tried to influence me to enter the seminary. When the subject was brought up, it was usually about what the family would think and what they'd tell people if I did leave the priesthood. In the late sixties there was a stigma in a priest leaving the priesthood, and families were afraid of losing face. But when push came to shove, I knew that they would support whatever decision I might make. I was right!

Columbia University

I never dreamed that I would attend one of the eight Ivy League universities, but there I was a doctoral student at Columbia! Their of School of Social Work is the oldest social work school in the United States, with its roots dating back to 1889, when the New York Charity Organization Society offered its first summer course. After several moves, it was located in 1949 at 2 East 91st Street at Fifth Avenue in Manhattan. This was the former Andrew Carnegie Mansion.[6] It was ironic that social work students were being taught in a mansion of such extraordinary elegance; that a profession that championed the rights of workers was located in the former home of one of the "robber barons"; that the former owner was counted along with names like J. P. Morgan and John D. Rockefeller, all of whom were as well known for their opposition to unions and workers' rights to a "fair day's pay for a fair day's work" as they were for their charity.

Most of the rooms had been made over into classrooms and offices, but there was one room where the doctoral classes met that was the former "sewing room." I remember being told that one of the sewing cabinets that remained attached to a wall had been imported from Thailand and cost $20,000. For those days that seemed lavish to me, even for a robber baron.

Since I was on a leave of absence and in good standing with the diocese, the good nuns let me have my old room back at St. Patrick's Home for the Aged. Monsignor Reardon was delighted to have me back. He would have someone to play his pranks on, except that I was not as naive as I was when I believed that Nolan was at the six-day bicycle race.

Our first class was Issues in Social Security with Dr. Eveline M. Burns. Dr. Burns was a giant in the field of Social Security. She was an economist who taught social welfare at Columbia for almost forty years. She authored three important books on Social Security and was appointed by the Roosevelt administration as the first training consultant for the Social Security Board in early 1936.[7] She was a good example of the caliber of the instructors. We had her class in the morning for three hours once a week. She would usually try to have lunch with a few of us. I remember one day she was talking about how she and her husband had decided to move to St. Thomas in the Virgin Islands when they retired. They had been spending summers there for a number of years. They observed early on that food was more expensive there, but liquor was less expensive, and as they got older they needed less food and more booze.

It surprised me how down-to-earth this distinguished scholar and straitlaced English woman could be. At that time she was approaching sixty-five and told us, "After forty years teaching, they were getting ready to give me the boot. They'll give me a title of professor emeritus and put me out to pasture." That was the policy of the university. I'm sure they would have liked to have kept her on because of the status she brought to the program, but apparently they didn't have a choice. She received a position at New York University's School of Social Work and taught there for another eight years.

After the first months of classes, I had serious doubts that I would ever finish the program. My nemesis was statistics. I had never been that good in math. Luckily, one of my classmates, Donald Feldstein, the smartest boy in our class, volunteered to tutor several of us who were mathematically impaired and, thanks to him, I managed to get through the class with a B minus. I did well enough in my other classes to bring my average above the required B. I was beginning to think there was some hope for me.

As I recall, we started with fourteen in our class, and only three of the fourteen were women—a very small percentage by today's standards. One of the women, Aracelis Francis, was a very striking woman with a charming smile from the Virgin Islands. I had learned my lesson from my experience at Fordham, and, although I was very attracted to her (she reminded me of the late Dorothy Dandridge), I never pursued a romantic relationship with her. We did become very good friends, studied together, met for dinners, went to movies, and stayed in touch for several years after we graduated. I Googled her recently, and I was not surprised to read that she had had a very distinguished career for over thirty-five years. She taught at several universities and held administrative positions both in the States and the Virgin Islands.

On most weekends I went back to Albany Diocese to help out with Masses at the Immaculate Conception Church in New Lebanon, New York. The pastor was Father Curt Hughes, who became one of my best friends, confidants, and mentors. The rectory was a refuge from Columbia, my daily struggles, and my unresolved future. I can still remember driving toward the rectory from New York and seeing the steeple of the church getting closer and closer. It always felt like I was coming home.

New Lebanon was only fifteen minutes from two of the Berkshire's finest ski resorts, Jiminy Peak and Brodie Mountain. Our favorite was Brodie, mainly because it had night skiing and manmade snow when needed. Brodie was where I first learned to ski, under the tutelage of Curt Hughes. Curt was one of those people everyone liked. Besides being a good priest, he was an avid golfer and skier and knew how to enjoy life. He had dozens of lay friends through his sporting activities, and his rectory was a haven for his parishioners, his golfing and skiing friends, and his brother priests.

We called it the Fun Farm. It was not unusual for Curt to bring half a dozen friends or acquaintances home from the slopes to have dinner, and if someone could play the piano we'd sing or just listen to good music. He was also a good dancer from his college days and loved to dance. His living room was like a club room with a card table, comfortable sofas and chairs for group conversations, an ample supply of liquor and wine, and room for dancing. I wasn't much of a dancer, but there was always a female guest who was willing to try to overcome my two left feet. Most of the women were there with their husbands, and everyone would help preparing the meal. Curt would cook the steaks on his outside barbecue grill, someone else would be preparing a Caesar salad from scratch, and vegetables were cooking on the stove. It was just like a family dinner.

My old friend from St. Patrick's Home for the Aged, John Gavin Nolan, was a frequent visitor. He was now Monsignor Nolan and

Secretary of the Catholic Near East Welfare Association, which he had inherited from the former secretary, Archbishop Joseph Ryan, his and my close friend and at that time the archbishop of Anchorage, Alaska. In Nolan's position as secretary for the Near East Association he had one office in Beirut and another in New York City. He reported directly to the pope, who at that time was Paul VI. I remember that at one of his visits to the Fun Farm, we were playing gin rummy, and out of the blue he announced that he had the pope's tiara in the trunk of his car. Of course Curt and I didn't believe him, thinking it was one of his usual practical jokes. He insisted he was telling the truth that the pope had divested himself of that extravagant three-tier crown as a demonstration of his humility. We called his bluff, only to find out he was not kidding. There it was in a velvet-lined leather case, right where he said it was. The pope had let him take it to raise money for the Catholic Near East Association, and he was making a national tour with the tiara as his prop.

Phil and Lisa Moore were two of the people I met at the Fun Farm. Phil was famous for a jazz quartet that he created and led—the Phil Moore Four. He spent the late 1940s as accompanist and musical director for singers such as Lena Horne, Dorothy Dandridge, and Diahann Carroll. Curt and I met the Moores in a small restaurant near the parish where he was playing for one of his up-and-coming singers before she performed in Las Vegas. The Moores had a summer home nearby and Curt, who loved jazz, got friendly with Phil, and had him and Lisa for dinner several times. Phil provided the entertainment by playing the piano and reminiscing about some of the stars he had accompanied early on in their careers. They knew I was studying at Columbia, and they had an apartment in New York City, so they promised to have me over sometime.

I really never expected to hear from them, but two or three months later I received a call from Lisa, and she asked me if I'd meet for a cup of coffee at a neighborhood place on the West Side. She didn't mention Phil or why she wanted to meet, but I agreed without asking any questions. When I met her, she was obviously distraught and looked like she had been crying. After we got our coffee, she apologized for calling me but said she thought that, given my background, I might be able to help her. I explained to her that I could help her as a friend but not as a professional because of ethical issues. She understood that and went on to tell her story—how Phil had been married a number of times, that she was twenty-eight and he was almost thirty years older than she, and how he was unhappy with the relationship and wanted to get a divorce. She was trying to get started in a modeling career, and he kept accusing her of having affairs with every photographer or agent that she saw. She vehemently denied that this was what was happening, but he seemed to be getting more and more suspicious and had bugged their phone and hired a private detective to follow her around. Most of her friends were mutual friends of hers and Phil's, and she couldn't talk to them, so she thought I might help. Without going into details, it seemed as if he wanted out of the marriage, and she thought he was attempting to find her unfaithful so he wouldn't have to make any settlement in a divorce. I explained that New York was a "no-fault" state, so even if she were unfaithful, that wouldn't count against her. I suggested she might want to consult with a lawyer if she had not already done so.

I couldn't do much more than suggest a lawyer and be supportive and just let her vent. We left without any plans to meet again. I told her if she needed to talk more, to feel free to call me. As soon as the words came out of my mouth, I wondered if I had opened a door that would have been better left closed. Lisa was a very attractive woman from a Eurasian background, with high cheekbones and striking brown eyes and a model's body. She was half Asian and, I suspect, half British Indian. If you saw her, you wouldn't be surprised that she was a model. Ordinarily she had a very vivacious personality mixed with a naïveté that didn't seem to fit with her otherwise sophisticated demeanor.

Several weeks later I did get a call from Lisa. She sounded much more in control than the last time I spoke with her. She told me she checked with a lawyer, and he told her Phil was just trying to intimidate her as she had expected. She had moved out of the apartment and was temporarily living with some friends. The big news was that she had a small role in a movie, *For Love of Ivy*, with Sidney Poitier, that was being filmed in New York City. After bringing me up to date on how the divorce was going, she asked whether I wanted to come down to the set where they were filming and maybe meet Sidney Poitier. I reluctantly told her that I had classes, and it was getting close to exam time. Her tone seemed disappointed, but she promised to give me a rain check. I had to make a great effort not to accept her invitation, but I knew it was a good decision. I had a sense that she wanted to spend time with me, not because of the divorce but because she wanted to spend time with me. I was flattered but also confused. Why me? I assumed that she knew dozens of men who would have loved to date her. It was indeed a mystery, but not for very long!

She called the next weekend. After some beating around the bush, she wanted to know whether I was interested in seeing a movie that a friend of hers was in. I thought to myself, *A movie is harmless enough,* so I agreed to pick her up at her new apartment at West Broadway and 102nd Street. I don't remember what the name of the movie was, but I do recall that, as they were running the credits at the end of the movie, they listed someone as "so and so" in her first starring role. Lisa nudged me and said, "See so and so's billing, that's going to be me some day!"

"I'll put money on that!" I replied.

She suggested we have dinner at a little Chinese restaurant around the corner from her apartment on Broadway. At that point I had only had Chinese food twice in my life, and the only dish I was familiar with was chicken chow mein, so I let her do the ordering. It was a great meal. After we finished, we sat there nursing our wine as she shared her hopes and dreams for a career in the movies. At one point she put her hand on my hand, closed her eyes, and seemed to be in a deep reverie. Later on, I asked her *the* question rather awkwardly, "You know, I've been wondering,

I certainly enjoy your company, but with all the men you know, how come I'm here with you?"

She squeezed my hand, looked into my eyes, and softly said, "Because you're the only genuine man I know." There were a few seconds of silence where we continued to gaze at one another until I finally said, "I'm really flattered—no, more than flattered; I'm privileged."

"You're the sweetest man I ever met. Most of the men I come in contact with are not gentleman. They don't respect me. They just want to take advantage of me. I've never met anyone like you."

Wow! All I could think of was that my heart was touched. *I am a goner!* I felt like Caesar crossing the Rubicon, there was no turning back. Even though intellectually I knew getting involved with someone who was in the process of being divorced was a hazardous step to take.

Her apartment was a converted hotel—one bedroom, kitchen, dining area, and living room area. Very cozy! We sat on her couch and listened to tapes of her friend Diahann Carroll. We talked more about her singing and dancing lessons, and she showed me several albums of pictures, mostly of her growing up in Georgia. She gave me a composite of pictures of six poses that she used for interviews. I told her about my plans after Columbia. I explained to her all about celibacy and how I really was too immature when I went into the seminary to see celibacy in the context of a relationship and family. Her response was, "I'm glad to hear that's not a problem." We cuddled and kissed a little before I said, "I better get going, or you're not going to think I'm a gentleman." Her answer was to take me by the hand and lead me into her bedroom. I woke up the next morning to the aroma of bacon and eggs.

For the next few months I was in "Limerence." (You remember Limerence from chapter 8.) Lisa and I spent a lot of time together—movies, plays, dinners together and with friends, walks, and just hanging out. It was a special time in my life. Then along came Flip Wilson. Yes, Flip Wilson the comedian, "the devil made me do it!" and *The Flip Wilson Show* and the characters he played, "The Rev.

Leroy" and "Geraldine Jones." Well, Flip was a friend of Lisa's through Diahann Carroll. At that time he was performing at the Rainbow Room, an upscale nightclub on the sixty-fifth floor of the GE Building at Rockefeller Center. Lisa asked me whether I would like to see his performance. Why not?

I had never been in such a fancy place. It even had a revolving dance floor. After his first show, Flip came over to our table and had a drink. Wow! People must have been wondering who this couple was that Flip Wilson would join them for a drink. Lisa introduced him to me as "her friend," blah, blah, blah, and I found him to be a real down-to-earth guy. This was a couple of years before he got his weekly program, but he had already developed a national reputation from being on *The Johnny Carson Show* several times and a regular on *Laugh-In* and *The Ed Sullivan Show*. During the course of our visit, he mentioned that he might have some work for Lisa in California for five or six weeks that summer. He didn't go into the details, but she was excited just at the thought of being out in California, where everything was happening.

I was not happy with the thought of her being away so long. I had always suspected that her career would trump our relationship if an opportunity came along for a job. I also had a touch of jealousy or self-doubt at the thought of her rubbing elbows with movie-star types in Hollywood. She tried to assure me of her faithfulness, but I still had fears of losing her. I took her to the airport, and my old family rule of "no mush at the airport" didn't work. She gave me a big hug and kiss and the keys to her apartment, which made me temporarily feel a little more secure.

Keeping Busy

I had been offered a summer job at Mobilization for Youth (MFY) in the Neighborhood Youth Corp program on the Lower East Side of New York City. The area was a predominantly poor, African-American and Puerto Rican community. This was a very exciting and challenging experience. The program was based on "opportunity theory," whose premise was that the more opportunities you created for youth, the lower the rate of delinquency would be.[8] Mobilization for Youth was the precursor for some of the programs for Lyndon Johnson's War on Poverty. My job was to connect teenagers with one of the many agencies in the area so they could learn the basic skills needed for being in the work force and at the same time make a contribution to the community. Being immersed in a racially diverse and low-income community on the Lower East Side was a terrific learning experience for me.

In addition to it being an opportunity to put into practice what I had been learning in school, it helped keep my mind off Lisa, whom she might be meeting, and what she might be doing. We'd exchange letters and occasional phone calls, but that didn't seem to put to rest my sense of impending doom.

I sensed something was different when Lisa got off the plane from California. On the way back to the city, she talked about all the job possibilities. She had one firm offer for a small part in a movie that would start shooting in three weeks, and she had made good contacts for modeling jobs. She sounded very enthusiastic about the possibilities. The more she talked, the more it sounded as though she planned to move to California permanently. It wasn't until we got to the apartment and she had showered and did some unpacking that she sat me down to drop the bomb. She prefaced her remarks by telling me how much she had missed me while she was away and how she agonized over having to tell me that she was going to move to California. "I hope you understand how difficult this is for me. You're the last one in the world I want to hurt ..." She got teary as she spoke, and I ended up having to comfort her. I thought she was sincere when she said she hoped that once I got my PhD, I could find a job in California, and we could be together. Even though that was a long shot, it gave us both an out for having to face the reality that we probably wouldn't ever be together. And we could be close for the time we had before she left. And that's what we did. We lived in our dream world most of the time.

Occasionally we'd talk about being apart but it always ended with the same refrain: "It might take some time, but we'll be together." I think we both were in a major state of denial.

Lisa left for California, and I was numb for weeks. The calls and letters became less and less frequent. I saw her one more time when I first moved to Arizona. She came over for a long weekend to visit, and it was wonderful. It was almost like we had never been separated. We took up where we left off. Perhaps we were both a little more realistic, but we were both living in the moment. I never saw her again. When I Googled her to bring me up to date for writing this section, I found out that she had died in 1989. She was forty-nine years old. I have no idea of how she died at such a young age. I found out that she had appeared in minor roles in TV shows from *Charlie's Angels* to *Streets of San Francisco,* along with twenty "B" movies. Sadly, she never fulfilled her dreams of becoming a star. May she rest in peace.

The Student Strike at Columbia

I was attending a late-afternoon sociology class on utopian societies at Hamilton Hall on the main Columbia campus. The class was taught by Professor Diamond, who was lecturing on the Shaker Society. The reason I remember all the details was because in the middle of the class four or five undergraduate militants barged into the classroom and notified us that they were taking over the building, and we needed to get out. With a weak protest from Professor Diamond, the whole class picked up their notebooks and marched out. This was in late April of 1968 and the beginning of the student strike and occupation. In addition to the student protests against the Vietnam War, Columbia had its own issues to protest. There were actually two issues, both concerned with racial disputes. The first was Columbia's plan to construct a gymnasium on city-owned land. One of the concerns about the gym's proposed design included access for Harlem residents through a back door to a community facility on the building's lower level. The design was interpreted as segregationist and labeled "Gym Crow."⁹ The Students for a Democratic Society (SDS) took up the cause to change the plan for the gym primarily as a means to mobilize the student population of Columbia. The Student Afro Society (SAS) was concerned about the gym issue, but they also were equally concerned about Columbia addressing the race issue. At the request of the SAS, the two student groups separated their protest activities. That way SAS could establish a separate identity.

The protests came to a conclusion in the early-morning hours of April 30 after six days of occupation. The New York Police Department violently quashed the occupation. They cleared the SAS students in Hamilton Hall peacefully. The buildings occupied by the SDS students were cleared violently, as approximately 150 students were injured and taken to hospitals and 700 protesters were arrested.¹⁰

Although the School of Social Work was not on the main campus, the students and many of the professors boycotted classes during the occupation. My oral exam to qualify to move on to the second year of required courses was scheduled during all that unrest. They changed the venue to a local drug store, where I met with three professors who proceeded to grill me on topics from my major classes. I must have done okay, since they gave me a passing grade and a ticket to the second year and renewed my scholarship.

The second year went very quickly. Lisa and I communicated less frequently, but we did stay in touch. I had to focus on maintaining a B+ average and beginning to prepare for my qualifying exams, which would take place the following October. These exams consisted of two days of written exams in each area of my specialization and an oral exam on the material in the written exam. Passing the exams was a prerequisite for starting on my dissertation, along with having a prospectus of the dissertation approved.

During my last semester, I saw an ad on the bulletin board for the position of assistant professor in the department of sociology at Arizona State University. They wanted someone who could teach sociology 101 and had a doctoral degree or all but a dissertation in social work. That sounded like me. So I sent them my curriculum vitae (resumé), letter of interest, and references. A few weeks later I got a call inviting me for a site visit and interview. I was on the short list of applicants, which meant I had a chance for the position.

The site visit was for three days, and I decided to stay another three days to check out the area. For the first three days I met with the faculty personnel committee, gave a lecture, met with a student committee, and met with staffs of several agencies. My final interview was with the dean of the liberal arts college, who seemed very curious about my clerical background. I remember him asking me what kind of priest I was, and I responded, "A good one!" He liked that.

The last evening they had a little cocktail party with the department members. After that I went out for dinner with the director of the social work program and the dean of the Graduate School of Social Service Administration. I was worn out when they told me that they were going to have a breakfast trail ride the next morning. Luckily I had learned to ride a horse at Marian Lodge. There was a stable just outside of Phoenix. We saddled up and took a leisurely ride into the desert until we got to where the wranglers were preparing a real down-home breakfast. It was a real treat.

The interview was during spring break. When I left New York there was snow on the ground and less than pleasant weather. After a week in Phoenix, with the sun shining every day and people at ASU being so nice to me, I said to myself, *If they offer me the position, I don't care what the salary is, I'm saying "yes"!* At the time, I thought I'd spend a couple of years out West, finish my dissertation, and then go back East. Well, here I am forty years later, still in living in Phoenix. I think I'll stay!

Reflections

I experienced a number of different feelings while writing this chapter. After discovering that Lisa had died, I was taken by surprise by how sad I felt. I wondered: how she had died at such a relatively young age? Had she been stricken by a deadly disease or was her death caused by an accident? Did she suffer? Did she die alone, or did she have a loved one to care for her? If she was sick for a period of time, had she thought about contacting me, and if she did, why didn't she get in touch with me? At the time she died in 1989, I was single and had no romantic relationship. I even thought that somehow I would have taken care of her. Mingled with my sadness was a touch of guilt. Why hadn't I stayed in touch with her over the years? I hoped she would have known that even though the embers of our love had faded, I still thought of her as a dear friend and cared for her, and after twenty years would have been willing to be there for her. I guess, at least on my part, even though the sparks had been dormant for many years, they were easily reignited.

Another feeling that was reactivated was my dissatisfaction with Rome for not honestly dealing with mandatory celibacy and a married clergy—the feeling was anger. I wasn't sure whether I was angrier about Rome not making any changes in the discipline or about the fact that John Paul II made it clear throughout his long reign that, as far as the Vatican was concerned, discussions about obligatory celibacy were off the table; mandatory celibacy was not negotiable. Pope Benedict XVI reaffirmed mandatory celibacy for priests as a nonnegotiable job requirement. Another example of the principle, "Rome has spoken, the cause is finished." No one suggested that optional celibacy for those who were given the charism of celibacy should not be a choice. Rather it should be encouraged for those who have that gift. As Father Donald Cozzens and other theologians believe, only "some few men and women appear to possess the charism of celibacy, a graced call from God to pledge themselves to celibate living."[11] The National Review Board of the United States Conference of Catholic Bishops acknowledged that "There can be no doubt that while it [the charism of celibacy] is a gift to some, celibacy is a terrible burden for others, resulting in loneliness, alcohol and drug abuse and improper sexual conduct."[12]

Cozzens describes the years between 1400 and 1600 as the nadir of clerical immorality. After portraying the immoral activities of several popes and their relatives whom they appointed cardinals at very young ages, he adds that this period was by no means the only historical period where clergy not blessed with the charism of celibacy "scandalized the faithful and tragically assaulted the innocence and faith of the most vulnerable and defenseless of believers."[13] Sounds like the clerical sex scandal that the media exposed in the early 2000s.

Christianity has a history of being suspicious of sexuality, dating back to St. Augustine, the prime mover of Christianity's negative view of human sexuality. After his misspent youth of sexual and other indulgences, he seemed to be tainted by Manichaean and other dualistic philosophies. These systems or doctrines taught that a superior spirituality was to be found in the practice of asceticism and most particularly in sexual abstinence. Judging by many of the statements about sexuality that John Paul II made over his years as pope, I suspect that he had been infected by a touch of Manichaean philosophy. A negative attitude in matters of sex and an obsession about the sexual behaviors of both married and unmarried couples and individuals permeates Rome's teachings before and after celibacy was made mandatory. To mention just a few examples, pre-celibacy and post-celibacy: married priests were admonished not to have sex before offering the Eucharist, as if sex was dirty and the celebrant/husband would be soiled by having sex with his wife; women have traditionally been treated as inferior to men; women have been denied leadership roles and have been told to be submissive, and church doctrines are used to control them; sex and sexuality are often treated as if they were inherently evil.[14]

As recently as 2002, when Benedict XVI headed the Congregation of the Doctrine of the Faith, rather than assigning Rome any blame for the scandal of the pedophilic priests, he shamefully shifted the blame for the molestation scandal to the media by stating, "I am personally convinced that the constant presence in the press of the sins of Catholic priests, especially in the United States, is a planned campaign."[15]

A much more honest approach to the scandal, along with solutions, can be found in Bishop Geoffrey Robinson's book, *Confronting Power and Sex in the Catholic Church: Reclaiming the Spirit of Jesus*. In the introduction of his book, which caused shock waves around the world, Robinson wrote:

> Sexual abuse of minors by a significant number of priests together with the attempt by many Church authorities to conceal the abuse, constitute one of the ugliest stories ever to emerge in the Catholic Church. It is hard to imagine a more total contradiction of everything Jesus stood for.[16]

How refreshing to have a Catholic bishop model the type of transparency and honesty that I would like to hear coming from the Vatican. Bishop Robinson has managed to free himself from the elitist mind-set that has characterized the hierarchy, often referred to as "clericalism," which takes it for granted that bishops and priests are intrinsically superior to other members of the church and deserve automatic deference. Some liken it to a feudal or military system that demands absolute loyalty and fidelity and commitment to Rome if one is to maintain one's elite status and advance in rank. A structure that demands such blind adherence to authority is destined to rely on secrecy, deceit, and extreme privacy in dealing with outsiders. [17]

The cardinals who head each of the nine Congregations that comprise the Curia hold an inordinate amount of power. Unfortunately, we still have a Vatican I model of Curial elitism, with bishops as branch managers and the lay faithful as disenfranchised customers who pay for services from a monopoly: don't ask questions, don't critique your superiors, and don't think. I hope the efforts of lay organizations like Voice of the Faithful, Call to Action, and Future Church will not be discouraged by small changes and will keep moving forward one step at a time.

As we've seen above, mandatory celibacy was promulgated at the second Lateran Council in 1139, so it has only been around for less than 900 years of the church's more than two-thousand-year history. It was then that Pope Innocent II pronounced that all clerical marriages were invalid, and the children of such marriages were bastards.[18] Four hundred years later, in 1545, the Council of Trent was convened, with celibacy on its agenda to be reaffirmed but not discussed. Does this sound familiar? Interesting that Trent added marriage to its list of sacraments, even though it declared celibacy and virginity to be nobler callings than marriage. Here we have St. Augustine and his Manichean philosophy and distorted and negative views of sex to thank for that. It boggles the mind to think that the person who believed that original sin was passed on through the male semen could have such an influence on Rome for centuries after his death.[19] Others of the church fathers had equally negative views about sex, even in marriage. For example, St. Jerome (AD 331–419) considered marriage to be an invention of Satan and actually encouraged married couples who converted to Christianity to renounce their marriage vows and to become "eunuchs by their own accord through their desire to serve the kingdom of heaven." St. Iranaeus (d. AD 202) taught that Adam and Eve were banished from the Eden for copulating and that Jesus redeemed the world by remaining celibate and not copulating.[20] Without going into their statements, which were equally bizarre, Origen, Tertullian, John Chrysostom, Ambrose, and a host of early "theologians" found in Augustine one who could articulate better than anyone what they all believed, that sex is the root of all evil, even though Jesus had said that greed was.[21]

It's hard for me to believe that these revered men who lived centuries ago still have such a strong influence on the teaching of the church today as it relates to sexuality. This is despite the fact that society has moved so far beyond what the early fathers of the church were teaching in philosophy, science, technology, and all the physical and social sciences.

To allow their negative attitudes to be a major consideration in sexual behavior, especially as it relates to the discipline of mandatory celibacy, is beyond my comprehension. It would be the same situation as if we had never accepted Copernicus's (1473–1543) theory, which looked at the universe in a very different way than the Bible. The church taught that the sun revolved around the Earth, rather than the Earth rotating on its axis and revolving yearly around the sun. And, perhaps more important, Copernicus argued that the planets also circled the sun.

In addition to the negative views of sex that some of the early church fathers had about sex and obligatory celibacy, they continued to make the connection between Christ being celibate and celibate priests not having to be concerned with a wife and family so they could devote all their time to their ministry. Well that seems to work for those who have the gift of the charism of celibacy, but, as we've seen, relatively few who take the vow have that gift. In reality, the main reason for obligatory celibacy continues to be administrative. To mention just a few of those reasons: it would be much easier to move a single priest from parish to parish than a priest with a family; nor would they have to provide a salary that would support a priest and his family or deal with a priest's family if he died and they had to move another priest's family into the rectory.

For me, from the time of "my calling" when Father Hines sent me to the chancery office to talk with Monsignor Rooney, my talks with my spiritual directors in the seminary were limited to their telling me not to worry about the doubts I was having about dealing with "impure thoughts"; they would go away when I was ordained and it was just the devil that was tempting me. That is a sad commentary on the pre-Vatican II church.

Thankfully there is a more realistic view about preparing seminarians for living a celibate life since Vatican II. In talking to a small group of seminarians when I visited St. Mary's Seminary in 2005, I learned that not only are future seminarians vetted more thoroughly before being admitted to the seminary, but once admitted they openly discuss mandatory celibacy in small groups in classes and are treated more as adults who need to share their concerns and get feedback from their peers and their spiritual advisors. I was impressed when the same seminarians told me about their having to read all of A. W. Richard Sipe's books. He is one of the most prolific and knowledgeable scholar/practitioners on celibacy. At the time, they were reading his most recent book, *Living the Celibate Life: A Search for Model and Meaning*, which he wrote in 2004. Sipe doesn't focus on the debate about mandatory or voluntary celibacy. This book is more for anyone considering celibacy as a possible way of life. He provides potential celibates with the right questions to ask themselves for determining their ability to lead a celibate life. This type of responsible discernment is encouraging for the future of the church. To personalize Richard Sipe's position, I believe that if I had had those same opportunities to discern my appropriateness for celibacy, I would have been able to make an informed and responsible decision and would not have pursued the priesthood.[22]

The Ordination of Women Priests

The other issue that is equally influenced by the church's negative views about sexuality is the ordination of women. In order to bring myself up to date before I reflected on this issue, I needed to study more recent research on the topic. I knew that the church had opposed women as priests for centuries; that all the popes during my lifetime had made statements supporting the party line; that John Paul II had put an end to the debate, but I had forgotten how strong and binding his opposition was. On May 22, 1994, he issued an "Apostolic Letter on Reserving Ordination to Men Alone." The letter is titled *Ordinatio Sacerdotalis*. After reminding us that priestly ordination has been reserved to men alone, that women had their own important role in the church and how this teaching had been preserved by the constant universal tradition of the church and consistently taught by the magisterium, he pointed out that "in some places it is nonetheless considered still open to debate ... [and] considered to have merely disciplinary force."[23] He then proceeded to lay down the law:

Wherefore, in order that all doubt may be removed regarding a matter of great importance, a matter which pertains to the church's divine constitution itself, in virtue of my ministry of Confirming the brethren (cf. Luke 22:32) I declare that the church has no authority whatsoever to confer priestly ordination on women and that this judgment is to be definitively held by all the church faithful.[24]

This statement by the pontiff is just short of a declaration that he is speaking ex cathedra. He attributes his position to divine inspiration, thus making his teaching infallible. By stating that the church had no authority to confer ordination on women, this declaration was not merely a disciplinary matter but was a doctrine of the church.[25] Unless the church changes the way it does business, two hundred years from now some pope will be quoting John Paul II's apostolic letter to prove that the church has no authority to change the doctrine that women are excluded from being priests. As I also mentioned in the last chapter, when the pope or an office of the Vatican wishes to "prove" the reasonableness and authenticity of a teaching, they tend to use references that they believe apodictically prove their point. They usually fall back on the magisterium (in this case the pope's apostolic letter) or their interpretation of a biblical quotation or tradition. I'm not sure why the pope chose that particular biblical citation from Luke, since Jesus had just admonished Peter that "you in your turn need to strengthen your brothers." Perhaps because it didn't mention his "sisters," it therefore proves there were no women priests. At any rate, I'm suspicious of relying not only on the interpretations of Scripture but also on tradition and the magisterium and abandoning our reason and even common sense. As we've seen, the magisterium has not always made correct decisions, and just because tradition reports that one or more of the fathers of the church in the first century spoke out against ordaining women, doesn't mean that this principle should apply in 2010 and beyond. Judging from Jesus' devout following of women in the gospels, it seems to me that if he lived in another time, in another land, he could have chosen women to be equal with men for ordination.

On a more optimistic note, I am hopeful that the voices of the many theologians, priests, progressive groups of the Catholic faithful, and women's groups will be heard in Rome, and the authorities will recognize that women priests in the twenty-first century can play an important part in the reign of the Kingdom.

Chapter 11
Go West, Young Man

As you probably surmised, I was offered the position at Arizona State University. One of the reasons I chose to accept their offer was that the sociology department had a federal grant to do research on minority students in undergraduate education. I intended to write my dissertation on the recruitment and retention of minority and disadvantaged students in undergraduate social work programs in the United States (a catchy title), and I could use the grant to collect data for my dissertation. That was a bonus.

I planned to spend most of the summer after I completed my course work, preparing for the qualifying exams in October and putting together a draft of my dissertation prospectus. But Rita Ortiz, the director of the Neighborhood Youth Corp program, called me to ask whether I would like to have the summer job at Mobilization for Youth (MFY) that I had had the previous summer. I quickly re-evaluated my plan for the summer and said yes. I had learned a lot from Rita the previous summer and enjoyed the experience. I thought it was an excellent opportunity to assist individuals living in a very poor environment make changes in their lives, as well as in the neighborhood itself. One of the hallmarks of the social work professions is the need to deal with the person in their environment (PIE).

One of the first things we had to deal with that summer, before the program even started, was that the City of New York was cutting the budget for the youth programs. After a number of meetings with city officials, it was obvious that they were not going to budge on the budget. Rita and I and other department heads determined that our only alternative was to organize a protest that might get the city fathers to listen to our requests. We decided on a demonstration outside of Governor Nelson Rockefeller's New York residence on Fifth Avenue. We mobilized East Side neighborhood activists, including youths who already had jobs, oriented them on how to handle themselves in a demonstration, especially about matters of safety, and we were on our way in four or five buses. Our media staff had notified the press and TV people so we would have good coverage. What I remember most is about two hundred of us walking in a large circle outside Rockefeller's apartment carrying placards and chanting "More Money, Olé, Olé" and such vulgarities as "Up the Ass of the Ruling Class, Power to the People"!

I'm not sure whether Mohandas Gandhi or Martin Luther King Jr. would have appreciated the vulgarities, but the demonstration was nonviolent and apparently got the attention of the governor's office, who found some money to give to the city for more slots to accommodate more participants in the program. We did get good media coverage for a program that a few years before was accused of being influenced by communist ideology. In the early days of Mobilization for Youth, the press and the power elite were not too happy with MFY's social protest–focused community action approach, which was similar to the civil rights strategies to effect social change. Even though the program's focus was on reducing the delinquency rate among youth on the Lower East Side, it was a hard sell to those in power. Perhaps because they understood that one of its underlying assumptions was that the community needed to expand the democratic participation of the lower income inner-city residents of color. It was obvious that when they did realize that federal funds were paying the salaries of the community organizers, they pressured Washington to change the job descriptions of what the indigenous leaders could and could not do. One of the things that the new regulations changed was that community organizers could not lead demonstrations against any level of the government. So much for power to the people!

Helen of the Dominican Republic

My contract with MFY was for a four-day work week so I could have a three-day weekend to work in the library on preparing for the qualifying exams and have time for myself to relax.

One Friday early in the summer, I was having lunch by myself in the school cafeteria when the secretary for a professor I had done some work for asked if she could join me. Even though I had a book propped up for reading while I ate, I told her I'd appreciate the company. I had been in the library most of the morning and was getting tired of my own company. I had known her for most of the last semester but only as someone with whom I dropped off the papers that I had corrected for Professor Brager's master's students. As we began talking, it was obvious that she knew much more about me than I knew about her. She knew that I was a priest, that I lived in a home for the aged, that I had been offered a job in Arizona, and that I was in the process of leaving the priesthood. I asked how she knew so much about my background. She replied, "Talking about single, male doctoral candidates is a major indoor sport for the secretaries."

Somewhat taken aback, I responded, "That's not fair! All I know about you is that your name is Helen, you're from the Dominican Republic, and you've always been very friendly when I drop off the grades For Dr. Brager's students." I didn't tell her that I couldn't help but notice her attractive good looks, her ready smile, her shapely body, and her striking red hair. She went on to tell me that she was divorced and had no children; her maiden name was Martinez; she still had a home in the Dominican Republic; she was working on her master's degree in education part-time at

Hunter College in the Manhattan branch and hoped to get her degree in another year and teach in the New York City school system. It sounded as if she were reading from an ad in a singles magazine or meeting someone for a first date. Whatever ... I was impressed with her both being a master's student and working at the same time, and I told her so.

We were just finishing our lunches, and I asked if she was free Saturday night to go out for dinner. She quickly answered, "Yes. If you hadn't asked, I was going to ask you the same question."

I told her, "I like your straightforward response. It tells me you don't play games."

"You got that right," she replied

This was the beginning of a summer relationship. Looking back, it was another example of my retarded adolescent sexual development. At the time I didn't see it that way. I convinced myself it was healthy for me to be in a relationship, even if it was unlikely that it would last. After all, we were two consenting adults, and it was the 1960s.

Helen and I enjoyed one another's company. She had a wonderful temperament. She was always very positive about life, and I never saw her in a bad mood. She was a very thoughtful and understanding person. It was a joy to be with her. We spent time talking about everything from religion to politics, two subjects that I always heard shouldn't be discussed if you wanted to keep your friends. We enjoyed movies and dinners, and Helen even introduced me to the opera. In the process, I learned that Helen had a touch of larceny in her.

We had made plans to go to the Lincoln Center for the Performing Arts to see a performance of the Metropolitan Opera. The only seats we could purchase were about as far away from the stage as you could get. She told me not to worry and brought me down to Macy's, where she purchased two very expensive pairs of binoculars. I thought it was rather extravagant for a night at the opera, but again she told me not to worry. Despite my hesitancy, I enjoyed my first opera more than I thought I would, perched high in the uppermost balcony. The next day, back we went to Macy's with the binoculars. I watched as she convinced the salesperson that they were just not what we needed, and she got a refund. I would never have had the chutzpa to carry out that caper, but apparently she had mastered the art of the refund by practice. She admitted that this was her most expensive exchange, but she never doubted that she could pull it off.

Toward the end of the summer we used a long weekend to take a trip to Montreal Canada to visit what had been Expo '67. Even though it closed in October of 1967, the site and most of the pavilions lived on as an exhibition during the summer months from 1968 until 1981. The exhibition was named Man and His World—a sexist title—but remember, we were still in the sixties. Helen was disappointed but not surprised that the Dominican Republic did not have a pavilion at the Expo, but she viewed all the pavilions with the enthusiasm of a young girl.

I grew very fond of Helen during the short time we had together, and the feelings were mutual. We both recognized that there would be only a small chance of her moving to Arizona after she finished her degree or my moving back to New York in the near future. We discussed the possibility of a long-distance relationship, with letters, phone calls, and trips back and forth, and decided to give it a try. Recognizing the perils of a long-distance relationship, we agreed that we could see other people.

Retrospectively, I think I was putting off closure. Even though there was a remote possibility that a long-distance relationship might work, this was my way of not dealing with good-byes. As you know from the last chapter, this wasn't new behavior for me. Not to be too analytic, but I'm sure it related to fears of abandonment I had since Judson Street. But knowing the cause doesn't in itself cure the problem. I knew even then it was something I had to deal with and eventually did.

Helen and I said our good-byes, both hoping that we could work something out. We could at least look forward to my returning to New York City in October for my qualifying exams.

I also knew that I needed to learn how to deal with separations in a more responsible and mature manner.

On the Way to Arizona

I had three days to spend in Albany to get my stuff together for the big trip. My brother, Jim, generously volunteered to drive out with me in my 1968 Mercury Cougar. I didn't have enough stuff to need a truck or even a little trailer, so I rented a U-Haul container that I could strap onto the roof of my car. It was big enough to hold all my earthly belongings except for some that we piled in the backseat. Jim and I took turns driving. We tried to cover four or five hundred miles a day, with the hope of making the whole trip in five days at the most. It was a bonus that he had a better sense of direction than I did, or we would have ended up in Mexico.

When we reached Phoenix on August 15, it was 115 degrees. We found out later that it was the hottest day of the summer up to that point. We were lucky enough to find a Holiday Inn on Washington Avenue and 24th Street, which, unbeknownst to us, was the city's red-light district.

After a good night's sleep and a lumberjack's breakfast we headed to Tempe to find an apartment. I found a furnished, two-bedroom apartment with a pool about a mile from the university. It had the romantic name of Villa Viento; at that point, I thought anything Spanish sounded romantic. Best of all, the rent was only $165 a month, including utilities, with a year's lease. From there we headed to the campus. We parked the car, grabbed several bags full of school stuff, and walked to the sociology department in 118-degree heat—another record day. My brother asked, "Are you sure that you really want to live in this heat?" I gave the pat answer that I learned when I made my visit last March, "Well, it's a dry heat."

He looked at me as if I were already brain-dead from the heat and responded, "If it's a dry heat, how come I'm sweating bullets?"

We found the secretary's office for the sociology department, and Miss Fisher, a matronly, middle-aged woman welcomed me, gave me a key to my office, and asked whether I had any questions. I asked whether any of the faculty were around. She informed me they were probably up north to avoid the heat and wouldn't be back until the beginning of September when school started. So much for the warm welcome I expected.

We went up to the third floor to check out my office and to get rid of some of the stuff we were carrying. I felt a touch of pride when I saw my name on the door—Professor Fausel. Wow! It was a small though adequate office with a window looking out on the campus mall, but it was my office.

Over the years Jim had grown from being my "little brother the nuisance" to my good friend. He had the same sense of humor that my father and his brothers had had. He always made me laugh. Not only that, he was a good driver! He spent a few days helping me get settled in my new apartment. Since I had never lived on my own (that's interesting at age thirty-nine) we had to purchase everything needed for a first apartment. I remember shopping for pots and pans, sheets and pillows, and toilet paper and laundry soap—you name it. When we got to the checkout register, the checkout person said, "Looks like you guys are setting up a new apartment."

Jim was quick to reply, "We're brothers. It's his apartment. I'm going back East tomorrow." It was as if he was afraid that the checkout person was questioning our sexual orientation, and he wanted to make sure she knew that we were straight.

I drove him to the airport, and he insisted that I didn't have to go in to wait for the plane's departure. It was as if he didn't want to risk any tears. A quick hug and an "I'll see you at your Christmas break" and he was on his way. I had already told him how much I appreciated his making the trip with me. I'm glad I did because I wouldn't have had time at the airport; he was gone so fast. It was just another vestige of the family rule, "No mush at the airport!"

Professor Fausel

During that first semester, I had three courses to teach. I still have the rosters for each of those classes. Each class met for three hours a week. What I had forgotten was that I had an average of forty students in each class. This meant three different preparations, 120 papers to correct and term papers to read, and 120 students to advise. I remember carefully practicing the pronunciation of the names of the 120 students before the first class so I wouldn't mispronounce any names.

There are three areas that faculty is required to excel in for tenure and promotion as well as merit increases: teaching, research/publications, and community service. I loved teaching, and my evaluations were positive.

The expectations for research/publications are that you have two publications or presentations at refereed professional conferences a year. During the first year I had one article published and gave two papers at professional conferences. I was also working on a book of readings that I published the second year. Since books take more time than articles in professional journals, they were given more weight and more time to complete.

The second year I focused on community service. I started with the Welfare Rights Organization and was elected president of Friends of Welfare Rights of Maricopa County. We were part of the National Welfare Rights Organization (NWRO), a movement started by Dr. George Wiley, an African-American with a PhD in organic chemistry, and a former professor at the University of California at Berkeley and Syracuse University. Dr. Wiley left academia to accept the job of associate national director of the Congress for Racial Equality (CORE), making him second in command to the national director, James Farmer. Wiley left CORE to become a full-time activist, moving with his family to New York City's Lower East Side.

In Phoenix our chapter of NWRO organized a protest at Arizona State University's 1970 graduation that was held in the school's football stadium. The reason for choosing the graduation, was that the keynote speaker was Robert Finch, who was Nixon's secretary of the Department of Health, Education, and Welfare, as it was known at that time, or as William F. Buckley referred to it, the Department of the Healthy, Wealthy, and Wise. There were many welfare issues being considered in Washington, and we thought it would be a good opportunity to demonstrate. As president of the Maricopa chapter of Friends of NWRO, I was asked to join with the recipient's group along with our members. This was my first graduation ceremony at ASU, and instead of participating inside the stadium with other faculty, I chose to march outside in my academic robes with the welfare recipients. While Secretary Finch was giving his address inside, we were outside chanting slogans like, "Finch is a bird, Finch is a bird." Since I was the only one with a cap and gown on, I was interviewed by reporters from several different TV stations and the local newspaper.

During that same period of time, there was a professor/ activist, Morris Starsky, in ASU's philosophy department who was receiving a lot of press because he had dismissed a class to attend a demonstration in Tucson against the Vietnam War. The Board of Regents terminated his contract, despite the fact that each level of the university, including the president, agreed to grant him tenure. If the truth were to be known, the real reason for his dismissal was not that he dismissed his class, but because he was an avowed Communist. Even though he had been in the papers and on TV for weeks, people coming out of the stadium who saw me demonstrating in my academic robes thought I was Professor Starsky. They started to shout at me, "Starsky, you're a Communist bastard," or "Dirty Communist, get a real job," usually with other four-letter words attached. Aside from my new colleagues asking me if I were nuts, after the TV and press coverage came out, I never heard a thing from anyone at any level of the administration.

Another event that we sponsored was a "Live on Welfare Week." This was a joint effort of Friends of NWRO and the social work students at ASU, whom I mentored. First we figured out what the budget for a welfare recipient of a family of four, given their welfare check. At that time it came out to thirty-six cents a day or twelve cents per meal. We hoped to recruit as many volunteers as we could who would be willing to try to live on a food budget of thirty-six cents a day and then share their experience in a qualitative research project. Qualitative research does not rely on statistics or numbers, which are the domain of quantitative researchers, rather it collects people's stories.

At the end of the week we planned with the welfare recipients to have a "Live on Welfare Dinner" that the welfare mothers would prepare from their surplus commodity food.

I got in touch with Dr. Wiley, and he agreed to be the main speaker at the dinner. I picked him up at the airport with Ida Noble and her husband, the leaders of the local NWOR. I never knew her husband's first name because she always called him Mr. Noble. We had arranged a TV interview for Dr. Wiley at Channel 5 about forty-five minutes after his arrival. In my effort to get him downtown on time, I wasn't paying attention to how fast I was driving. Before I knew it, there was a red light flashing and a siren blaring behind us. When the officer came over to my window, I politely explained, "This is Dr. Wiley, and I need to get him to Channel 5 for a TV interview."

His response was, "I don't give a damn if he's Dr. Seuss. Show me your driver's license and your registration."

I wondered whether, if I weren't driving three African-Americans, the officer would have stopped us. I'll never know. The important thing was that we made it to the TV station on time, despite the delay.

The dinner was great. The rice, cheese, and canned goods and other surplus commodities provided by the welfare department, plus the cooking skills of the welfare mothers, made it a meal to remember. Dr. Wiley gave a factual but emotional talk about what it was like to live on welfare, and the press gave him great coverage. A week or two later the students prepared and presented a one-hour TV show on the local public TV station to cap off "The Live on Welfare Week." I acted as the facilitator for their panel. I also described how I had cooked a large pot of stew at the beginning of the week that I rationed it out at every meal. At the end of the week, I was so sick of eating stew that I never wanted to see a bowl of stew again. Plus, it was downright depressing to eat the same meal over and over.

Extracurricular Activity

Most of the sociology faculty was married. The one person who wasn't was Hans Sebald, a tenured faculty member who had been at ASU since 1963. He befriended me and introduced me to the singles scene in Arizona. Hans was born in Germany and often told the story of how he arrived at Manchester College in Indiana in 1954 with one suitcase and twenty-five dollars in his pocket. He was a card-carrying atheist, or, at the very least, an agnostic. Although he had written five other books and numerous articles, he was most famous for his book *Witchcraft: The Heritage of a Heresy*. Halloween was his big time of the year for being called to do interviews with the press, radio talk shows, and TV. We became lifelong friends until his death in 2002, after a long battle with angiosarcoma.

Hans introduced me to the singles dances. They were held every weekend at one of the hotels. After trying several of these affairs and seeing how all the women loved to dance with Hans and would politely agree to dance with me, I realized that dancing was not my forte, and if I wanted to meet someone, it wasn't going to be on the dance floor. Tennis, maybe, or even a night at the opera, but not dancing!

One of my most memorable experiences with Hans was when we met two women at one of the dances. Their names were Lillie and Millie. They both worked for the telephone company and apparently went to this particular dance every week. They were really quite enjoyable company despite their names sounding like a vaudeville team. At the end of the dance, I ended up taking Millie or was it Lillie home, and Hans took her friend home. The next morning Hans called to see how the evening went. I reported that Millie or Lillie, whoever it was, threw up all over me just as we were about to become amorous. That was the last time we saw Millie and Lillie.

Other colleagues and a married couple in my apartment complex fixed me up with dates. With few exceptions, these dates went nowhere. I did have several platonic relationships that were good for companionship, but since I was still in my late thirties, I was hoping for something more.

One good thing about not being in a relationship was that it gave me the time I needed to prepare for my qualifying exams at Columbia. If I didn't pass the exams, I would not be able to work on my dissertation and that would probably be the end of my academic career. When I got back to Columbia for the exams, I had little time to spend with my friends or with Helen. During the two months I had been in Arizona the long-distance relationship had cooled, but we did have a chance to have a more than cordial dinner one night after my tests. She understood the stress I was under and didn't expect us to have the same good time we had in Montreal.

I was exhausted after spending six hours a day filling up blue books. The oral exam was equally stressful, with four professors, each an expert in his or her own field, interrogating me on the answers I had given on the written exams. After we finished, they excused me so they could discuss my future. I waited, as instructed, in Professor Florence Hollis's office to get the jury's verdict. After what seemed like hours, she came in to point out my strengths and weaknesses and finally gave me the good news that I had passed. She congratulated me with a stiff handshake, and that was it. She had been my faculty advisor for two years, but I never found her to be a very warm person. At that moment I felt like giving her a big hug even though she wasn't the hugging type. I think I made the right decision in vetoing that thought.

There was one other thing I had to attend to. With the help of Father John Ross, who was a canon lawyer for the Albany Diocese, and a friend since St. Thomas Seminary, I applied to Rome for my dispensation. John told me it might take a little time, but it ended up taking two years before I heard anything. At least that gave me plenty of time to better prepare my parents and friends. Finally, I heard from the Vatican. I didn't actually hear from the Vatican; I received a phone call from the canon lawyer of the Diocese of Phoenix to let me know they had received my papers from the Vatican granting me a dispensation. He asked me to come down to the chancery to pick them up. I asked if he could mail them, and he told me that he was afraid they might get lost in the mail. I thought that was odd, but I complied with his request. I was received at his office efficiently, as if I had just come to pick up a check. He showed me the document, which was all in Latin. I thought, *Even if it was lost in the mail, no one could read it.* Oh well, at least it had arrived, and now I was officially free to marry, but whom?

A Ready-Made Family

I met my future wife, Madge, at one of the workshops I was conducting. I think it was the one on perfectionism, "Be Ye Perfect: Mission Impossible." After the workshop, Madge came up to talk with me. She had been trying to get a scholarship to ASU. She had read my bio for the workshop and knew that I taught there. She thought I might know of someone who might help. I told her I couldn't think of anyone right now but I'd try to get the information and call her. She gave me a copy of her resumé and her transcript from a college in Seattle where she had completed two years.

I called her a few days later. I had the number of someone in the financial aid office that I thought might be helpful. I also had a number for the work incentive program that was run by the Department of Economic Security, which was a possibility, even though she had a job. She thanked me and asked if we could get together for a cup of coffee to discuss the differences between social work and psychology. Perhaps I was just rationalizing, but I agreed to meet at the cafeteria at ASU.

Madge was a very bright woman, as her college transcript showed. She was also a very attractive woman in her early thirties. I was impressed with the numbers of interests she had. Sitting and having coffee was for me a much better way to get to know someone than the dance floor. Since I sensed some mutual attraction, I invited her to dinner that weekend. From there we started dating on a regular basis. After five or six weeks dating, I was anxious to meet her children. Up to this point she had either come to my place or I picked her up at work.

She had three boys—Michael, who had just turned one and was still in diapers; Joe, who was three; and Tony, who was five. Their father had left them when she was pregnant with Michael, and she had no idea where he was, nor did she want to find out, even to get child support. Apparently he was a philanderer, and she didn't want to have him involved in the children's lives.

Our first "family date" was to go out for pizza with the three boys. I picked Madge up at her apartment, and the boys entertained me until she was ready to go. Apparently Madge hadn't had any gentleman callers meet the boys. They seemed very curious about me. I was sitting on the couch, and Joey came over and asked, "Do you like airplanes?" When I responded that I did, he went into his bedroom and came back with a toy airplane; he proceeded to tell me all about his favorite plane. Then Tony went into his bedroom and got one of his favorite toys, and they surrounded me on the couch as if they were starved for male attention.

I wasn't sure what precipitated it, but after we received our pizza and coke, for some reason Joey ended up on the floor, kicking and screaming as if he were having an epileptic seizure. With the whole restaurant watching his performance, Madge finally calmed him down. I found out that the episode was apparently about the unequal distribution of the pizza. It probably should have been a red flag for me, but I thought, *I can handle that by convincing Joey that there are better ways to deal with his frustrations.* That isn't unusual behavior for a middle child; but handling things, how wrong I was!

Despite that episode, we started to spend fun times together as a "family." We'd go to movies and took trips to Payson to ride huge truck-tire tubes down the hills in the winter snow, to Prescott to go camping, and to Sedona to Slide Rock for the kids to enjoy the challenges of sliding on the slippery rocks without breaking an arm or leg.

In 1972, after the dispensation arrived, we asked to be married in the church. The only way the bishop's office would agree was if we were married "secretly" in the chapel at the chancery office. It was like they were afraid of creating a scandal if we were married publically. Several of my priest friends were so angry at the rigidity and need to control of the local bishop that they offered to perform the service at their church. I appreciated their offer but I didn't want to get them in any trouble with their bishop. We decided to go along with the chancery. Looking back, I probably should have pressed the issue or just got married in a civil ceremony but I think I thought that a marriage in the church would make it easier for my parents. So we had a nice semi-private wedding with just my brother and sister-in-law and my old friends Marge (the old plug) and Al Port, who were visiting for the winter.

After a weekend honeymoon in Carefree, Arizona, my new family all moved into the small, three-bedroom house that I had bought six months before. I'll never forget my first night as a step-parent. We had all gone to bed when Michael, who was almost three, woke me up when I heard a little voice yelling from his bedroom, "I want a Twinkie!" So much for my serenity!

Madge enrolled at ASU in the psychology program and finished her last two years for her bachelor's degree with a perfect 4.0 average. She received the outstanding student award for her accomplishment. She applied to the doctoral program in the psychology department. The following fall she was accepted into the PhD program with five other students out of over a hundred applicants. This was another honor.

I finally finished my dissertation and flew back to New York City to defend it. This was another do-or-die situation as far as my academic career was concerned. I had butterflies just thinking about the possibility of failing. The Columbia system was that you worked only with your chairperson until you finished writing the dissertation. The other members of the committee—two from the School of Social Work and one from another department within the university—were only present for the defense. In going through my correspondence from Columbia for the defense, I was reminded that the outside committee representative was Donna Shalala, a professor of politics and education at Teachers College at Columbia. In 1993 she was appointed secretary of Health and Human Services by President Clinton.

The worst part of the dissertation defense was that, after all the committee members had a chance to ask questions, they'd request that you leave the room while they determined your fate. When they invited me back, my chairperson gave me the good news that I had passed, pending some minor changes. I was even more elated when I arrived in Phoenix, and Madge and the boys were all there, and Michael, with Madge's coaching, came running up to me and said, "Congratulations, Doctor Daddy."

Our favorite family activity was camping in the summer. We had a large tent and a Volkswagen camper with a sink and sleeping quarters. We set up camp in most of the campgrounds in northern Arizona. Also, the boys and I became members of the YMCA's Indian Guides. This was and is a program developed to support a strong relationship between fathers and sons. They have a very structured organization throughout the country with educational, recreational, and spiritual programs for its members. We even learned how to treasure the environment and the rituals, values, and cultures of the various tribes in Arizona.

Even though we looked like a normal, happy family from the outside, it seemed to me that as Madge got seriously involved with her doctoral program she experienced more and more stress. The more stress, the more she distanced herself from me and the boys. Her one glass a night of wine gradually increased to three or four. It got to the point where I started to go to meetings of Al-Anon because no matter how I tried to help her recognize the problem, it didn't seem to work. I don't mean to make Madge the bad guy, because I firmly believe that alcoholism is a disease. Although she happened to be the one with the disease, I was the one enabling her with my misguided efforts to help. It was as if she had diabetes, and I was encouraging her to eat sweets. Here's an example of how things were deteriorating in our family.

The Great Cover-Up

It was around 11:30 PM when I was awakened by the sounds of a Neil Diamond record that Madge was playing in the living room. It blared throughout the house. There was another sound that puzzled me. I wasn't sure, but it sounded like furniture being rearranged. What was she up to now?

I mused, *How the hell am I supposed to get any sleep? Is she doing this just to annoy me? She knows I hate Neil Diamond!* Even today I hate him. If one of his songs plays on the radio, I automatically switch stations. I realized that Madge must have been drinking pretty heavy; she only played Neil Diamond that loud when she was doing her heaviest drinking. Now he was singing "Sweet Carolyn"! I still hate that song!

As I tossed and turned in my attempt to get back to sleep, I had a movie-like flashback to the time when we were married four years earlier. I didn't have a clue that Madge had a drinking problem, let alone that she was addicted to alcohol. For the first year and a half that we dated, we both enjoyed our nightly glass of wine. At that time I didn't know much about alcoholism or alcoholics. In particular, I didn't know much about their behaviors. I believed many of the stereotypes—that they were just weak; that they had no willpower; that they were too self-centered and didn't see how their drinking could ruin relationships. The time I spent at Al-Anon was very enlightening for me. Before this incident happened, I had accepted the fact that alcoholism is a disease and, even more important, that the spouse of an alcoholic or anyone who enables the alcoholic is crazier that the alcoholic. Amen to that! Let me get back to the story to show you exactly how crazy I was thirty-five years ago.

I finally let my curiosity get to me. I went to the living room to see what was going on. As I looked around the room, I was shocked to see that all the furniture had vanished, except for a sofa and a favorite chair. I stood there with my mouth wide open in disbelief. If I hadn't known better, I would have thought that we had been burgled. Where were the end tables, the bookcase, the TV, the coffee table, the lamps, our stereo, and where was my dear wife?

After recovering from my initial shock, I started searching the rest of the house. As I approached Madge's office, I heard a noise coming from the direction of the garage. I quickly made my way back to that end of the house, and, sure enough, there she was struggling to get our stereo into the VW pop-top van.

Trying to control my temper, I stammered, "Madge, what the hell are you doing out here?"

She looked at me through glazed eyes and replied, "I'm leaving!"

I took several deep breaths and responded sarcastically, "Can I ask where you're going?"

Apparently that was not the right question to ask. She gritted her teeth and looked at me as if I were the village idiot and yelled, "That's the trouble with you, buster—you have no idea where I'm going."

Feeling like I had just taken a punch in the stomach, I shrugged my shoulders and, with a touch of sarcasm in my voice, replied, "Ya know, you are absolutely correct. I'm clueless. I have no idea where you're going. Would it be too much to ask for you to just give me a little hint?"

With a grimace of disgust, she responded, "I told you a long time ago my favorite place in the world was Grant's Pass in Oregon. You don't pay attention to anything I say!"

I vaguely recalled that, five years ago, when we were dating, she had mentioned Grant's Pass as her favorite place. To my recollection, she had never mentioned it again. I didn't like to patronize her, but I thought I needed to reply. Again, with a touch of sarcasm in my voice, I said, "Come to think of it, you did mention that, about five years ago. I guess I just forgot. Stupid me! I'm sorry."

"You're goddamn right I did. And I told you that I wanted to go back there someday."

She started to come back into the house but tripped and fell flat on her face. She fought off my attempt to help her get back on her feet and struggled to make it up by herself. It was as if she were trying to show me she was capable of navigating on her own.

I stuffed back a few ugly words that popped into my head and said instead, "Look, Madge, I know you want to get to Grant's Pass, but why don't you wait until the morning? It's almost 1:00 AM, you'll feel better with a good night's sleep." Knowing that nothing I said would make sense to her at this point, I still felt compelled to say, "Now doesn't that make sense?"

Trying to steady herself by leaning against the wall, she answered curtly, "Have it your way, baby cakes," and started inching her way toward our bedroom.

Baby cakes! Where the hell did that come from? She never called me baby cakes or anything close to it. I wasn't sure if it was a term of endearment or of opprobrium. I suspected the latter but wasn't about to make an issue of it. I was both surprised and relieved that she had accepted my suggestion so easily. I never knew how she would react when I made any type of suggestion. Lately a suggestion like that could just as easily have started World War III. Too many of our conversations—discussions—arguments were more adversarial than productive and ended without a resolution. But, I had learned in Al-Anon, it was useless to have a discussion when she was drinking. I tried very hard to avoid that trap.

By the time Madge got to our bedroom, it was after one o'clock. I was not about to join her in bed and, given my state of agitation, I knew I probably wouldn't get much sleep. I sat down in my comfortable Lay-Z-Boy recliner in the family room and began to process the great furniture caper.

The first ones up the next morning were my three stepsons. My expectation when we were married was that our family was going to be just like the TV show *My Three Sons.* Just substitute "stepsons." How unrealistic I was.

When I heard the boys getting up, I quickly got up to cushion their shock when they discovered the empty living room. By the time I got there, they were standing in the middle of the room with their eyes wide open as if it were Christmas morning, and Santa hadn't left any presents.

As I walked into the living room, they broke out in a staccato chorus of questions, "Dad, where's all the furniture? Who took our TV? Where's our stereo? Did someone rob us?"

I gathered them around me and gave them my cover-up rendition of the great furniture caper. "Okay, okay, calm down. This is what happened. Your mom and I were trying to see how much furniture we could fit in the VW van." I couldn't believe I said that. *Your mom and I …?* I was taking partial credit for the caper. I was lying.

They looked at one another as if they had their own secret code and were furtively saying to one another, *Who does he think he's kidding?* They weren't stupid! I'm sure they knew their mom had a drinking problem and that I was lying through my teeth to cover up for her. Even though my lies were to protect their mother and them, I was still l-y-i-n-g!

Tony spoke for the rest of them: "What's for breakfast?" That's the way he had learned to deal with expressing feelings in our stepfamily. We usually didn't talk about the proverbial elephant in the living room. Like most dysfunctional families, we just walked around it.

I went on with my cover-up. "Well, before we have breakfast, let's surprise your mom and put the furniture back in the living room. Then I'll make you some French toast." Reluctantly, they all helped as if it were one of their regular weekend chores.

It was close to noon before Madge got up. I greeted her with a cheery, "Good morning, how ya feeling?"

"I got a god-awful headache. Do we have any Alka-Seltzer?"

I resisted the temptation of bringing up last night. Apparently she didn't notice that the furniture was all back in place, and life was back to normal. At least for the time being!

I reported to her that Tony had a soccer game, and I would take him and Mike and Joe with me. She seemed relieved to know that we would all be out of the house. She grunted and drank her Alka-Seltzer.

I didn't have any time that day to really think much about the goings-on the previous night, but when I did, it was clear to me that my behavior that night and in the morning wasn't all that new. I recognized that I was the great enabler, and I was actually teaching the kids to lie. What I had heard so often in Al-Anon meetings finally sank in: "You can't change anyone else's behavior; you can only change your own." Now you know what I meant when I said before that I was crazier than Madge. I needed to change my behaviors.

When we got home from the soccer game, Madge had transformed into the other Madge, a different person than she was the previous night. She was now the sober Madge; the Madge I fell in love with five years ago; the talented, bright, charming, beautiful Madge. As she worked on the lasagna she was preparing for dinner, the sauce was simmering on the back burner sending out mouthwatering aromas. Without being distracted by the cooking, she asked about the soccer; who was there? blah, blah, blah, and then she surprisingly suggested that we get a babysitter and go to the movies by ourselves that night. I responded to her suggestion with an enthusiastic, "That's a great idea. I'll check the movie schedule and call the babysitter."

I knew this wouldn't solve our problems, but it certainly wouldn't hurt. I realized that the precipitating events that sparked the drinking, which then prompted my enabling, were often different, but our reactions to the events were always the same. It was like the laws of physics—action/reaction. It was as if we were following a script that was deeply imbedded in our DNA.

I began to realize more clearly that if we didn't deal with that elephant in the living room, we'd just keep repeating the same behaviors over and over, expecting different results. Isn't that the definition of insanity, or, if you will, craziness?

I promised myself that I would take responsibility for asking Madge to sit down with me at a more appropriate time and, without blaming or shaming one another, have a rational discussion of our behaviors and agree on solutions. But that would be for another day. Tonight we would just enjoy one another's company and, I hoped, a good movie.

This was not atypical behavior for both of us. We tried counseling, and that didn't work. So, after five years of marriage, we divorced. Even though I hadn't adopted the boys as I always intended to do, Madge agreed to give me regular visitation rights. I agreed to pay her alimony until she finished her doctoral program. After we sold our house, I bought a town house, and she moved into an apartment a few blocks away. The boys would stay with me on weekends and one night during the week. I realize I'm writing this very cognitively, as if I had no feelings about these major losses. That's far from the truth. I felt sadder than I ever had—verging on depression. I felt I was a failure at the most important roles in life—being a spouse and parent. I had experienced losses from other failed relationships but nothing like this. At times I was immobilized. The most creative thing I could do was stuff envelopes. I had no zest for life. Luckily, I had a good support system. My brother and his wife, Diane, were very supportive. I remember their patience in listening to my "poor me" stories and my staying at their home when I didn't want to face going back to an empty house. My good friend Hans was there for me. I spent more than one night at his place, while he would talk to me like a Dutch uncle. My old school chum from St. Thomas, Pat Healy, had left the priest business and moved to Arizona. He and his wife, Sandy, were very open to my stopping in unannounced for dinner to listen to my story of woe. Madge and I had gone out with them many times while we were married, so they knew us both well and were both good listeners. I remember sitting at the counter in their kitchen as Sandy did the cooking and Pat poured the drinks. It was very healing. I called it "healing at Healys."

I also continued to go to Al-Anon. That was probably the best move I made. The group wouldn't let me stay on the "pity pot," as they called it. At the same time, they were very supportive and caring, having gone through similar situations themselves. Their philosophy of "take what you want and leave the rest" outweighed their "tough love" appearance. Though it took almost a year, thanks to my Higher Power and help from my friends, I eventually bounced back to close to normal.

On a happier note, several years ago I received a letter from Madge with a newspaper clipping. She had moved to the state of Washington a few years earlier. She had grown up in Seattle and had family living there. The clipping was about the great work she was doing as the director of a substance abuse program. It described her work with a particular family whose lives had been torn apart by an alcoholic parent. She ended the letter by saying, "I hope what I've been doing for the last few years brought honor to the Fausel name." I treasured that letter.

Reflections

As I recalled my early days in Arizona, I was reminded of the important part Native American spirituality played in my life, bolstering my own faith tradition. Soon after my arrival in Arizona, I was introduced to Native American spirituality by Naomi Harwood. As I mentioned earlier, one of the reasons I took the job at Arizona State University was that Naomi Harwood, who was then the director of the undergraduate social work program, had received a grant to recruit and retain ethnic minority students and asked me to work with her on the grant, since my doctoral dissertation at Columbia was on that topic. It would be a bonus and a pleasure to work with Naomi, who was an exceptional woman. She was Mrs. Social Worker of Arizona. I was fortunate to have her as my mentor. From the time we first got together after my arrival, my informal education began. On our first visit, Naomi launched into a homily on the cultures of the American Indians and the Hispanic people. The next day when I met with her, she had a stack of books for me to read to familiarize me with the culture of the Southwest and its diversity.

Even after Naomi retired, she continued to be a social activist and, in 1988, she led the successful impeachment effort to oust Governor Evan Meacham from office. One of her grievances with him was his arrogant attitude toward minorities. To give you an idea of her energy and commitment to social change, I remember coming home from a trip back East. It was about 11:00 PM, and there was Naomi at the airport terminal, trying to convince the embarking passengers to sign a petition to impeach the governor. At that time, she was in her early eighties, with poor eyesight and not as mobile as she used to be. We need more people like Naomi in this world.

I religiously absorbed the resources she provided, and I felt great respect when I read about the spirituality of the American Indians. I was even more impressed when Naomi introduced me to shamans and other leaders of the Navaho Nation, and I had the occasion to actually talk with them about opportunities for American Indian students to obtain a degree in social work and go back to their reservations to work with the Navaho people. At that time this was an innovative program that was a dream that Naomi had and was willing to share with me.

I believe that there are no teachers, just learners. When the Native American program started, I soon found out that I was learning as much or more from the students as they were from me. They didn't give me lectures or homework, but just being able to experience the impact their spiritual practices had on them was an education. Their stories of what I would have considered deprivation had a lasting impact on me. It was obvious from listening to them that the spiritual support of extended family and the wisdom of their elders strengthened them to the point that they were able to enter the university, not just for themselves but for all their relations.

I remember one discussion with a group of five or six students just back from the reservation, where they had spent the spring break. One casually mentioned "walking the Red Road." I knew from my reading that the Red Road was a term that Native Americans used to describe the spiritual path that each individual travels during his or her lifetime on Mother Earth. Without trying to be intrusive, I asked, "You know, I'm familiar with the term the Red Road, but if you feel comfortable, would you share what that means to you?" To a person, they were able to describe experiences of how they had integrated the teachings of the Red Road in their lives. Through their own unique stories, they described how walking the Red Road taught them to stand on equal ground with all living things; that because we are human, we have been given superiority over nothing; how, under the guidance of an elder, they had come to understand that we can all learn from the rivers and mountains, the stone people, the wind and animal people, because they all know something that we don't know; that all these different levels of being are void of evil thoughts; the students do not wish vengeance on anyone, they seek justice; accumulating "stuff" was not that important; the spiritual journey on the Red Road can be hampered by material things.

Despite temptations to become obsessed with the values of the dominant culture of consumerism, they had incorporated a code of living from their nurturing culture that I envied. The reverence they expressed for the land and their sacred places has only recently been translated into sustainability and taking more responsibility for our environment. Their commitment to the wisdom of their ancestors and the importance of extended family was refreshing. They brought "walking the Sacred Red Road" alive for me and their commitment to ancient ways has stayed with me for over three decades. Their philosophy fit well with my own faith tradition. For me it was similar to "the way" that Jesus taught and lived.

My First Sweat Lodge

After Naomi retired in 1979, one of my colleagues at Arizona State University, John Red Horse, took up where she left off. John became my informal tutor in Native American healing traditions and eventually a good friend. His academic area of expertise was the Native American family, but his life experiences as an American Indian were equally important.

I remember John telling me that whenever he needed to renew himself spiritually or was just feeling low, he would go to the reservation, where he had a shaman who would guide him through a cleansing process that he called a sweat lodge. The fact that he described the sweat lodge as such a positive experience made me interested in experiencing a sweat myself. (The ceremony is usually referred to as a "sweat.") After he explained more about what went on at sweat, he gave me a booklet that I read, and I thought, *Why not? It sounds interesting, and it can't do any harm.*

What I had learned in my reading was that a sweat lodge is a place for spiritual, mental, and physical healing. The lodge itself is a wickiup made of a frame that is usually covered with animal hides, blankets, or whatever material is available. It is about ten feet in diameter, four to five feet high at the center, with a pit in the center about two feet in diameter and a foot deep. The lodge itself is symbolic of a mother's womb. To do a sweat is to return to the womb of Mother Earth and the innocence of childhood. Once the ceremony is under way, the lodge is dark and moist, hot and safe.

John introduced me to a shaman who led sweat lodges at the Gila River Reservation at Sacaton, Arizona. At the shaman's invitation, I attended my first sweat, along with about ten other folks. As much as I had read and as much as John Red Horse had explained, I was not prepared for the actual experience.

Once we got to the reservation at Sacaton, we stripped down to bathing suits and formed a circle around a bonfire with a number of large rocks being heated in the middle. Following the shaman's lead, we started slowly dancing around the fire and chanting. Even though I had no idea what we were chanting, I quickly picked up the beat. I felt as if I had been transported back in time and found myself really getting into the chanting and dancing. I mean really getting into it. The more familiar I became with the chant, the louder I chanted and the more vigorous were my dance steps. It was mesmerizing. I found out later that we were preparing the rocks for the ceremony in the lodge. When the rocks were prepared, one by one we crawled into the lodge on all fours through a small entrance. This in itself was a lesson in humility. Upon entering, each person said, "I'd like to greet all my relations!" The greeting acknowledged not just our human relatives, but included our four-legged relations, the rock people, and all spirits. There was a strong sense of reverence, respect, and our interconnectedness with all creatures created by the Great Spirit. Inside the lodge, we then crawled clockwise to take our places, where we sat with legs crossed and our backs against the lodge wall.

As soon as everyone was in place, the leader gave some brief rules and described the structure of the sweat. There would be four rounds/sessions that would make up the evening's sweat. Each round would last approximately thirty minutes. I remember thinking, *That sounds like a piece of cake. I can do that.* The leader then asked for a short period of silence. After the silence, he recited a prayer. A typical prayer might be:

Great Spirit, Sacred one!
Put our feet on the holy path that
leads to you, and give us the strength and will
to lead ourselves and our children
past the darkness we have entered.
Teach us to heal ourselves, to heal others, and heal the world.

Even today, I often meditate on those words. Not that there aren't similar expressions in Christian prayers; I can't explain it, but these words give me the inspiration I need to help center myself.

The shaman then smudged each of us with cedar smoke as a sign of cleansing. Then, one by one the sacred rocks were brought into the lodge on shovels and put in the pit in the middle of the lodge. The shaman started chanting, accompanied by a drum beat that produced an atmosphere of otherworldliness. When he gave the word, water was poured over the rocks. The flap on the lodge was closed, and, except for the last remaining glow from the rocks, the sweat became pitch-black. Gazing at the rocks before the water extinguished their bright, red glow, I thought I could see the image of my Grandfather Fausel. Later, when it came my turn to talk around the circle, I would speak about him. More water was poured on the rocks to the point that there was no red glow, just steam filling the lodge. From that point on, I was immersed in the darkest dark I had ever experienced. After ten minutes or so, it seemed as if we had been in the sweat for hours. I wasn't sure if would survive the first round. I had to get as close to the earth as I could to breathe. But thankfully I made it through the first round. They opened the flap, and we had a ten-minute break.

We reentered the lodge for the second round, following the same procedure we had for the first round. Knowing that I had made it through the first round gave me the confidence that I could make it through the rest of the rounds.

I was about in the middle of the circle, so before my turn, I listened to the others tell their stories. I only have a vague recollection of what anyone said, but I do remember that I was impressed with their openness and sincerity. The content of what some had to say presupposed a great deal of trust in that they exposed their deepest feelings.

When it came my turn to speak, there were a number of things I could have talked about. I chose to speak about my grandfather. I'm not sure why. Before I started the sweat, I didn't have the slightest thought of speaking about him. I started by sharing with the group the vision I had of my grandfather in the glowing rocks and went on to say, "I guess I have some unfinished business with him." This was a surprise to me. I don't think I ever thought of any unfinished business I might have had with him. I continued, "I knew from my father that Grandpa was an alcoholic, but my experience with him was positive." He died when I was fourteen, and my picture of him was of a very kindly, elderly man who always wore a tie and vest, even in the middle of the summer when he was relaxing at home. I expressed my reverence for him as an ancestor and wanted him to know that whatever failings he had while he was on earth, my father had a great love and reverence for him and missed his presence. I felt that I was being a liaison between him and my father. I had a strong sense that the purpose in my being at this sweat was to serve the role of mediator and resolve any unfinished business between them. After the sweat, I mentioned this to the shaman, and he nodded in agreement with a whispered, "Yes." I attended other sweats and talking circles, which I always found purifying and personally therapeutic but I never again felt I had to be a liaison between my father and grandfather.

Becoming involved with Native American spirituality was the first step on my journey toward integrating the spiritual practice of other faith traditions, whose perspectives inspired in me a more person-centered and socially engaged understanding of Christianity. Over the years I learned that if we engage other faiths with complete honesty and openness, we recognize that we don't have the market on truth or faith. In the spirit of Thomas Merton, who in his later years drew spiritual strength from a variety of Eastern religions, I believe that an enlivened Christianity can result from encounters with other religions. I will share more about that in the next chapter.

Chapter 12
The Seventies and Eighties

A colleague of mine told me that I made a second career out of my divorce. I tend to agree with her. One of the ways I did that was by offering workshops on topics I was dealing with or had dealt with personally. I brought to those workshops not only my professional background on the subjects but personal experiences from my married family and my divorce. Here are the titles of a few of those workshops that were related to my experience of being a stepparent and dealing with my stepchildren after our divorce, as well as single parenting after a divorce: *Thriving and Surviving as a Stepfamily*; *Children of Separation and Divorce*; *The Single Family after Divorce or Separation*. Preparing for these workshops was one of my ways of attempting to understand myself and my patterns of behavior. It supports the old adage, "We teach what we want to learn."

In addition to the workshops related to divorce and different family structures, I began to narrow my focus more on stepfamilies as a sub-specialty, partly because in 1984 a magazine called *Impact Parenting* offered me a contract to write a monthly article on stepfamily issues. The overall title for the series was, "Getting and Staying in Step." Each month from June 1984 to February 1987, I had to come up with a headline for the article over my byline and three and a half pages on a specific "step" subject. As an example, the title for the first issue was, "The Instant Family." I also began to write "step" articles for professional journals. I began to run groups at Jewish Family Services in Mesa, Arizona, for "step" couples. So, with the workshops and groups, and the magazine and journal articles, I became the local guru on stepfamilies. Pat McMahon, a local talk-show host, often called on me to appear on his show as an expert on "step" issues. In addition to my professional expertise, I could always pull a real-life story from my memory bag. For instance, Pat might ask for an example of a stepparent who took over the discipline of the family too quickly from the birth parent. That was me!

My favorite anecdote of trying to change the family rules was focused on Joey, who had a habit of eating each item on his plate one at a time until he finished. For example, if our meal consisted of potatoes, meat, and peas, Joey would first eat all his peas, then all his potatoes, then all his meat. Of course that wasn't the way I learned to eat. I learned at my father's table to take a little bit of peas, a little bit of potatoes, and a little bit of meat and continue until I had consumed the last forkful of meat, potatoes, and peas. When I took into consideration just how important Joey's way of eating was in contrast to what I had been taught, I had to consider: Was what I had learned from the authority figure in my family of origin the only way to eat correctly? Where did my father get the rules for the proper way to eat? Did he go back to the early fathers of the family? To the bible of good manners, who, at that time, was Emily Post? Perhaps those beliefs of the Fausels and McCarrolls regarding eating etiquette were passed down from generation to generation? You might call that "tradition." Does the process sound vaguely familiar?

Besides the serious concerns I had for Joey and Emily Post, I was getting indigestion from having the same argument every night with Joey about the proper way to eat. Was I concerned that someday in a fancy restaurant he might embarrass me when the other guests saw him gobbling down all his peas without touching

the main entrée? I finally decided that the issue was not worth
my getting ulcers over, so I just let it go. Strangely, after I let the
issue go, Joey decided on his own that there must be some value
in the ancient tradition that had been handed down through the
generations: "a little bit of this and little bit of that." He joined the
faithful who followed what was written in *Emily Post's Etiquette*
(the bible of etiquette, the Good Book).

The President

I was on the board of the Grand Canyon chapter of the National
Association of Social Workers (NASW) and was elected president
in 1974. This required me to plan for our monthly program/
business meetings and provide a monthly column on topics that
were significant for social workers. Here is an excerpt of one
message I wrote in 1976. During that time period, Arizona was
the last state in the Union to have a Medicaid health program
for low-income folks. The state legislature was still debating the
underlying philosophy of Medicaid. This is an excerpt of my
president's message to rally the support of our members. Like a
"Yes We Can" message that candidate Obama used in his election
campaign for president in 2008.

An Apple a Day ...

> "Health of mind and body is so fundamental to the good life
> that if we believe that men have any personal rights at all
> as human beings, then they have an absolute moral right to
> such a measure of good health as society and society alone is
> able to give them."
>
> For $64,000, which of the five listed below was the
> author of that statement?
>
> 1) Plato 2) John F. Kennedy 3) Richard Nixon
> 4) Aristotle 5) Hubert Humphrey

If you chose Aristotle, you win. That's correct, the same Aristotle who was the pupil of Plato, the tutor of Alexander the Great, who lived between 384–322 BC and who spelled out society's obligation to provide health care some 2,300 years ago.

Cultural Lag?
Meanwhile back in Arizona, at this writing [1976], forces seem to be mounting to keep the medically indigent as second-class citizens as far as health care is concerned. Although Medicaid is far from a perfect system in other states, it does offer an accessibility of services, with the recognition that health care should be a social utility, like our libraries and parks are.

We Can Make the Difference!
If Medicaid is to be a reality in Arizona, the voices of professional social workers must join other concerned citizens to be heard above those of the ultraconservative politicians and media who oppose its implementation. Rather than just deplore the fact that we are the only state without a Medicaid program, our social action committee will be asking each one of us to express our concerns to our individual legislators that this legislation be passed. This is our opportunity to join with Aristotle and other progressive thinkers to operationalize our professional philosophy.

Don Fausel, President

I'm happy to report that the legislature passed a Medicaid bill that session. They chose to call it the Arizona Health Care Cost Containment System (AHCCCS) rather than Medicaid. Remember this was in the mid-1970s, and we were living in Barry Goldwater country, the "pull-yourself-up-by-your-bootstraps state." I suspect that the legislators wanted to let the rest of the country know that we weren't liberals like that guy Aristotle; they wanted to show, even in the title of the bill, that its purpose was to "contain costs" not that to acknowledge that "those people" had rights to health care. It interesting that as I sit here writing in 2010, the same issues are being discussed on a national level as we debate President Obama's health care bill.

One of my major tasks as president of the Grand Canyon chapter of NASW was to unite with the Southern Arizona chapter in Tucson and have one state organization. The rationale was that we could have more political clout if we joined together, and we could save resources by having one organization. This required months of meetings, bargaining, and compromising about the constitution, the by-laws, and the composition of the state board before we finally became the Arizona chapter of NASW. During the same time period, we were lobbying our legislators for increases in funding for social service programs, and we started the long process of having social workers licensed.

Foster Care

I was appointed by Governor Fife Symington of Arizona as a member of the initial State Foster Care Review Board (FCRB) in 1977. The board was a response to the concern that Arizona's foster children were being "lost" in out-of-home care and staying too long in temporary placements. The state board was made up of chairs of local review boards of each county in the state. The larger counties had more than one board, each reviewing a hundred children in foster care. The state board's major responsibility was to make recommendations to the Arizona Supreme Court, the governor, and the legislature regarding foster care statutes, policies, and procedures by producing an annual report. In contrast to Arizona's position as the last state to have legislation for Medicaid, we were the first citizens volunteer review board in the country to be appointed by a governor. For me this was an opportunity to be able to be an inside advocate in changing the foster care system, which had been dysfunctional for years, both at the policy level and as chair of one of the local boards that had responsibility for monitoring one hundred foster children. Many of these children had been shuffled from foster home to foster home where the foster parents were not qualified to meet their needs and were not receiving even the minimal services required under the law from their appointed social workers.

Around this same time I received a two-year grant from the Department of Economic Security (DES) to provide training manuals for foster care workers, most of whom had no educational background in social work or foster care. The only requirement for being hired was that you have a bachelor's degree. It didn't matter what your major was; it could have been in music, and they would hire you. The grant included a budget to hire a supervisor, a secretary, and three researchers/writers for the project, along with the cost of a furnished office. I was the primary author, and we produced eight training manuals for foster care workers. The titles of the training manuals included: *Decision Making in Foster Care; Evaluation of Foster Families; Data Collection and Documentation in Foster Care; Educating of Foster Parents; Assessing Foster Family Dynamics; Role of Licensing Worker and Others in the Foster Care System; Recruitment of Foster Homes; Policies and Procedures for Licensing Foster Homes.* We tested each of the programs with current foster care workers. The responses from the workers were positive but only after making the recommended changes did we turn the manuals over to DES. Our hope was that the training would contribute to positive social change in the Arizona foster care system.

The Administrator

Naomi Harwood (whose energy for social change I described in the last chapter) retired as director of the undergraduate social work program in 1974, and I was appointed to take her place. Large shoes to fill! That same year the undergraduate program moved from the College of Liberal Arts to the School of Social Work. Administratively it was a good move, but becoming part of a larger unit meant that we lost some of the family-like atmosphere that we enjoyed in the department of sociology.

During my thirty years at ASU I was appointed to other administrative positions, none of which I sought. It usually happened when a new dean was appointed. For example, when Jesse McClure was appointed, he asked me to serve as director of the MSW program. Jesse was one of those people that it was hard to get mad at or say no to. I told him I'd rather work on my publications. I felt good that I was able to say no. But that was short-lived. We had a party that night to welcome new faculty members. Jesse cornered me and proceeded to tell me how he had talked to faculty members, and they all trusted me and thought I would be the best person to do the job, etc. I finally said, "Look, if you can't get anyone else, I'll consider it."

He put his arm around my shoulder and said, "You won't regret it. I'll take good care of you." The next day we had a faculty meeting, and Jesse announced to the faculty that I had accepted the position of director of the MSW program. I received a round of applause, probably because no one else wanted to do it. So much for my newfound assertiveness!

The Private Practitioner

Early on, I started a private counseling practice that included working with individuals, families, and groups. My main reason besides extra income was to keep my skills current, so I would not be teaching from an ivory tower. Besides the workshops I described above, I developed other workshops on shame, anger, making peace with the past, helping the helper heal, and codependency, all of which were issues I had dealt with myself. I gave most of them at the Franciscan Renewal Center in Scottsdale. The workshops also kept me honest because I was relating to real people with real problems.

My Personal Life

In about 1978 I was lounging in the pool at the Villa Patrician, where I had bought a town house after my divorce, when I started chatting with one of my neighbors whom I hadn't met before. John Rusnak was soon to become a lifelong friend. At that time he was finishing his dissertation for his PhD in counseling psychology at ASU. After chatting for a while about where we were from (most people living in Arizona are from someplace else), what we were doing, etc., I began to suspect that he had been a priest in a former life. The only clues I had were that he mentioned teaching in Costa Rica in a Catholic high school for seven years (this was the clincher) before coming back to the States; that he had been married and was divorced; and that he had a master's in counseling and had worked as director of a rehab program for prisoners in New Jersey. No one but another former priest would ever have guessed. What's that old saying, "It takes one to know one"? I think I was the first one to mention that I had been a priest in Albany, and he immediately responded that he had been ordained as a Franciscan in the Albany Cathedral of the Immaculate Conception the same year as my brother, Jim. We have been friends from that time on. He would invite me to parties at his town house, where I mingled with his ASU classmates and met several single women whom I dated for a while.

I was one of the "best persons" at his marriage to Pepper McLaine. The other best person was his friend Punch from his days in Costa Rica. So there were two best persons and no maid of honor.

Besides giving John some wise advice on his dissertation, I also suggested he get a new committee chair. We did several workshops together on anger management. I shared his wonderful Slavic cooking around the holidays. There were times I was feeling down and he was up and times that he was down and I was feeling up, so we were a mutual support system. John and Pepper were, and are, great hosts, and since I was single they usually invited me to their events, which were many. They even arranged dates for me with several of their single women friends, which unfortunately never worked out.

In 2002 John and I went to Dallas, where the bishops were holding their annual meeting right after the scandal of the priest pedophiles became exposed in the media. We were part of Call to Action, a lay group that had been attempting to make changes in the church. I remember that during the flight to Dallas, after we settled in and the cabin door was closed, I asked, "Why the hell are we going to Dallas?" John shrugged his shoulder as if to say, "It beats me" and answered, "Good question!" I thought, *Well, at least I'll get to see my niece Laura.* She moved to Dallas for her first job. I was her "American Father" and looked forward to seeing how she was doing.

Actually, in addition to visiting Laura, I'm glad we went. We attended a number of sessions that Call to Action and other advocacy groups presented, which were very enlightening. We marched with the protest group (placards and all) against the way the bishops were handling the outrage that many Catholics felt. The anger was not just toward the perpetrators but toward the bishops themselves for the devious ways they had tried to cover up their mistake of moving the offenders from one parish to another, giving them the opportunity to abuse more innocent children.

One light note about the protests. After we marched from a local church to the luxurious hotel where the bishops were staying and having their meetings, there were barriers to keep us out of the hotel. We congregated across the street from the hotel and continued to demonstrate by singing and getting the attention of the TV cameras. After a couple of hours, I needed to go to the men's room. So I furtively made my way across the street, only to be spotted by a policeman who wouldn't let me beyond the barriers. After I told him I needed to get to a rest room, he reluctantly let me slip under the yellow tape barrier. When I got into the hotel, there was another barrier blocking my way to the men's room because it was just outside where the bishops were meeting. In order to reach my goal and do my business, I had to forfeit my driver's license temporarily. Luckily, I made it to my destination before wetting my pants.

The New Ministry

When I first came to Phoenix, there was a group of former priests who had formed an organization they called The New Ministry. A majority in the group had expectations that the church would change its rules on celibacy and welcome former priests back to the ministry. They probably also still believed in the tooth fairy. I should talk! I remember talking to Tom Briedenback, a former member of the group and a good friend. He recalled how he was so sure things would change that around the time of Vatican II he started reading his Breviary in English instead of the required Latin. I replied, "I was so sure, I started dating." My point is that for a long time I had the same unrealistic expectations, and it took me years to face the reality that mandatory celibacy for priests was unchangeable in the minds of those who made the rules in Rome.

The group, despite its expectations, was a very caring and supportive source, especially for someone like me who had just moved to Arizona. Sometimes we met in a member's home and had our own liturgy. Other times we had dinners and discussions. Even after I was married to Madge, we went to their monthly meetings at the Franciscan Renewal Center, where the friars supplied the booze, and we all brought a dish for a potluck dinner. Bill Murphy was a native Arizonian and a member of the group, and he and his wife, Ann, organized trips to points of interest throughout the state. One of the members, Cappy, had been a monsignor in Chicago, and he and his wife, a former parishioner, sponsored a fancy dinner at the clubhouse at their condo. I was surprised that the bishop of Phoenix, Bishop McCarthy, attended and gave a welcoming talk after dinner. It was as if he wanted us to know that even though the Vatican had no intention of letting former priests function as priests, as far as he was concerned we were not stigmatized because we had left the active ministry; we were still part of the church with gifts to offer.

Soon after that dinner, I was appointed by the bishop as a member of the Catholic Campaign for Human Development (CCHD) for the Diocese of Phoenix. The group's goal and mission of providing grants to organizations whose focus was to empower the poor through a methodology of participation and education for justice certainly resonated with my commitment to helping change the conditions of the oppressed and disadvantaged. I was very pleased to be asked to be part of the local effort. I saw it as an opportunity to "preach the social gospel" and to mirror the compassion that Jesus showed to the disenfranchised during his aborted public ministry. I served two terms on the committee, which in many ways brought me closer to my faith tradition.

A Step-Stepmother

Meanwhile, back in Tempe, I continued to be the noncustodial father for the boys. This arrangement went on for almost six years. I became quite a good cook and housekeeper. My regular dishes were goulash, stew, hamburgers, and grilled cheese sandwiches. As the boys became pre-teens and teenagers, house rules and expectations were more of a problem. The rules in Madge's house were more lenient than mine. The double message "It's okay to smoke pot" and "It's not okay to smoke pot" was confusing for the boys. This was before she became "clean and sober," as they say in AA.

Madge eventually moved back to the state of Washington with the boys. This was heart-wrenching for me, but it didn't last too long. After trying to deal with the three boys for several months, Madge asked me to let Michael and Joe, who were having a hard time adjusting to their new environment, move back with me. Again, the enabler in me automatically said "Yes" without any written agreement. Here I was, a single parent with two stepsons who had just gone through several difficult adjustments and were entering their teenage years. Is there any question that I'm a slow learner? That's a rhetorical question.

One evening soon after they came back, Joe was out with his friends, and Michael and I were home watching TV. He came over to me and, out of the blue, said, "Dad, if Mom wants me to go back to live with her, tell her I want to stay with you." I turned the TV off and acknowledged how difficult it must have been for him to say that because I knew he loved his mother, and I would do everything I could to respect his wishes. We had a very adult conversation about the effects alcohol and drugs have on how a person behaves and how we needed to have the same kind of compassion for his mother as if she had any other kind of a disease.

Soon after Joe and Michael moved in with me, I met Barbara. I was introduced to her by my friend Ken Chin, who had worked with her in the Social Security office, where she was a client relations representative. We hit it off from the first time we met. She had been divorced for several years and had no children. She owned her own home, where she lived quietly with her German shepherd dog, seeming very content with her single life. She was very attractive but hadn't dated for over a year and wasn't really looking for a romantic relationship. We began to do the usual dating activities—movies, dinners, etc.—and we seemed to be very compatible. We also did fun things with Michael and Joe—fishing in Encanto Park Lake, eating at the Miner's Camp Restaurant in Apache Junction, and horseback riding in the desert—all family stuff that Barbara seemed to enjoy as much as she seemed to enjoy Mike and Joe. We all went for a weekend to a lodge up near the Grand Canyon and had a great time taking tours with guides who provided interesting information about the Canyon and the variety of birds and the animals who lived there. Barbara even mentioned that she had never wanted her own kids but that she wouldn't mind being a "step-stepmother." That was her definition of what her relationship with the boys would be. Her rationale was, since I was their stepfather, she would not just be a stepmother, she would hold the rank of step-stepmother.

We even bought a house together, both paying half, with the expectation of getting married. It was a large, round, white house that had been built and lived in by an architect. We got it at a great price, and it was actually a good investment. It had four bedrooms, and two of them were master bedrooms, so there would be no arguments about bedrooms for everyone.

All seemed to be going fine until I went to a conference back East for several days, and Barbara volunteered to take care of the kids. I guess that was the acid test. They were there to pick me up at the airport, and we stopped at a Burger King to have a bite to eat. On the way home she seemed a little downcast, which was unlike her usual cheerful self. I soon found out why she looked so glum. She started the conversation off with a pre-scripted opening. "This has nothing to do with you. You're a great guy, and I've loved the time we've spent together, but …" blah, blah, blah. You know the rest of the speech. To make me feel better, she proceeded to take all the blame for our breaking up. "You know while you were gone, I realized that I was just not made to be a 'step-stepmother'. The kids weren't all that bad; they weren't devils, but they weren't angels, either. [That phrase has always stuck in my mind.] I don't know, it must be that I'm not the mothering type." There were a few tears, and I tried to comfort her and suggested she not write herself off on the mothering question but that even if she were right, that wasn't all that bad. I went on to tell her I had known a lot of women who have lived very happy and useful lives single.

Looking back, whatever I said seemed stupid. We did have a much longer discussion before we went to bed, each in our own master bedroom, but before we retired, I said something to the effect of, "Look, I'm not going anywhere in the near future. If you have any second thoughts or just want to talk to an old friend, let me know." The only talks we had from then on were how we were going to sell the house and everything that that entailed. Some of my friends, John in particular, voiced their impressions, which boiled down to "I never knew what you saw in Barbara; you're better off now."

Another Ready-Made Family

This is beginning to sound like a soap opera, but the relationship I'm going to recall is a little different but very much the same. I met another woman with three children at an NASW meeting. Her name was Sheri, and she had a master's degree in social work from Michigan State and had moved to Arizona recently after an amiable divorce followed by a relationship with a psychiatrist in Michigan. Her husband had primary custody during the school months, and the children lived with her during the summer and the Christmas and Easter school vacations.

At that time, only Michael was living with me, since Joe had gone back to Seattle to live with his mother and Tony. A friend of mine, who was also a friend of Sheri's, thought she and I would enjoy meeting. My friend had discovered a great weekend bargain at one of the local resorts. She told me that Sheri and her three children were going to join her and she could get a suite-like room for me and Michael. I thought it was a great idea and readily agreed to join them. Sheri's children were a few years younger than Mike: twin boys of nine and a daughter who was eleven. We all had a great time, enjoying the amenities of the Pointe Hilton Resort. Most of our time was spent in one of their luxurious pools or playing miniature golf. Mike immediately became like a big brother—a big step up for him, since, having been the youngest of three, he was now promoted to the oldest of four.

For the rest of the summer, our two families got together most weekends and often during the week to do activities that were "kid-centered." Sheri and I never really had a date. It wasn't until after her kids went back to Michigan that we really went out on our own. We still did things with Michael, but he was getting into his teens and often had things to do with his peers.

Sheri was working as a therapist at a drug rehab program at a local hospital and also had a private counseling practice. As social workers we had many common interests, even though we often didn't agree with one another. I tended to be more liberal on social issues, and she was usually more conservative. Our relationship gradually moved from friendship to a romantic connection, with talk of marriage. I liked the fact that we just didn't jump into a more intimate relationship as I had often done in the past. We seemed to be able to handle what were often volatile reactions on both sides. This, too, was new for me. I wasn't always sure what precipitated our reactions, but we were able to step back and look at things more maturely. An example of these volatile responses is that we would be having a romantic-type dinner in a restaurant when all of a sudden Sheri would respond to something I said by getting so upset/angry that she would storm out of the restaurant, leaving me there alone, wondering what the hell I had said that pushed the wrong button. This happened more than once. It probably should have been one of those red flags that I missed in other relationships, but since we always eventually resolved whatever triggered the reaction, I thought, *Well, everything is okay. We're able to patch up our differences, and that's a good sign of a mature relationship, and there are so many good things about our relationship, not to worry.* So, I went ahead and proposed to her, diamond ring and all.

Her children came back for the Christmas holidays, and we picked up right where we had left off. They were happy about our engagement, as was Michael, who liked his role as the No. 1 sibling. By the way, I really liked her children, and Sheri liked Mike. Her children were all very respectful of me, and I had learned from my previous "step" experience that I didn't have to set all the family rules. We had "family" meetings to discuss matters and to get the children's opinions. One thing I admired about Sheri, among others, was how she dealt with her role as long-distance parent. She would phone regularly to talk with each of the children. I was always impressed with the side of the conversation that I could hear. These were not just obligatory calls; she used the time with each child to talk intimately about what was going on in their lives. I knew it was hard for her to be separated from them, and I think the children realized that, too.

She was usually sad for a while after the calls, but that did not deter her from making the calls.

Soon after her children went back to Michigan, we started looking for a house for the six of us. After looking at a number of houses, we finally agreed on a four-bedroom house in Scottsdale. Our problems started when we began to discuss the bedroom arrangements. Sheri insisted that one bedroom would be for the twins, one for her daughter, and another for Michael, and the master bedroom for us. I had always had an office in my home and suggested that, since her children would only be in Arizona for two months out of the year, we could use her daughter's room during the other ten months as my office. Given the size of the bedroom, I thought there would be room for a single bed, plus my desk and books and even a lounge chair. She would not even consider that and was adamant that her daughter needed to have her own room all year round, even when she was in Michigan. Again, I suggested it could be her room while she was here but my office for the other ten months. Sheri told me I had an office at the university, and I could use that. There was to be no compromising on the bedroom issue. Even though I tried to convince her that there were three days a week, including the weekend, when I wouldn't even go to the university, and the way my schedule was I usually only stayed there a half a day when I did go. It was a standoff! When that became apparent, she took her engagement ring off and dramatically handed it back to me.

Even though she broke our engagement, Sheri and I still had other extended discussions, but they always ended in a deadlock. I remember one discussion where we each agreed to list all the good things about our relationship. We were both surprised with the number of things we liked about the relationship. But when push came to shove, I thought she was unreasonable about the bedroom distribution, and I'm sure she thought I was unreasonable. We finally both agreed to take a break and give one another time to look at where we wanted to go with our relationship. It just occurred to me after all these years that neither one of us suggested a compromise—that we could get a five-bedroom house. This makes me wonder if we really wanted to stay together and just used the four-bedroom issue as an excuse for breaking our engagement. She eventually moved back to Michigan, married the psychiatrist she knew before she moved to Arizona, divorced him after a few months, and moved back to Arizona. I saw her for lunch a few times, but there never was any talk about our getting back together.

My sister-in-law always invited me and whomever I was dating to Thanksgiving and Christmas dinners. She often reminded me that she had a box full of place cards for the table with names of different women. I guess she was right. For seven or eight years, my relationships with women were mostly for companionship. I dated a number of women, had a long-term platonic relationship that was very satisfying as far as companionship was concerned but that didn't meet my hopes for a physical bonding. That was okay at that time in my life. I guess I had given up my quest for someone to share my life forever. I wasn't even looking for that person. But that would change.

Reflections

As I reflected on my professional life during the seventies and eighties, I realized that, despite the fact that I had left the priestly ministry, I was still trying to promote the social gospel through the professional and volunteer activities I chose to be involved in. The social action activities I described in this chapter were in one way or another guided by the Sermon on the Mount, described in the Gospel of Matthew 5:1–12, also known as the Beatitudes. It was my attempt to live the Beatitudes. I recognized that this was a journey that I started back in the sixties when I:

- began to critically study the primacy of conscience;
- began to question seriously many of the ***prescribed beliefs*** that I learned from growing up in an

environment that accepted whatever the church taught and chose to listen to my conscience to arrive at a ***responsible adult faith;***

- began to make a distinction between beliefs and faith;
- became skeptical at relying on the magisterium and the fathers of the church as reliable sources for providing evidence that established what I must believe;
- began to question the doctrine of infallibility;
- began to challenge the prescription of obligatory celibacy and recognized that I did not have the gift or charism of celibacy but that I did have the charism of service;
- was disillusioned by the way Pius VI discounted the sense of the faithful with his encyclical *Humanae Vitae,* in which he banned any form of artificial birth control;
- challenged the church's position on the ordination of women;
- began to study the image of God and the cosmology that I had been taught, as opposed to the new cosmology;
- began to study other religions to determine what they could add to my faith tradition;
- questioned the utility of the monarchical structure of the Vatican and pursued changes leading to a more democratic structure.

The journey continued as I processed what I've learned and determined the need for more depth or other areas I needed to explore. I still derive nourishment from the Seekers. As I write these reflections, for the last two months we have been studying and practicing Roger Walsh's book *Essential Spirituality.* His book provides exercises from the world's major religions to help us cultivate kindness, love, joy, peace, vision, wisdom, and generosity.[1] His approach fits well with the Beatitudes. As Robin Meyers points out in his book, *Saving Jesus from the Church: How to Stop Worshiping Christ and Start Following Jesus*, "Consider this: there is not a single word in the sermon (on the Mount) about what to believe, only words about what to do ... Yet when the Nicene Creed became the official oath of Christendom, there was not a single word about what to do, only words about what to believe!"[2]

Along the same lines, in his book *The Future of Faith*, Harvey Cox suggests that patterns of beliefs that we held at ten or twelve are not identical with the ones we hold at fifty or seventy-five. He takes his point further by stating, "To focus Christian life on belief rather than faith is simply a mistake. We have been misled by [those] who taught that faith consists in dutifully believing the articles listed in one of the countless creeds they have spun out. But it does not."[3] Cox speaks of faith in the same sense that the early Christians experienced it, before the Council of Nicaea in AD 325. Under the watchful eye of the Emperor Constantine, the bishops codified beliefs, while faith is a way of life! As a matter of historical fact, the early Christians called the Jesus movement, "the Way."[4] They were more interested in what Jesus believed and did, rather than what others said we should believe. The more I thought about it, the more I realized that I never lost my faith, but I lost my beliefs in many doctrines (creeds) over the years. I have found the distinction between beliefs and faith very helpful.

For me the Beatitudes provide a way to rekindle a sense of the early church's focus on faith as opposed to beliefs. The Beatitudes are Jesus' recipe for how to follow in his steps. Reading the Beatitudes reminds me that I need to look at: How are they reflected in my life? How do I live them? How can I lead others to them? Am I reluctant to experience them because I fear what I might have to give up or that I might have to make changes in my life? The Beatitudes are a commitment to compassion—the compassion that Jesus modeled for us in his life on earth. Compassion for *les miserables*—those who are hungry or thirsty, who are homeless, who mourn, who are sick and alone, who are persecuted, whose rights for justice are denied.

I recognize that compassion should not be confused with the caricature of the bleeding-heart liberal social worker handing out public dollars to a welfare mother of multiple children—the so-called Cadillac Welfare Queen. Interesting that President Reagan, in a bogus story that he repeatedly told, was the one who labeled the "Cadillac-Driving Welfare Queen." I couldn't resist sharing that little bit of information. But the point is that when we speak of compassion, we are not referring to a sloppy emotional concept. Compassion, according to Karen Armstrong, the acclaimed author of a number of books on religious topics states that compassion "requires a serious intellectual effort to learn about one another, even if it's unflattering to ourselves."[5]

In her Charter of Compassion, Armstrong writes:

> The principle of compassion lies at the heart of all religious, ethical and spiritual traditions, calling us always to treat all others as we wish to be treated ourselves. Compassion impels us to work tirelessly to alleviate the suffering of our fellow creatures, to dethrone ourselves from the center of our world and put another there and to honor the inviolable sanctity of every single human being, treating everybody, without exception, with absolute justice, equity and respect.[6]

My days of marching in demonstrations or being physically active in advocacy are over. But I still have the opportunity to be active in cyberspace, the virtual global community through the magic of the Internet. I can help to create social change through the Charter of Compassion, living the beatitudes and practicing the principles of compassion in my daily life. "Yes we can!"

Chapter 13
The Nineties and the
New Millennium

In 1992 Jesse McClure resigned as dean and Emilia Martinez-Brawley was appointed by the vice president of ASU as the first woman/minority dean. She was not the candidate that a faction of the faculty chose. She had impressive credentials. She was a full professor at Penn State; had published extensively; was an expert in rural social work; was on the board of the Council of Social Work Education, but she did not have experience in administering an undergraduate/graduate program. The other finalist in the search was a woman who had been the dean of a school of social work for many years as well as having experience as vice president of a major university. Emilia's tenure as dean started under less than favorable conditions. The faction that had opposed her candidacy was uncooperative from the very beginning. She had a very strong yet charming personality, with an agenda for change that didn't sit well with the dissidents.

At the faculty retreat we had at the beginning of the academic year, she made a point of coming over to where I was sitting to tell me she had heard a lot of good things about me and wanted to talk to me after the retreat. I thought to myself, *Oh, no, I hope she doesn't want me to serve in any administrative position. I'm sixty-three years old and plan to retire in a few years.*

I met her the next day in her office, not knowing for sure why she wanted to see me, but I was prepared to say no if it were to offer me an administration position. When we got down to business, I braced myself, suspecting what she was going to ask me. Sure enough, she wanted me to be either assistant dean or director of the MSW program. I told her I appreciated her offering me the positions but I intended to retire in two years and wanted to spend more time on my publications. She tried to convince me that it would be best for the school, but I responded that after all these years I had to figure what would be best for me. I stood my ground. A wife of one of the dissenters took the position for a year. After she completed the year, she resigned the position, and Emilia offered me the position of associate dean, which was a step up from assistant dean. By that time, in my opinion, the dissenters had been giving Emilia an undeserved hard time. I didn't believe she deserved the treatment she was receiving. I felt that if I could give her some relief by being the associate dean for troubles, I could do it for a year or two at the most. Five years later, I was still associate dean in charge of troubles. Don't ask me why!

When I was getting near my retirement date, Governor Jane Hull appointed me to the Arizona Board of Behavioral Health Examiners (BBHE), which was responsible for licensing marriage and family counselors, substance abuse counselors, professional counselors, and social workers. More trouble! When I agreed to serve, I thought, *Well, this would give me something to do when I retire.*

The board had been established by law in 1987, and after the original executive director resigned in 1996, three other executives were appointed, but all three served for less than three months. They either resigned or were let go before they finished their probationary period. Frequent turnovers in the administration and staff created a very chaotic atmosphere at the agency. During my first year on the board, things settled down as we hired a new executive who brought good management skills and was able to work well with the board.

During my second year I was elected as chair of the Social Work Credentialing Committee. Even though the committee met only once a month for the whole day much preparation was needed to be able to give each complainant a fair hearing. The meetings are open to the public, as is the content of each individual case and the decisions for each complaint. The hearings are semi-judicial in form, and often there were lawyers representing the professional and the plaintiff and witnesses for and against both parties. I remember one situation where the complainant was so contentious that we had to call the security guards to escort him out of the hearing room.

All information about each complaint is included on the Board's Web site. Below are examples of the typical type of complaints that the credentialing committees would hear. A professional:

- having a sexual relationship with a client;
- failing to keep proper records on clients;
- committing breaches of confidentiality;
- treating a client outside of the professional's scope of practice;
- making billing errors;
- giving false information on application or license renewal.

The resolutions of the complaints could include an order of censure; suspension of a license for various lengths of time with requirements to be supervised during suspension; the requirement to take a graduate course in ethics; or revocation of license. As chair of the committee, I had to run the hearings and the discussions by the members to determine the resolution of the complaint. It was often a very stressful role, which I did not enjoy.

The Coco Connection: East Meets West

While I was busy with my professional life, I sort of put my social life on the back burner. I don't mean I became a hermit and was completely immersed in work in and outside of the university. I continued to be involved with my spiritual quest, and, as I suggested in the last chapter, I dated and had platonic relationships that were rewarding but not completely fulfilling. I was not looking for an ongoing, meaningful, interpersonal relationship. This went on for almost ten years. They were good years but rather dull for a memoir. Then along came Jane. This was purely an accidental meeting; no one fixed us up with a date, nor did we meet at one of those singles dances or other activities. As the scientists might say, it was simply serendipitous. Or, as the person on the street might say, it was unexpected, unforeseen, unanticipated, just a matter of chance.

Usually when she and I meet people for the first time, they ask, "How did you two meet?" I'm not sure why they ask, perhaps because Jane is Chinese, and I'm Caucasian, and they think we must have met in China. In case you're wondering how we met, here is the answer that we give, without all the details.

It was during the spring break on March 17, 1993 (St. Patrick's Day). I had just finished making a home visit to one of the stepfamilies with whom I had been working. I decided to have lunch at Coco's Restaurant in the town of Paradise Valley, Arizona, which is an upscale town between Phoenix and Scottsdale. For those of you not familiar with the Coco chain, it's not a fancy restaurant; it's just one step above Denny's. After lunch I was waiting in line to pay my bill behind a very attractive and friendly Asian woman with striking, dark eyes and dressed impeccably. She started a conversation and by the time we got to the cash register I had given her my business card, with the hope that I would hear from her. As I found out later, Jane is one of those people who never met a stranger. So it was not unusual for her to strike up a conversation with this stranger. Since then I've seen her do it over and over. I've come to believe that it was providential that it was a long line and we couldn't finish our conversation because Jane had to get back to J. C. Penny's, where she was employed in the accounting office. My only regret at the time was that I hadn't asked for her phone number. She told me after she got to know me that she probably wouldn't have given it until she checked me out a little more.

That night I received a phone call from Jane to continue the conversation we were having as we stood in line. After a long telephone conversation, I invited her out that weekend for dinner. We had dinner at Chianti's, a small but authentic neighborhood Italian restaurant. After an enjoyable meal, we went to the Royal Palms resort where Maxine Andrews, one of the famous Andrews sisters, was performing as a solo act. When I Googled the Andrews sisters, I found to my surprise that Maxine was seventy-seven years old at that time and died two years later. She could still belt out a song when we saw her, but it was not the same without her sisters. In addition to singing some of their hit songs, she did a brief monologue about her sisters and some of the famous leading men they had performed with like Bing Crosby and Bob Hope. Her older sister, LaVerne, had died in 1967, and I had recently read in the paper that her younger sister, Patti, had just turned ninety-two. It was nostalgic to see and hear Maxine sing some of the songs I grew up with during World War II.

Maxine had her own pianist to accompany her, but after her performance, the Royal Palms had a trio for dancing. Before we got out on the dance floor, I warned Jane that dancing was not my forte and asked for her indulgence. Jane loved dancing and was a great dancer. She could even accommodate my two left feet. Despite my being dancing-impaired, with Jane I felt like I was a great dancer. It was a wonderful night. From that night on, we started to go out on a regular basis.

During the week our dating ranged from her inviting me for a home-cooked meal to our going out for a meal at a Chinese restaurant. As time went on, I felt comfortable enough to stop by after school with a stack of exams or term papers and work on them while she talked on the phone in Chinese to her family or friends or read the paper. On weekends we usually went to a play or movie or to a fancy restaurant. I remember taking her to a very up-town restaurant called the Wigwam in Litchfield Park on her birthday. We had a very romantic dinner. They had a band of vintage aged musicians from New York City who played all the old favorites. We sat right next to the dance floor, and I think we danced to every song they played. I couldn't believe it! I was a dancer. I knew even then that this was the woman I wanted to be with and dance with for the rest of my life.

If I were to marry Jane, I had to pass inspection by her family. The first step was to meet her mother. Mama Li, as she was affectionately known by the family, lived in a very attractive one-bedroom apartment at the Honling House, which was an apartment house for elderly Chinese. She was a very distinguished woman in her early eighties at the time—the matriarch of the Li family. Her husband had died in his early sixties. She had lived with Jane for a number of years until she moved into the Honling House. She loved it because there were always friends available that she could play Mahjong with. Sometimes they'd play for six or eight hours a day.

When Jane brought me to see her, she was dressed in the traditional Chinese dress, the cheongsam. She spoke very little English, and I had a very limited vocabulary in Mandarin Chinese. She was delighted when I responded, *"Xie xie"* (thank you) when she offered me a cup of tea. Jane reported back to me after the meeting to tell me that Mama Li liked me and told her she should marry me. Her main reason was that I have big ears, which are a sign I would live a long life. God bless Mama Li.

Jane had told her I was a professor, so when she spoke to Jane about me she always referred to me as "the scholar." When Jane and I were married, and Mama Li would phone, and when I answered, our conversation would go something like this:

"Donald?"

"Mama?"

"Jane home?"

"She's shopping."

"Thank you!"

The next time she'd talk to Jane, she'd tell her, "The scholar and I had a nice conversation."

Jane shared with me the tragic death of her son, Billy. He had been murdered by the former boyfriend of a girl he had just started to date. From what everyone told me, he was an outstanding young man with great promise. He was only twenty-two, an engineering student at ASU, in the forefront of computer technology for the eighties, with a cheerful and caring personality, like his mother. I can't begin to imagine how extremely difficult it is to lose a child. I know from others that you never recover from it completely. I think Jane handled it as well as anyone could. At the same time, there's not a day goes by that she doesn't remember him in her prayers. The person who committed the murder was given a flat sentence of twenty years in the penitentiary. Every month until he was released after he served his sentence, Jane would call the Department of Corrections to make sure he had not been released.

When we first met, I went with her to a support group, Parents of Murdered Children, which she had attended since Billy's death. I had participated in a number of different support groups over the years but nothing like this. The stories that the participants shared were heartrending and depressing. We still go to their annual Christmas remembrance but stopped going to the support group on a regular basis.

Soon after Billy's death, Jane's husband, who had been sick for most of their married life, died of cancer. Another loss! Again her strong faith in an eternal life helped get her through her grief.

I met Jane's daughter, Sandra, and her fiancé, TY, just before they were married. Jane made their wedding day very special, with a church ceremony, a reception right after the service, and a banquet in the evening. I had a chance to meet more of her friends and relatives and enjoy a feast of many Chinese dishes. It was outstanding. Sandra graduated from ASU as an RN. She and I connected right away. Jane said it because we both like to read a lot and had common interests in some of the same authors.

Sandra and TY's son, Alex, is now fourteen. He's very bright, well mannered, and has broad interests in a number of subjects but seems to be focusing on science. Jane and I are both proud of our grandson.

Besides being the focal point for her family, Jane also was and is the hub of her Chinese women friends. Ten years ago she founded a group she called the Over Fifty Chinese Women's Club. Most of the women at that time were well over fifty and getting close to sixty. Now it could be called the Over Seventy Chinese Women's Club.

In 1994, after courting for almost two years, we decided to get married on New Year's Day, 1995. I remember telling my friend John Rusnak that in my whole life, I was never surer about any major decision I made as I was about marrying Jane. After sixteen years of marriage, I still believe and feel that same way. We had a beautiful outdoor wedding at the Doubletree Resort in Scottsdale, with John Rusnak performing the ceremony. My brother was the best man and Jane's friend of forty years, Nancy Wang, was the maiden of honor. After the ceremony we celebrated with a four-course dinner, with our nieces Lisa and Angela providing the entertainment on the Chinese zither and the piano.

We bought an older house before we were married. I moved in a month or so before our wedding, but Jane waited until after we were married because she thought that was the proper thing to do. It wasn't a pretentious house, but it was in a nice area, with John McCain living a few blocks west of us and Barry Goldwater a couple of miles to the east. We had great views of the mountains in back and the beautiful Arizona sunsets in the front. Jane enjoyed gardening and made the backyard into our oasis in the desert. I even taught her to swim in our pool, and we would enjoy a pre-dinnertime swim after a day of triple-digit temperatures.

We both enjoyed entertaining, and our house became the party place for relatives and friends. Get-togethers on Christmas, birthdays, Chinese New Years, and Super Bowl Sundays became traditions. We had a ritual for celebrating Mama Li's birthday. After our meal, she would enthrone herself in all her glory in a dining room chair. First, all her children would approach the throne, kneel down, kowtow (bow) three times, and Mama Li would hand each a red envelope with a gift of cash. Next the grandchildren would go through the same ritual, followed by the sons and daughter-in-laws. She loved it.

As I suggested above, Jane was the hub of her family. Soon after she came to America, she brought over her parents, in addition to all her siblings and their spouses. Not only did she bring them to America, but she gave them all American names—Jeanne, Joanie, Jimmy, and Philip, the only one whose name didn't start with a "J". She believed it was important to have American first names that were easy to pronounce, rather than a difficult Chinese first name, especially one that began with X. She also made sure they all either had jobs or finished their educations. As an example, she tells the story of how her brother Jimmy arrived in the United States on a Tuesday and was working for J. C. Penny's on Wednesday in the stockroom. He could hardly speak any English then, but like his other siblings, he learned quickly. To their credit, they all did well over the years and became good American citizens, owned properties in addition to their homes, paid taxes, raised their children, and contributed to the community. I'm very honored and happy to have inherited such a wonderful extended family.

In 1996 her brother John escorted his daughter Laura to America to continue her education. He stayed for a few months and left Laura in our good hands. She lived with us for almost four years while she worked on her bachelor's degree in electrical engineering at Glendale Community College and Arizona State University. It was a delight for me to see her adapt to her new environment. Although she had taken English courses in China, she had to work harder than American students who had the advantage of years of education in the States. After she finished her bachelor's degree with honors, she moved to live with her sister Linda, who Jane also brought to the United States. Laura was accepted into the master's program in engineering, and Linda enrolled in the master's program in computer science. Linda hadn't had the advantage of practicing her English in a community college, so her command of the language left a lot to be desired. I thought to myself, *I don't know how she'll be able to get through the first class, let alone complete her degree.* Much to her credit and my surprise, she not only finished the first class but received her master's degree with a 4.0 grade point average.

To me, Jane's No. 1 brother, John, was the family hero. Jane's father was in the air force, headed by the anti-communist Chiang Kai-shek. When the rest of the family was forced to move to Taiwan with Chiang, after Chairman Mao Zedong took over China, John was left behind at the age of eleven to take care of the grandparents. After the family migrated to Taiwan, he was considered "the son of a traitor" by the communist regime. He was arrested and placed in a hard labor camp, where he remained for seventeen years. After Mao died in 1976, John was released, and he returned to his village. He married his wife, Sue, who had a young child, Linda, and they soon had Laura. We brought him and his wife to the United States in 1999. He was always so respectful of me that if I walked into a room, he would immediately stand up. As often as I discouraged him from standing, he would still stand. He enjoyed being with his family. They took him to Las Vegas and the Grand Canyon, and when Laura moved to Texas for her first job, he, his wife, Sue, and Linda spent a week there. After several tries, he passed the exam to become an American citizen. He was so proud of that accomplishment. I remember that after the exam he was beaming. I asked him, "What were some of the questions on the exam?" He answered in Chinese to Jane, "Where does the president live?"

"What did you answer?"

"The president he live in White Home."

Toward the end of his life, John was diagnosed with prostate cancer. When Jane pointed out that he never complained, he responded, "If I thought crying would help, I'd cry." He died in hospice care at his home with his family. I often think of him and the struggles he had in life and how he was an example of acceptance. Despite his physical pain, he never asked the question, "Why me?" When I asked, "Do you ever think 'Why me?'," his answer was, "Why not me?" I felt honored to know him.

The Travelers

During a period of ten years before I met Jane, I presented papers, did training, or lectured in Brazil, Costa Rico, Mexico, and Yugoslavia in addition to attending conferences and giving workshops throughout the United States. (Maybe that's why I didn't have a significant romantic relationship.) After we were married, Jane and I took a number of ocean cruises and land tours, but the most memorable trip of all was when I was on sabbatical in 1996. We spent six weeks in Taiwan and China. I combined the trip with lectures in Taiwan at the National Taiwan University and the National Cheng-Chi University; in China at Peking University in Beijing and Nankai University in Tianjin. After each lecture they would have a banquet where they presented me with their university's plaque, and we toasted one another's countries. I felt like a diplomat.

When we finished the lecture tour, we took a wonderful cruise down the Yangtze River through the Three Gorges across the area soon to be submerged. The grandeur and beauty of the perpendicular cliffs as we headed toward the first gorge was spectacular. At that time the controversial Three Gorges Dam was in its early days of construction. When it is completed, it will be the largest dam in the world and will eventually form the world's largest hydroelectric power facility. What I didn't realize was that when the project is completed, 13 cities, 140 towns, 1,352 villages, and 650 factories will be under water, and 1.8 million people will need to be relocated.[1] I thought it would just cover farmland and individual homes. Some of the cities we saw that would be submerged had ten-story high-rise buildings. So much for preserving the environment!

I had been reading *The Private Life of Chairman Mao: The Memoirs of Mao's Personal Physician*, by Dr. Li Zhisui. As we cruised down the river, I imagined Chairman Mao as Dr. Li described him, floating in the murky waters of the Yangtze, surrounded by his entourage of flunkies. At one point, we took a side trip in a sampan that accommodated about twenty people. Halfway through the trip I had to urinate, as they say in polite company. I was directed to the back of the sampan, where there was a private area. What I didn't expect, when I relieved myself, was that my pee went right into the river. So there is a little bit of me mixed into the water of the ancient Yangtze River.

Retirement

I woke up one morning and realized it would soon be thirty years since I started teaching at ASU. While I was associate dean, I only had one class to teach, and the rest of my time was devoted to administration. The contentious atmosphere at the School of Social Work still prevailed. I loved teaching the class on family therapies but had had enough of the political battles. At the same time I realized that I had devoted a good part of my professional life to two institutions, the church and the university, that were not immune from the same type of power politics that we expect from corporations and politicians. It was disheartening for me to admit that the clerical culture of the church was often motivated by self-advancement, greed, and egotism, and that the coin of the realm was control and power.

I let Dean Martinez-Brawley know early enough so she could start looking for a replacement. She decided to take a sabbatical, resign from her position as dean, and go back to her teaching position as professor of social work and be awarded the John F. Roatch Distinguished Community Service Scholar. I felt honored and somewhat vindicated, despite the disdain of the dissidents, when in my final year I received the Faculty Achievement Award for Outstanding Service from the university's Alumni Association. The fact that I was chosen from over two thousand faculty members was a great honor. The award was given at a large banquet on Founders' Day and in addition to a bronze plaque I received a check for $3,000.

Other honors included: a certificate of appreciation from the governor of Arizona for my contributions to ASU and the community; a lifetime achievement award from the state chapter of the National Association of Social Workers; and the one I treasured the most—a plaque presented by the Association of American Indian Social Workers, which read, "For Outstanding Service to the American Indian People of Arizona." It was a nice way to start my retirement.

Another milestone in my life was my seventieth birthday. Jane organized an unforgettable party. She made arrangements to have it at the University Club at ASU and gave the one hundred guests a choice of three entrées. Their name tags were color coded, so the servers knew which guest got which meal. The meal was preceded by a happy hour with a variety of hors d'oeuvres and our niece Lisa Prout playing the Chinese zither. During the meal there was a string quartet from the School of Music at ASU. My sister-in-law, Diane, said the blessing for the meal; my brother, Jim, did a great job entertaining the guests as MC, and my friends Hans and John and cousins Bob Brew and Mary Anne Tommaney from New York took the occasion to "roast" me. It was a great gathering of kith and kin, and a good time was had by all. I had come a long way from 8 Judson Street in the last seventy years.

We continued the celebration with a trip to Italy with Hans and his bride-to-be Karen. Our tour started in Rome, where we spent three days and went along the Amalfi Coast to the Bay of Naples, where we stayed in Sorrento and visited Pompeii, Salerno, Naples, Posetano, Ravello, and the Isle of Capri. This was an outstanding trip with many happy memories, but unfortunately I don't have the space to fill in the details.

Walden University

What to do during my retirement? As the actual date for retiring approached, I began to look at options for how I would spend my time. I certainly wanted to travel with Jane, but that might be only one month out of the year. I hadn't played golf for forty years, and I had left my clubs back in Schenectady with my dentist, who never shipped them out to me. I had played tennis and joined a gym, but how much time could I spend I playing tennis or exercising? I intended to do more writing, but at that time I was thinking of doing a book on stepfamilies. I even looked into joining the Civil Air Patrol and went to a couple of their meetings, but the commitment was a little more than I was prepared for.

While I was weighing these options and others, I received a letter from Walden University, inviting me to apply for a part-time position on their faculty. I accepted an invitation to a three-day orientation in Minneapolis, which was where the administration offices were located. I liked what I heard and saw. I particularly liked their focus on social change and their practice model of "the scholar/practitioner." A short time after the orientation, I received an offer to join their faculty.

At that time, Walden was an online PhD program with four different departments: Health and Human Services, Education, Administration, and Psychology. There were approximately two thousand students and one hundred faculty located in different parts of the country. My appointment was to teach in the Health and Human Services program. In addition to the course work, there was a requirement for thirty-two hours of residency where students met face-to-face with faculty; attended seminars; and enhanced their writing, research, and critical thinking skills. These residencies were held throughout the country on four weekends a year and two weeks in the summer at the University of Indiana (UI) in Bloomington. I particularly enjoyed the summer sessions on the campus of UI. Not only is it one of the most beautiful campuses in the country, but it also provided me with two weeks away from the three-digit heat in Arizona. Even more, I enjoyed the face-to-face interaction with the students and faculty.

I also attended one or two weekend residencies throughout the country. Faculty had to prepare two workshops for each residency, in addition to being available for meetings with students. The students were mostly from the States, but a number were from other countries. They were midcareer students who didn't have the luxury to take time from their jobs to go a traditional "brick and mortar" university. I remember one South African student whose dissertation committee I chaired. I had never met him until his graduation ceremony at UI. When they called his name to receive his degree, I was stunned to see him make his way up the ramp in a motorized wheelchair. He was a paraplegic, even though we had a program to assist the physically impaired, he had never mentioned it in the two years we worked together on his dissertation. When I asked him later, at the reception, why he hadn't told me, he humbly replied, "I didn't want any special treatment because of my disability. I needed to know I could make it despite my being in a wheelchair." I told him I was honored to be his chairperson.

Of all the presentations I made at Walden residencies over a period of ten years, my most memorable one was a plenary session that a colleague and I put together back in 2002. Bruce Lackey, who was a faculty member from Philadelphia, and I started at Walden in 1998 and became very close friends. Bruce always brought his guitar and banjo, plus his station wagon full of speakers, microphones, and karaoke equipment to the residencies. From our first summer session, we had hootenannies for everyone who liked to sing. It was a great way for folks to get to know one another and to have fun after a long day of straining our brains. Many of the songs we sang were folk songs. The thought occurred to us that since social change was one of Walden's hallmarks, and we believed that some of the protest songs that were popular in the sixties motivated people to social action, we should put together a plenary session on protest songs and social change. I agreed to research music and social change, since we needed an academic base in order to make the presentation.

I found a number of authors[2] who believed that social protest songs have been used by leaders, from slavery to the environmental movement, to inspire communities to mobilize for social action. I also found that there were a number of universities throughout the United States that had departments of ethnomusicology, which is the systematic approach to study of music in a cultural context— that is, the study of music wherever it may be found or in whatever time.[3] This became our rationale for making the presentation legitimate. With Bruce accompanying us on his guitar, we had a PowerPoint presentation and sang songs of some of the more well-known artists of the sixties: Woody Guthrie's "This Land is Your Land" and Pete Seeger's "Everybody's Got a Right to Live," "If I Had a Hammer," and "Where Have All the Flowers Gone?"[4] And the anthem of the civil rights movement, "We Shall Overcome!"

As the years went by, Walden was bought by Laureate, Inc. and soon after, I became disenchanted with the new corporate environment. It was not the Walden I had joined. The new administration added bachelor's and master's degrees to the four PhD programs, along with a number of new disciplines with multiple levels of degrees. They now have six colleges and schools; ten doctoral programs; eighteen master's programs; and thirteen bachelor's programs. The number of students worldwide grew to over 225,000 in a period of four or five years.

I stopped taking new students, and after all my students finished their dissertations, I resigned in 2008. Just as I did when I retired from ASU, I looked at all my options for a fulfilling second retirement.

I decided I would write my memoir. In order to make the transition from academic writing to memoir writing, I took a twelve-week online course on how to write a memoir. There is obviously a big difference between the two writing modalities. Unless you're doing qualitative research, you don't tell stories. You certainly don't share intimate information about your life.

The course was interactive via e-mails. I had assignments every week that the instructor and the other four students critiqued. I in turn critiqued their assignments. It was a good learning experience for me. Perhaps you should be the judge of that.

Aung San Suu Kyi

I continued to be involved with social justice issues. One of the causes I had been interested in for some time was the plight of the world's only imprisoned Nobel Peace Prize recipient, Aung San Suu Kyi. She is one of the world's most renowned freedom fighters and advocates of nonviolence. She has served as the figurehead for Burma's struggle for democracy since 1988. For over thirteen years, she was under house arrest by order of the ruling military junta of Burma.

I joined with two hundred plus members of the US Campaign for Burma around the world to place myself under voluntary "house arrest" for twenty-four hours to celebrate her sixty-second birthday. I sent invitations to friends, family, and colleagues to join me for a portion of my "arrest" to view a documentary film on Aung San Suu Kyi and the crisis the people of Burma face every day. The purpose of the arrest was to share information about Burma and, I hoped, to further her message of peaceful change.

Unfortunately Jane had surgery a week before my "arrest," and I had to cancel the house arrest. I was, however, able to raise $800 for the US Campaign for Burma. I was happy to learn recently that the military junta has agreed to release Suu Kyi from her house arrest in November of 2010. I felt that in a very small way I had contributed to her release.

Bouncing Back

During 2007 and 2008 both Jane and I had surgeries that altered our lifestyles. Jane had a lobe removed from her left lung. She became the Mayo Clinic's poster girl for lung cancer, and her picture and story appeared in the *Phoenix Magazine* and several other local magazines promoting Mayo, where she received chemotherapy. Thankfully, she has been cancer free since her last chemo treatment and just needs to have regular checkups. She continues with her water aerobics five or six days a week at a local health spa, and most people would never guess that she is a recovering cancer victim. She has been a model to me of how to fight back when you are diagnosed with cancer.

A year later, I had major surgery to remove part of my colon. This came as a surprise after a routine colonoscopy exam. There were some signs of non-Hodgkin's lymphoma, which was very scary. I can remember being in the oncologist's office at Mayo waiting for the verdict. The oncologist walked into the room with an expression that was hard to read. I felt like a prisoner waiting to hear the judge pronounce the verdict. He pulled his chair next to me and said, "Now I'm only going to say this once. I want you to pay close attention. You have a very mild version of lymphoma. I'm not going to prescribe any treatment. I just want to see you in three months so we can do the same tests again." To say I was relieved is a major understatement. My tests have been negative for the past year, and I am very grateful for that.

Sadly, while I was in the hospital recovering from my surgery, my brother, Jim, had surgery for colon cancer in another hospital. His prognosis was not good. I was able to visit him shortly before he died. Jane and I stopped on our way home from the Mayo Clinic. Diane, Jimmy, and Paul, Jim's stepson, was there, along with Father Eric, the pastor of St. Patrick's Church, where both Jim and Diane were very active. Father Eric left soon after we arrived, so we could be alone. Jim was sitting up in bed. His color was very white, and he was very weak but still responsive. He asked Paul to help him out of bed into a chair. It was almost as if he were trying to show me that he was still mobile despite his colostomy bag. After Paul had settled him in the chair, with Jimmy's help, Jim made some witty observations about what he had gone through and made comments about the nurses. When it was time to go, I went over to his chair, gave him a hug, kissed him, and told him I loved him and to get better soon. He whispered, "I love you, boss." He always called me "boss" when we talked on the phone.

I dreaded getting a phone call from Diane that Jim had died. Even though I prepared for the worst, I prayed for his recovery.

Jim had survived other serious operations, including coronary bypass and prostate surgeries, so I actually thought he might have a chance to recover. Despite thinking I was ready for the worst, it was a shock when Diane called me from the hospital to tell me that Jim had died. I never thought when I said good-bye at the hospital that it would be our last good-bye. I was glad I had told him I loved him and heard him respond that he loved me. We both always knew that, but we didn't trade endearments very often. Jim was a great guy, and I miss him very much.

Diane and the folks at St. Patrick's Church in Scottsdale prepared a touching evening memorial service for Jim and a beautiful liturgy the following day. The church was packed for both events, which included moving words from friends and relatives. It was a real tribute to Jim and the life he lived. I was not strong enough yet to do any public speaking, but Diane's sister Liz read my "Ode to Jim" for me.

The Beatitudes Campus

After much thought and prayer, Jane and I finally decided that maintaining a large house was getting to be too much for us to handle, and it was time for us to move into an independent living facility. This wasn't an easy decision. Next to 8 Judson Street, I had never lived in a house as long as I did in our last home. I never thought I was that attached to it until the time came to move. It was more difficult than I thought it would be to leave the home, which held so many happy memories. It was like saying good-bye to an old friend.

We had considered a move before our surgeries and had looked at a number of options in the Phoenix/Scottsdale area. We finally settled on The Beatitudes, a retirement community, which offers a continuum of care from independent living through assisted living to skilled nursing care. It was a good decision.

The Beatitudes is only four miles from where we lived. The campus is on twenty-two acres, with everything within walking distance. We live in a very comfortable four-room, two-bathroom apartment with a small but adequate kitchen. There are three restaurants, ranging from informal, come-as-you-are dining at the Bistro to Elaine's Fine Dining. There are more social, cultural, educational, spiritual, and recreational programs than we could ever take advantage of. We even have Mass every Sunday in the Life Center, which is only a three-minute walk from our apartment. No more hassle with parking the car and fighting to get out of the parking lot at the end of Mass.

The staff, from the CEO on down, is committed to creating a caring community for all the residents. Also, one of the first things we noticed when we moved in is how friendly the residents are. This makes it easy to make new friends, whether you meet on the elevator, in the dining room, or while attending a meeting of the "Good Fellars."

Life at The Beatitudes is stress-free. It gives us the chance to do the things we want without worrying about the water heater breaking down or the roof leaking. Now we just dial "0" for maintenance, and voilà, someone is there to fix whatever needs fixing. On a practical note, The Beatitudes provides for the time when our physical condition does not allow us to enjoy life as we've known it. For me that time would be when I am not able to share the deep connection I have with my wife, Jane, and other loved ones, because of either physical or mental illness.

At this point, I am fortunate to be able to continue my journey of seeking. I have lived beyond the course of my biblically allotted three score and ten by ten years. Although I'm still counting, I can't think of a better place to live out whatever time I have than at the Beatitudes campus, with my lovely wife, Jane.

Reflections

A few days ago, I was half-asleep and half-awake when the thought came to me, *If there is such a thing as reincarnation, I couldn't wish for a better life than I've had.* Not that I didn't have struggles and experience losses, but who doesn't? I can't complain! Health-wise, since they operated on my tonsils in 1935, it's been seventy-four years between surgeries; financially, we are very comfortable and fortunate enough to have been able to create a Charitable Remainder Trust, with St. Joseph's Hospital as the beneficiary; spiritually, I went down many paths but eventually found my way back to my faith tradition and still meet every other week with the Seekers. I do not accept all the prescribed beliefs from my youth; my journey has brought me to a more responsible faith. I know some people might call me and thousands of others like me, cafeteria or smorgasbord Catholics, because we have followed our informed consciences and rejected particular teachings of the church. Labeling us or calling us derogatory names, and dismissing our right to follow our consciences, however, is not a rational response.

I discussed the primacy of conscience in chapter 9 and have spent hours debating this with myself and others since I started to think critically. Years ago I made the decision that the primacy of conscience was the underlying reason for being able to dissent particular teachings of the church, while making every effort not to "throw the baby out with the bath water," an idiom for not getting rid of what is good along with what is bad when you're trying to improve something—in this case, the church. I thought about those people who ask, "Why do you still call yourself a Catholic if you don't agree with all the teachings from Rome?" This prompted me to revisit the research and other sources I had used to develop an informed conscience and apply it to where I am today.

Whenever someone who knew I had been a priest would ask a similar question—"Do you consider yourself Catholic?"—I would facetiously respond, "I suppose if I found myself in the hospital and they asked my religion, I'd say I was Catholic."

At that time, I wasn't sure what faith community I would join if I left the Catholic Church. I did know that I needed the support of a community of worshippers as much as I needed my individual time for prayer, spiritual reading, and meditation. John Rusnak and I went on a mission to check out other worship communities. We went from mainstream Protestant churches to Orthodox services; from Baha'i to New Age. We visited with an Imam at a Muslim mosque and observed their prayer session.

Despite the eccentricities of some of the faith traditions we visited, there was usually something I admired about each one. It made me wonder more why we minimized the positive aspects of other religions. Thankfully we had abandoned the ultraconservative position that Father Leonard Feeney, S. J. had preached during the late 1940s in Massachusetts: *Extra ecclesiam nulla sollus* ("Outside the church there is no salvation"), arguing that no non-Catholics could be saved, that they were damned to eternal suffering. Not a position that promotes ecumenism or even helps to create an atmosphere that would be conducive for a constructive dialogue. Father Feeney was eventually silenced by Rome. I believe that this was one time when the Vatican used its authority appropriately.

I thought about Father Feeney when I recently read a book by Rabbi Brad Hirschfield entitled, *You Don't Have to Be Wrong for Me to Be Right*. The subtitle is *Finding Faith without Fanaticism*. Before I read the book, I found that just meditating on the title was very helpful. It reinforced my opinion that the Catholic church did not have the corner on the market of "the truth" and that we could benefit from studying other religions. That became eminently clear to me when I read how Thomas Merton's interest in Buddhism had enriched his spiritual life. He is quoted as saying that he wanted "to become as good a Buddhist as I can."[5] For him, that meant being a Christian more profoundly than ever.

Merton was also influenced by Gandhi, who believed that we can find the deeper roots of our own religious tradition by becoming immersed in other religions and then returning "home" to see our own heritage in a transformed way, with a new consciousness.[6] What impressed me was that, even as Merton's study of Buddhism went into more depth, he had no intention of leaving his faith tradition. Just as the early Christians had to face the influence of Greek thought and, later in history, the rise of modern science, the contemporary church has to take seriously the other religions of the world and the reality of pluralistic cultures.[7] This is even more apparent now in this age of globalization.

Merton was further motivated by the decree from Vatican II, *Nostras Aetate* (NA), which was meant to alter the church's attitude toward our relationships with other religions. This was no longer Father Feeney's church. The decree "legitimatized" what Merton and others had been doing for some time: recognizing the value and validity of other religions by having dialogues on theological issues on an interreligious basis. I found the words of the decree very encouraging:

> The Church therefore has this exhortation for her sons: prudently and lovingly, through dialogue and collaboration with the followers of other religions and in witness of Christian faith and life, acknowledge, preserve and promote the spiritual and moral goods found among these men, as well as the values in their society and cultures.[8]

Notice the pastoral tone of the decree. It certainly differs from the authoritarian prose and dogmatic positions of pre-Vatican II documents.

Another source along the same line that I found inspiring was a book by Paul F. Knitter. He is currently the Paul Tillich Professor of Theology, World Religions and Culture at Union Theological Seminary in New York City and a leading advocate of globally responsible interreligious dialogue. He was given permission to leave the priesthood for the same reasons as I was—mandatory celibacy and blind obedience. I found the title of his book to be very seductive: *Without Buddha, I Could Not Be a Christian*. The book is, as it is described on the back cover, "a moving story of one man's quest for truth and spiritual authenticity; from the nature of prayer to Christian views of life after death."[9]

Knitter describes how the Buddhist perspective can inspire a more person-centered and socially engaged understanding of

Christianity. The emphasis of the book is on religious experiences rather than rigid dogma and ritual; and how that approach can enliven Christianity and benefit worship, social action, and engagement with the Christian tradition. I found his book a great source of meditation.

The Loyal Opposition

During the past few years, I've read a number of books and articles by prominent theologians and former priests who wrote on the topic of why they still considered themselves Catholics, even though they held views contrary to the teachings of the church. I went back to my notes and files and reflected on how they justified their positions on the doctrines that they had publicly opposed. Not only was I curious, but I wanted to see how their rationale for dissent compared with mine. Perhaps I just wanted to be assured that I had taken the right steps in forming my conscience. These were all distinguished authors whom I admired. I also reviewed authors who were critical of dissenters who identified themselves as Catholics. I recognize, as with any of the topics I've discussed in this book, it is difficult to reduce any issue, from abortion to celibacy, into a few pages, when each topic is the subject of volumes of theological debates. Let me say again that my purpose is to describe the process I used to form my conscience, not to suggest that it is "the way."

I plan to focus on one of the most vocal dissenters and just briefly identify some others. Hans Kung is thought of as one of the most distinguished and widely acclaimed theologians of our time. Father Kung has a long history of dissent. He first got in trouble with the Vatican with the publication of a book in 1971 that questioned papal infallibility. Eight years after the book was published, he was stripped of his license to teach as a Catholic theologian. From 1960 to his retirement in 1996, he was professor of ecumenical theology at the University of Tubingen. He founded the Global Ethic Foundation in 1990 after the publication of his book *Global Responsibility* and serves as its president. The goal of the foundation is to promote intercultural and interreligious research, education, and dialogue.[10]

The first book of his that I read, over fifteen years ago, was *Why I Am a Christian*. The book contains a laundry list of teachings of the Vatican with which he strongly disagrees. He prefaces his list by stating that he can't believe that Jesus of Nazareth would take the same attitude as the Roman authorities. He then goes on to include the church's teaching on birth control, women priests, mandatory celibacy, premarital sex, homosexuality, and masturbation.[11] Overall, he objects to any monarchical exercise of power by the Vatican. Despite the many teachings of the church that he has publicly disputed, he has never left the church and continues to be an active priest.

When Cardinal Joseph Ratzinger was elected pope and became Benedict XVI, very early in his papacy he invited his former colleague Hans Kung to a four-hour session that stretched out over dinner. As Kung told us at the dinner of the Jesuit Alumni in Arizona (JAAZ), the two old friends who had taught together at the University at Tubingen and were both *periti* (theological experts) at Vatican II, as part of the broad progressive majority, decided to discuss things they agreed on and not their differences. Kung described the session as "very joyful," with no reproaches. He regarded the meeting as a "sign of hope for many in the church with the same vision as mine."[12] Apparently, the fact that Kung had hired then Father Ratzinger at Tubingen outweighed his once comparing him to the head of the KGB in his position as the Vatican's top doctrinal enforcer.

Dissent has a long history in the church. One of the books that I used in my research was Robert McClory's *Faithful Dissenters*.[12] The book includes stories of men and women who loved and changed the church by taking contrary opinions on one or more of its teachings. The subjects of the eighteen stories range from Galileo, who was probably the best-known dissenter in the history of the church, to John Courtney Murray, S. J.

All the stories had several things in common: each one was inspirational; all the dissenters suffered emotional abuse for their dissent; they all remained in the church through thick and thin; they did not reject the concept of church authority in general but just how it was applied to particular teachings; the issue on which they dissented was eventually resolved and, more often than not, had ramifications that benefited the whole church. The resolutions did not usually just apply to their issue but established principles that could be applied to other doctrinal disputes. I was so impressed with how Father Murray handled his clash with church authorities that I want to share his story briefly.

In fighting for the separation of church and state, he was challenging the teaching of Pius X, whose encyclical *Vehementer Nos,* on the French Law of Separation (of state and church) was diametrically opposed to Father Murray's. In article 3, the pope stated that it was absolutely false that the state should be separated from the church and characterized the law as a most pernicious error.

I had known about the influence Father Murray had at Vatican II as a *periti* for the American bishops and the part he played in fighting for a clear definition of the church's teaching on the proper relationship between church and state, particularly regarding freedom of worship. I was aware that he publically challenged the deeply established teaching of the church that the state had an obligation to recognize the Catholic church in its constitution specifically, by giving it preferential treatment in public affairs and suppressing anyone who opposed the teaching of the church. In 1847 Pius IX (the pope who made himself infallible) taught in his *Syllabus of Errors* that the state must recognize the Catholic religion as supreme and dissenters must be punished or forced to conform to the church's requirements. This relationship between the church and state became known as the *Catholic Thesis*. It was upheld by Pope Leo XIII as the ideal for America.[13] What I didn't know was that, prior to being called to be a *periti* at Vatican II, Father Murray was silenced by Pope Pius XII for his writing, which basically challenged the

Catholic Thesis, and for his belief that "primacy of conscience could be affirmed not against the community (outside the church) as Catholic anathemas had warned for a century, but (only) within the (Catholic) community."[14] If you are interested, I highly recommend James Carroll's book, *Practicing Catholic,* pages 84–95. Carroll is a former Paulist priest who left the priesthood because of his conscience and the church's expectation of blind obedience—also to become a writer. He became a prize-winning author with ten books of fiction and six nonfiction books.

Vatican II's *The Declaration on Religious Freedom: Dignitatis Humanae,* on the right of the person and of communities to social and civil freedom in matters religious, was spearheaded by Father Murray. Not only was it a victory for church-state relationship, but it was another example that the church's teachings could be changed. It is also reflected in the Catechism of the Catholic Church (CCC) in its section on conscience. In section 1782 the primacy of conscience is again recognized as the judgment of reason that trumps authority:

> Man has the right to act in conscience and in freedom so as personally to make moral decisions. He must not be forced to act contrary to his conscience. Nor must he be prevented from acting according to his conscience, especially in religious matters.[15]

This statement also makes it clear that individual conscience is inviolable and cannot be coerced through an appeal to blind obedience or through threats. Rather, it must be formed through reflection, prayer, and reason. Secondarily, it underscores the premise that we can't have freedom without its necessary concomitants of dissent and dialogue. I believe it gives the Christian faithful the right and even at times the duty to make clear to the authorities their opinion on matters that pertain to the good of the church. To paraphrase the *Association for the Rights of Catholics in the Church,* those who are involved in the disciplines of theology and scriptural study have a lawful freedom of inquiry and a duty to express their opinions on matters in which they have expertise.[16]

Perhaps I'm being naive to think that the dissent of the faithful is going to change the hierarchy. Although we've seen instances of change in the church, judging from the past, the Curia is still entrenched in a pre-Vatican II posture that expects the faithful to just "pray, pay, and obey" as the old saying goes. An absolute monarchy where the pope is king, the bishops are lords, and the members of the Curia are courtiers does not give up its power and control easily and become a democratic form of governance that takes into account the *sensus fidelium*—what the faithful believe, accept, or reject.

I remember just a small example of how autocratic these shepherds of the flock can be. When Voice of the Faithful (VOF) first started in Massachusetts soon after the scandal of child molestation by priest pedophiles became national news in 2002, John Rusnak and I went to the early VOF meetings in Phoenix. As in many other locations, we were not allowed to meet in a parish facility. We had to meet in a public library. This was not a radical organization. Its mission statement was supportive of the church; it was an effort to reclaim the voice that had been ignored by the hierarchy over the years. The group's mission statement reads, "To provide a prayerful voice, attentive to the Spirit, through which the Faithful can actively participate in the governance and guidance of the Catholic Church."[17] The group's goals are to support survivors of sexual abuse; support priests of integrity; shape structural change within the Catholic Church. Aha! That last one is the red flag that prompts the hierarchy to close ranks. Just to suggest structural change is apparently sacrilegious enough to exile us from the parish to a public library for our meetings. This is minor compared to the silencing and persecution of those theologians and scriptural scholars who have attempted to express an understanding of faith that better reflects the sense of the faithful. The more I reflect on the abuse of power

by the hierarchy, the more I'm convinced that the time has come
for the people of God to take a stronger stand on what Cardinal
Newman identified as our right to make sure that the faithful are
taken seriously by the hierarchy before imposing doctrines for us
to believe and follow sheepishly.

A Reawakening of the Role of the Faithful

There is no doubt in my mind that the church leaders need to
follow the spirit of Vatican II as outlined in the documents of the
Council. They have not acted in an accountable or transparent
manner in dealing with the worldwide scandal of pedophile priests
and the bishops who protected them, rather than protecting the
children and young adults who were their victims. The Curial-
run church is not going to loosen its grip on power voluntarily.
I believe that it is up to us to become active in one or more of
the faith groups that have already organized to challenge the
hierarchy for our lawful right of full membership as designated in
the Vatican II documents *Lumen Gentium,* on the nature of the
church, and *Gaudium et Spes*, the church in the modern world.

   Lumen Gentium made it clear that the church isn't just an
institution run by bureaucrats. It described the church as the
"People of God". No longer is the model of the church a caste
system, with the pope, bishops, and clergy on one level and
the laity on a secondary level. The Council proposed a more
egalitarian vision of the church. Through renewal we were to leave
the medieval church behind us and be revitalized.[18]

   Gaudium et Spes proclaimed that the aim of the church is to
establish God's reign of peace over all creation. Justice, equality,
truth, love, and peace on earth would characterize his reign.
Through God's people, global inequality would become a reality.
God's reign would find ways of establishing peace through human
rights rather than escalating the arms race. We are all called to be
part of that renewal.[19] Just meditating on the Reign of God with
those expectations is a peak experience. But is it just a utopian

fantasy? I think not, even though, in many ways, the momentum was scuttled by the reign of John Paul II.[20] I believe that the Reign of God is not just at the end of the world. It is happening right now. We need to plant the seeds for its global development.

One of the reasons for my optimism is that there seems to be a coalescing of the dozens of Catholic reform groups. While maintaining their own identity, they are uniting under the banner of a newly formed movement called the American Catholic Council (ACC). The impetus for this organization came from members of the Voice of the Faithful. Although VOF has grown rapidly since it was founded eight years ago, it only has about 30,000 members. Call to Action, one of the early reform groups, has 22,000 members. Put them together and you only have 52,000 members. ACC already has added to its list groups like Future Church, Takebackourchurch.org, Association for Rights of Catholics in the church, Catholics Speak Out, the Women's Ordination Conference, the Survivor's Network of Those Abused by Priests (SNAP), and the list is growing. Imagine if each group comes to the table with 20,000 or 30,000 members, we'd be more likely to get the Vatican to listen to us. If the Tea Party Movement, which seemed to have come from out of nowhere, can mobilize 500,000 for a political protest, I believe that ACC can mobilize the faithful for religious protests that would open the door of the secret chambers of decision-making in the Vatican.

Some of the reform groups committed to ACC have been working for years to be heard and taken seriously, but to no avail. Basically they all share the same values and goals: "to fulfill the promise of Vatican II; to create a more responsive, accountable church that calls on the active participation of the people and more closely models the American experience."[21] I was very encouraged by ACC's Web site. It does not challenge the faith or the essential beliefs of the church. What the group does object to is the monarchical governing structure of the church that promotes the evangelical role of the laity but excludes the rights of the faithful to be taken seriously when it comes to their contributing to the magisterium.

ACC and its members seek a church that: is inclusive, compassionate, trustworthy, and representative; listens to the Spirit in its people; addresses the spiritual hunger of all Catholics, including marginalized and former Catholics; is willing to reform the governing structure of the church so that it reflects the better aspects of the American experience; has a democratic spirit concerned for human rights, supports freedom of speech and assembly and a tradition of participation and representation. The members of ACC believe that Jesus called all to the Reign of God without reservation. They take as their norm the Gospel and the life-giving elements in their tradition, especially the earliest history of their church and the rebirth promised by Vatican II.[22]

ACC is not a bunch of anti-Catholic wackos who want to secede from the church.

They're highly educated women and men, successful in their chosen profession/occupations, who have been loyal members of the church and who see a serious deterioration in the life of the Catholic Church because of the way it is governed. One of the members of ACC, Robert Blair Kaiser, covered Vatican II for *Time* magazine. Five of his thirteen books deal with church reform. I read recently his very thorough and thoughtful article about the unfulfilled hope of Vatican II, which was published on the Web site of the American Catholic Council. The title of the article is "A Look Back Almost 60 Years." In assessing the condition of the faithful's position with the hierarchy today, he is quite clear that we don't need to "go into schism" in order to effect change. He states, "We are members of a church that has always found a way to reform. Vatican II showed us the way. We are the church. We speak out. We say what we want. I see American Catholics doing this soon."[23] He goes on to explain how his position is compatible with enculturation of the Gospel; the documents of Vatican II, especially *Lumen Gentium* and *Gaudium et Spes*; prominent theologians; and the teachings of Jesus.

On a lighter note, I thought of a novel that Kaiser wrote, *Cardinal Mahony*. It is an intriguing story of an American cardinal who is kidnapped and taken to Latin America, where he is tried for sins against the people, with a jury of five Latin American bishops. The trial is televised internationally, and the cardinal is found guilty as charged. His sentence is "to become a Christian." He is injured during a military attempt to rescue him and after his recovery is a changed man. In the rest of the book, Kaiser uses the "born again" cardinal to provide a recipe of how to create a democratically structured church. It's a very enjoyable read, with a message that fits with my view of a reformed Catholic Church.

On the Road to a Responsible Adult Faith

My journey started with the prayers my parents taught me before I was introduced to the Baltimore Catechism in the first grade at St. Patrick Institute almost seventy-five years ago. During those years I have been down many paths to arrive at where I am today. Often the paths I chose were dead ends where it was difficult to find my way out. Other times it was easier to get back on track. Whether I went down the right or wrong path, they were all turning points, and I always learned more about the Reign of God that helped me continue my lifelong journey. Writing this memoir has been a wonderful experience, which has given me the opportunity to put these turning points in perspective.

I decided it would be helpful, at least for me, to end this chapter and the book by briefly reviewing the underlying concepts that affected my decisions on specific teachings of the church. The following concepts are the basic ones that guided me in moving from the beliefs prescribed by the church to a process of reasoning and critical thinking that led me to a more a responsible faith.

The Image of What God Is. The first belief that I re-examined was my image of God and how it differed from what I was taught. In his book *Tomorrow's Catholic: Understanding God and Jesus in a New Millennium,* Michael Norwood points out, "The way we image or imagine what God is like forms the foundation of our religious beliefs."[24] It makes sense to me that if we change our image of God, we change our way of thinking about God. We also change our way of thinking about ourselves and our relationship with God.

I took a class in the seminary on cosmology, the study of the universe as a system and our place in it. But that was in the early fifties—almost sixty years ago. Our knowledge about the universe has increased by leaps and bounds since then. Especially since 1990, when the Hubble space telescope was launched, our knowledge about space, other galaxies, and the big bang theory has multiplied beyond our imagination. The old cosmology has earth as the center of creation; heaven is up, and so is God; hell is below, along with the devil. That worldview no longer has any credibility. Scientists have identified more than 300 billion galaxies in the universe. In 1920 astronomers were trying to cope with just the one galaxy that earth was part of.[25] The question then is, What does this new scientific knowledge do to our image of God? The answer is, each of us needs to resolve that for ourselves using the best scientific knowledge available. What we do know is that the old cosmology just doesn't fit with what we have learned about the universe since the middle of the last millennium.

The Difference between Beliefs and Faith. I also had to change my understanding of the difference between faith and beliefs. The renowned theologian Harvey Cox, professor emeritus at Harvard Divinity School, describes in his most recent book, *The Future of Faith,* how he was first puzzled by a friend who told him he was "a practicing Christian but not always a believing one." To call oneself a practicing Catholic but not necessarily a believing one acknowledges the certainties and uncertainties that mark the life of any religious person. To support that statement, Cox tells the story of Cardinal Carlo Maria Martini inviting him to his annual Lectureship for Nonbelievers. He goes on to quote the cardinal, who shocked him by saying, "The line between belief and unbelief runs through the middle of each of us, including myself, a bishop of the church."[26]

He also mentions the struggle that Mother Teresa had for years, when she harbored troubling doubts about the existence of God. And how Krista Hughes commented that Mother Teresa "exemplifies the living aspect of faith, something sorely needed in society where Christian identity is most often defined in terms of what a person believes rather than how he or she lives. Shouldn't it be the other way around?"[27] I say, "Yes it should!" The more I thought about it, the more I agreed with Dr. Cox when he writes, "To focus the Christian life on beliefs rather than on faith is simply a mistake. We have been misled for many centuries by theologians who taught that 'faith' consists of dutifully believing the articles listed in one of the countless creeds ... this came as a welcomed liberation."[28]

Indeed, it did! I realized that for a number of years I had believed what Dr. Cox put into print. The more I studied the teaching of the church through the magisterium, tradition, and the fathers of the church, the more I came to the conclusion that many of the teachings from my pre-Vatican II background did not pass the litmus test of my conscience. My faith was in the Jesus of what Cox calls the Age of Faith, the first three centuries after Jesus died, when the early church was more interested in following Jesus' teachings than in making obligatory what to believe about Jesus. This is the Jesus that my faith is grounded in—the Jesus who gave us the Beatitudes and his example of how to live; the Jesus who was focused on compassion for the disenfranchised. If you will, it is the Church of the Beatitudes.

The Primacy of Conscience. As I mentioned in previous chapters, I could not be part of a church that did not recognize the important part conscience plays in making adult decisions about what the magisterium teaches. I believe that the primacy of conscience is quite clear in the Catholic faith tradition. What has concerned me in recent years is that there are some clerics who seem to be intent on repealing that teaching, at times for political reasons and at other times as a feeble attempt to maintain power.

Even though in US Catholic Bishop's Conference's statement on *Faithful Citizenship: A Catholic Call to Responsible Citizenship*, the bishops suggests that they are not trying to tell anyone whom to vote for and acknowledges Catholics' conscience, their agenda seems clear. They don't mention names of any catholic politicians, but anyone who follows the news knows whom they are talking about. Not only are they attempting to influence politicians' votes, but they also imply that for Catholics to vote for candidates who don't agree with their reasoning puts them in danger of sin. It sounds to me as if they are trying to create a theocracy.

Another example is Cardinal George Pell of Australia, who advocates that the church should abandon the doctrine of the primacy of conscience because young people and homosexuals use it to justify "doing their own thing" rather than following the papal dictates of the church."[29] This is despite the strong statements of Benedict XVI on conscience that I previously mentioned, *Gaudium et Spes,* and the Vatican II's *Pastoral Constitution of the Church in the Modern World,* which I have already referenced. Apparently it's okay for Cardinal Pell to be a dissenter.

Sensus Fidelium. The strong position of the Blessed John Henry Newman, the champion of the *sense of the faithful* that Vatican II supported, speaks for itself. This is despite the statement that Pius X made during his reign in the beginning of the twentieth century. In his encyclical letter, *Vehementer Nos,* he wrote, "The laity have no other rights than to let themselves be guided and to follow their pastors in docility." Docile indeed! When I read that, I thought, "Docile Don"—that could have been my nickname during all those years when I allowed myself to be led by whatever the good fathers told me was *the* truth.

The Reign of God. Since I left the seminary, there have been major advances in the study of the Scriptures. Groups like the Jesus Seminar have made available through books, lectures, articles, and ongoing research by biblical scholars, anthropologists, and theologians, information that was never available fifty years ago. They recognize that there is an intelligent, educated laity who can understand controversial and complicated studies. Their work is now more accessible to the general public. These historical Jesus scholars aim to investigate the social, religious, political, and cultural climate of the early first century in order to place the human figure of Jesus within the structures of those times.[30] One of the major areas of conflict among Jesus scholars is the proximity of the Kingdom of God or, as some scholars prefer calling it, the Reign of God. There are scholars that believe it is in the future, at the end of the world, while others believe that when Jesus said in Luke 17:22 that "the Kingdom of God is within you," he meant that the Reign of God was already in us as it was with him. That is an awesome view! We don't have to wait until the end of the world; the Reign of God is with us right now. Imagine that, God is in us! As I'm sitting here right now, God's Reign is within me. As you're reading this right now, God's Reign is within you. I can't think of a better mantra than "The Reign of God is within me."

Who is welcomed into the Kingdom of God? Jesus made the answer clear in Matthew (25:35–46). He insisted that those who fed the hungry, gave drink to the thirsty, clothed the naked, welcomed strangers, and visited the sick and those in prison, would be welcomed into the Kingdom of God. I took note that he doesn't exclude adulterers, those who practice birth control, gays or lesbians or others who follow their conscience and reject beliefs prescribed by the church by not going to Mass weekly or contributing to the support of their pastors or any other church-made laws. It's not that some of those laws aren't good but that they aren't what Jesus identified as necessary for being part of the Reign of God. I recalled that he did not approve the adulteress's behavior in John's Gospel, but he did not condemn her. He forgave her and showed his compassion and mercy for someone who had violated a law. The Lord has mercy!

In considering the teachings of the church on infallibility, birth control, sexuality, abortion, and the understanding of the

Scriptures, I need to keep in mind what other religions have to
offer my faith tradition. This includes the abuse of authority by the
institutional church; equal rights for women, including ordination
to the priesthood; and the rights of gays and lesbians, or whether
the church is an affirming and welcoming to its members. I
keep in mind the primacy of conscience and the *sensus fidelium*.
I don't ignore the magisterium, including the teachings of the
early fathers of the church, nor do I ignore the encyclicals of the
popes or the Councils of the church. But I look at them with a
critical eye and weigh my decisions with reason and reliance on
the Holy Spirit. As you might recall, when I made a decision on
abortion, I carefully read the church's position and ended up
agreeing with their conclusions. It was not the church's position,
however, that convinced me that abortion was not acceptable.
My conclusion was built more on my serious scrutiny of scientific
information. I finally decided that no one could determine the
exact time when the fetus became a human being, and therefore
I gave the benefit of the doubt to the fetus. In my decision on the
subject of artificial birth control, I carefully examined the position
of the Commission on Birth Control appointed by John XXIII
that voted to change the church's position, as well as theologians
on both sides of the issue, along with the encyclical of Pius VI,
Humanae Vitae. I made the decision that I could not support the
church's ban on artificial birth control, mainly because it did not
take seriously the sense of the people.

I am also disappointed that the leaders of the church derailed
many of the most important teachings of the documents of Vatican
II. I will continue to join those who want to see a real rebirth and
renewal that the spirit of Blessed Pope John XXII envisioned when
he called for Vatican II. His hope was for an *aggiornamento*, a
bringing the church up to date of which resonated with thousands
of Catholics who are now faithful dissenters.

I agree with the position Charles Curran states in his book
Loyal Dissent: Memoir of a Catholic Theologian. "My problems are
with particular church teachings, not with its core dogma or broad

theological approach."[31] Charles Curran is an ordained Catholic priest and probably the most well-known and controversial Catholic moral theologian in the United States. Father Curran remains a committed Catholic, a priest working to reform the pilgrim church, despite his dissent on a number of official teachings of the church. Even with all his achievements, he is perhaps most remember for leading the opposition against the ban on contraceptives, which caused him to be removed from his teaching position as professor of Catholic theology at the Catholic University of America; by a decision of the Vatican's Congregation for Doctrine of the Faith, then headed by the present pope.[32]

In my view Father Curran could have been included in the book *Faithful Dissenters* if it was not for the fact he is still alive. I look at him as a role model for anyone who disagrees with any doctrine of the church but still considers him or herself a Catholic. He has suffered at the hands of the church for his dissent—not physically, like the victims of the Inquisition, but he experienced mental anguish, which is apparent from reading his memoir. His ability to forgive his persecutors is admirable and worthy of imitation.

Closing Thoughts

In the words of Carl Rogers, "This has been an irreversible experience." After being sequestered in my office at the computer for a little over two years, writing, researching, rewriting, and rewriting, I'm finally at the point to paraphrase a newspaper editor's slang, "It's time to put this baby to bed." I had a few unanticipated interruptions during my writing journey—the death of my brother, Jim; major and minor surgeries; shingles; Jane's major surgery; my being attacked by the treadmill in the exercise room and ending up in the emergency room for stitches; not to mention downsizing from a 2,400-square-foot home to a 1,100-square-foot apartment. Oh, yes, there were also two audits by the IRS that really threw me off track; then there were Jane's and my frequent visits to the Mayo Clinic for checkups; numerous visits to this, that, and the other specialist—a predictable part of the aging process. What can an octogenarian expect?

Not only have I enjoyed this experience, but it has been very helpful for me to take a look at my life and how I got from where I started, at 8 Judson Street in Albany, New York, to the Beatitudes campus in Phoenix, Arizona. Not just the physical trip, but the spiritual, emotional, and theological experience. I hope I've answered some of the questions about why I and others are still Catholic, despite our dissent. I hope by reading my stories and reflections you have a clearer idea of how anyone could spend eight years in the seminary and not realize until later in life that he didn't have the charism of celibacy or that he didn't agree with all the beliefs he had learned from grammar school through his seminary training.

At age eighty, I have no personal investment in mandatory celibacy and certainly not in the practice of birth control or many other doctrines regarding sexuality taught by the church. It has been decades since I "sowed my wild oats," as my Grandma Fausel used to say. Ironically, I think that freed me to view these issues from a point of personal detachment. I do, however, have strong intellectual and theological positions on many of the church's Manichean attitudes about sex that affect thousands of today's Catholics. I also have an ongoing interest in changing the monarchical structure the church has functioned under since around the fourth century. I plan to volunteer to be a member of Voice of the Faithful's initiative committee for Universal Reform in the church. They currently have three initiatives. The one I'm most interested in is on bishop selection. I believe that the major reason we are so deadlocked is the centralized way bishops are appointed. Vatican officials, of whom Cardinal Bernard Law is one, tend to appoint bishops in their own image and likeness. This provides little hope for change. In the early church, bishops were appointed locally in a democratic fashion; they were chosen by the people in their area. That way they didn't have to pass a litmus test. I believe that having local democratic elections for bishops would be a step closer to a democratically organized church. As they say in the twelve-step programs, "One step at a time."

Before I close, I have just one more observation. It relates to age and continued activism. One of my heroes was Granny D. She exemplified a role model for the elderly (including me) staying active in social change. If you don't remember her, she was a social activist whose real name was Doris Haddcock, from Dublin, New Hampshire. She died peacefully in her home at the age of one hundred. In 2000, at the age of ninety, Granny D. walked 3,200 miles across America to raise awareness about a campaign for political finance reform. At the age of ninety-four, she crisscrossed America registering women to vote in swing states. In her later years, she wrote a book entitled, *You're Never Too Old to Raise a Little Hell.* I think we need more people with Granny D.'s spirit working for change in the church. Amen!

Notes

Chapter 1

1. Quotes by Herbert Hoover, http://thinkexist.com/quotes/herbert_hoover.
2. The Great Depression and the New Deal, http://iws.ccccd.edu/kwilkison/Online1302home/20th%20Century/DepressionNewDeal.html. Retrieved 2/15/09
3. Ibid.
4. Abraham Maslow's Hierarchy of Needs Motivational Model. http://www.businessballs.com/maslow.htm 4page 16.
5. Fredric Bugliani, "In the Mind to Suffer: Hamlet's Soliloquy." *Hamlet Studies 17* (1995): 1–2.
6. Biomedical Process of the Zygote. http://www.zygote.com/biomed_main.php. Retrieved 2/20/09
7. Ibid.
8. Teachings of the Early Church Fathers. http://catholicism.suite101.com/article.cfm/the_early_church_fathers_of_the_catholic_church. Retrieved 2/20/09
9. Ibid.

10. Teachings of St. Thomas Aquinas on Abortion. http://faculty.cua.edu/Pennington/Law111/CatholicHistory. htm. Retrieved 2/20/09

11. Ibid.

12. Ending a Pregnancy. http://familydoctor.org/online/ famdocen/home/articles/846.html. Retrieved 2/23/09

13. The Abortion Debate. http:www.washington post.com/ wpdyn/content/article/2005/10/17AR2005101701311.html. Retrieved 2/23/09

Chapter 3

1. Robert Ichausti, ed., *Echoing Silence: Thomas Merton on the Vocation of Writing* (Boston, MA: New Seeds, 2007).

Chapter 4

1. Robert Fulghum, *All I Really Need to Know I Learned in Kindergarten* (New York: Ballentine Books, 2003).

2. Geoffrey Robinson, *Confronting Power and Sex in the Catholic Church: Reclaiming the Spirit of Jesus* (Collegeville, MN: Liturgical Press, 2008).

4. Earnie Larson on adult children of alcoholics, http://www. adultchildren.org/characteristics Retrieved 2/21/09

5. Ibid.

Chapter 6

1. George Santayana, *The Life of Reason* (New York: Dover Publishing. Vol. 1, 1905. p. 245).

2. Gilgamesh: A Spiritual Biography by W. T. S. Thackara, http://www.theosophy-nw.org/theosnw/world/Mideast/mi-wist.htm. Retrieved 2/20/09

3. Fordham Web site, http://www.fordham.edu/discover_ fordham/mission_26603.asp. Retrieved 2/25/09

Chapter 8

1. John F. Kennedy, First Inaugural Address, http://www.
bartleby.com/124/pres56.htmldress. Retrieved 2/20/09
2. Alfred Kinsey, *Sexuality and the Human Male.* Retrieved,
2/22/2009 http://health.discovery.com/centers/sex/sexpedia/
alfredckinsey.html.
3. Alan Petigny, Family, http://news.ufl.edu/research/
family/1Resarch. Retrieved 2/23/09
4. Birth Control Pills Helped Empower Women, Changed the
World, http:www.religiousconsultation.org/News_Tracker/
birth_control Retrieved 2/22/09
5. The Pill: Did It Really Change How We Live? www.
american heritage.com /articles/web/20060511-birth.contr
Retrieved 2/22/09
6. Ibid.
7. Ibid.
8. Erich Fromm, *The Art of Loving* (New York: Harper
Perennial Press, 2006).
9. Ibid., 17.
10. Rainer Funk, "Love in the Life of Erick Fromm." *The Art of
Loving* (New York: Harper Perennial Press, 2006), 21.
11. Ibid., 23.
12. Dorothy Tennov, *Love and Limerence: The Experience of
Being in Love* (New York: Stein and Day, 1979), 8.

Chapter 9

1. John W. O'Malley, J. W., *Vatican II: Did Anything Happen?*
(New York: Continuum Press, 2006).
2. Marin Luther King Jr.'s Assassination. Retrieved 3/9/09
www.history1900s.about.com/cs/martinutherking/a/
mlkassass.htm.
3. Robert Kennedy's eulogy for Martin Luther King Jr. Retrieved
3/10/09 http://www.historyplace.com/speeches/rfk.htm.

4. Edward Kennedy's eulogy for Robert F. Kennedy. Retrieved 3/10/09 http://www.americanrhetoric.com/speeches/ekennedytributetorfk.html.

5. The Military Assistance Command for Vietnam. Retrieved 3/10/09 www.jfklibrary.org/Historical+Resources/Archives/Reference.

6. Lyndon Johnson's Deployment of Troops. Retrieved 3/11/09 http://www.sparknotes.com/history/american/vietnamwar/section5.rhtml.

7. Tet Offensive. 1968. Retrieved 3/11/09 http://www.sparknotes.com/history/american/vietnamwar/section7.rhtml.

8. Daniel McMichael, "William Calley Apologizes for My Lai Massacre." Retrieved 4/2/09 www.lwsfwe-enquirer.com/news/story/813829.html.

9. Vietnam on Line, www.pbs.org.wgbh/amex/vietnam/timeline/tl3#a

10. Ibid.

11. J. Lewis and T. Hensley, "The May 4 Shootings at Kent State University: The Search for Historical Accuracy." Retrieved 4/20/09 http://dept.kent.edu/sociology/lewis/lewihen.htm.

12. Brian Martin, "The Legacy of the Pentagon Papers." Retrieved 4/20/09 http://www.bmatin.cc/pubs//03BRwhistle07.html.

13. Agent Orange. Retrieved 4/20/09 http://www.lewispublishing.com/orange.htm.

14. This Week at Vatican II. Retrieved 4/20/09 http://thisweekatvaticanii.blogspot.com/2009/10/50-years-ago-announcement-of-council.html.

15. Second Vatican Council. Retrieved 4/22/09 http://www.answers.com/topic/second-vatican-council

16. Ibid.

17. Robert McClory, *Turning Point* (New York: Crossroads Press, 1995).

18. Ibid., 4.

19. Ibid., 102–108.
20. Ibid.
21. Ibid.
22. Ibid., 124.
23. Ibid., 127–128.
24. Pope John Paul II On Conscience. Retrieved 11/9/09 http://www.hprweb.com/index.php?option=com_content&view=article&id=206:pope-john –paul-ii-on-conscience&catid=34:current-issu.
25. Catechism of the Catholic Church. Retrieved 11/22/09 http://www.vatican.va/archive/catechism/ccc_toc.htm.
26. Syllabus of Errors of Pius IX. Retrieved 12/15/09 http://www.papalencyclicals.net/Pius09/p9syll.htm.
27. On Consulting the Faithful in Matters of Doctrine. Retrieved 1/25/10 http://www.fordham.edu/halsall/mod/newman-faithful.html.
28. Ibid.
29. Brian Lewis, "Primacy of Conscience," *Australian Journal of Theology*. 6 (2006): 1448. Retrieved 1/3/10 http://dlibrary.acu.edu.au/research/theology/ejournal/aejt_6/lewis.htm.
30. St. Thomas More: Trial and Execution. Retrieved 1/15/10 http://en.wikipedia.org/wiki/Thomas_More#Trial_and_execution.
31. Pope Benedict XVI on Primacy of Conscience. Retrieved 2/2/10 http://purplepew.org/blog/carey/pope-on-primacy-of-conscience.

Chapter 10

1. Economic Opportunity Act, August 1964. Retrieved 2/2/10 http://www2.volstate.edu/geades/FinalDocs/1960s/eoa.htm.
2. Ibid.
3. Cardinal Spellman's Quote on the Vietnam War. Retrieved 2/7/10 http://www.encyclopedia.com/doc/1G2-3468302463.html.

4. Ibid.
5. Father Dan Berrigan's Jailhouse Experience. Retrieved 2/10/10. http://www.jonahhouse.org/catonsville40/index.htm.
6. Andrew Carnegie Mansion. Retrieved 2/17/10 http://en.wikipedia.org/wiki/Andrew_Carnegie_Mansion
7. Social Security Administration. Retrieved 2/12/10. http://www.docstoc.com/docs/16197264/Social- Policy-and-Planning.
8. Mobilization for Youth. Retrieved 2/12/10. http://www.columbia.edu/cu/lweb/archival/collections/ldpd_4079120/index.html.
9. Student Protests at Columbia University, 1968. Retrieved 2/15/10. http://en.wikipedia.org/wiki/Columbia_University_protests_of_1968.
10. Ibid.
11. Donald Cozzens, *Freeing Celibacy* (Collegeville, MN: Liturgical Press, 2006), 21.
12. Ibid.
13. Ibid., 63.
14. How Religion Can Repress Women's Sexuality. Retrieved 2/17/10 http://atheism.about.com/od/religionwomensex/Religion_Women_Sex_How_Rel gion_Can_Repress_Women_and_Sexuality.htm.
15. A Hypocritical Church's Sex Lessons. Retrieved 2/19/10. http://www.thenation.com/doc/20050606/scheer0524/print.
16. Gregory Robinson, *Confronting Power and Sex in the Catholic Church: Reclaiming the Spirit of Jesus* (Collegeville, MN: Liturgical Press, 2007).
17. Russell Shaw, *Nothing to Hide* (San Francisco, CA: Ignatius Press, 2008).
18. Henry C. Lea, *History of Sacerdotal Celibacy* (New York: University Books, 1966).
19. Ibid., 264.
20. Benjamin Goldberg, *The Sacred Fire* (New York: University Books, 1958).

21. Mandatory Celibacy. Retrieved 2/19/10 http://www.ejhs.org/volume2/walsh/walshtoc.htm.

22. A.W. Richad Sipe, *Living the Celibate Life: A Search for Models and Meaning* (Liguori, MO: Triumph, 2004).

23. Pope John Paul II's Apostolic Letter on Female Ordination. Retrieved 2/22/10 http://www.religioustolerance.org/femclrg10.htm.

24. Ibid.

25. Kenneth D. Whitehead, "Church Authority: No Longer 'Authoritative'?" Retrieved 2/25/10 http://www.catholic.net/.

Chapter 12

1. Robert N. Walsh, *Essential Spirituality* (New York: John Wiley & Sons, 1999).

2. Robin Meyers, *Saving Jesus from the Church: How to Stop Worshiping Christ and Start Following Jesus* (New York: HarperCollins, 2009).

3. Harvey Cox. *The Future of Faith* (New York: HarperCollins, 2009).

4. Ibid., 77–78.

5. Karen Armstrong. Retrieved 2/27/10 http://www.youtube.com/watch?v=SJMm4RAwVLo&feature=related.

6. Karen Armstrong, *The Battle for God: A History of Fundamentalism* (New York: Ballantine, 2001). Front book cover.

Chapter 13

1. The Three Gorge Dam. Retrieved 2/27/10 http://www.kenexner.com/china.stml.

2. Thomas Lawson, "Music and Social Work," in *Encyclopedia of Social Work*, 19th ed., ed. R. L. Edwards, 1736–1741 (Washington, DC: National Association of Social Work, 1995).

3. William Gamson, *The Strategies of Social Protest,* 2nd ed. (Belmont, CA: Wadsworth, 1992).
4. Charles Seymour, "Struggle and Songs." Retrieved 3/1/10 http://www.peoplesmusic.org/Info/News.htm.
5. David Steindl-Rast, "Recollections of Thomas Merton's Last Days in the West," *Monastic Studies 7* (1969):10.
6. The Thomas Merton Connection, http://www.hundredmountain.com. Retrieved 3/5/10
7. Ibid.
8. *Nostra Aetate.* The Relation of the Church to non-Christian Religions. Retrieved 3/5/10 http://www.vatican.va/archive/ hist_councils/ii_vatican_council/documents/vat-ii_ decl_19651028_nostra-aetate_en.html.
9. Paul Knitter, *Without Buddha I Could Not be a Christian* (Oxford: One World, 2009).
10. Hans Kung, *Why I am Christian.* (New York: Continuum International Publishing Group, 1986), 14–15.
11. Ibid.
12. John Allen, "Hans Kung and Pope Benedict: Old Friends and Archrivals Have a Cordial Meeting." Retrieved 3/8/10 http://www.nationalcatholicreporter.org/update//bn092605.htm.
13. Robert McClory, *Faithful Dissenters: Stories of Men and Women Who Loved and Changed the Church* (Maryknoll, New York: Orbis Press, 2000).
14. James Carroll, *Practicing Catholic* (Boston: Houghton Mifflin Harcourt, 2009), 87.
15. The Catechism of the Catholic Church. 1782. Retrieved 2/9/09 http://www.vatican.va/archive/ENG0015/__P5Z.HTM.
16. Association for the Rights of Catholics in the Church. Retrieved 3/5/10 http://arcc-catholic-rights.org/dissentlen.htm.
17. The Voice of the Faithful. Mission Statement and Goals. Retrieved 3/5/10 http://www.votf.org/whoweare/mission-statement/98.

18. The Roaming Catholic. Retrieved 3/5/10
    http://theroamingcatholic.com/?p=187.
19. Ibid.
20. Robert B. Kaiser, "A Look Back Almost 60 Years Later."
    Retrieved 3/11/10 http://americancatholiccouncil.org/
    resources/notes-toward-an-essay-on/.
21. Historic Move for Voice of the Faithful and U.S. Catholics.
    Retrieved 3/11/10 http://www.votf.org/.
22. American Catholic Council Declaration of Reform. See link
    on Declaration. Retrieved 3/2/20
    http://americancatholiccouncil.org/.
23. Robert B. Kaiser, "A Look Back Almost 60 Years Later."
    Retrieved 3/11/10 http://americancatholiccouncil.org/
    resources/notes-toward-an-essay-on/.
24. Michael Morwood, *Tomorrow's Catholic: Understanding God
    and Jesus in a New Millennium* (New London, CT: Twenty-
    Third Publications, 2006), 8.
25. Ibid., 16.
26. Harvey Cox, *The Future of Faith* (New York: Harper One,
    2009), 16.
27. Ibid., 17.
28. Ibid., 18.
29. Primacy of Conscience, *Pell vs. Popes*. Retrieved 3/10/10
    http://slimpickens.wordpress.com/2007/06/08/primacy-of-
    conscience-pell-vs-the-popes/
30. The Kingdom of God or Reign of God. Retrieved 2/11/10
    http://en.wikipedia.org/wiki/Kingdom_of_God.
31. Charles Curran, *Loyal Dissent: Memoir of a Catholic
    Theologian* (Washington, DC: Georgetown Press, 2006),
    239.
32. Ibid.